Cyprus Before 1974

Cyprus Before 1974

The Prelude to Crisis

Marilena Varnava

I.B. TAURIS
LONDON • NEW YORK • OXFORD • NEW DELHI • SYDNEY

I.B. TAURIS
Bloomsbury Publishing Plc
50 Bedford Square, London, WC1B 3DP, UK
1385 Broadway, New York, NY 10018, USA

BLOOMSBURY, I.B. TAURIS and the Diana logo are trademarks
of Bloomsbury Publishing Plc

First published in Great Britain 2020

A catalogue record for this book is available from the British Library.

A catalogue record for this book is available from the Library of Congress.

ISBN: HB: 978-1-7845-3997-9
ePDF: 978-1-7883-1543-2
eBook: 978-1-7883-1542-5

Series: International Library of Twentieth Century History

Typeset by Integra Software Services Pvt. Ltd.
Printed and bound in Great Britain

To find out more about our authors and books visit www.bloomsbury.com
and sign up for our newsletters.

Contents

Acknowledgements

This book is a result of my doctoral research at the Institute of Commonwealth Studies, School of Advanced Study, at the University of London. Undertaking this research and writing this book might have been a long journey, during which many times I felt that it might never come to fruition. However, this journey was a rewarding one. I was lucky to have by my side many individuals who gave me their unreserved support and their invaluable assistance and to all of them I would like to extend my gratitude.

First and foremost, I would like to express my deepest gratitude to my PhD supervisor, Professor Robert Holland, for patiently guiding me along the right paths during this very challenging yet utterly fulfilling journey. I am especially thankful for his priceless academic advice and his overall support that enabled me to grow not only as doctoral student but also as a young professional. Without his guidance, his valuable feedback and our long discussions about the Cyprus affairs at this cosy café in Russell Square, in London, this book would have never been realized. Robert Holland, thank you for being a great mentor to me.

I would also like to express my appreciation to Professor Philip Murphy, director of the Institute of Commonwealth Studies, for his valuable contribution during the final and very critical stage of my PhD thesis preparation. Additionally, I would like to sincerely thank my viva examiners, Dr Klearchos Kyriakides and Dr Spyros Economides, who gave me valuable feedback and guidance, not only during the viva examination, but also after the completion of my doctoral research. I could not but thank my IB Tauris editor, Tomasz Hoskins, for his assistance and our very fruitful collaboration.

Many thanks to the staff of the Senate House Library, of the University of London, the National Archives of the United Kingdom in London, the Cyprus State Archives in Nicosia, the Library of Makarios III Foundation in Nicosia, the newspapers archive at the Public Information Office in Nicosia, and the Cyprus Development Bank archive in Nicosia.

It would not have been possible to complete this research without the immense support and love of my friends and family. I would like to thank each and every one of my friends and colleagues who encouraged and helped me to overcome any difficulties encountered along the way. Our endless discussions, our disagreements and our mutual concerns about the Cyprus problem were a true source of inspiration to me, motivating me to bring this project into life.

I am also grateful to Andria Ioannou for her selfless help with the manuscript. Likewise, I am deeply indebted to my sister, Alexia, who supported me in numerous ways during this research. My overwhelming thanks and love go to Nikos, who with his unconditional love and patience never stopped believing in me and giving me constantly strength and courage.

Last but foremost, words cannot express my gratitude to my parents, Varnavas and Pistoula, for their immense love, patience, as well as their moral and financial support that made everything possible during this long and rewarding journey of my life.

Abbreviations

AKEL	Ανορθωτικό Κόμμα Εργαζόμενου Λαού – Progressive Party of Working People
CoE	Council of Europe
DoS	(US) Department of State
EDEK	Ενιαία Δημοκρατική Ένωση Κέντρου – Unified Democratic Union of the Centre
EOKA	Εθνική Οργάνωση Κυπρίων Αγωνιστών – National Organization of Cypriot Fighters)
GDP	gross domestic product
MP	member of the Parliament
NATO	North Atlantic Treaty Organization
PIO	Press and Information Office (Republic of Cyprus)
TCA	Turkish-Cypriot Administration
TCPA	Turkish-Cypriot Provisional Administration
TMT	*Türk Mukavemet Teşkilatı* – Turkish Resistance Organization
TNA	The National Archives of the UK
UNFICYP	United Nations Force in Cyprus
UP	Unified Party

Introduction

In December 1963, only three years after the birth of the Republic of Cyprus, a violent, inter-communal clash abruptly terminated the already shaky co-existence of Greek-Cypriots and Turkish-Cypriots in the state apparatus of the island that had been envisaged in the 1960 Constitution. Thereupon, both communities' leaderships set in motion their plans for consolidating separate administrations, making Cyprus 'a simmering cauldron' which exploded ten years later, in July 1974. The purpose of this book is to explore the development of the Cyprus problem through the decade of 1964–1974 with a main focus on the goals and strategies, decision making and actions of the leaderships of the two main communities on the island.

It should be borne in mind that the Cyprus question, even before independence, had evolved through several phases closely entwined with the international context. The Cold War rivalries and the need of the West to keep Cyprus under its sphere of influence had inevitably affected the evolution of the Cyprus problem and exacerbated the internal rivalries within and between the two communities on the island. There is still a widespread perception, especially among Greek-Cypriots, that the island's fate was pre-determined according to the interests of the big powers and secret 'arrangements' between Turkey and the junta in Greece. There are several theories and studies that seem to confirm this belief. This book, however, through extensive archival research, focuses instead on the primary and decisive contribution made by specifically Cypriot players to the evolution of the Cyprus problem and the events that led up to July 1974. Through this study several elements are distinguished, which explain the compelling motives that drove the two communal leaderships, and how these moulded the political context of Cyprus. It becomes evident that a lack of rational political evaluation of internal problems and the international context, wishful thinking and the consequent misperception of threats led to a self-fulfilling prophecy. This proved catastrophic for the peaceful co-existence of the two communities in Cyprus.

The main underlying cause of the island's fragile situation during the period under examination can be detected in the background that led to independence and the nature of the constitution of the new state. As a former colony, the Republic of Cyprus had inherited several colonial legacies which made its existence very challenging. The rivalry and mistrust between the two ethnic communities exacerbated by Britain, the failings of political institutions and the dearth of good governance skills were some of the default characteristics of the new state. There was also an additional factor – the role of the Church and its involvement in the island's politics. More specifically, the role of the enigmatic figure of the President, Archbishop Makarios III, and his great influence on Greek-Cypriots. No other leader in the history of Cyprus had an analogous impact on the 'hearts and minds' of Greek-Cypriots, and that had given him, until recently at least, a sort of immunity for his political mistakes and miscalculations. The anthropologist Paul Sant Cassia argues that Makarios' policies were affected by his dual capacity as the spiritual and secular leader of the Greek-Cypriots, and that gave him 'immense popularity which never declined in spite of the ultimately disastrous effects his tight-rope walking policies led to'.[1] Therefore, both his personality and his policies are closely examined in this book.

Conversely, for the Turkish-Cypriot community things were very different. The lack of an experienced political leadership along with the isolation of a significant percentage of the Turkish-Cypriot community isolation within the enclaves after 1964 led to a constantly growing economic and military dependence on Ankara. It was only after April 1968, with the return from Turkey of the previously exiled Turkish-Cypriot leader Rauf Denktash, that it seemed Makarios would have to face a worthy political opponent. It should be stressed that although the Turkish-Cypriot community deeply relied on Turkey's diplomatic and economic aid, it was also true that it remained very much a distinctive entity, capable, albeit to a limited extent, of expressing its own views and positions.

The immediate background of this book begins with the adoption of the UN Security Council Resolution 186 on 4 March 1964, with which the UN peacekeeping force and the UN mediator were assigned to the island following the inter-communal crisis of December 1963. The resolution was in order, first, to maintain a peaceful *status quo* and, second, to seek for a solution to the Cyprus problem.[2] This Resolution is still considered by Greek-Cypriots as their most important diplomatic victory, since it gave international legitimacy to the entirely Greek-Cypriot-led state.

Our starting point lies in the arrival of the second UN Mediator, Senor Galo Plaza Lasso, in Nicosia in September 1964. From that point onwards, Plaza employed a new, more Cypriot-centric, approach to settle the inter-communal problem – all previous attempts to find a solution on the basis of a Greco-Turkish understanding were, at least temporarily, shelved. Thereafter, it seemed that focus was concentrated solely on the UN mediator and the two communities' leaderships. By March 1965, however, mediation was effectively terminated. Plaza's conclusions as expressed in his mediation report were used as an excuse by both communities to justify their preference for a negotiating stalemate on the island so as to give time to each side to upgrade its own bargaining position. Nonetheless, each year a series of new *faits accomplis* on the ground induced, according to the British, the 'benign stalemate'[3] and steadily reduced the chances for finding an acceptable settlement.

When in June 1968 the active peacemaking efforts resumed, it was evident that the situation on the island was very different from 1965. In 1969 the British high commissioner in Nicosia stated, 'Cyprus is partitioned in the most haphazard and intricate way between intermingled areas controlled by the Greek Government of Cyprus and the Turkish-Cypriot administration respectively, making the communal map of Cyprus look like the latter days of the Holy Roman Empire'.[4] This, however, was a reality that the Greek-Cypriot leadership failed to realize in its full implications, and which the Turkish-Cypriot leadership fully exploited. Therefore, the most crucial opportunity to settle the Cyprus problem in 1968 was to be missed mainly due to the misperceptions, inaccurate assessments and maximalist approaches of the decision makers of the two communities. Although the negotiations continued until they were violently terminated on 15 July 1974, as early as 1972, it was evident that the developments on the island, and especially the increasingly violent opposition against President Makarios, meant inter-communal discussions were dead in the water. Thereafter, the window of opportunity for a negotiated settlement closed.

During this decade world-changing developments were taking place throughout the globe. The Western powers, especially Britain and America, had to tackle many challenges in their foreign policy commitments. On the one hand, the great decolonization wave of the 1960s, Britain's economic problems and its decision to reduce its forces in the Mediterranean had inevitably reduced its previous hegemonic role, especially in the Middle East. On the other hand, American foreign policy was greatly pre-occupied with the Vietnam War. The year 1968 saw the Prague Spring, Soviet Union's invasion of Czechoslovakia and the Tet offensive in Vietnam – some of the most crucial developments in global politics. Still to come were the two Arab–Israeli wars, the Six-Day War of 1967 and the Yom Kippur War of 1973 which had almost led to a US–Soviet confrontation. As the historian Claude Nicolet argues, following the Six-Day War, 'the US discovered that even NATO allies were no longer as responsive to American pressure as they had been during the 1950s'.[5] That reality was particularly evident within the Greek and Turkish domestic politics and foreign policy formulation regarding the Cyprus problem in the 1960s.

Under this context, the Cyprus problem was just another challenge for the British and the American foreign policy decision makers that had to be urgently tackled, either by peacefully closing it or by prolonging the 'benign stalemate' status. Most importantly for the United States and Britain, stability in the region was imperative and thus the Cyprus question had to be resolved without upsetting their relations with their two North Atlantic Treaty Organization (NATO) allies, Greece and Turkey. Both Western powers were not willing or even capable of forcing the two motherlands into any other direction than restraint, especially until 1972. At the same time, a large-scale war between Greece and Turkey over Cyprus had to be prevented at all costs, Turkey's rapprochement to USSR had to be monitored and contained, and the Cyprus president should not be seemed as if he was sidelined, since all of these prospects could have allowed a Soviet foothold on the island.

What is of great interest in the Cyprus case, however, is that the Cyprus policymakers usually underestimated the importance of the shockwave developments that were taken place inside and outside of Europe, and the strategic interests at stake of the Western allies and Soviet Union in the region. That element had a detrimental impact on the formulation of the strategy of, especially, the Greek-Cypriot community vis-à-vis the Cyprus question before 1974.

The post-independence history of Cyprus has only recently become the focus of proper academic study. Nevertheless, the history of the inter-communal conflict of Cyprus, interacting as it did with Cold War rivalries and regional diplomacy, is a subject that invariably dominates the existing secondary literature of that period. What is presently not extensively studied in the historiography is an analysis based on primary documentation, where available, and relevant secondary literature, on the issue of the divergent evolution of the two communities and subsequently of the Cyprus problem from 1964 until the landmark year of 1974. More specifically, the interactive effect of the development of the Cyprus question on the separate socio-economic, political and administrative development of the two communities and vice versa needs to be much more clearly distinguished. Furthermore, the period between the two severe inter-communal clashes of 1964 and 1967 is not examined from a Cypriot-centric angle. This, however, is a period and a scope that form a central part of this book. Likewise, this study aims to fill in the gap of the most crucial effort to settle the constitutional problem on the island of the period 1968 and 1971, with a comprehensive analysis of the negotiating strategies of all the parties involved, as well as a simultaneous analysis of the evolution of the inter-communal dialogue and the internal developments within each community.

Undoubtedly, the existing literature, including memoirs and collections by leading protagonists of the period, provides a vital and general background of the period under examination. It should be kept in mind, however, that most of the current literature was produced before the lifting of classification restrictions of official documentation.

Although the use of the available secondary literature was unquestionably of vital importance for shaping the necessary background, there have also been an extensive use and analysis of primary resources. The archival material cited at The National Archives of the United Kingdom at Kew, London (hereinafter called TNA) has been undoubtedly the most crucial source of information. The official correspondence held at the TNA contains the most insightful narratives and analyses of events and personalities from all the interested parties.

Besides possessing an interest in the smooth functioning of the Sovereign Bases, and also being a Guarantor Power of the independence of Cyprus, the British still had vital concerns at stake on the island. Therefore, the archival material kept in the Dominions Office (DO), the Foreign Office (FO) and – after the merger of the Commonwealth and Foreign Office in 1968 – in the Foreign Commonwealth Office (FCO), as well as the documents from the Prime Minister's Office (PREM), provided detailed reports and evaluations of administrative and economic aspects of the Republic of Cyprus, and for each community in particular. Meanwhile, there is, where relevant, a precise focus on various diplomatic and military crises and the crisis management of various players. The weekly, quarterly and annual dispatches of the five successive British high commissioners in Nicosia were also essential for this project, along with the detailed minutes held following the discussions of various British diplomats with key political figures from Cyprus, as well as from Greece, Turkey and the United States. Intelligence reports kept by the War Office (WO) also provided some key information on specific security incidents and the prevailing conditions on the island, elements that give a more lucid image of the internal affairs of Cyprus.

Supplementary to the study of the British archives, the publication of certain archives from the US Department of State especially for the period 1964–1968 proved to be also crucial. The online publication of the US Government's *Foreign Relations of the United States, 1964–1968, Volume XVI, Cyprus; Greece; Turkey*[6] was a source of additional information on discussions and meetings of American diplomats with key political figures of the three interested countries, as well as of official correspondence of the British and American diplomats concerning the Cyprus issue.

Although extensively consulted, the State Archives in Nicosia, Cyprus, gave mostly a general background of most important events with limited information about daily problems within the Greek-Cypriot community and inter-communal relations in general. It remains the case that it is the British and American archives which yield the most accessible information on the internal policies of both main communities and the diplomatic goals of the Republic itself. Still the comprehensive study of Greek-Cypriot and Turkish-Cypriot newspapers held in the Makarios III Foundation and the Press and Information Office (PIO) in Nicosia, as well as the multi-voluminous collection of Makarios III Foundation containing official documents, press releases and interviews given by President Makarios III during his presidency (*Άπαντα Αρχιεπισκόπου Κύπρου Μακαρίου III*)[7] vividly illustrated the intense day-by-day situation, the internal rivalries, the propaganda games and the constant polarization of public opinion on both sides.

Critical for the period 1968–1969 was also the personal archive of Glafkos Clerides,[8] which contained minutes of the two negotiator's meetings during the inter-communal talks, notes from Clerides' discussions with other political figures as well as correspondence between the various ministries of the Republic of Cyprus.

Lastly, certain oral interviews with Greek-Cypriot politicians of that period were conducted as a purely supplementary source. There were of course certain practical limitations, since recollection of historical events or even facts almost fifty years later is prone to distortion.

The main body of this study is divided into two parts, where there is a clear distinction between the phases of the Cyprus problem. Part One deals with the period from 1964, when Galo Plaza assumed the mediatory role in Cyprus until the eve of the November 1967 inter-communal clash. Part Two focuses on the immediate aftermath of the November 1967 crisis by tracing the new dynamics set in place, the initiation of the inter-communal talks in 1968 and the development of the first Cyprus talks until their violent termination in July 1974.

Chapter 1 presents the first attempt of the UN mediation in Cyprus of 1964–1965. The chapter provides an analysis of Galo Plaza's strategies and achievements, the reasons that led to the termination of his mediation and the impact of his conclusions in the later evolution of both the peacemaking efforts and the negotiating policies of the contested parties.

Chapter 2 analyses the internal restructuring of the Cyprus state after the separation of the two communities in 1964. It highlights the goals set by each community's leadership according to the new state of affairs and how these were pursued from 1964 until 1967. Throughout this period, Greek-Cypriots effectively holding the political reins of the island succeeded in overcoming the previous administrative obstacles of the constitution. Conversely, the Turkish-Cypriot leadership, isolated in the enclaves, managed to establish its own, separate administrative structures on the island, while arguing that this was a necessity deriving from the Greek-Cypriot *faits accomplis*. As it is indicated in Chapter 6, the new realities of this period came to haunt the negotiating process of 1968–1974.

Subsequently, Chapter 3 goes on to explore the socio-economic situation of the two communities during the same period of 1964–1967 and the impact of this particular context on the evolution of the inter-communal problem.

Chapter 4 deals with the prolonged diplomatic efforts inside and outside the island to break the stalemate created after the submission of Plaza's report. It briefly explains the dynamics of the sterile dialogue between Greece and Turkey, initiated in May 1965 and lasted until September 1967. Nonetheless, the most important part of the chapter analyses what had been discussed in Cyprus simultaneously with the Greco-Turkish negotiations and explains why, despite their constant efforts, the UN secretary-general's representatives failed to recapture the initiative or find even the minimum common ground between the two communities. In this chapter, the role of President Makarios in 'defusing the power' of the *Enosis* dream is also highlighted.[9]

Chapter 5 coincides with the beginning of the second part of the book. Initially, there is a brief analysis of the November 1967 crisis which is considered a turning point both for the peacemaking process and for the political development of the two communities. By April 1968 the UN secretary-general convinced the parties to accept a constructive inter-communal dialogue, which began two months later. Parallel with this development were very significant changes within the island. This chapter explains the aims of the parties in the eve of the talks and their negotiating tactics as these were transformed after this 'reshuffling of the deck'.

Chapter 6 explores extensively the first round of the inter-communal talks, from June 1968 until December 1971. The chapter evolves simultaneously with the analysis of the developments on the negotiating table and the political developments in Cyprus, which crucially affected the pace and progress of the talks. By mid-1971, however, the first round of the talks collapsed and the UN secretary-general tried to find a suitable way to break the impasse. We shall argue that the first round of the inter-communal talks was one of the most important opportunities missed for settling the Cyprus problem.

Lastly, Chapter 7 provides an overall perspective on the inter-communal talks from January 1972 until July 1974, held under a new procedure. Nonetheless, the problems created within the Greek-Cypriot community and the seeds of division that had been pervasively cultivated during the previous phase of the talks reduced the second round of the negotiations to what became a mere safety valve for avoiding the threat of violence should talks collapse altogether. The internal developments led to three detrimental pauses during negotiations. Paradoxically, however, progress at the negotiating table was unprecedented. By July 1974 there was a compromise legal formula for all constitutional aspects. Nevertheless, even if the *coup d'etat* or the Turkish invasion was ultimately averted, a mere legal formula and a constitutional compromise would not have been sufficient for providing an authentic and lasting political solution to the Cyprus question.

By reviewing the various threads of the argument, we will locate the real cause for the failure within the post-independence political culture of the island. The alienation of a segment of a population had created severe challenges to the most critical phase of the island's history: the transition from the internal turmoil of the colonial period until the consolidation of peace and democracy within a newly founded state. These lessons from the past could be of particular importance to the still ongoing efforts for the reunification of the island.

Historical background

February 1959 constituted a critical landmark for Cyprus. This small British colony in the eastern edge of the Mediterranean became independent, during a period when self-determination movements were gaining ground, new independent states were emerging and Cold War rivalries helped to shape the political development of the newly founded states. It was in this context that the Republic of Cyprus emerged after a four-year struggle against the British colonial rulers. However, independence and the creation of a new autonomous state was not what the majority of the inhabitants of the island wanted or believed in. This majority was of Greek origin and believed for many years that the final destiny of their island would be *Enosis*: unification with their motherland Greece. Nonetheless, there were critical factors and interests at stake which barred the fulfilment of their ideal aim.

An important part of the background of this study is that during the almost 300 years of Ottoman rule on the island (1571–1878), a small but important Ottoman minority was formed, which at independence in 1960 was recognized as an entity almost equal in political rights and privileges to those of the majority of the nascent republic. Despite their substantial cultural differences and the fact that they were never truly socially integrated, the Christian Orthodox and Muslim population of Cyprus had co-existed peacefully for years.[10] Since 1830, when Greece gained its independence and then in 1843 when the campaign for the '*Megali Idea*' was launched, Cyprus' Christian Orthodox population pursued an often-subdued but nonetheless consistently expressed desire to be joined to a Hellenic motherland. The struggle for *Enosis* intensified during the 1940s and continued, if often covertly, after independence but was terminated in 1974 after the Turkish invasion.

Before presenting briefly the recent history of the conflict of these two communities on the island, it should be borne in mind that the Greek community of Cyprus over a long period not only underestimated the Turkish-Cypriot presence on the island but also developed a strong tendency to overlook the fact that Cyprus geographically is located under the 'soft underbelly' of Turkey, only 40 miles away from its southern cost. Thus, Turkey's strategic interests inevitably came to play a significant role in the determination of the island's destiny.

The pursuit of Enosis

Since 1878, when Cyprus came under British rule and then in 1925 became officially a Crown Colony, the Greeks of Cyprus actively sought the fulfilment of their national obligation. The Orthodox Church and the right-wing circles had the leading role in this campaign. Determined to take the matter to the United Nations, Archbishop Makarios III, after his enthronement in October 1950, pursued an intensified unification campaign and decided to initiate a mission of internationalization of the Cyprus issue. The left-wing circles and the communist party of AKEL (Ανορθωτικό Κόμμα Εργαζόμενου Λαού – Progressive Party of Working People), passing through many stages since 1926 as to the optimum solution for the island's destiny, by 1950s also came to support this campaign.[11] The Greeks of Cyprus believed that their numerical superiority (80 per cent) of the island's population legitimated their struggle for *Enosis*. That, however, was nullified by Britain's determination not to accept any radical change in the *status quo* on the island, the opposition of the Turkish minority of Cyprus and the increasing influence of Turkey at a regional level.

During the political fermentation of Greek-Cypriots throughout the 1950s, the role of Archbishop Makarios proved to be crucial and indeed he managed to hold the political reins of his community until his death in 1977. It should be stressed that since Ottoman rule in Cyprus, the Church and in particular the Archbishop had been the *Ethnarch*, and thus he was perceived as the 'natural leader' of the Greeks of Cyprus.[12] However, Archbishop Makarios breathed a new life into an often moribund *Ethnarchy*. His intelligence, charismatic personality and great oratorical skills allowed him to build up an immense popular appeal.[13] Through the *Ethnarchy*, Archbishop Makarios III was above any institution, and he soon became the undisputable political leader of the Greek-Cypriots. The most determining moment, for the political predominance of the *Ethnarchy* and of Makarios III in Greek-Cypriot politics and society, according to Sia Anagnostopoulou came in January 1950.[14] Makarios, who was still merely the Bishop of Kitium, along with the Church, in January 1950 led the campaign for the referendum on *Enosis*, through which 90 per cent of the Greek-Cypriots voted in favour of *Enosis*.

By 1955 the Greek-Cypriots' efforts for unification with Greece had borne very limited fruit due to Britain's refusal to discuss 'self-determination' of the island within the UN. The Greek-Cypriots then decided to take a more radical initiative. On 1 April 1955, the National Organization of Cypriot Fighters, known as EOKA, initiated a guerrilla campaign against the colonial rule aiming at *Enosis*.[15] EOKA was organized under the military leadership of the fervent nationalist General Georgios Grivas, a Greek-Cypriot officer of the Greek army, known also for his strong anti-communist feelings, and under the political leadership of Archbishop Makarios. Although the British initially tried to negotiate a political compromise with Makarios, they failed and in March 1956 the latter was deported to Seychelles. His exile, according to Sant Cassia, increased immeasurably his popularity among his community, while 'it was seen as a point of passage marking the transition from an "otherworldly" priest to a "this-worldly" politician'.[16]

Conversely with the Greek-Cypriot community, the threat of *Enosis* sparked the acceleration of political activity among Turkish-Cypriots during the 1940s.[17] Alongside a growing Turkish-Cypriot apprehension of union with Greece and simultaneously, through Kemal Ataturk's dominance in Turkey, went a distinct Turkish consciousness, the enhancement of secularism and by the end of the 1940s the gradual prevalence of the Progressivists (Kemalists) over the old political elite of traditionalists among Turkish-Cypriots.[18] Unification of Cyprus to 'motherland Turkey' became the essential goal of the progressivist youth among Turkish-Cypriots. Leading figures of this movement were Dr Fazil Kuchuk and the young lawyer, Rauf Denktash, who later became the leaders of the Turkish-Cypriot community. The culmination of this activity came in November 1948, when the first Turkish-Cypriot demonstration was organized against *Enosis*.[19]

Ultimately this Turkish-Cypriot opposition became an integral feature in British tactics to address the Greek-Cypriot upheaval. In September 1955 Turkey was officially established as an equal political partner on the Cypriot issue alongside Greece, when Britain organized a tripartite conference to discuss the island's future in the wider context of the eastern Mediterranean.

Moreover, in December 1956, the British Secretary of State for the Colonies, Alan Lennox-Boyd, stated that in case the right of self-determination is exercised by Greek-Cypriots, then Turkish-Cypriots would equally have the right to decide their future status on the island.[20] Notwithstanding, as the EOKA campaign evolved and intensified, several Turkish-Cypriot extremists with the encouragement and practical support of Ankara formed in 1958 the most effective hitherto resistance movement, the paramilitary organization, called TMT – Turkish Resistance Organization – aiming at the fulfilment of the so-called KIP project (*Kıbrıs İstirdat Planı* – Plan for the Reclamation of Cyprus). According to this project, TMT would 'reclaim the land which had previously belonged to Turkey.'[21] Since its formation, TMT remained clandestine, actively pursuing its aim through underground activities. It was not until the breakdown in the stability of Cyprus after December 1963 that it was to come into the open.[22]

At the beginning of 1959 it was decided that Cyprus would become independent. Although a new state was about to be established, the most important ingredient for the nascent Republic, that of a common Cypriot ethnic identity, had still been missing.[23] As the political analyst, Niyazi Kizilyurek very interestingly explains, the island's independence marked the failure of both Greek-Cypriot and Turkish-Cypriot nationalist elites and this failure downgraded Cyprus for all Cypriots to just a 'useless geography.'[24] Additionally, due to the lack of political institutions in Cyprus, EOKA and TMT were about to become the organizational prototypes and ideologies for the secret armed groups formed within the island between 1960 and 1974. Inevitably, even after independence, violence and clandestine activities constituted the natural default position for many ex-EOKA and TMT fighters for achieving their 'national' goals. Inevitably, Cyprus democracy was built upon fragile foundations, while the rule of law was not properly entrenched in the Cyprus' political culture. This reality was profoundly evident throughout the decade under examination. Moreover, the cultivation of mistrust and fear during the last years of the British rule were also critical factors that hindered the smooth functioning of the new independent state.

The transitional period

Ultimately, the compromise agreements – the Zurich–London Agreements – that traced the outline of an independent state in Cyprus excluded both *Enosis* and partition.[25] Its basic constitutional framework along with several elements about its international status and its relations with the two motherlands and Britain were incorporated in the new Constitution and three founding treaties: the Treaty of Alliance which gave the right to Greece and Turkey to station military contingents in Cyprus for defence purposes; the Treaty of Guarantee with which Greece, Turkey and Britain guaranteed the territorial integrity of the Republic of Cyprus, either jointly or solely; and the Treaty of Establishment which envisaged the establishment of two British Sovereign Base Areas on the island. These treaties were signed by all interested parties, including the two Cypriot communities, at the Lancaster House in London on 19 February 1959.

After three years in exile, on 1 March 1959, Makarios arrived back home and was met by a massive welcoming demonstration. As the historian Diana Markides notes, the 200,000 Greek-Cypriots that lined up from the airport to the Archbishopric Palace 'were not paying homage to the signatory of the Lancaster House Agreements, but acknowledging the *Ethnarch* who had led them out of colonial servitude.'[26] Although independence was not what Greek-Cypriots were aiming for in 1955, Makarios in his speech tried to inspire his people that a new, better era now lay ahead.[27] That did not alter the fact that these agreements were considered by many Greek-Cypriots and certainly by Georgios Grivas,[28] a painful and an unfair compromise that had to be accepted in order to avoid further bloodshed. Not only *Enosis* was not achieved, but the Turkish-Cypriot minority, which represented only 18 per cent of the Cypriot population, gained significant political privileges and a disproportionate representation in all pillars of the new state.[29] Therefore, for Greek-Cypriots, the Turkish-Cypriot constitutional power was an obstacle that undermined the fulfilment of their own destiny on the island.[30]

The 18 months of the transition from the colonial rule to independence was, indeed, a very crucial period.[31] All pending constitutional and other relevant issues had to be finalized; elections had to be conducted while inter-communal hostilities and antagonism had to be contained. The strong bi-communal character and the inherent divisiveness of the constitution were making these tasks even more complex. Addressing these was very difficult since nationalist factions from the two communities were constantly sabotaging the efforts of the working committees established in order to lead the island smoothly towards the official Independence Day.[32]

The brittle inter-communal relationship and the disagreements over the implementation of various ambivalent provisions of the 1959 Agreements were not the only challenges. Political rivalries within the Greek-Cypriot community overshadowed the transition. In order to entice several young ex-EOKA fighters, Makarios assigned them to key posts within both the transitional government and his later Cabinet. That proved crucial for two reasons. First, by actively engaging those who had previously fought for *Enosis* with the new state's apparatus, had weakened Grivas' later efforts to sabotage the birth of the Republic. Second, the old political elites, who were also disappointed by the 1959 Agreements, were excluded from the new administration and so fuelled further resentment among various Greek-Cypriots factions. In this context and with the prospect of the first Presidential elections of December 1959, two different political campaigns were initiated among Greek-Cypriots which led to several unstable coalitions and the first post-EOKA political formations.[33]

Soon after the signing of the Agreements, Makarios encouraged the formation of a political organization by ex-EOKA fighters and other right-wing members, designated as the Unified Democratic Front of Recreation, EDMA (*Ενωτικό Δημοκρατικό Μέτωπο Αναδημιουργίας*). Nonetheless, due to various internal quarrels EDMA in a few months was transformed into a new organization called Patriotic Front (*Πατριωτικό Μέτωπο*).[34] The Patriotic Front, although not a full-fledged political party, constituted a loose coalition of Makarios supporters, representing the broader right wing of Greek-Cypriots. By giving their active support for Makarios' candidacy during the December elections, the Patriotic Front also supported the implementation of the Zurich–London Agreements.

On 13 December 1959 the first elections for the president and vice president of the Republic of Cyprus were held. As expected, Archbishop Makarios III prevailed against the anti-Zurich–London movement led by Ioannis Clerides and AKEL.[35] Makarios won by gaining 66.85 per cent of the Greek-Cypriot votes and became the first president of the Republic of Cyprus. In the separate elections held within the Turkish-Cypriot community, Fazil Kuchuk was elected unopposed as the vice-president.

A few months later, on 31 July 1960, the elections for the fifty members of the House of Representatives (thirty-five Greek-Cypriots and fifteen Turkish-Cypriots) were held. For the Greek-Cypriot seats there was a loose pre-electoral agreement between Makarios, the Patriotic Front and AKEL, in which it was decided that thirty seats would be allocated to the former and the five remaining seats to the latter. After the presidential elections, AKEL and Makarios proceeded to establish a mutually beneficial alliance, which lasted until the latter's death.[36] Although AKEL enjoyed the support of a significant percentage of the Cypriot population, its representation within the Parliament had to be contained. It should be kept in mind that it was a period that Cold War rivalries were reaching a peak and a strong communist party in the Cyprus Parliament would have been an 'anathema' for the West. Besides, Makarios constituted for AKEL the only guarantee that Cyprus would not fall under NATO's influence – mainly by declaring imminent *Enosis* with Greece.[37] Nonetheless, this agreement was equally important to Makarios, because it enabled him to establish his complete dominance over Greek-Cypriot politics. The AKEL–Makarios alliance had another important effect. Being essentially Makarios' greatest supporter throughout his presidency, AKEL did not manage to evolve a distinctive role of its own in the island's politics. Therefore, the lack of any threat for the expansion of the left party's influence over the island even though it was the sole properly structured political party in Cyprus perhaps was one of the underlying reasons for the absence of the need for a properly structured right-wing party. Therefore, it could be argued that AKEL's containment was also one of the factors that affected the normal development of political institutions on the island.

The fifteen Turkish-Cypriots seats were taken by the Cyprus Turkish National People's Party of Fazil Kuchuk.[38] Neither the selection of the Turkish-Cypriot members, however, was purely democratic since those who were not previously approved by Ankara were forced to withdraw their candidacy.[39] As in the Greek-Cypriot community however, the selection of the Turkish-Cypriot members of the parliament had not been conducted under a purely democratic process. The Turkish-Cypriot candidates who had not been previously approved by Ankara were forced to withdraw their candidacy. It is noteworthy that one of the most influential Turkish-Cypriot political leaders, Rauf Denktash, remained outside the central governmental machinery of the new state. The truth was that Denktash never believed in this new bi-communal state and refused to assume a post, either in the executive or in the Parliament, that would have promoted institutional inter-communal cooperation.[40] Instead, he became the president of the Turkish Communal Chamber, an institution that dealt exclusively with Turkish-Cypriot affairs.

By early August 1960 everything was set for the official inauguration of the Republic of Cyprus. It should be noted that the initial date for the transfer of sovereignty was set for exactly a year after the signing of the Zurich–London Agreements on 19 February 1960.[41] The negotiations, however, over the implementation of several constitutional arrangements, and mainly the negotiations over the size of the British Sovereign Base Areas, had not been concluded when expected, and thus the date for the inauguration was repeatedly deferred. After several postponements, 16 August 1960 was set as the effective date for the Independence Day of Cyprus.[42] Nevertheless, there was certainly nothing exceptional or enthusiastic about the independence celebrations on that day. The inauguration of the new Republic was overseen by the Governor of the island, Sir Hugh Foot, with a short procedure.

It is rather doubtful if the occasion was indeed a celebration for any of the parties concerned.[43] It seemed a 'business handover' to Makarios.[44] The Greek-Cypriots failed to achieve *Enosis*, while the Turkish-Cypriots did not secure partition or the transferring of the island to its previous owner. The

British for their part had worried that independence might prove even worse than *Enosis*.[45] This fear was valid to a degree since independence implied the dominance of Makarios in the internal affairs of the island and thus of policies characterized by ambivalent intentions not only towards the future of their Bases, but also for the extent of Soviet involvement on the island. The transitional period that led up to the official transfer of sovereignty and the 'celebration' planned for that day were a clear indication of the lukewarm feelings both of communities and of the ex-colonial power. Such ambivalence was also illustrated in 1963 when it was decided by the Council of Ministers to move the Independence Day commemoration to 1 October due to the fact that the 16 August was during the main summer holiday period. It was not until 1979 that 1 October became officially a public holiday.[46]

Furthermore, it was still an unspoken but shared assumption for both communities that independence was not a permanent settlement. It was just an interim path towards their unfulfilled but continuing and contradictory goals. While Greek-Cypriots believed that as a majority they would eventually have the right for *Enosis,* the Turkish-Cypriot leadership argued that the Zurich–London Agreements recognized them as the co-founders of the new state and not just a minority with certain rights, as the Greek-Cypriots wanted them to be.[47] That was their strongest negotiating card until 1974. Nonetheless, the separatist elements which permeated the fundamental structure of the constitution enhanced the communal mistrust not only among the elected political leaders of the two communities but also among the people themselves. In this way the cultivation of a common Cypriot identity was hobbled at the start.

'Constitutional breakdown'

The already limited signs of goodwill of the Greek-Cypriot and Turkish-Cypriot leaderships for the smooth functioning of the state and the constitution were, therefore, subject to erosion from the outset. Lack of cooperation between the leaders of the two communities, mostly at the executive level, increased the difficulties created by the enhanced bi-communal nature of the constitution. Glafkos Clerides, the president of the Parliament, stated,

> Although there was a considerable degree of cooperation in the House [of Representatives] on a number of issues [...] the main problem was that no feeling of trust was created between the two leaders, the President and Vice-President, which could have started at the top and worked its way down.[48]

The assumption that goodwill could have solved the main political difficulties of the first three years of the Republic might be questionable but the possibility is still relevant for our analysis. Clerides explains that during 1960–1961 there were clear signs that through the necessary compromises in all three pillars of the state the constitution could have worked.[49] Nevertheless, the main problems, that eventually led to the breakdown, were first the constitutional need for separate majorities for the adoption of the tax legislation and second the establishment of separate municipalities in the five main towns of the island. These were the main issues to which the two communities' leaderships were unable to find a compromise solution.[50]

Besides these political differences, the fundamental need to build bridges of cooperation and trust was also hampered by another factor. Both communities were secretly importing arms, making ammunition and enhancing the numerical strength of their secret armies by bringing in mainland Greeks or Turks.[51] The paramilitary organizations formed under the command of Greek-Cypriot officials, like the underground army of the Minister of Interior, Polikarpos Yorkadjis, and the other two under the command of Nikos Sampson and Vassos Lyssarides, both members of the Parliament, were a clear indication that the Cyprus problem had not been solved in 1960. In the Turkish-Cypriot community similar tendencies were at work.[52] The TMT focused on the aims set in 1958 and continued to recruit fighters, until time was 'right' for action.[53] The time was 'right' by the end of 1963, when the explosive situation needed a small spark to lead to the inter-communal violence that followed.

Because of the lack of the necessary compromise to address the constitutional impasse, Makarios in November 1963 decided to take a radical step and made a proposal to the vice-president for certain amendments – the famous 'Thirteen Points' – on the basic constitutional framework, which according to the former were necessary for the smooth functioning of the state.[54] The immediate and strongly negative response of Turkey gave little room for manoeuvre to the Turkish-Cypriot leadership which seemed willing to, at least, study Makarios' proposals.[55] Therefore, the Turkish-Cypriots rejected them and the tense atmosphere created on the island led swiftly to an inter-communal clash, on 21 December 1963, and to the subsequent constitutional breakdown.

It is essential here to say more about the 'Thirteen Points' of Makarios. These were indeed aiming at reducing the disproportionate constitutional privileges of Turkish-Cypriots and enhancing the unitary character of the state. Through the account of the development of the inter-communal negotiations of 1968–1974 in the later chapters, it will be evident that most of the points that were strongly rejected in 1963, in fact, came to constitute the first Turkish-Cypriot concessions during the first inter-communal negotiations that started in 1968. Moreover, by 1974 through the inter-communal talks there were legal compromise formulas which settled on paper many problematic issues of the constitution. That, however, seemed impossible in 1963. This element illustrates that in policymaking and especially in a context of hostility and mistrust, rationality in evaluating all the possible consequences, the value trade-offs and the 'ripe moment' for any kind of radical changes are of crucial importance. Unfortunately in the negotiating history of the period examined in this study, these qualities were often absent from the decision-making processes of the leaders of both communities.

In December 1963 the power-sharing model of the constitution collapsed. All the Turkish-Cypriots employees of the state promptly withdrew from the government and from their public posts, and a large percentage of the Turkish-Cypriot population retreated into enclaves created in several strategic parts of the island. For Greek-Cypriots, these withdrawals were perceived as acts of rebellion. For the Turkish-Cypriot standpoint, this was an act of necessity for their physical protection.[56] However, the truth, as always, lies somewhere in the middle; but whatever the exact truth might have been, these deeply contested versions have determined the competing discourses at the international level and within the separate political universes of the communities themselves.

Establishment of UN peacebuilding operation

The escalation of violence between the two communities in December of 1963 posed severe problems for the Guarantor powers and the wider stability of the region. The danger for the eruption of a Greco-Turkish war was looming, since Turkey was threatening to intervene in Cyprus in order to protect the Turkish-Cypriot minority. A while later, Makarios declared that both the Treaty of Alliance and Guarantee were the main source of the anomalous situation and thus his government decided to abrogate them.[57] Conversely, Vice-President Kuchuk stated that the December crisis bore out primarily that the two communities could not live peacefully together, the constitution was dead and partition was the only viable solution.[58] It was urgent, therefore, especially for the British and the Americans, to find a way to reconcile the wide gap in both communities' perceptions before the crisis further deteriorated and negatively affected their own security interests in the area. Initially, Britain took the lead and invited the interested parties to a conference in London, which ended in failure. After several debates about finding the most appropriate forum to discuss and find the relevant mechanisms to settle the problem, Britain decided to take the matter to the UN Security Council.[59]

From 18 February until 4 March 1964, there was an intense debate in the Security Council in New York about how to address the Cyprus crisis. The bipolarity of Cold War rivalries was evident throughout.[60] Nonetheless, by 4 March the Security Council adopted the Resolution 186 unanimously, which made provision for establishing a peacekeeping force, to be called United Nations Force in Cyprus (UNFICYP), and the appointment of a UN mediator.[61]

It is true that the Resolution 186 is perceived to be a landmark for the Cyprus problem.[62] First and foremost, it constituted one of the most important diplomatic victories for Greek-Cypriots because it initially prevented NATO's active involvement in the Cyprus question, as favoured by the Western powers and Turkey and, second, it recognized the Cyprus Government, even without the Turkish-Cypriot representation in it, as the only legitimate party responsible for the maintenance and restoration of the law and order on the island. Conversely, the Turkish-Cypriots, disregarding American and Turkish suggestions, decided even after this Resolution to remain isolated, thereby missing an important face-saving opportunity to return to their abandoned posts.[63]

Soon, however, it was evident that both the UNFICYP and the UN mediator were unable to lead the parties towards a stable solution. During the first months of UNFICYP's assignment in Cyprus, both communities' militias hampered its smooth functioning. Cyprus became essentially a 'powder keg', while bombing and shooting incidents remained a constant theme on the daily news.[64] Turkey threatened to militarily intervene on several occasions, while the island was brought twice to the brink of a war. In June 1964, Ankara was ready to intervene, when the Americans, with the notorious letter of President Johnson, stopped them at the eleventh hour.[65] This for Turkey was diplomatic humiliation. Nonetheless, the crisis had not been completely averted. Each side's forces tried to intercept the military plans of the opponent for expanding *de facto* control over certain areas on the island. By August this led to a recurrence of inter-communal fighting and subsequently to new Turkish air raids over Cyprus, which seriously threatened again the peace of the region.

Meanwhile, the first UN Mediator, Sakari Tuomioja, almost a month after assuming his post in Cyprus, admitted that he was at a complete impasse, unable to make any breakthrough to restore normality. Both he and the UN secretary-general, therefore, discreetly allowed the United States to take the lead in the mediation.[66] The Americans still considered that the Cyprus problem should have been dealt principally between

Greece and Turkey, overestimating Athens' ability to manipulate Makarios. Given the constitutional breakdown, both the Americans and the British then concluded that some form of *Enosis* with territorial concessions for Turkey was the most appropriate, and from their point of view, pragmatic solution that would probably be acceptable to both NATO allies and more importantly secure Western interests in the area.[67] Consequently, after the June crisis, the United States under the mediation of the American policymaker Dean Acheson engaged in a series of negotiations with Athens and Ankara. The outcome of these were two plans in Acheson's name, which proposed two successive versions of *Enosis* with certain territorial exchanges for Turkey. Nonetheless, Acheson's mission ended in failure after both of his plans were rejected, the first version by Athens and the latter by Ankara. Moreover, Makarios' rejection of both versions highlighted once again that the primary responsibility for the island's future lies solely with the Cyprus Government and the UN. At the same time Makarios turned towards the Soviets for further military and diplomatic support. After Acheson's failure and the sudden death of Tuomioja, the UN secretary-general decided to take back the lead in the mediation on the island. A new UN mediator was appointed and the Americans decided to gradually disengage from actively seeking for a long-term solution to the Cyprus question.[68]

Constitutional breakdown, serious inter-communal clashes and a buffer zone dividing the Greek and Turkish sector of the capital of the island, known as the Green Line,[69] were the price Cyprus paid for this inter-communal crisis. Turkey for the first time in January 1964 used as a pretext the Treaty of Guarantee to intervene in Cyprus. The United States and Soviet Union were actively engaged with the Cyprus problem, while the two communities' leaderships in Cyprus were completely estranged, having almost all official channels of communication closed. The violent event of 1963/1964 was an early indication of what was about to follow ten years later. The power-sharing model, as had been articulated, in such a fragile manner at independence had collapsed in violence-creating refugees, missing persons and physical destruction. Very ominously for the future, the different paramilitary organizations saw in this the opportunity to enhance their own authority and goals. In this situation the two political leaderships were already becoming pre-occupied with their own extreme factions, underpinning inflexible positions and creating conditions for the failure of UN mediation in March 1965. After that, the impasse – above all an impasse within the island's political culture itself – was to shape the political landscape of Cyprus for the ten dramatic years ahead. The ensuing experience, with its principally internalized focus, will be the focus of our treatment.

Part One

1964–1967

Galo Plaza Report, 1964–1965

Origins and Consequences

The events of December 1963 indicated that the Zurich–London Agreements not only failed to produce a lasting and peaceful solution to the Cyprus question, but on the contrary triggered a new unstable era. The internal turmoil led to a complex situation that widened the perceptions' gap about the optimal settlement between the two communities. Since the initiation of the peacemaking effort in March 1964, the United Nations (UN) officials had been well aware that the variables surrounding the Cyprus question included elements such as the interests at stake of various important players, a fragile balance which threatened the region's peace and an already precarious co-existence of the two communities. In addition, the latter's lack of trust and genuine will to compromise progressively shaped a very difficult and challenging task for any prospective mediator. Although himself not optimistic on arrival, the second UN Mediator in Cyprus, Senor Galo Plaza Lasso, still felt able to say that he saw some 'rays of hope'.[1]

A few months later, on 26 March 1965, Plaza submitted his report, containing what he characterized as 'directions which they themselves should explore in the search for a peaceful solution and an agreed settlement'.[2] By clarifying that these directions were to be considered neither as recommendations nor as concrete suggestions, he highlighted the need for the immediate initiation of direct talks between the two communities.[3] However the parties' perceptions, regarding not only the nature of these directions but their content as well, were diametrically different to Plaza's view. Although this report sought to bring the parties towards a constructive basis for direct negotiations, it drove them further apart. A 'comfortable' impasse for both leaderships – that is, one which both could see as not hindering their respective long-term aims – was then created, which unavoidably led to the acceleration of the separate political and social evolution of the two communities on the island.

In order to have a clear insight into the situation and the determining nature of the mediator's report for the later evolution of the Cyprus question, it is important to identify the reasons that led to Plaza's failure in 1965.

This chapter, therefore, initially examines the prevailing atmosphere upon his assuming of the mediator's post in Cyprus, along with the negotiating objectives and agendas of the conflicting parties. Subsequently, Plaza's assessments are identified along with the reactions raised by the conflicting parties and the aftermath of his short-lived mediation. Before these, however, it is important to sketch out a brief background to the appointment of Galo Plaza in September 1964.

The new mediator in Cyprus

In terms of reaching a functional settlement, the Cyprus question is inevitably perceived as one of the conspicuously unsuccessful missions of the UN. It is for that reason that this problem has usually been characterized as the 'diplomat's graveyard'. Perhaps it was indeed a bad omen the sudden death of the first such mediator, the Finnish Diplomat Sakari Tuomioja, on 9 September 1964, only a few months after his assignment to Cyprus. Finding a suitable mediator back in March 1964, acceptable to all of parties concerned, was not an easy task for the UN secretary-general. U Thant, in particular, admitted that he was 'completely stuck'.[4] After the new wave of inter-communal clashes in August 1964, the failure of Acheson's initiative and Washington's gradual disengagement from the active efforts to broker an agreement, there was again a pressing need for the UN secretary-general to recapture the initiative over the mediation efforts, not least by finding a suitable successor of Tuomioja.

Having previously been the political advisor of United Nations Force in Cyprus (UNFICYP), apparently familiar with all the peculiarities and complexities of the Cyprus problem, and without any other viable options, U Thant believed that Plaza was the natural alternative after Tuomioja's death. As the political advisor of the peacekeeping operation, Plaza's main task had been to effectively manage the daily tensions that occurred between the two communities, to negotiate short-term solutions with Greek-Cypriot and Turkish-Cypriot officials separately, and above all to head off any fresh recourse to violence.[5] Besides his previous post in Cyprus, Galo Plaza was an ex-president of Ecuador and an 'old hand at UN troubleshooting'.[6] He was assigned in 1958 as a chairman of a UN observation group in Lebanon and two years later as a chairman of a study group on the Congo problems.[7] He, therefore, had a good deal of experience of deeply divided and even collapsed societies.

Nevertheless, the name of the new mediator drew mixed reactions within the Turkish-Cypriot community and Turkey. Although generally considered as a skilled UN official, the Turkish side perceived that Plaza, through his UNFICYP post, thus far tended to favour the Greek-Cypriots. Besides, his Latin-American background made him instinctively anti-colonial and strongly supportive of the principle of self-determination. For that reason, before U Thant made public his final decision, Ankara discreetly but unsuccessfully lobbied in order to ward off Plaza's appointment.[8] Nonetheless, the British had convinced the Turks that U Thant's choice was perhaps the only viable alternative at that critical juncture. Turkey, therefore, grudgingly agreed to the latter's assignment, and on 16 September 1964 Galo Plaza officially succeeded the late Sakari Tuomioja. Nevertheless, the impartiality or otherwise of the new mediator continued to constitute a great source of concern for Turkey and Turkish-Cypriots, and from their perspective the final outcome of the report seemed to prove them right.

Lessons from Dean Acheson's mediation of summer 1964

I am not going into this blindfolded. I am very much aware of the difficulties involved in this complex task. However, if it is believed that I am in a position to make a positive contribution to the cause of peace, I find it a moral obligation to accept the assignment. If I fail, I will move on and let a better man to take over. Mediators must be understood to be expendable.[9]

With these words Galo Plaza opened on 17 September a new chapter in the peacemaking of the Cyprus problem. He knew that if he wanted to produce any concrete results, he had to follow a totally new approach to that of his predecessor. The developments that took place throughout the summer of 1964 and particularly the failure of the US mediation with Dean Acheson in Geneva gave important lessons that all parties had to take now under serious consideration. Primarily, the Cyprus problem was not an exclusively Greco-Turkish affair, and thus a solution on the basis of *Enosis* with territorial exchanges for Turkey was not as feasible as Britain and the United States believed.[10] Although after the summer of 1964 *Enosis* was still regarded by the West as the only solution that would guarantee stability in the area, the UN continued to seek out possible middle ground between the two communities and their motherlands. It should be stated that although Plaza sought American and British diplomatic support and their help to exert moderate influence on the parties, he also requested that they accept that mediation would be an exclusively UN initiative which only he would take responsibility for, if it failed.[11] The Anglo-Americans consented and decided to shelve the *Enosis* option for the moment, let the UN take the lead in seeking a solution that would focus first on preserving independence on the island and, above all, put a stop to any further destabilization.[12]

The most important lesson for Plaza was that Makarios and the Cyprus Government had to be maintained at the centre of the negotiating attempts since anything else was a recipe for failure.[13] Makarios had made plain that he was not going to accept any solution that would seem to be imposed from the outside, regardless of its benefits.[14] The Republic of Cyprus was a sovereign state, and, in principle, a solution had to be sought within the island according to Security Council Resolution 186 and with the UN in the driving seat. Besides, Makarios' political manoeuvres during the Geneva negotiations of Acheson provided evidence, not for the first time, of the falsity of the British, American and Turkish belief that Greece had the necessary leverage to force Makarios to accept a solution in the making of which he had not been involved.[15] It should be stressed, however, that throughout the following decade Turkey never really accepted this counter-thesis, while Greece tried unsuccessfully to reverse it by constantly trying to strengthen its military presence and political influence on the island.[16] Nonetheless, after Geneva the Greek Government, ostensibly at least, decided to follow a common line with the Cyprus Government, refused to have bilateral discussions with Turkey and argued that a solution should first be sought on the basis of independence.[17]

Despite all the above, the most important 'side effect' for the West of the Geneva negotiations was that it reinforced Makarios' turn to the Soviet Union. In August 1964 Makarios secured not only military support but also a diplomatic 'shield', with a statement confirming that 'if a foreign armed intervention takes place in Cyprus the Soviet Union will help Cyprus to defend its freedom and independence'.[18]

Acheson's mediation, meanwhile, had a negative effect on Turco-American relations. Following the diplomatic humiliation in June 1964, when President Johnson prevented Ankara from intervening in Cyprus,[19] the Turkish Government believed that Washington was letting them down again. Ankara was coming under fire at home for being too subservient to the Western alliance, including over Cyprus. In these circumstances, *Enosis* in any form became impossible for Turkey.[20] While never abandoning the belief that Cyprus was a matter to be dealt primarily between Greece and Turkey, the Turkish Government now seemed willing to go along with UN mediation, while harbouring misgivings about Plaza.[21] It hedged its bets, however, on making fresh declarations about the inviolability of the Zurich–London Agreements and, at the same time, on arguing that any new constitutional arrangement in Cyprus had to be a federal one.

Having all these realities in mind, in taking up the reins, Plaza's basic idea was to concentrate principally on the leaders of the two communities with the concept of thrashing out a solution without an absolute winner or absolute loser.[22] Absoluteness, however, remained the nub of the matter. Plaza soon began to discover that each of the Cypriot parties was not preoccupied with an urgent agreement to sooth existing discontents, but rather with gaining time to strengthen their own negotiating positions through outside alliances and, most essentially, a series of *faits accomplis* on the island. Meanwhile, polarization of their public opinion was essential for this 'game'.[23] The American ambassador in Ankara caught the essence in November 1964 reporting that

despite Galo Plaza's inveterate optimism and political virtuosity, including close rapport with Makarios, his multiple conversations with all parties concerned have not resulted in any narrowing of gap [...] but instead have served [to] reveal that gap greater than was thought.[24]

The parties' agendas

It could be argued that the developments of the first half of 1964 had nonetheless secured the diplomatic preponderance of the Greek-Cypriot community vis-à-vis the Turkish-Cypriots. The Security Council debate in March 1964 saw the Cyprus Government in its purely Greek-Cypriot synthesis henceforth and thus the Greek-Cypriot position broadly victorious. The Greek-Cypriots controlled the state's machinery enjoying the international recognition given to them by the Resolution 186, while the Turkish-Cypriot leaders who withdrew from the Cyprus Government were internationally isolated, without any official voice in the government and fully dependent on Ankara's diplomatic, and even potentially physical, support.

Nevertheless, a second diplomatic battle within the UN was anticipated by both sides. Particularly, after September 1964 both sides were getting prepared for a General Assembly debate. Their preparation activities, however, to some extent, overshadowed Plaza's negotiations.[25] At this point, we shall briefly define the objectives of each party and the mechanisms employed in order to achieve them during Plaza's mediation.

First, Greek-Cypriot leaders agitated in favour of an independent, unitary, integral, demilitarized and sovereign State with adequate safeguards for minority rights and respect for the legitimate right of the people of Cyprus to determine their future without outside interventions.[26] There should be, however, a particular emphasis on the latter part of this assertion. The respect of the right of self-determination for the Greek-Cypriot leadership naturally meant that as soon as unfettered independence was consolidated, the Greek-Cypriots should have the right to pursue freely unification of the island with Greece. Nevertheless, this *Enosis* was very different from the one that the Greek Government and the West had sought.[27] For the Cyprus Government it meant primarily unconditional *Enosis,* without any territorial exchanges to Turkey and, second, that Cyprus would enjoy a special status within Greece's administration, since it would not be bound by any of the latter's international commitments.[28] Makarios already knew that this was indeed impractical. Nevertheless, he could not openly admit that *Enosis,* which was still perceived by Greek-Cypriots as the only road for national salvation, was an illusory dream.[29] Although he continued to pay constant lip service to this illusory dream, Makarios decided to put it into cold storage for the moment and work towards the consolidation of the first goal: an independent, unitary state with minority rights for the Turkish-Cypriots. As will be explained, the first step towards that goal was to institutionally re-organize and economically develop the state along the lines he favoured, by removing all the contentious provisions of the Constitution. The absence of the Turkish-Cypriot factor was going to make this task easier. Second, he had to find ways to get rid of the 1960 Treaties of Alliance and Guarantee, which for him not only undermined but also posed a real threat to the sovereignty of the Republic. Finally, he had to force the Turkish-Cypriot community into accepting the minority status on offer, but without provoking military intervention by Turkey.

In order to achieve the latter, the Cyprus Government decided to impose a series of measures aiming to tighten the pressure on the Turkish-Cypriots residing in the enclaves created after the inter-communal clashes of December 1963. More specifically, the embargo of the so-called 'strategic materials' that could have been used for building arms and fortifications – such as iron, tiles, cement, several types of clothing and raw materials, building materials, fuel, batteries and so on – and restrictions of movement were an indispensable part of the government's attrition policy towards the isolated Turkish-Cypriots.[30] In February 1965, however, a few months after the strict embargo, President Makarios argued that he was ready to discuss with the Turkish-Cypriot leaders but solely on the basis of minority rights.[31] All other procedures, seemingly, were rejected.[32] We shall see that this proved to be a highly ineffective policy.

Makarios' second goal of nullifying the two 1960 treaties was practically very difficult due to its wider legal and international implications. Immediately after the December 1963 clash, Makarios unilaterally declared that the treaties were no longer valid for the Cyprus Government, but this statement was not accepted by the other signatories, especially Britain and Turkey.[33] The treaties had been signed by the two communities themselves and the three guarantors, while their abrogation or amendment needed the consent of all the signatories. Nonetheless, the Cyprus Government was determined to eliminate all the obstacles to its sovereignty and believed that the forthcoming UN General Assembly debate and resolution would provide a stepping stone in that direction.[34] It tried, therefore, to secure diplomatic support by initiating a 'good-will mission' towards the Non-Aligned countries – where the quest for self-determination was highlighted – and towards the Soviet Union – stressing the West's allegedly sinister and divisive plans in the region.[35] In the meantime, the Cyprus Government tried to incapacitate the Treaty of Alliance by creating obstacles and setting pre-conditions for the rotation of Turkey's troops on the island.[36] In October 1964, when the troop rotation issue came up, Ankara appeared flexible and accepted some of the Cyprus Government's pre-conditions. However, in February 1965, when that issue re-surfaced, the Turkish Government was determined to show a firm hand, even in indicating a preparedness to intervene if the rotation was hampered.[37]

On the other side of the buffer line, as already stated, there was an isolated and internally weak Turkish-Cypriot leadership. By rejecting their characterization as a rebellious minority, the Turkish-Cypriots tried to convince the international community that they were in fact the victims of what they depicted as a repressive and illegal Greek-Cypriot Government, which was planning their complete domination.[38] The imposition of what was characterized by Ankara as a criminal blockade on the Turkish-Cypriots who lived in the enclaves was seen as a proof of the Greek-Cypriots' determination to condemn them to live under concentration camp conditions until they were brought to their knees.[39] Moreover, the constant rhetoric of *Enosis* by the Greek-Cypriot leaders (increasingly formulaic though it may have been for some of them) was a firm indication for Ankara and the Turkish-Cypriots that the sole adequate mechanism for ensuring their safe existence on the island was the physical and geographical separation of the two communities through a federal state or even partition.[40]

In fact, the conditions for the establishment of a federation, such as defined and geographically coherent areas where Greek-Cypriots and Turkish-Cypriots might carry on a separate existence, did not exist. On the contrary, Turkish-Cypriot and mixed villages were spread throughout the island and the creation of a federated state would have implied a compulsory movement of population. As in 1956 when Lord Radcliffe, the constitutional expert, assigned to prepare proposals for a Cyprus Constitution, now Plaza was constantly emphasizing to the Turkish side that the above reality confirms that a federal system in Cyprus would not be functional.[41] The Turkish-Cypriot leadership, including Turkish Resistance Organization (TMT) under Ankara's guidance, sought to effect the necessary conditions. The creation of strategic enclaves in several parts of the island and Turkish-Cypriot isolation in them was a prerequisite for such consolidation. The main ones were in Nicosia and the villages of Limnitis, Lefka and Kokkina. In addition, securing the control of the main road which connected Nicosia and Kyrenia was perceived as a key development for the Turkish-Cypriot aims. This road enabled them to concentrate the necessary military equipment and to forbid the Greek-Cypriot movement throughout their own sectors.[42] Such a heightening of the minority's sense of security was essential to maintaining its morale.

For ensuring the separation of the two communities on the ground, the TMT leaders and Turkish military officials imposed severe restrictions of movement outside these enclaves, trying thus to cut off inter-communal contacts and prevent any fraternization with Greek-Cypriots. Pamphlets were occasionally circulated throughout the Turkish-Cypriot enclaves regarding fines and punishments for association with Greek-Cypriots.[43] Simultaneously, Turkish-Cypriot military and political leaders initiated an aggressive propaganda proposing their distinctive version of the present situation and the events which had shaped them.[44] For that reason, it was essential to promote the strengthening of a common Turkish consciousness, especially during the first months of the separation, by engaging as many Turkish-Cypriots as possible with the separate administration and the fighters' corps.[45] Additionally, the cultivation of mistrust for the 'common enemy' and the physical elimination of voices in favour of peaceful co-existence were also crucial parts of their plans. Simultaneously, the Turkish-Cypriot leadership was able to point to the economic restrictions imposed on them to give evidence of their victimization by Makarios' Government. This was also illustrated in several UNFICYP commanders' reports, recalling visits to the Kokkina caves inhabited by refugees, so allowing the TMT leaders to claim that the situation was worse than it really was.[46]

With their own leverage faltering, both within the island and in the UN debates, the Turkish-Cypriot leaders felt threatened, and to counter-balance this weakness Ankara initiated an internationalization strategy designed to maximize its limited political assets. Through this strategy the Turkish Government sought to portray the illegitimacy of the Cyprus Government and the inability of the two communities to live together under a unified state.[47] It was essential for Ankara to gain outside support in order to prevent a General Assembly resolution which could diplomatically strengthen Makarios' position, especially on the aspect of the 1960 treaties. Ankara's first stop was Moscow, where the Turkish diplomacy 'played' the *Enosis* card. Although the Soviets in August 1964 had given assurances to the Cyprus Government for support in case of an external aggression, at the same time they wanted to prevent any type of *Enosis,* since that would have brought Cyprus under North Atlantic Treaty Organization's (NATO's) protection. Ankara and Moscow, therefore, were ready to form a common front against *Enosis* were it to become at all imminent. The Turco-Soviet rapprochement of autumn 1964 secured two important gains for Turkey: first, in November 1964 a joint *communiqué* which made reference to both communities' legal rights and the inviolability of the 1960 treaties[48] and, second, in January 1965, a statement by the Soviet Foreign Minister, Andrei Gromyko, favourable to the concept of a federal solution for Cyprus.[49]

Moscow's support for Turkey's position in this sense had affected to some extent the dynamics of the Cyprus problem. As the American ambassador in Turkey explained, the Turco-Soviet rapprochement alleviated the previous American concern for the growing Soviet influence over Makarios' Government.[50] As a result, it reduced America's previous sense of urgency to find a solution on the basis of *Enosis.*

After a series of negotiations and a shuttle diplomacy between the interested parties, the UN mediator had a clear image of both their overt and hidden agendas.[51] It should be re-emphasized, however, that at that juncture it was the Greek-Cypriots who held a tight rein of the island. Although the Greek-Cypriots genuinely believed that their objectives as the majority of the 78 per cent on the island had been legitimate, deriving from the undisputable right of self-determination, the Greek-Cypriot leaders crucially failed to make accurate and pragmatic evaluation about the objectives and position of their 'opponents'.[52] One of these mistakes was the erroneous beliefs of the Cyprus Foreign Ministry about the primary concern of Turkey and Turkish-Cypriots. The Greek-Cypriots underestimated the importance of safeguarding Ankara's own prestige and the security concerns of the Turkish-Cypriots in any prospective settlement; they also overestimated the UN's capabilities for providing adequate guarantees and anything other than moral support to the parties. Spyros Kyprianou, the Cypriot foreign minister, reiterated his belief that Turkey's '*sine qua non* in the Cyprus problem' was the rights of the Turkish-Cypriots themselves. After securing the latter, Ankara would have probably sought a solution that would have satisfied its security concerns and finally a compromise that would have constituted an honourable exit from the Cyprus impasse.[53] Kyprianou concluded that

> the Turkish Cypriots for the most part, do not have a preference as to independence or enosis but are most interested in where they can get

reliable guarantees of human rights. He [Kyprianou] thought that they would be happy to accept these if they involve some degree in autonomy and religion, culture, education, and personal status, combined with some Government financial assistance.[54]

These assessments were proved to be mistaken but they would continue to highly affect the Greek-Cypriot decision-making process until 1974.[55]

The truth was really an inversion of this ranking. The Cyprus problem had become a huge liability for Turkey; therefore, the first and most important concern for Ankara was to find a face-saving way out both for its public opinion and for the armed forces.[56] A second concern was Turkey's broader geopolitical and security interests, insofar as Cyprus had any relevance from them, and very much last was the well-being of the Turkish-Cypriots 'with the latter being much the weakest point', as the Turkish Prime Minister, Ismet Inonu, confessed to Plaza.[57]

It should also be borne in mind that Turkish general elections were scheduled for October 1965 and that inevitably increased domestic pressure. This was not the first time that the Cyprus issue had a great impact on Turkish politics. Since the 1950s, the Cyprus issue had continuously affected Turkey's domestic and foreign policy. Admittedly, Cyprus was only one of several territorial issues in which Turkish interests were involved in the wider region, stretching into Asia and the Caucasus, and which also raised the possibilities of tension with the Soviet Union. Of these various engagements, however, Cyprus was the one where the risks could be more easily calibrated and, whenever necessary, kept within bounds.[58] Furthermore, the 'threat of extinction' of the Turkish-Cypriot community bound up with the Greek-Cypriot claim for *Enosis* became a convenient tool for mobilizing new followers and popular support for new political movements and parties in Turkey itself. These movements were actively seeking not only to energize public opinion among the Turks but also to encourage Turkish-Cypriots to fight against *Enosis*. The Turkish press campaign towards that goal was an element that clearly had a purely domestic political dimension. The press created internal pressures on the Turkish Government to evolve a more effective and radical strategy towards the 'unredeemed' Turkish-Cypriot population.[59] This factor had become increasingly significant over the second half of the 1950s and continued throughout the following decade.

Having in mind the totally inflexible positions of Nicosia and Ankara, Plaza could have only succeeded if he could manage to simultaneously lead the parties towards moderation with the same face-saving formula. Was that possible?

Galo Plaza measures his options

Pursuing their respective strategies, and positioning themselves for the looming General Assembly debate, by the end of 1964 both Greek-Cypriots and Turkish-Cypriots remained inflexible during their consultations with the mediator.[60] Although Plaza had reached several tentative conclusions, about the most functional and lasting solution for the Cyprus problem and for the most appropriate procedure towards it, he decided to let the 'storm' of the expected UN debate fade and then to make known his conclusions. However, by early February 1965 it became known that the General Assembly on Cyprus would not take place and thus Plaza set about drafting his report. The latter also calculated that the previous Turco-Soviet rapprochement would constrain mainly the Greek-Cypriot reactions to his report and in particular that Makarios would line up behind it.[61] Since at that point the international balance was seemingly changing, Plaza believed the time was ripe to introduce the element he considered vital for success all round. He explained that the parties needed a 'face-saving device to explain why they had abandoned apparently entrenched positions'.[62] This device for Plaza was his report which he believed that would help in

> dislodging the present impasse without risking any serious deterioration of the situation and in particular in creating the necessary conditions for a new phase in the mediation process, including the possibility of multilateral talks.[63]

What, then, were the main options for settlement and the relevant factors that Plaza had to consider? First of all, there was *Enosis*, entailing two important implications. Although it was the best possible solution for the West, essentially what Athens wanted and what Greek-Cypriots favoured for the distant future, it was not possible for a UN representative to effectively recommend the dissolution of a member state of the UN organization.[64] Its own membership would not permit any such dangerous precedent. *Enosis* was perhaps only possible if it was the outcome of a referendum but not from a unilateral UN proposal.[65] Even in that case, however, there was one crucial element missing: a clear understanding between the Greek Government and Makarios as to what *Enosis* actually meant.[66]

Alternatively, there was the option of independence under a federal state with physical separation of the two communities as Turks and Turkish-Cypriots favoured. Plaza ruled out this option since it was 'utterly repugnant' to the majority of the Cypriots.[67] Also, it would have required forced movement of population along with the creation of more displaced persons.

This would have damaging financial consequences, especially for Turkish-Cypriots, who would be forced to look even more towards Turkey for economic and material aid. That reality could easily lead to full partition and that was contrary to the philosophy of the UN Charter of Human Rights.[68]

Lastly, there was the option of a solution on the basis of independence with adequate UN guarantees for the Turkish-Cypriots and demilitarization of the island.[69] Plaza saw this as potentially acceptable to all parties since it would have satisfied the Turks on the grounds that the Zurich–London Agreements were still valid and was essentially what Makarios was in favour of, even if he could not yet say so openly. Simultaneously, the Turkish-Cypriot rights would have been effectively guaranteed. Lastly, demilitarizing the island and preventing *Enosis* helped to satisfy Turkey's security interests.[70]

Nonetheless, this type of settlement required some form of negotiations. But this was where the problems really began. Since it was imperative that Makarios remained in the centre of any negotiations, these had to be conducted between the two communities. This option, however, was constantly rejected by Turkey. Meanwhile, Makarios agreed to negotiate as the president of the Republic of Cyprus and not as a community leader opposite some Turkish-Cypriot counterpart. Arguably, the most efficient negotiating method was through direct exchanges between Makarios and Turkey who held effective control within their respective communities. Nevertheless, this was an option that primarily clashed with the principles set by the contested parties and was impossible for the UN mediator to suggest.[71] Both the UN mediation and Western diplomacy increasingly sought in vain to 'square the circle' of any type of negotiations over Cyprus.[72] Plaza's report appeared to be the 'last hurrah' in such an exercise.

On the eve of the submission of the mediator's report, there was no sign that the latter was succeeding in bringing the parties towards a common ground. The Greek-Cypriot side was at least content that the looming report had overtaken a UN General Assembly debate in which Turkey, after the Turco-Soviet rapprochement of November 1964, might have mobilized support. The Greek-Cypriots were confident that Plaza's conclusions would veer in their direction and, even though likely to be rejected by the Turkish-Cypriots, could reinforce their own future bargaining positions.[73]

Conversely, the Turkish Government had a very different perception not only about the timing of the publication of the report but also about its content. Ankara expressed strong reactions to the possibility of Plaza submitting a possibly unfavourable report before the forthcoming elections in Turkey of October 1965.[74] Ankara was anxious to ensure that even if the report was published, the mediator should merely reiterate basic historical and current facts, without making any substantive proposals.[75] Otherwise, the Turkish foreign minister had threatened Plaza to reject it in advance.[76] The Turkish ambassador in Britain explained:

> The Mediator's report should not contain a clear cut solution, or even a basis on which the solution could be achieved [...] the Turks were asking that the Mediator should be encouraged to say that the problem was insoluble and that he had nothing to suggest.[77]

The Turkish-Cypriots for their part, according to the British High Commissioner in Nicosia, Sir David Hunt, did not expect much from Plaza since they believed that he was 'a willing dupe of Makarios'.[78] Hunt explained the general attitude of the Turkish-Cypriot side as follows:

> Let us wait and see what he [i.e Plaza] has to say but whatever it is we stand on our constitutional rights as a community and [we] are ready to negotiate only if the three Guarantor Powers are involved.[79]

It seemed, therefore, that the Turkish authorities, even more than the Turkish-Cypriots, were almost bound to react strongly to Plaza's report. Finally, aware that the mediator's report would probably be inclined towards the Greek-Cypriot position and afraid of the Turkish reaction, Britain and the United States were sceptical even about its necessity.[80] However, by March 1965, tension had again increased on the island and there seemed no other alternative than to sit and wait in the hope that some good might come out of it.

The UN mediator's report

A few days before the publication of his conclusions, Plaza explained that his report

> would be a detailed analysis of each element in the situation and it was to be hoped that it would stimulate a flow of ideas which might help to move the various parties away from their present entrenched position. It would be the end of one chapter and the beginning of a new one. The report would not contain any positive suggestions. I am a mediator rather than an arbitrator. But I would lay down certain guide-lines. I was not able to accept the Turkish view that the report should be merely a historical account. I had tried to persuade the Turkish Government that if they wanted the mediation to continue it

was essential to open up certain avenues along which future progress might be made in negotiations.[81]

On 26 March 1965, the report was unveiled at a UN Security Council meeting.[82] After making a brief historical background, an analysis of the previous mediation effort and the objectives of the parties, the mediator proceeded with his conclusions and 'indications of the possible future course'.[83] Trying to deflect Turkish reactions, he emphasized again that he was not an arbitrator and that nothing should be imposed upon the parties. He stressed that the views contained in the report were purely personal.[84]

Guided primarily by the UN Charter, most of his observations indeed favoured Makarios' position. Unsurprisingly, this infuriated the Turkish Government. Plaza particularly recommended that a solution should be sought primarily within Cyprus with negotiations between the two communities, on the basis of an independent, demilitarized state with special guarantees for minority rights, that would be supervised by a UN commissioner for as long as necessary, and autonomy for the Turkish-Cypriots in religious, cultural, educational and personal status affairs.[85] Nevertheless, he proposed that there should also be a second stage of negotiations with all the other signatories of the Zurich–London Agreements.[86] The mediator stressed that although the treaties and the Constitution were still legally binding, the recent events bore out that they could not be fully implemented and thus should be either abrogated or at least modified. Moreover, it was stated that *Enosis* should be voluntarily renounced due to its wider implications.[87] Contrary to Ankara's arguments, he concluded that federation and geographical separation of the two communities were neither realistic nor feasible.[88]

Against Plaza's previous hopes for fresh momentum, the intensity of the Turkish reactions deeply disillusioned the UN secretary-general and the mediator. Rejecting immediately all of Plaza's conclusions out of hand, Ankara explained that the publication of his report brought the immediate termination of his services.[89] The issue that primarily provoked this strong reaction was the recommendation for talks between the two communities.[90] Both the Turkish Government and opposition in Ankara followed a common line that Cyprus was a Greco-Turkish affair, and only negotiations between the two motherlands were acceptable.[91]

The UN, the United States and Britain quickly set about trying to tone down Turkey's hostility to the report. The Americans were particularly disappointed by Ankara's reaction.[92] They believed it was an irrational and impulsive decision and placed the Turkish side in a disadvantageous position, especially in a future Security Council or General Assembly debate. They even saw some positive elements within the report for Turkey. For example, the validity of the Zurich–London Agreements was highlighted, and, although not as explicitly as Turkey wished, *Enosis* was rejected. In addition, although there was a clear preference for inter-communal talks, Plaza did not exclude negotiations between the two motherlands.[93] It was utopian for Turkey to expect that Makarios be excluded from active negotiations about the future of the island. By vehemently rejecting this report and by not accepting any form of negotiations in Cyprus itself, Ankara had given further credibility to Nicosia's and Makarios' arguments that there needed to be much greater recognition of Cyprus' unfettered independence.

The Turkish Government, however, was in no mood to show any such moderation. A few days later it informed the UN secretary-general that Plaza had exceeded his mandate without having obtained the consent of all parties concerned and that his services were perceived to be terminated.[94] Although the UN secretary-general tried to defend his mediator by explaining that Plaza had acted in complete accordance with his mandate under Resolution 186, he wholly failed to pacify Ankara's reactions.[95]

The immediate and negative reaction of the Turkish Government gave little room for manoeuvre to the Turkish-Cypriot leaders. Therefore, the Turkish-Cypriot response was shaped by Ankara's inflexibility.[96] The Turkish-Cypriot leaders criticized the inadequate guarantees proposed by the mediator for the protection of the Turkish-Cypriots, which they still argued that they could only be guaranteed under physical separation.[97] The report, they additionally claimed, sought to curtail the partnership status conferred on Turkish-Cypriots by the 1960 Constitution. However, according to British Intelligence Reports, 'the Turkish-Cypriots would ideally have wished to take a less hostile attitude to the report but were compelled to do so by Ankara's statement'.[98] It was also suggestive that the Turkish-Cypriot leadership did not immediately endorse the Turkish position for the termination of Plaza's mediation and privately certain moderate Turkish-Cypriot leaders did not fully reject the possibility of having direct talks with some Greek-Cypriot leaders.[99]

Although initial indications coming from the Greek-Cypriot leaderships were favourable to the report, internal reactions were more mixed. Plaza's call for a voluntary abandonment of *Enosis* held within it the seed of considerable controversy. It was exploited by the right-wing press in order to attack the Greek-Cypriot leadership.[100] The government's ambivalence towards *Enosis* was clearly exposed in the public domain since the mediator had reported that 'neither the President nor the Government of Cyprus, in their discussions with me as the mediator actually advocated for *Enosis* as the final solution to the Cyprus problem'.[101] Instead, they had in private pursued the aim of an unfettered independence. The internal unrest between the right-wing and Makarios' Government was intensified after Clerides' statement of 31 March 1965 that 'time had come to stop telling people that *Enosis* is round the corner [...] we must be adult enough to give up wishful thinking, and realize we have an adult population and treat them as such'.[102] Extreme right wingers called for Makarios' resignation because he failed to renounce Clerides' statement,[103] while General Grivas was said to have commented 'that damned priest is letting us all down'.[104] Aware of the intense atmosphere in the aftermath of Plaza's report, and in order to prevent any further causes of friction, *The Economist* reported that 'western correspondents accepted an unusual degree of pressure not to write anything about this split out of which Grivas supporters could make capital'.[105]

The official response of the Cyprus Government, which came a few days later, was nonetheless positive. Trying to appease concerns internally, however, the Cyprus Permanent Representative to the UN, Zenon Rossides, sent a letter to the secretary-general in which he emphasized his country's only reservation; it was inconceivable for the Cyprus Government to accept the self-restriction of their right for self-determination and *Enosis,* merely because of Turkey's threats to use force in such a case.[106] That element for the Greek-Cypriots was a clear violation of the UN Charter of Human Rights.

Finally, as was the case with the Turkish-Cypriots, Greece's reaction was also determined by the hostile reaction of Turkey. Although for the Greek leaders the mediator's findings were to some extent satisfactory, any acceptance of his proposal for voluntary renunciation of *Enosis* was domestically still perceived as political suicide.[107] Hunt vividly recalls:

> While both Greek parties were hesitating and consulting each other they were saved from embarrassment by Ankara which, without giving the Turkish-Cypriots time to utter a word, denounced the whole plan and declared Galo Plaza was no longer acceptable as a mediator. This was not a clever move. The advice of the Turkish Foreign Service, a well-trained and shrewd body of men, had plainly been overruled by the government, which was weak in Parliamentary terms and accordingly thought it vital to take a strong line. They would have put Athens, though perhaps not Nicosia, in a much more difficult position if they had accepted the report at least as a basis for discussion. As it was the Greeks, much relieved, were able to put themselves on the right side with the United Nations.[108]

Both Nicosia and Athens, therefore, expressed reservations about the *Enosis* self-renunciation but, nevertheless, indicated their willingness for the continuation of Plaza's mediation and of his constructive efforts to settle the Cyprus problem. Turkey's rejection, however, forced the UN peacemaking efforts on the sidelines once again and led to the awkward necessity of a new mediator. Nonetheless, the latter option was rejected outright by Makarios.[109] The impasse was, therefore, unavoidable and, as later proved, very difficult to be bridged. Up until 1968 it was impossible for the UN secretary-general to achieve a compromise even on the question of a new mediator.

Conclusion

The publication of Plaza's report marked the beginning of the end of the first UN mediating attempt in Cyprus. After several discussions to find a suitable exit from the new impasse, Plaza's services effectively ended although he only officially resigned in December 1965.[110] However, he left an even more suspicious atmosphere. Interestingly, Oliver Richmond, a political scientist who dealt extensively with the UN peacemaking in Cyprus, believes that Plaza's failure had 'set a dangerous precedent'.[111]

There were two particular elements that should be kept in mind when examining the failure of Plaza's mediation: the conclusions themselves, which infuriated the Turkish side, and the unfortunate timing of their publication. More specifically, the latter factor proved to be a double-edged sword. Although Plaza calculated that the Greek-Cypriots at that time would be more amenable to accept inter-communal talks without pre-conditions and abandonment of *Enosis*, it seems that he had underestimated the importance of prestige and honour concerns of the Turkish Government at that particular juncture. While the latter was in a weak position internally, the successful overtures of Ankara towards the Soviet Union in November 1964 and January 1965 gave a great boost to the Turkish morale and confidence in its quest for federation. All these helped to consolidate on the part of Turkey an uncompromising attitude towards the mediator and especially on the aspect of inter-communal talks.

Simultaneously, internal developments and the prevailing context on the island in February–March 1965 were further diminishing any chances for convincing the parties to show moderation. As will be explained in detail in Chapter 2, after some months of relative calm, during the first months of 1965 tension increased again due to several provocative statements and actions of the Cyprus Government as well as due to the military confrontation of the National Guard and the Turkish-Cypriot fighters in various areas of the island. Adding to all these, Ankara's strong views over the content of the mediator's report were gaining an extra edge in the run-up to the elections of October 1965. It should also be stressed that during this period both Britain and the United States believed that they were unable to substantially press the Turkish Government not to reject Plaza's suggestions *in toto* because their own leverage towards Turkey had diminished since the summer of 1964.[112]

Accordingly, publishing a report in this shape under the circumstances, without any 'coercive resources or major incentives' to convince Turkey to accept it, was to run a big risk.[113] The UN Under-Secretary for Special Political Affairs José Rölz-Bennett, who tried to sound out the parties in order to take their approval for a new mediator in 1966, explained that the Turkish side was particularly sensitive on the issue of making public the conclusions of any prospective mediator.[114] Perhaps, according to Rölz-Bennett, 'if Plaza's report had not been published and the Turks had been given time to consider it, they might have been less hostile towards it, especially as it came down against *Enosis*'.[115] Inevitably, the Plaza episode generated a deep mistrust of the Turkish and Turkish-Cypriot side which was constantly reflected in Turkey's foreign policy regarding Cyprus' future.[116] Until 1972, Turkey sought to prevent the direct involvement of the UN in the political aspects of the Cyprus problem.

Along with the bad timing of the publication, the substance of the mediator's conclusions eventually brought mediation to naught. This element was decisive for the later development of the Cyprus problem. A key reason for this was that Plaza's conclusions made Makarios even less keen to abandon what he saw as a position of strength, without first securing the *de facto* capitulation of the Turkish-Cypriots. Newly confident, in subsequent years Makarios never relaxed his pre-conditions over talks, while even after 1968, when he eventually accepted the inter-communal talks, his negotiating position was shaped on the basis of Plaza's conclusions.[117]

Although Turkey's prompt and negative response was characterized as irrational by the Americans, Ankara achieved its main goal from the UN mediation's ultimate deadlock. It succeeded in downgrading the UN involvement on the political aspects of the Cyprus problem, while the focus again shifted to the bilateral Greco-Turkish dialogue initiated in May 1965. Despite their previous adamant position for the contrary, both Athens and Nicosia agreed to the motherlands' dialogue and justified this *volte-face* on grounds that it was one of the mediator's suggestions. In that respect, therefore, it could be argued that indeed Plaza's report constituted a face-saving device for the initiation of negotiations. However, these negotiations were not conducted between the two communities but between the two motherlands and were not on the basis of independence but on the basis of *Enosis*.

Meanwhile, due to the disagreement over the successor to Plaza between the Greek-Cypriots and Turkish-Cypriots, the UN secretary-general was forced to downgrade his mediation to simply those of good offices and to accept the primacy of the Greco-Turkish dialogue.[118] This was a setback for the UN itself. Nonetheless, Makarios' reluctance to accept any direct contacts with the Turkish-Cypriot leaders throughout the following years made the good offices of the secretary-general totally ineffective. The only active UN operation was UNFICYP, which tried to maintain at least a peaceful atmosphere on the island.

More than fifty years after the publication of Plaza's report, the Greek-Cypriots still perceive it as probably the most acceptable and balanced report that has emerged from the UN since the initiation of its efforts to the Cyprus problem. On the contrary, the critical perceptions of Ankara and the Turkish-Cypriots remain rooted in the belief that Plaza was prejudiced in favour of the Greek-Cypriots. It is certainly hard to validate the assertion in one source that Plaza's contribution was 'successful in the face of extremely difficult circumstances'.[119] Such a view probably reflects a desire on the UN's own part to lay claims to a positive track record in the sphere of conflict resolution. Inevitably, the recollections of the protagonists themselves are prone to distortion and inaccuracy as to the real sequence of events. This is clearly illustrated by an interview that the mediator himself gave in 1984 about his report. He recalled,

[*sic*] Before I left I wrote a report on what I thought was a way to solve the problem between the two communities and hence between the two countries. That report is valid up to this day and has been used at the different meetings at the UN anytime the Cyprus problem has come up. I resigned at the time because the Greek Government, for internal political reasons, did not agree with the report. But they agreed since. Both communities have agreed with the report but at the time they did not [...] The idea was to give the Turks a greater hand in the government of the country and also a greater presence in the area that they occupied themselves. So it would give them greater participation in [the] government and they did not think of themselves as being totally controlled and absorbed by the Greeks to a position where they might eventually become the owners of the country and the country added to Greece in what they called *enosis*; that is something the Greeks never accepted.[120]

It seems that by 1984, intervening events had affected Plaza's recollections. Despite the contested versions of all the players and the serious problems and limitations of the UN, goodwill and trust were the most important elements absent from all the contested parties. Goodwill was absent before 1960; it was absent during this first mediation attempt; and it was to continue afterwards.

Progress towards a settlement in the 1960s – as later – hinged on goodwill expressed openly in a power-sharing state. Richard Haass, a Senior American policymaker and political scientist closely involved in the peace process in Northern Ireland, explains that distrust between communities is translated into an often unspoken preference for the *status quo*[121]: Indeed the fact that this preference for tactical reasons must remain unspoken on all sides helps to make a continuing situation even more muddled. Although events in the period 1964–1965 in some respect prevented an opportunity to row back from the alarming prospect opened up by the crisis of 1963–1964, the prevailing context – or zeitgeist – of the time, both on the island and abroad, did not allow the parties to grasp the hazards of letting the *status quo* worsen. The stalemate that followed the Plaza episode led to the consolidation of communal separation and the perpetuation or establishment of divergent institutions as political formations. By the time a new UN initiative was to be launched in 1968, fresh realities were to hamper the effort. This only validated the British prediction made in February 1965 that 'inaction after report is presented would allow Makarios to consolidate present *de facto* position, continue erosion of Constitution and weaken the Turkish community on the island by economic and other pressures'.[122] This further deterioration in the likelihood of an agreed basis for a settlement in Cyprus will be explored in the following chapters.

1964–1967: Reshuffling the Deck

The Restructuring of the State

The dawn of 1964 had marked a new phase for the Cyprus question. The withdrawal of the Turkish-Cypriots from the state apparatus led to a reshuffling of cards in relation to the political problem. The Greek-Cypriots were left to govern the Republic of Cyprus, while the Turkish-Cypriots barricaded themselves into enclaves where they administered their own areas. The former now had the opportunity to create the type of state they sought by amending all parts of the 1960 Constitution they considered problematic. Having as a legal shield the Security Council Resolution 186, this state would be internationally recognized and, while operating smoothly without the obstructing Turkish-Cypriot vetoes, further emphasis could be given to its economic development. These factors placed the Greek-Cypriot leadership in a position of strength vis-à-vis the Turkish-Cypriots, who remained completely isolated during the first three years of separation. Therefore, the only element missing for the Cyprus Government to ensure its desired solution to the Cyprus question was to encourage, and even coerce, more and more Turkish-Cypriots to retreat into this 'limbo-land' without provoking a Turkish military response. In fact, in February 1965, the British high commissioner commented,

> Makarios seems to be labouring under the delusion that if he avoids physical attacks on Turkish Cypriots and does not declare *Enosis* he can get away with any sort of political or economic pressures, and progressively erode constitutional and treaty provisions until he achieves independent unitary state on lines which he and Greek Cypriots alone will determine.[1]

Wholly convinced that 'the right is on our side', both Makarios and the Greek-Cypriot leaderships overestimated their own ability to achieve their goals – this was either *Enosis* or a purely Greek-Cypriot-led unitary state – along with the ultimate pliability of Turkish-Cypriots. By the same token, however, they critically miscalculated the determination of Turkish-Cypriots to cope with the isolation and the implications of this *status quo*.

This chapter reviews the efforts made by the Cyprus Government from 1964 to 1967 to restructure the state machinery by transforming it into what amounted to a purely Greek-Cypriot unitary state along the lines of Makarios' previous 'Thirteen Points'. That inevitably drove the Turkish-Cypriot leadership into setting up and gradually consolidating a separate *de facto* administration on the island. This presentation makes clear that the nature of the institutional evolution of the two communities during the three years in question – along with their socio-economic development and the lack of a strictly political settlement, presented in the following chapters – must be a vital aspect of the narrative. By 1968, when new efforts for settlement began, the conflicting issues were far more complicated than in 1964, during Plaza's mediation.

This chapter analyses the most important changes in the three state pillars: executive, legislative and judicial. Meanwhile, there is an analysis of the organization of the Turkish-Cypriot enclaves. Afterwards, particular emphasis is given to two key junctures in the evolution of the Cyprus problem: the issue surrounding the holding of elections in 1965 and the termination of inter-communal cooperation in the judiciary in the summer of 1966. Finally, the critical effects of the reorganization of the Security Forces of the Cyprus Government are also presented. Through this it is demonstrated that the military strengthening of the Republic became a double-edged sword for Makarios' Government. This was the element which sowed the deep mistrust between Athens and Nicosia, while constantly leading to provocations and violent inter-communal incidents throughout the island.

1960 Constitution revised: The implementation of the 'Thirteen Points'

Immediately after the clash of Christmas 1963, and due to the withdrawal of all Turkish-Cypriot officials and public servants to incipient enclaves, an administrative and constitutional gap had been created that had to be filled or in some cases to be completely improvised. The Cyprus Government and the House of Representatives benefitted from an important 'tool' to address the difficulties of the proper functioning of the state and the continuation of the legitimate existence of the Republic of Cyprus. The Supreme Court decision *Attorney-General of the Republic v. Mustafa Ibrahim and others,* in November 1964, recognized that developments in Cyprus generated 'a necessity as a source of authority for acting in a manner not regulated by law but required, in prevailing circumstances, by supreme public interest, for the salvation of the State and its people'.[2] Through this decision a legal precedent had been established which justified deviation from normal constitutional mandatory provisions. The otherwise compulsory separate majorities in the Parliament and the consent of the vice-president for many decisions were no longer applicable. This made the work of the Parliament and the government much easier. New institutions were established, new personnel appointed and new legislation adopted. In other words, a new process had begun which flowed naturally from Makarios' famous 'Thirteen Points'. For the Turkish-Cypriots, however, all these moves were a flagrant breach of the Constitution. Every new legislation and alteration triggered more or less the same reactions by the Turkish-Cypriot leadership: formal protests, sometimes stronger or milder, towards the United Nations (UN) and the Guarantor Powers about the alleged illegality of Greek-Cypriot actions. Our analysis begins with the amendments to the executive and, in particular, in the make-up of the Council of Ministers. We then note the modifications of the highly contested issue of local governance and the changes in the civil service of the Republic.

The first significant modification in the executive authority was the formation of a new ministry (the eleventh) responsible for educational, cultural and religious affairs. Until then, these matters had been under the jurisdiction of two quasi-independent organs of the state, the two Communal Chambers. By late 1964, however, the government decided that the Greek Communal Chamber should be dissolved, its responsibilities given to an executive portfolio within the new Ministry of Education and Culture, with Dr Constantinos Spyridakis, the former head of the Communal Chamber, as minister.

The centralization process of these matters effectively met the previous criticism that a Communal Chamber which represented 80 per cent of the population in Cyprus had no *reason d'être* mainly for two reasons. First and foremost, it hindered the unity of the state.[3] More importantly, however, it was proved that having such a separate organ responsible for the majority of the population in Cyprus, operating outside the government's main fiscal and social programming, created serious educational, economic, administrative and social setbacks to the state and an additional heavy burden to the Cypriot taxpayer.[4]

Henceforth, it was obvious that the government's educational, cultural and fiscal policies had to be coordinated with its wider political programme. The work of the new ministry was especially significant for the promotion of Hellenism within Greek-Cypriot schools. We should note that Spyridakis was a long-time 'champion' of Hellenic education. Well before the coming of independence he had worked for the transformation of the colonial educational system towards a more 'hellenocentric' form of education by implementing the same annual syllabuses, books and types of schools as in Greece.[5]

Spyridakis was a strong supporter of *Enosis* and during his ten-year tenure at the Ministry consistently opposed adopting policies or creating institutions that would undermine the purely Hellenic character of the state and thus could have led to the cultivation of a separate Cypriot consciousness.[6] The minister of education expressed rigid and extreme *enosists* views in his speeches, often against the official line of his government.[7] Nonetheless, his appointment was highly significant according to an ex-member of the Parliament and the Patriotic Front, Mr Lellos Demetriades.[8] Setting up smoothly a newly born independent state, lacking solid foundations and with an embittered Greek-Cypriot community, had proved a very delicate task for Makarios. Unity within his community had to be preserved at all costs, and the educational orientation of the government was essential to that goal. An educational policy promoting Hellenic ideals was one way to avoid further divisions of the Greek-Cypriot community and thus the disruption of the Cyprus state. The Greek-Cypriot community was not in any mood to openly accept a common Cypriot consciousness.[9] Yet the Spyridakis approach was to carry costs.

Meanwhile, the new ministry was not only about the strengthening and consolidation of the Hellenic character of the island. It also sought to have an important role in the efforts of the Cyprus Government towards economic growth. An important problem was the lack of skilled workers for several sectors of the economy and endemic under-employment. Hence, Spyridakis introduced several innovative elements to Cyprus' educational system in order to adapt to the developing nature of the island. Career Centres for students were established in High Schools, in order to help and guide them towards productive sectors of the economy that needed skilful employees.[10] In addition to, in close collaboration with the Ministries of Labour and of Commerce, Industry and Tourism, a significant amount of government spending was allocated towards the creation of vocational training secondary schools and other relevant institutions of higher level education, such as the Higher Technical Institute or the Hotel and Catering Institute.[11] In this way, Spyridakis aimed to marry a very conservative Hellenic educational philosophy to more modern requirements.

The creation of the eleventh ministry was not the only modification in the composition of the government's Cabinet. Three months after the Turkish-Cypriot withdrawal from the administrative structures, Makarios announced the appointment of acting ministers in the three hitherto Turkish-Cypriot posts, of the Ministries of Defence, Health and Agriculture and Natural Resources, that remained vacant. These Ministries could not have remained 'headless' for long, while the ministers who boycotted the government could hardly have continued to be paid by the state's funds.[12]

Additionally, Makarios was at pains to underscore Greek-Cypriot control on all the sectors of the government so the refusal of the Turkish-Cypriots to return to their posts merely served his purposes. The US Secretary of State, Dean Rusk, remarked that had Kuchuk and his ministers returned to their posts by March 1964, they could have been a serious embarrassment for Makarios.[13] However, Rusk acknowledged that 'Makarios' tactics will probably succeed if [the] Turk[ish]-Cypriots continue to sit on [their] hands and feel sorry for themselves'.[14] It should be stressed that both the British and Americans, along with several Turkish officials, had tried to convince the Turkish-Cypriot leadership to return to their posts precisely in order to forestall Makarios' plans, especially after the establishment of the United Nations Force in Cyprus (UNFICYP) on the island, but to no avail.[15] Arguably also, the persistent refusal of Turkish-Cypriots to return to their previous state responsibilities only served to give credence to Makarios' Government's allegations of a rebellious minority.

Although the above ministerial replacements were considered temporary, it was not until April 1966 that they became a legal reality. The Doctrine of Necessity was then applied for the official replacement of the Turkish-Cypriot ministers. In 1966, Makarios appointed George Tombazos as the new minister of agriculture and natural resources and assigned Tassos Papadopoulos to the health portfolio along with his existing duties as minister of labour. This move was considered as a double provocation by Kuchuk, who appealed to the UN secretary-general, and by Turkey which ineffectively threatened to use its treaty rights to restore the constitutional order on the island.[16] Kuchuk claimed that these appointments were *a fait accompli,* an effort to obliterate the partner status enshrined in the 1960 Constitution and reduce Turkish-Cypriots to a 'mere' minority. In addition, the Turkish-Cypriot leadership believed that Tombazos was especially hostile to the Turkish-Cypriot community and had been selected partly because of this.[17] The British officials shared the view that this appointment was a reward for Tombazos for his former services during the National Organization of Cypriot Fighters (EOKA) struggle in the 1950s and the inter-communal struggle of 1963.[18] Nonetheless, it should be stressed that Makarios avoided appointing a new Greek-Cypriot minister of defence (or even a Greek-Cypriot director-general for that ministry) since this was a particularly sensitive portfolio for both communities. The formal replacement of that Turkish-Cypriot minister would have provided a more obvious move away from the *status quo.*[19]

Besides these changes within the Executive, additional amendments were pursued in the local government structures and public service. Undoubtedly, one of the major constitutional problems created in the aftermath of independence was that of the separate municipalities in the main towns of Cyprus. The local governance and the municipalities had been paralysed since 1962 when the relevant temporary law expired and an agreement between the two leaderships on this issue proved impossible. The Greek-Cypriots argued that the separation in the local government should be abolished, while for Turkish-Cypriots, and mainly Ankara, this was a 'red line'. However, the constitutional provision for double municipalities in the five main towns of Cyprus constituted a major administrative and financial burden for both communities and the state's funds. Inevitably, that complex issue proved to be the Trojan Horse of separatism as Diana Markides has fully evoked.[20] The changes that the Greek-Cypriot side wanted to pursue on this matter were eventually set in place in November 1964, when the House of Representatives voted the Municipal Corporation Law of 1964. This abolished the separate municipal councils in the main towns and made provision for common rolls for Greek-Cypriots and Turkish-Cypriots in future elections for the local government officials.[21] This was in contradiction with Article 173 of the Constitution, leading to the usual Turkish-Cypriot protest to the UN.[22]

Although the new legislation for local governance did not have any immediate effects and there were no forthcoming municipal elections, the amendments within the Public Service were of practical significance. Throughout 1964, the government planned important changes within the internal structure of the public sector, aiming at a full reorganization. New legislation and a new Code of Conduct were adopted, in order to ensure the better safeguarding of labour rights/benefits and more efficiency overall.[23] Moreover, the structure of the Public Service Commission, the organ which according to the Constitution was responsible for the appointment, status and promotions of the civil servants, was restructured. According to Article 124, this Commission had ten members, seven Greek and three Turkish-Cypriots, all appointed jointly by the president and vice-president. However, on 9 December 1965 the Parliament enacted an amendment envisaging that this should be constituted by five members appointed solely by the president.[24] This law was initially stated to be provisional, but the later modifications of October 1966 and June 1967 made it permanent. The enactment of the December 1965 law marked the chronological implementation of the 'Thirteen Points'.[25] Having concluded all the important changes in the state apparatus, Makarios set in motion what was in effect a purely Greek-Cypriot state, with its main remaining concern the economic enhancement of the Republic and – since this was an inherent goal of the wider strategy – the eventual capitulation of the Turkish-Cypriots. Consistent with his usual tactics, Kuchuk on all these amendments appealed to the UN secretary-general, protesting about the violations of the 1960 Constitution by the Greek-Cypriots.[26]

At the lower levels of the public service, by 1963 the constitutional staff ratio of 70:30 per cent was impossible to implement fully because of the lack of fully qualified Turkish-Cypriots employees. Statistical data confirmed that by December 1963 the Turkish-Cypriots employed in the government sector were approximately 24 per cent.[27] Although after the 1963 crisis, the Cyprus Government appeared determined to abolish this problematic ratio,[28] in practice it was unnecessary since all Turkish-Cypriot public servants had already abandoned their posts – either voluntarily or forced by their Turkish-Cypriots or Greek-Cypriots counterparts.[29] Their withdrawal naturally led to the termination of their salaries.[30] Zafer Ali Zihni, the president of the Cyprus Turkish Civil Servants, made a series of protests to Britain. By early 1964 he persistently declared that termination of their salaries was unjustifiable since the Turkish-Cypriot civil servants continued to 'serve the public in offices which have had to be set up in the Turkish sector with the object of rendering essential public services to the besieged Turks to whom such essential public services have been denied by the Greek elements of the Government'.[31] Despite the negative financial consequences, he highlighted his community's determination

> not to fall into the trap of Greeks and not resume attending their offices in the Greek sectors even if the Greeks give assurances as to their safety. Previous experience has shown that assurances given by the Greeks cannot be relied upon. In any event it is quite out of the question to work in the midst of E.O.K.A infested hives which is virtually what Government offices have become since Independence.[32]

The Society of the Turkish Civil Servants tried repeatedly, but unsuccessfully, to be compensated by the Cyprus Government for their services. A few months after *de facto* separation, however, Ankara gave them the very much needed financial support. In particular, it provided £30 per month for male civil servants, while by the end of 1965 it was increased to £40.[33] The fact that in some ways, very reluctantly, ordinary Turkish-Cypriots felt driven to put reliance on Turkey as a 'motherland' was one of the several causes that Makarios' strategy to economically grind down the Turkish-Cypriot community finally produced the opposite effect from his desired outcomes. After 1963 Turkish-Cypriots were totally dependent, both politically and economically, on Ankara, which provided them with at least the minimum resources needed to prevent their capitulation to Greek-Cypriots. By the same token, the official Turkish-Cypriot leadership came progressively 'dance to the tune' of Ankara.

Conversely, there were two important exceptions from the general Turkish-Cypriot withdrawal from the Public Service in 1963: first, the judicial officers and servants of the courts remained in place until June 1966 (to be discussed later) and, second, a very sensitive sector, the Diplomatic Service of Cyprus. The Turkish-Cypriot diplomats did not voluntarily withdraw but some of them were gradually dismissed by the Cyprus Government on the grounds that they would undermine the interests of their country both internally and abroad.[34] In particular, by 1963 there were thirteen Turkish-Cypriot senior diplomats and some more junior diplomats employed in the Diplomatic Corps. A year later, eight of the senior diplomats were dismissed, although the other five remained in place. The remaining Turkish-Cypriot diplomats were in posts mainly in London and Ankara. Although these were perceived as very important positions, those who occupied them, of whatever ethnicity, were unable to make any practical difference to the conduct of Cyprus' interests.[35] Quite apart from the significance of diplomacy, it may be said that the Cyprus Government's actions in this sphere revealed the 'jobs for the boys' – or rather jobs for the professional Greek-Cypriot elite – that was also part of the push to new state formation in Cyprus after 1963–1964.

The organization of the Turkish-Cypriot enclaves

The constitutional breakdown and the ensuing violence proved to be a turning point for Turkish-Cypriots which redefined their own existence on the island. Their confinement into the enclaves and their engagement with a *de facto* state-within-a-state under mainly Turkish Resistance Organization (TMT) command eventually led to the critical transformation of their cultural and national identity, as well as of their social, economic and political status on the island. From that point onwards, Turkish-Cypriots expected that sooner or later their motherland will militarily intervene to rescue them. Nonetheless, they were soon disillusioned. It proved that Turkey was not planning to get engage soon in a military operation in Cyprus, and according to Rebecca Bryant and Mete Hatay 'as Turkish Cypriots established a peculiar form of self-sufficiency in the enclaves, a new attachment to a Cypriot homeland emerged'.[36] In this section we shall examine the formation of the enclaves after 1963.

Within only a few weeks after the inter-communal clash, almost half of the Turkish-Cypriot population was barricaded into enclaves, formed in several strategic locations of the island. By August 1964, 25,000 Turkish-Cypriots abandoned their villages, while seventy-two mixed and twenty-four Turkish-Cypriot villages were completely evacuated and eight mixed villages were partially evacuated.[37] One of the main questions in both communities' ethnic narratives for the Cyprus question was whether this an *en masse* displacement was a spontaneous movement or the implementation of a well-calculated plan of the Turkish-Cypriot leadership. For the Cyprus Government, this movement was organized and encouraged by the Turkish-Cypriot leadership as a measure to facilitate their plans for partition/federation. The Turkish-Cypriot leadership on the other hand rejected these claims.[38] Nonetheless, there are sources that confirm both contested versions. Although there are testimonies indicating that in several occasions TMT leaders forced Turkish-Cypriots to abandon their jobs and houses,[39] Richard Patrick's field research conducted in 1970–1971 explained that probably there was not official administrative organization to direct the 'refugee' movements but 'there is ample proof that Turk-Cypriot political and military leaders controlled the return of refugees to their former homes'.[40] Another factor however, which prevented the return of the displaced in their villages, was the looting and the significant damages of the abandoned Turkish-Cypriot properties by the Greek-Cypriot militias during the crisis.[41]

Although usually downplayed in the relevant historiography, it should be highlighted that the formation of these enclaves was not a static process. U Thant in December 1964 reported that the enclaves covered 1.5 per cent of the island's territory with 59,000 population. By the early 1970s the previous figures were significantly different. The enclaves were geographically expanded, and the percentage of Turkish-Cypriots living outside the Cyprus Government's control was probably around 90 per cent.[42] This was to be a remarkable turnaround from the still very 'mixed' demography that prevailed on the island prior to 1963.

It should be stressed that besides those living inside the enclaves, there was also a considerable remnant of the Turkish-Cypriot population that continued to live in their villages in areas under the government's control – at least until the late 1960s. There were two perceptions about the reasons as to why these Turkish-Cypriots did not move into the enclaves. On the one hand, many Turkish-Cypriots remained in their villages because they still had very good relations with their Greek-Cypriot neighbours and wanted to resist their leadership's partition plans. On the other hand, Patrick argues that many Turkish-Cypriots remained outside the enclaves because they lived in areas which the Greek-Cypriots were simply unable or unwilling to penetrate.[43] He continues that most Turkish-Cypriot villages that were under the government control did not really recognize the legitimacy of the Cyprus Government and remained outside the government's *de facto* administrative structure.[44] Those villages were more or less administered on their own. In such cases, the government's main concern was for the villages to remain quiet and to pay all of their taxes and fees to the government bodies.[45]

As soon as separation was imposed, the Turkish-Cypriot leadership decided to set up its own administrative structures for the areas under its control. In coordination with TMT, the political leadership and the active involvement of almost all the enclaved Turkish-Cypriots by May 1964 those structures had already been established and set in motion.[46] In Nicosia, the biggest enclave, an executive body of thirteen officials, the 'General Committee', had been formulated. Head of the Committee was the Vice-President of the Republic, Fazil Kuchuk, and the other participants were former members of the government such as the Turkish-Cypriot ministers, the members of the Parliament, the Judiciary and the Executive Committee of the Turkish Communal Chamber.[47] As a second tier of the Turkish-Cypriot administration were the sub-committees, which constituted a quasi-ministry formation, and the District Committees established in the five main towns: Nicosia, Limassol, Famagusta, Larnaca and Paphos. Municipal and village councils were placed under the District Committees. Executive decrees issued by Kuchuk and the District officers, along with regulations issued by the Communal Chamber and the Turkish-Cypriot members of the Parliament, were used for the administration of these areas.[48] Nonetheless, after summer 1965 the latter two (members of the Communal Chamber and of the Parliament) formed a quasi-parliament issuing 'official legislation' for the enclaves.[49] The basic 'legal framework' for the operation of the 'General Committee' was the 1960 Constitution and all the decrees and 'laws' issued by the Turkish-Cypriot administration after 1963.[50]

Kuchuk insisted that his community was forced to form a separate administration because there was no other way for maintaining all the essential public services.[51] The main task of the 'General Committee' and the Communal Chamber was the issue of decrees regulating daily affairs. Nonetheless, by the end of 1964 the Communal Chamber became effectively the main financial authority of the enclaves, controlling the enclaves' budget and was responsible for the collection of the income tax from Turkish-Cypriots, the issuing of motor licences and the collection of all relevant fees.[52] That was another step to strengthen both the economic viability and the consolidation of their separate administrative structures.

One of the biggest problems of the 'General Committee', however, was its practical inability to exert effective control over the majority of the enclaves. In fact, there were seventeen enclaves scattered throughout the island, and both due to their policy of isolation and the embargo imposed by the Cyprus Government, there was no proper telephone communication or postal services between the Central Authorities and all the other enclaves and villages.[53] Thus, in most enclaves TMT leaders assumed a *de facto* administrative leadership having in that way both the military and political reins of the enclaves.[54] According to Patrick, the administration of the enclaves was of 'a civil-military synthesis'.[55] This inevitably had profound effects not only on the nature of Turkish-Cypriot decision making, but also in the cultivation of a specific culture of Turkish-Cypriot politics. Yael Navaro-Yashin characterizes this culture as 'the spirit of the TMT' and the culture of terror which to some extent exists until nowadays.[56]

The TMT commander, the '*Bozkurt*' (*Bayraktar*), was Kenan Choygun – with the code name Kemal Coshkun – and as soon as the crisis erupted and TMT came into open, he became the most powerful man in the enclaves. Certainly most of the key political and military decisions were taken by him, making Kuchuk something of a figurehead within his community.[57] Needless to say, this had led to a constant power struggle between Coshkun and Kuchuk. The latter, however, still enjoyed the political support of Ankara. It should also be stressed that the alternate strong man of the Turkish-Cypriot community, Rauf Denktash, since February 1964 was banned from the island by the Cyprus Government and thus remained exiled in Ankara from 1964 to 1968. Despite that, Denktash actively supported Coshkun in this power struggle against Kuchuk, through his close associate Dr Shemsi Kiazim who presided the Communal Chamber in his absence.[58] By 1966 this power struggle had deteriorated.[59] By January 1967 the Turkish Government announced that Coshkun was no longer the commander of the TMT and he was recalled and replaced.[60] Nonetheless, Coshkun's successors did not manage to establish the same political authority within the enclaves mainly due to Denktash's return on the island in April 1968. It was reported that since Denktash's return, the latter had managed to confine *Bozkurt*'s powers mainly on the military and security aspects of the enclaves, reducing thus his political powers.[61]

In spite of their own internal cleavages, and indeed to overcome them, the Turkish-Cypriot leadership and the mainland military commanders constantly sought to effectively extend their control in wider geographical areas, causing severe clashes with the Cyprus Government's militias.[62] At the same time they exploited Greek-Cypriot policies to justify actions that in effect further consolidated the administrative separation of the two communities. Two of the most important events, the issue of the electoral law of 1965 and the termination of the judicial inter-communal cooperation in June 1966, will now be discussed.

The electoral law of 1965

As already stated, up to the summer of 1965 the Cyprus Government had introduced several important modifications to the state apparatus. An important matter that sparked further political problems between the two communities and diplomatic unrest between the Guarantor Powers was the issue of the forthcoming end of the five-year tenure of the executive and legislative authority in August 1965. The crucial question for the Cyprus Government was whether then to hold the presidential and parliamentary elections. The debate about the feasibility of elections sprang from an interview that President Makarios gave in early February 1965 stating

> I think [...] that the term of office of the Government should not be prolonged beyond the period which people gave it a mandate through elections. People should be called upon to vote. But elections will not be held under *the separatist provisions* of the defunct Zurich-London Agreements. Electoral law should be passed providing for unified elections on the basis of a Common Roll. People will be called upon to vote as a whole, and not separately as Greeks and Turks.[63]

Makarios' statement triggered several reactions primarily because of his aim to press on with elections, but most importantly because of his intention to use common electoral rolls for the two communities, instead of separate, as envisaged in Article 63 of the Constitution. It was even reported that high-ranking members of the Greek-Cypriot leadership, such as the president of the Parliament and the attorney-general, were not aware of Makarios' intentions.[64] Then again, Grivas, the commander in chief of the Cyprus Army, was opposed to any elections because the effect was bound to be the further consolidation of independence rather than *Enosis*.[65]

According to the British, the timing of this announcement was crucial. Makarios decided to announce his intentions when criticism against his handling of the Cyprus issue, especially from the right wing, was gaining ground. Constant accusations about his policies and his prevarication, even · evasion, towards *Enosis* from the right-wing press were strengthened after the notorious Soviet statement of January 1965, which leaned towards the Turkish argument for federation. Therefore, in order to avert the danger of factionalism that was increasing against him and in order to 're-create unanimity within his community', Makarios wanted to direct public attention towards the amendment of the electoral law and thus towards his policy designed to nibble away at the Turkish-Cypriot position.[66]

The Greek Government was also taken by surprise by Makarios' statement because there had been no prior consultation. At this point, it should be noted that the relations between the Greek Premier, George Papanderou, and the Cypriot president were already strained due to both differences over the previous Acheson episode and generally their divergent opinions on the Cyprus issue.[67] In order to avoid political embarrassment for its inability to control Makarios, the Greek Government felt it had no choice but to ostensibly go along with the Cyprus' Government plan for elections.[68] This was a classic example of Makarios' habit of seeking to force the Greek Government's hand to publicly agree with his own strategies and, thus, by a seemingly endless series of *faits accomplis*, make Athens a mere follower of his decisions. This clashed directly with Papandreou's thesis of Athens as the 'National Centre' from where all decisions should derive.[69] After the February statement, however, the latter privately tried to persuade Makarios to avoid holding them at least at that point. Following bilateral consultations, they came to an agreement of deferring the final decision until May 1965.[70] It was not only Athens that tried to dissuade Nicosia from acting provocatively. U Thant also had advised the Cypriot foreign minister to avoid holding elections under a common roll.[71]

Both the Turkish Government and the Turkish-Cypriot leadership reacted strongly on Makarios' statement. Elections on a common roll in their eyes meant the official abandonment of the 1960 Constitution and the Zurich–London Agreements. This issue was perceived by Turkey – and also by Britain – as the most fundamental challenge to the 1960 constitutional structure.[72] A common roll would provide a new ace up Makarios' sleeve. Specifically, it was believed that Makarios could have then legally based his government's legitimacy on the new electoral mandate and not on the 1960 Constitution, in effect asserting beyond contradiction its defunct character.[73] The possible participation of some moderate Turkish-Cypriots residing in the government-controlled areas could strengthen this contention. Feridun Erkin, Turkey's foreign minister, stated that Makarios again revealed his true intentions of destroying the basic principles of the Constitution and sow the seeds of partition. Meanwhile, he attempted again to actively implicate Greece and Britain in this dispute, threatening that 'the responsibility for the dangerous development which this situation will produce will fall entirely on Makarios and on the other guarantor powers who should prevent him from pursuing this course'.[74] Osman Orek, the Turkish-Cypriot minister of defence, initially commented that if elections were held by Greek-Cypriots, then Turkish-Cypriots would proceed to have their own elections and declare a new state with the Turkish Communal Chamber as their Parliament.[75] Nonetheless, he also explained to the British high commissioner, Major-General Alec Bishop and the Political Advisor of UNFICYP, Carlos Bernardes, that several Turkish-Cypriot leaders had receptively thought of the possibility that Progressive Party of Working People (AKEL) might invite them to participate in elections on the basis of unified rolls. As he explained, AKEL claimed to have the support of the two-fifths of the electorate of the

Greek-Cypriots and probably one-fifth of the Turkish-Cypriots. In such a case, AKEL might conceivably win the elections. Therefore, if the Turkish-Cypriot leadership could reach an agreement beforehand with AKEL about the status of Turkish-Cypriot community after elections – a guaranteed separate identity and a large measure of autonomy within a federal state, as supported by the Soviets – then their leadership could accept AKEL running the rest of the island as it wished.[76] Such a scenario was to revive ideals of an AKEL/Turkish-Cypriot orientation that had broken up in the later 1940s and 1950s, if not before, but which had certain folkloric status. There is no evidence that AKEL at this time had any such intention or plan to part company from President Makarios' supporters.[77] Nor is it likely that the Western powers or Greece would allow a communist party to rule the island, even if that meant a lasting agreement on the Cyprus problem between the Greeks and Turkish-Cypriots.

Nevertheless, Makarios now had to thoroughly calculate all the pros and cons of proceeding to elections. In addition to all the modifications he pursued within the state's structure so far, elections under a common roll would have emphatically confirmed that Makarios was perfectly able to fully transform the Republic of Cyprus into an independent unitary state without separatist provisions and with the Greek-Cypriot community as the sole master of its house. Furthermore, without the renewal of its mandate, the Cyprus Government would probably lack solid legal foundation. This could have become a valuable argument for Makarios' opponents both within Cyprus and abroad.

Conversely, he also had to assess that proclamation of elections would considerably sharpen his differences with two internal fronts: the Turkish-Cypriot leaders, who had already began protesting, and the Greek-Cypriot extreme right under General Grivas. An electoral campaign at that stage would have been another validation or expression of Cyprus as a self-standing independent state. Bearing also in mind the public debate that followed the publication of Plaza's report and the internal upheaval cultivated by the rivalry between the political and military leadership of the Greek-Cypriot community, as we shall see later, a catastrophic disruption between the supporters of instant *Enosis* and Makarios' followers would have been certain.

It was not until 20 July 1965 that the government clarified its final decisions about this issue; on 23 July during an extraordinary plenary session, the House of Representatives would have extended with a legislative act the term of office both of the president and the members of the Parliament.[78] Besides this extension, a new electoral law would have also been put for vote, with interim provisions for elections under unified electoral rolls for the two communities.[79] On the hearing of these decisions, the Turkish-Cypriot leadership requested from Carlos Bernardes to notify the president of the House that the Turkish-Cypriot MPs wished to attend Parliament on that occasion. However, Clerides responded that their request would only be accepted if they agreed on three conditions: (a) acceptance that the laws enacted by the House hitherto will be applicable to the whole island, including the *de facto* Turkish areas, (b) regular future participation in the normal business of the House and (c) recognition that the House no longer worked on the basis of separate majorities.[80] Not surprisingly, on 23 July, three Turkish-Cypriot MPs, Umit Suleiman, Djemil Ramadan and Ahmet Berberoglu, who met with Clerides, rejected these conditions and said that they were ready to return only if the 1960 Constitution was fully applied.[81]

Hence, on 23 July 1965, during the afternoon plenary session of Parliament, the two Bills were duly voted by Greek-Cypriot MPs, without any serious opposition.[82] AKEL was the only political party that expressed concern about one element of the new electoral law: the majority voting system. More specifically, AKEL members argued that this system was a remaining legacy of the colonial governance and now had to be amended into a proportional voting system.[83] This could benefit smaller parties, principally AKEL itself, which presently had only five representatives. In fact, since any future Turkish-Cypriot parties would have benefitted from such provision under unified rolls, the Greek-Cypriots might have thrown a substantive concession to the other side. In the event AKEL voted the law without pressing the amendment.[84] The law that extended the term of the president and of the House, but not of the vice-president or Turkish-Cypriot MPs who lacked any legal status for Greek-Cypriots, made explicit reference that this would last for a maximum of twelve months. Hence, elections had to be arranged at some point until August 1966.[85]

Once again the positions taken by the parties concerned on these laws were polarizing. All of them talked about a *fait accompli*. As regards the Turkish-Cypriots, Kuchuk's first reaction was to send a formal protest about the illegality of the Greek-Cypriot laws to the British high commissioner.[86] Representing the voices of the extreme Turkish-Cypriot leadership, Denktash asked for partition and the declaration of a separate state. The official Turkish-Cypriot policy, and Ankara's instructions, nevertheless, remained opposed to *de jure* separation. Instead, they continuously stressed that they did not wish to act outside the existing Constitution except when absolutely necessary.[87] In this case they claimed to have no other option than to convene on 23 July an extraordinary meeting of the Turkish Communal Chamber and of the Turkish-Cypriot MPs, in which they voted a 'law' extending their own and the vice-president's terms of office. Simultaneously, they decided that this first formal 'legislation' should be promulgated with a Turkish-Cypriot *Gazette*.[88] According to the Turkish-Cypriot MP, Suleiman,

> the decision to publish the *Gazette* now, rather than say, a year ago, was due to the refusal of the President of the House [of Representatives] to allow the Turkish Cypriot members to participate in the debates on the electoral bill and extensions of terms of office laws. This is regarded by the Turkish Cypriots as the breaking point after which they must protect their position by separate action even if this involves some departure from the Constitution.[89]

This move had a deeper meaning regarding the administrative organization of the Turkish-Cypriots. For the first time the Communal Chamber and the Turkish-Cypriot MPs acted as a separate 'parliament'. Meanwhile, the Turkish-Cypriot 'General Committee' from now on would use the *Gazette* as a new tool in order to make public and enforce all of its future 'legislative' acts. That inevitably meant a further step towards the consolidation of *de facto* partition.

Athens, which was amidst of a serious political crisis then, was also disturbed by the new legislation of the Cyprus Government. The former was piqued, since, according to Greek officials, Makarios acted contrary to his promise. Particularly, the Greek Ambassador in Cyprus, Menelaos Alexandrakis, stated that on 5 July, during their meeting, Makarios promised that he would not take such an action before consulting Athens. Greek leaders then had agreed that 'this kind of brinkmanship is dangerous ... and Makarios should not confront us with a *fait accompli*'.[90] Henceforth, the most important thing for Athens was to restrain the Cyprus Government from giving effect to the new electoral law.[91] Except from its own domestic crisis, Greece was at the moment engaged in bilateral negotiations with Turkey regarding the Cyprus issue and feared that this development would negatively affect its position towards the negotiations.

These developments also created a lot of suspicion in both Britain and the UN. They both believed that Nicosia's action appeared to have been taken in bad faith, while Bernardes was constantly expressing the UN's anxiety over the Greek-Cypriot moves.[92] Britain perceived that the Greek-Cypriots deliberately misled them about their true intentions on the matter, while sending a formal protest to the Cyprus Government under the pretext of the Treaty of Guarantee. Makarios consistent to his 1963 declaration that the Treaties were no longer applicable replied that Britain's protest had constituted an unacceptable interference in the domestic affairs of the Republic of Cyprus.[93] Yet, as already stated, this gambit gained no credence in Britain, Turkey or the international community in general. The high commissioner had a revealing conversation with Makarios regarding this development. David Hunt complained that the government's actions were provocative and contrary to the Security Council Resolution of 4 March 1964 and particularly its provision to avoid any actions that could worsen the situation. Makarios' perceptions, as indicated in the following abstract of Hunt's report, were totally different:

> [Makarios] reacted strongly to [the] reference to the UN resolutions. These, he said, referred only to fighting and he had scrupulously kept the peace. I said that I could not agree with this interpretation; and [the] enactment of the electoral law was as provocative to the Turkish-Cypriots and to Ankara as any shooting incident. He said the Turks could not keep Cyprus forever in a state of suspended animation. '*What are we to do? The Constitution is unworkable and you say we cannot alter it and get onto a proper legal basis because Turks will stop us*'. I said what was [the] need for electoral law since they had passed a law on [the] same day extending the tenure of Deputies and officers of State. It was the fact that it was so unnecessary that made it so provocative. He said that the law providing for extension was just as unconstitutional as the electoral law so why was I not protesting against that? I said all departures from Constitution were no doubt deplorable but some were more provocative than others. He said Cyprus is a sovereign state, a member of the UN, and did not believe that the UN would agree to restrictions being put upon it which strangled its political life. Nor did he admit the right of Britain, Greece and Turkey to intervene.[94]

The government's action was indeed provocative and unnecessary at that moment. Nevertheless, removing one more contentious and divisive provision of the 1960 Constitution as the separate electoral rolls was a matter of principle for the Cyprus Government and one of its public commitments. It was impossible, therefore, to retreat without losing face. In any case Makarios was confident that he still enjoyed considerable diplomatic support from abroad, and if a Security Council was convened for that issue, he could have definitely mobilized this support to his government's favour.

Finally, Ankara perceived this new electoral law as the most serious provocation from Makarios' Government and asked both Greece and Britain to meet under Article 4 of the Treaty of Guarantee to discuss this issue. Greece, however, refused to meet under this pretext.[95] Ankara decided then to formally protest and warn about the consequences of Makarios' actions to the 'Greek-Cypriot administration' with a *Note Verbale* and simultaneously asked for a Security Council meeting to discuss the new developments.[96] Ankara believed that Makarios' previous diplomatic advantage, gained by Plaza's conclusions, was to some extent faltering because his recent actions had alarmed many people outside the island.[97] Nonetheless, both the British and Americans tried unsuccessfully to warn Ankara that a Security Council debate would probably benefit the Greek-Cypriots, since the Security Council was traditionally reluctant to get involved with the interpretation of constitutional issues.[98]

It was not only Ankara, however, that called for a Security Council meeting. Nicosia had also requested for a Security Council debate on the grounds that Turkey was once again interfering within the internal affairs of the Cyprus Government.[99] A Security Council meeting about the electoral law was eventually convened on 3 August. It was notable that before the debate, Greek-Cypriot diplomacy adopted a new tactic. The Cypriot foreign minister had contacts with British and American officials during which he made direct threats that unless diplomatic support was not given to the Republic of Cyprus, there would be consequences both for the British bases and for the US radio installations in Cyprus.[100]

The intense debate that followed between the interested parties led to an anodyne Resolution which reaffirmed UN Security Council Resolution 186 and called on the parties to refrain from any actions that could worsen the situation in Cyprus.[101] The Cyprus Government claimed victory and a personal success for the Foreign Minister, Spyros Kyprianou who, according to Hunt, was presented at home 'as the hero of a valiant fight against heavy odds'.[102] Nevertheless, the Turkish-Cypriots also drew comfort.[103] Indeed, even some of Makarios' Greek-Cypriot critics on the right wing shared the view that the only effect of the UN debate was to further circumscribe the Cyprus Government's freedom of action for the conduct of elections in the future.[104] To some extent this was probably true since elections were not held until early 1968, and even then the 1965 legislation was skilfully not used.[105] It should also be noted that Kyprianou's 'warnings' towards the British and American officials had irritated rather than affected the latter's position during the debate.[106]

What was really the outcome of the new electoral law on the island and on the Cyprus issue in particular? Although formal complaints to the UN was the 'default' response of Turkish-Cypriots each time Greek-Cypriots amended the constitutional provisions, this new legislation triggered stronger reactions and had deeper implications. This is why we have traced it in such detail. Most importantly, however, once more the Greek-Cypriot actions had given to the Turkish-Cypriot leadership a pretext to further consolidate administrative partition by officially transforming their own Communal Chamber to a legislative assembly and creating new mechanisms to underpin a separate administration. The Turkish-Cypriot newspapers, themselves absolutely critical in shaping a distinctive 'voice' for a minority perceiving itself as now increasingly 'besieged', were handed a propaganda advantage.[107] From the start of 1966 they stepped up their campaign towards the declaration of a separate state within Cyprus underpinned by the military contribution of Turkey.[108]

Nevertheless, in some other respects the outcome reinforced Makarios' position both internally and abroad. Once more he had in effect acted entirely unilaterally and had taken both Greece and the other Guarantor Powers by surprise. In spite of the right-wing criticism, being able to dictate developments on the ground was his great advantage. By 'holding tight' to Resolution 186 and to the previous mediator's report, Makarios had further consolidated the existence of the Republic of Cyprus as defined by his own vision enshrined in the historic amendments. This was definitely a victory. In addition, he could use the developments of that summer in his search for allies in the forthcoming UN General Assembly, in which the Cyprus problem and Galo Plaza report were going to be discussed. Targeting the Afro-Asian states, with their sensitivity to issues of sovereignty and self-determination, Makarios could argue that events had demonstrated that Cyprus provided a classic instance of a new state struggling to assert its own legitimate rights.

Fragile agreement on the judiciary

The Turkish-Cypriot judges had also withdrawn from their posts in December 1963. Yet, crucially a few months later the minister of justice and the attorney-general along with the Greek-Cypriots and Turkish-Cypriot judges and leadership resumed inter-communal cooperation in the still-unified courts with certain modifications to 1960 practice. It was vital that the judiciary was an independent and impartial authority and the majority of the professional judges of both ethnicities operated above political considerations. Apparently judicial officers from both communities still enjoyed cordial relations.[109] This agreement was very important since it offered a constructive basis for the resumption of inter-communal contacts in other sectors of state. Unfortunately, the eruption of petty violence on the ground between rival militias and the resulting combustible atmosphere meant that such judicial cooperation did not survive beyond the summer of 1966. In retrospect, the fact that legal institutions ultimately failed to provide a counter-model to the disintegrative dynamic in other spheres of Cypriot public life was to be highly significant.

To begin with, the constitution envisaged that judicial practice was based on communal criteria. That is, the judges tried cases with litigants from their own community, while in mixed cases the trial was conducted by judges from both communities. In addition, there were two supreme courts – the Supreme Constitutional Court with one judge from each community and the High Court with two Greek-Cypriots and one Turkish-Cypriot judge – both presided over by foreign judges.

After the constitutional crisis of 1963, the Turkish-Cypriot judges were compelled to follow their leadership's policies and withdrew from their posts in the government-controlled areas of the island. Nevertheless, they continued to try purely Turkish-Cypriot cases only in the District courts of Nicosia since these were situated within the enclave's boundaries. Their withdrawal, therefore, along with the restriction of movement in and outside the Nicosia enclave meant that great delays were caused in the trials of mixed cases.[110] Further delays were also created at the appellate-supreme courts due to the fact that the posts of both the president of the Constitutional Court and of the High Court, the first in May 1963 and the second in May 1964, remained vacant.

In order to bridge the gap and deal with the resulting practical problems, the Parliament voted in July 1964 the Administration of Justice (Miscellaneous Provisions) Law no. 33, which introduced several important changes. This law provided the merger of the two superior courts into one – the Supreme Court – and abolished the communal criteria for the composition of lower courts and of the hearing of cases.[111] The post of the president of the Supreme Court was assigned to the most senior judge, and one of the moderate political voices within his community, the Turkish-Cypriot Mehmed Zekia. The first reactions of the Turkish-Cypriot leadership were predictably hostile to the new law, which was voted without its consent and in its views, contrary to the Constitution. Nevertheless, both the Turkish-Cypriot judges and, after a while, Ankara realized that this law was a practical solution to the judicial problem, which affected equally both communities. In order to appease the Turkish-Cypriots leaders, the Cyprus Government reassured them that the arrangement was temporary.[112] The final response of the Turkish-Cypriots came on 28 September 1964, when Kuchuk appealed for the necessity of returning to the constitutional order 'within a reasonable period' but also said,

> In order not to suddenly confront the difficulties [of this situation] those members of the Turkish and Greek communities who are involved in judicial proceedings, the Turkish Judges and other personnel engaged in the administration of justice may be prepared to continue during the

aforesaid *reasonable period* to perform the duties of their high office [...] If this appeal is not met with the spirit in which it is made and positive steps are not taken to ensure that justice is again administered in accordance with the constitution, the Turkish Judges [...] may find it contrary to their oath, conscience and sense of justice to prolong the unconstitutional state of affairs indefinitely.[113]

The Turkish-Cypriot judges, therefore, returned to the Republic's Courts.[114] Despite that, a few days later some Turkish-Cypriot litigants during the hearing of their case challenged the validity of recent legislation and the changes it introduced. This case, the well-known *Attorney General v. Mustafa Ibrahim,* led to the first decision of the Supreme Court of Cyprus recognizing that the Doctrine of Necessity applied in the legal, as well as the administrative, system of Cyprus.

Resuming cooperation in this sector at a time when the rest of the public machinery had sheared apart was undoubtedly something that both communities could have used to build upon for the future. Nonetheless, it was not long before the increase of tension on the ground snuffed out the fragile cooperation. On 1 June 1966, following a series of explosions, a new ban on movement in and out of the Turkish quarter of Nicosia was issued by the Cyprus Government. Until then, it was common practice that the Turkish-Cypriot judges were explicitly excluded from any restrictions of movement, except under specific conditions.[115] During this ban, however, Polycarpos Yorkadjis, the minister of interior, gave instructions to the police to also prevent the Turkish-Cypriot judges from passing the checkpoint. On 2 June the judges were sent back to the Turkish quarter of Nicosia. One of them, however, evaded police checks and went directly to the courts, but on being recognized it was reported that 'he was pursued and a police sergeant turned him out with a certain amount of contumely.'[116] When the Minister of Justice, Stella Soulioti, learnt about the incident, she intervened and strictly gave instructions to the police to exclude the judges from the ban. Although the judges immediately returned to the courts, the above incident touched a raw nerve. The next day, the 'General Committee' of the enclaves issued a new decision informing Greek-Cypriots that the Turkish-Cypriot judges would no longer continue working in the courts of the government-controlled sectors. A Turkish-Cypriot spokesman emphasized that their judges had accepted out of goodwill the arrangement of 1964 but that had been only for 'a reasonable period'.[117] He continued that their judges had been placed in an embarrassing position practising their duties in an impossible position while waiting patiently for a solution to the problem. However, the recent events have proved that the Greek side has no regard, or any respect for the personal freedom, dignity and honour of the Turkish judicial officers [...] in order to save the Turkish Judges from further humiliation and embarrassment as well as from continuing to act against their judicial conscience, the Turkish Cypriot leadership found no other alternative but to conclude that the reasonable period [...] has come to an end and that the Turkish judges should be free to discontinue attending their offices in the Greek sector, if they so wished.[118]

The Greek-Cypriot action had certainly been provocative and Makarios himself intervened to try and convince the Turkish-Cypriot judges to return to their previous responsibilities. He put out a statement that the matter had been rectified very quickly and that the judges had been able to attend their courts in the usual way.[119] But this did not satisfy the Turkish-Cypriot leadership, and thus on 3 June 1966 the inter-communal cooperation in the judiciary was officially terminated.

Nevertheless, there were still moderate voices among the Turkish-Cypriot judiciary. Among them was the President of the Supreme Court, Judge Zekia, who decided to announce his retirement in order to avoid voting for his leadership's decision, and two judges: Vedat Dervish, a judge of the Supreme Court, and Ozar Beha. The last two appeared willing to return to their duties but were forced by the Turkish-Cypriot leadership to reconsider.[120] Finally, when they were asked by their leadership to resume duties in the Turkish-Cypriot sector, they asked to be given permission to leave for Britain.[121] It is noteworthy that Sean MacBride, the secretary-general of the International Committee of Jurists and senior Irish Politician, tried to mediate this dispute by presenting several proposals but his efforts did not bear fruit. During the negotiations with the various actors, MacBride reported that he felt that the Turkish-Cypriot leadership was willing to resume contacts if Ankara issued such a directive.[122] This did not happen.

In September 1966, the Cyprus Government made some further modifications to streamline the Cyprus courts after the Turkish-Cypriot withdrawal.[123] Here was yet another example of a reformed and even partially modernized Cypriot public system, but one driven through without Turkish-Cypriot participation. Not long afterwards several 'courts' were set up in the Turkish-Cypriot enclaves to give them the basic elements of judicial recourse. However, they were suggestively named as 'Arbitration courts', as any other form of courts would have meant a violation of the constitution.[124]

The Turkish-Cypriot withdrawal from the judiciary meant that henceforward all three pillars of the state were now totally Greek-Cypriot-led while the Turkish-Cypriot leadership prepared its own quasi-state structures. Undoubtedly, inter-communal cooperation in the judiciary provided a critical test in the evolution of the Cyprus problem. Although the Turkish-Cypriot leadership continued to plead that the Cyprus Government was not legitimate and that all the modifications set in place were unconstitutional, the fact was that for two years the Turkish-Cypriot judges continued to operate under the 'unconstitutional' framework of Law 33/1964 and the decision *Attorney General v. Mustafa Ibrahim.*[125] This was a good opportunity, which, if grasped by both leaderships, might have provided a less drastic way out of the impasse. Indicative was also the fact that during the first round of the inter-communal talks of 1968–1971, every time a deadlock was imminent, the two negotiators focused on the issue of judicial cooperation which was perceived as the least difficult of all constitutional questions. Nonetheless, as in the later period of local talks, in 1966 mistrust, suspicion and provocation prevailed and a relatively minor violent incident was to have important political repercussions in a regressive direction. This last 'beacon of hope' for resuming inter-communal contacts in a wider political context was extinguished.

Restructuring of the security forces of the Republic of Cyprus

Transforming the Republic of Cyprus of 1960 into an independent unitary state along the lines President Makarios wished meant that there was still another sector of the state that had to be urgently strengthened: the security forces of the Republic. The Constitution provided for the establishment and the organization of the security forces and, in particular, the formation of an army of 2,000 men, with representation of 60 per cent Greek-Cypriots and 40 per cent Turkish-Cypriots, along with a police force and a gendarmerie with a representation of 70:30 per cent respectively. According to Stella Soulioti, the formation of this army was only for ceremonial reasons and for ensuring employment to Turkish-Cypriots in the public sector.[126] Nonetheless, three years after the birth of the Republic, it proved impossible for the two communities to agree on the specifics for the creation of this army. The Greek-Cypriots insisted for an army with mixed units, while the Turkish-Cypriots wanted units formed under communal criteria. Although by 1963 the police and gendarmerie were fully operational, there were not any other efficient or well-organized security cadres or defence infrastructure. Conversely, each community organized and trained its own forces. Since 1959, several private armies were secretly formed by Greek-Cypriots, ex-EOKA fighters and several politicians but without any official coordination or strategic planning for their actions. With the help of military personnel from Ankara, the Turkish-Cypriot leadership also secretly retained and strengthened their TMT fighters. It was not long before this underground rivalry, and the increase of hostility between the two communities' militias led to several reckless actions and then to the first serious inter-communal clashes of December 1963.

The achievement of an uneasy truce a few days after 1963 clashes, the constant small breaches of the ceasefire in the following months, along with the concentration of the Turkish-Cypriot fighters into enclaves, showed that the need for well-trained security forces and defence structures was more pressing than ever. Therefore, by February 1964 a new policy emerged for the defence of the Republic: forming an army, building fortifications and purchasing military equipment in order to protect the island from external or internal threats. The key players in this process were the Cyprus and Greek governments along with General Georgios Grivas.

From 1964 until 1967 the defence system of the government-controlled part of the island grew rapidly in effectiveness and manpower. Nonetheless, this process produced an important side effect. While it created some insurance against external threats, it also created two internal and serious fronts: the inter-communal violent incidents and the Greek-Cypriots' split. Regarding the former, armed confrontation was usually sparked between Greek-Cypriots and Turkish-Cypriots around sensitive areas which were considered strategically vital for both sides. Throughout these three years provocative actions from both sides led to confrontations of varying scale with implications for political aspects of the Cyprus problem. Prominent among them was the incident of June 1966 and the even more severe clashes in November 1967. The second front, however, was still more dangerous because it enhanced division and political unrest within the Greek-Cypriot community itself. The incipient fault line had derived from the antagonism between the political leadership of Makarios and the military leadership of Grivas, who was backed by the Greek Government, regarding the modalities, and even the overarching priority itself of the national aim of *Enosis*. In the following paragraphs we will explore how issues of defence raised tensions between Greek-Cypriots and how this then reverberated on relations between the two communities.

To begin with, a constituent part of Makarios' 'Thirteen Points' and of the Greek-led Cyprus Government after 1963 was the amendment of certain provisions about the security forces and the formation of a well-structured defence system of the island. On 25 February 1964, the Cyprus Government announced the formation of a force on a voluntary basis, named as the National Guard.[127] Simultaneously, however, it was decided between the

Greek and Cyprus governments and Grivas that the National Guard should be transformed into a tactical army under compulsory conscription. Athens and General Grivas took up the reins of this transformation process. More particularly, it was decided that a new division, the Cyprus Special Mixed Staff, responsible for the defence planning of Cyprus, was going to be established within the Greek Ministry of Defence, under the command of Grivas. A retired Lieutenant-General of the Greek Army, Georgios Karayiannis, was assigned as the chief of the National Guard. To reinforce the National Guard, the Greek Ministry approved the secret assignment of a division of Greek soldiers to Cyprus. This was contrary to the provisions of the Treaty of Alliance for a Greek Contingent of only 950 Greek soldiers. It should be stressed that Turkey did not initially protest against this. The main underlying reason for the division's assignment to Cyprus was to increase the Greek Government's leverage on Makarios' regime.[128] These new soldiers were about to come to Cyprus with fake Cypriot passports claiming to wish to volunteer in the National Guard.[129]

It should be noted that Grivas had gone back to Athens in March 1959, but by 1964 was anxious to return to Cyprus to lead the armed forces of the island and complete his own perceived destiny as the architect of *Enosis*.[130] The Cypriot president, however, did not favour Grivas' return both due to their strong disagreements on the handling of the Cyprus issue and due to the Turkish negative reactions in case of his return. Bearing in mind Grivas' past, the Greek Government was also reluctant to allow him to go back in Cyprus. Despite everybody's reservations they all knew that only Grivas could have exerted effective control upon all the irregular armed groups formed from 1959 onwards, in order to incorporate them within one strong force. His return to Cyprus was only a matter of time.[131]

By 1 June 1964, the legal framework for the establishment of National Guard was voted in Cyprus' Parliament. All men from 18 to 50 would serve a six-month service – which in December was increased to twelve months, in June 1965 to eighteen and in November 1967 to two years. Additionally, the Parliament voted for the compulsory service for all males aged from 16 to 55 and females from 20 to 40 in the civil defence services of the Republic.[132] The decisions about the reorganization of the security forces, therefore, had been taken and the legal framework set in place. In the light of these developments, Grivas was now more anxious than ever to return to the island. He did so secretly on 12 June 1964 with the pretext of inspecting the armed groups of the paramilitary organizations.[133] Nonetheless, his main goal was to assume full control of the Cyprus army and to remove every obstacle in the road towards *Enosis*, even if that meant getting rid of Makarios as well. However incipient, this was full of ominous possibilities in Greek-Cypriot political life. Although initially the Greek Government ordered him to return to Athens, Grivas did not comply. With much public expectation of cooperation between these two seminal figures of the 'national struggle' before 1959–1960, the president felt he had little choice but to welcome Grivas and host a public reception for him.[134] In doing so, Makarios surely had fewer illusions about the likely relationship ahead.

It should be clarified that although Grivas remained in Cyprus, he had no administrative powers over the National Guard. He remained only responsible for the operational command of the Cyprus army in case of war.[135] However, this changed after August 1964 and the serious inter-communal strife near the Mansoura-Kokkina enclave. Karayiannis, chief of the National Guard, hitherto loosely under Grivas' control, resigned due to their worsening relationship. In a series of articles that Karayiannis published in June 1965 in the Greek newspaper *Ethnikos Kiriks,* he explained the background of the August 1964 clash and highlighted the responsibilities of the National Guard's actions which later led to Ankara's intervention and to the indiscriminate air bombing of the area with many civilian casualties. Grivas' decision making during these days made impossible any cooperation between the two men; this led to Karayiannis' resignation. It is noteworthy that the latter publicly accused Grivas of erratic methods and behaviour, giving rise to doubts over his psychological balance.[136]

After this incident Grivas had effectively, though not officially, taken full control of the National Guard, thus achieving his initial aim. By then he had become convinced that the Cyprus Government had abandoned *Enosis* and was working towards the consolidation of independence. According to Spyros Papageorgiou (one of Grivas' closer associates), Grivas was 'assailing' the Greek Government and the Greek King with reports accusing Makarios and his entourage of obstructing the effective organization of the National Guard and preserving their private armies in order to undermine the *Enosis* struggle.[137] By this stage Grivas was already issuing veiled threats to resign himself from the National Guard and lead a guerrilla struggle – effectively against Makarios – for *Enosis.*[138] As indicated in the following abstract of a letter that Grivas sent in September 1964 to the Greek Premier, the former was ready to use all possible mechanisms to fulfil what he believed to be his national duty:

If you give me your permission, I will try to organize political propaganda in order to influence and direct the masses towards *enosis.* I believe that progress could be achieved. Contrary to what is happening in Nicosia where the anti-*enosis* propaganda has affected to a large extent Greek-Cypriot opinion, in most towns and villages the situation is better. Therefore, I would suggest the establishment of a Press Office in the Greek Embassy in Nicosia, which will work for the achievement of the national goal and in the meantime the assignment of a special Press Officer at my office.[139]

The Greek Premier agreed and duly sent a Press Attaché to the Greek Embassy in Nicosia. As stated above, Papandreou and Makarios themselves differed radically about the handling of the Cyprus issue. Makarios' disregard for the 'National Centre', and his tendency to act provocatively towards Turkey and Turkish-Cypriots, without consulting the Greek Government, was irritating for the Greek Premier.[140] Papandreou and his in-coming replacement, Stephanos Stephanopoulos, especially after Plaza's mediation, were anxious to solve the Cyprus issue as soon as possible via direct negotiations with Turkey aiming at *Enosis* with territorial concessions. To this end Makarios was becoming an annoying obstacle.[141]

By mid-1964, a secret operation was initiated and coordinated by the new Press Attaché; it aimed to increase anti-Makarios feelings among Greek-Cypriots.[142] The key tool for this operation was the Greek-Cypriot press. Several newspapers were funded and manipulated in order to propagandize against traitors in the Cyprus Government and condemn their anti-*Enosis* plans. This triggered a 'war' within the Greek-Cypriot press. The pro-government papers counter-attacked by issuing articles against the Greek Government and the Greek army officers in Cyprus who were conspiring to overthrow Makarios' Government.[143] The accusations and counter-accusations inflamed public opinion and spread more 'poison' within the Greek-Cypriot community. When Makarios was notified about the task of the new emissary of the Greek Embassy, he demanded his immediate recall by the Greek ambassador.[144] In an attempt to calm things down, the House of Representatives passed legislation in December 1965 envisaging that all newspaper editors had to disclose their regular and extraordinary income, while it prohibited the receipt of subsidies from foreign governments or citizens.[145]

Despite the government's efforts to soften this explosive atmosphere, it was evident that the situation was steadily getting out of hand. As long as there were press attacks against the Cyprus Government, large public demonstrations were organized within the Greek-Cypriot community in favour of Makarios' policies.[146] Makarios' relations with the new Greek Premier, Stephanopoulos, in 1966 were even more embittered than with Papandreou. On 9 March 1966, Stephanopoulos, without any prior consultation with Makarios, officially appointed Grivas as chief of all the Security Forces on the island, that is, of both the National Guard and the

Greek division. In this way, the Greek Government wanted to assert its control over the Cyprus problem.[147] Makarios responded immediately arguing that this was an internal affair not to be decided by the Greek Government, highlighting also that Grivas was dangerous and could tie the country into a Civil War.[148] The Greek Government did not accept Makarios' arguments. The political crisis between Athens and Nicosia had gradually moved into a more dangerous phase.

Makarios swiftly realized that he had lost effective control over the security forces of the island and decided instead to establish a paramilitary police tactical reserve strictly under his own authority. By November 1966 he came to an agreement for the purchase of Czechoslovakian arms to be allocated to this police force, later named as the Presidential Guard. Greatly alarmed, when Grivas, Athens and Ankara became aware of this development, they were at pains to ensure that these weapons would be immediately taken away from Makarios' control.[149] The episode that followed became known as the first Czech arms crisis.[150] Ankara threatened to retaliate if a satisfactory arrangement had not been reached soon, while Athens threatened to terminate its diplomatic relations with the Republic of Cyprus if the keys to the armoury were not given to the commander of the Greek forces on the island.[151] After a while, Makarios complied to the extent that the arms would be periodically inspected by UNFICYP. Contrary, however, to such assurances, Makarios secretly distributed some of the Czech arms without UNFICYP's prior knowledge. Reportedly those arms were distributed during the later Kophinou crisis of November 1967.[152] Additionally, Makarios took another action to reinforce his own loyalists. The Cyprus Government approved the increase of spending from the state's budget of 1967 for new recruits and the purchase of arms for the government-controlled police force.[153]

Inevitably such tendencies impacted on inter-communal relations, and violent incidents grew alongside them. The main sources of these clashes were the arms race, the construction of armed posts and the effort of both communities' forces to entrench their ground positions in strategically important parts of the island. The most problematic areas were those around Turkish-Cypriot villages or enclaves. Since the formation of the National Guard, one of the main military targets of the Cyprus army was to take over those areas. This is what had triggered the Mansoura crisis in August 1964. In addition, the extension of the National Guards' coastal defences, fortifications and the patrols in disputed areas became the spark of the serious Famagusta disturbances in both March and November 1965. Several similar incidents produced unrest and tension throughout the island, until a much more severe crisis was sparked in November 1967 in the mixed villages of Ayios Theodoros and Kophinou. Although the Cyprus Government persistently argued that the construction of fortifications was necessary for the defence of Cyprus in case of external attack, UNFICYP appealed several times to the National Guard not to site them in the immediate vicinity of Turkish-Cypriot villages. These actions were perceived by the Turkish-Cypriot fighters as provocative and they led to retaliatory actions, while the UN secretary-general repeatedly urged the parties to terminate the constant building.[154] David Hunt in his memoirs recalls,

> Confrontation between the Cyprus National Guard and UNFICYP was the sort of thing that kept us occupied most of the time. The Turks were capable of provocation but the majority of the incidents that kept us up late at night were the results of Grivas' restlessness. Since I left, and particularly since the 1967 affair when Ankara's ultimatum forced Grivas to leave the island, I have wondered whether Makarios may not have encouraged him not from any dislike for the Turkish Cypriots (which I doubt if he feels) but in the hope that he would go too far and pay the penalty […] At the time that the Grivas policy of digging trenches and erecting new strongpoints everywhere, and particularly in the neighbourhood of Turkish villages, was in full swing the Diplomatic Crops, especially the American and Greek Ambassadors and myself were liable to great bursts of activity by day and night with the wireless links to London, Washington, New York, Athens and Ankara working time. Alexandrakis [the Greek Ambassador] usually had the main role. Athens would let things take their course until it appeared there would be a severe clash at any minute between the National Guard and UNFICYP; then getting cold feet his Ministry would get on the telephone from Athens to rouse him out of his bed in the small hours with instructions to go and tell Grivas to calm down.[155]

Besides the defensive fortifications, turmoil was also produced with the constant supply of military equipment to both communities. The Cyprus Government was openly importing military equipment from abroad claiming that it was necessary for the defence of the Republic, while the Turkish-Cypriot fighters imported arms and ammunition from Ankara. The missiles' importation by the Cyprus Government from the Soviet Union was one of the most explosive incidents throughout 1965, which again threatened the stability of the area. This incident became known as the missile crisis of 1965 and it was generated only a few days before the submission of the UN mediator's report.

As already seen in the previous chapter, in August 1964 Nicosia turned to Moscow in order to secure military and diplomatic support in case of foreign invasion in Cyprus. In addition to the diplomatic support, the two governments came to an agreement for the purchase of military equipment including surface-to-air missiles.[156] When in March 1965 it became known that the missiles were about to be delivered to Cyprus – via Egypt – both Turkey and Turkish-Cypriots were greatly alarmed. Kuchuk stated in March 1965 that they were closer to war than ever before, while Turkey threatened again to intervene if such missiles were stationed in Cyprus.[157] This incident created diplomatic frissons in Washington as well, which exerted pressure to both Athens and Nicosia in order to prevent the stationing of missiles of Soviet origin in Cyprus and to avoid a direct Greco-Turkish clash over this. While Makarios had been under pressure from all sides not to bring the missiles in Cyprus, he stressed that he will not accept any threats.[158] For some time confusion was generated through the press about what will eventually happen. A few weeks later, however, it was evident that the government had abandoned its initial plan and the missiles remained in Alexandria.[159] The most surprising aspect of this missiles episode is that almost thirty years later history repeated itself. In 1997–1998 the Cyprus Government decided to purchase the Russian S-300 missiles. Because of Turkey's similar strong reactions, however, the missiles were eventually stationed in Crete.

The period from 1964 until 1967 was probably the most crucial period for the later formation of the Cyprus question. The different international orientations between the Cyprus Government and the Greek Governments and Grivas, along with their sharp disagreement about the best way to achieve *Enosis,* were reflected in the defence-planning process. Although in the first months of 1964 the army was formed, soon enough the key question was who was going to be in command of this National Guard. Control of the armed forces was for all parties the crucial element needed to help achieve their goals. Grivas wanted to control the National Guard: to lead it as a Trojan Horse for overthrowing Makarios and achieving *Enosis,* even if that led to an armed confrontation with Turkey. Conversely, the Greek Government wanted to achieve *Enosis* through diplomatic channels and without militarily provoking Turkey. Grivas was going to be their leverage for forcing on Makarios any perspective agreement with Turkey over *Enosis.* Finally, for Makarios, *Enosis* was not for the moment a feasible option. The aim was to strengthen the independent character of the island, while strengthening the defence capabilities of the country and simultaneously increasing pressure towards Turkish-Cypriots. The use of military violence against the Turkish-Cypriot fighters or Turkish armed forces, if necessary, could also be employed.[160] However, when he realized that he was losing control over the Cypriot armed forces and that there were conspiracies against him, he organized his own force. The catastrophic outcome of this rivalry became more obvious after 1971 with Grivas' clandestine return to Cyprus – after his forced withdrawal at the end of 1967 – and the realization of his previous threat for organizing a guerrilla struggle against those who shelved *Enosis*.

On the one hand, the internal cleavage between Greek-Cypriots unavoidably weakened an important internal firewall: the unity of the Greek-Cypriot community towards the 'allegedly' common target of self-determination. On the other hand, part of the Turkish-Cypriot policy was to appear in public united towards their common enemy and be determined to endure the hardships caused by their self-containment in the enclaves. The Turkish-Cypriot fighters continued to be trained and reinforced by the TMT and responded accordingly to any action considered provocative by the National Guard. The main aim of the Turkish-Cypriot leadership and fighters was to establish and preserve their superiority in the areas considered vital for their strategic interests. However, in two cases, when the National Guard tried to undermine the Turkish-Cypriot control near their enclaves, large-scale confrontation almost led to Turkish invasion: in August 1964 and in November 1967. Both confrontations changed the course of the Cyprus question.

Conclusion

It took two years for the Greek-Cypriot-controlled Government and the House of Representatives to transform the Republic of Cyprus administratively and militarily and run it along the lines they believed best from the vantage point of their own interests for the development of the state. For them, after all, it was inconceivable that a state could properly operate when a community of 80 per cent was politically equal with a minority of 18 per cent. Viewed in this way, the continued growth of the state necessarily meant remedying the inherent defects of the 1960 Constitution for the sake of the state's growth itself. That led to a radical restructuring of the state which completely disregarded the fundamental characteristic of the Constitution, its bi-communal nature. According, however, to Michael Dekleris, the Greek constitutional expert and advisor of the Greek-Cypriot side in the inter-communal talks of 1972–1974, if a solution was to be found at any later point, it was unrealistic for the Greek-Cypriots to believe that they could preserve this new type of state.[161]

Nonetheless, the reorganization of the state, along the lines of the previous 'Thirteen Points', along with its accompanying social logic, came with a cost:

the creation of a separate administration on the island which was steadily becoming more organized and effective within its own geographical area. In 1964 it was the 'General Committee'; in December 1967, it became the 'Turkish-Cypriot Provisional Administration'; in 1971 it was transformed into the 'Turkish-Cypriot Administration'; in 1974 it turned into the 'Autonomous Turkish-Cypriot Administration'; in 1975 it was named as 'Turkish Federated state of Cyprus'; and finally in 1983 the 'Turkish Republic of Northern Cyprus' was purportedly established pursuant to a Unilateral Declaration of Independence. Each phase indicated further consolidation of the inter-communal separation with which we are principally concerned in this study. From 1964 until 1967 Denktash expressed that, 'Makarios and Greece proved that *faits accomplis* could be used effectively'.[162] This proved to be Denktash's own justification and most effective tool for the reorganization of the Turkish-Cypriot administration after he came to Cyprus in 1968.

In order to have a clearer perception of the context and the divergent evolution of the two communities in the period 1964–1967, Chapter 3 will focus on the economic situation of the island. We will highlight the economic realities in Cyprus on the outset of 1960, how this changed until 1963 and how it was developed after the inter-communal strife until 1967. It will be evident that for Makarios' Government the shaping and manipulation of economic growth became a vital method for enforcing Turkish-Cypriot capitulation. The wider effects of this were to be critical for our subject.

1964–1967: Economic Development
of the Island

The struggle of the Cypriot people is shifting from the military to the
economic field. A basic prerequisite for success of our struggle in the
military and political fields lies in safeguarding our economic strength
and stability [...] However, further economic progress is impossible
without *freedom*.[1]

With these words, in December 1964, Tassos Papadopoulos, minister of
labour and social insurance, summarized the Cyprus Government's goals
for the following year. It was indeed true that by then the severe outbreaks
of inter-communal violence were diminishing and the Cyprus Government
could now focus on its development programme. However, in speaking of
freedom Papadopoulos was referring to *Enosis*, which in its strictly material
sense carved the significant implication of not being held back by Turkish-
Cypriots. Certainly the creation of a more explicitly Greek-Cypriot state
after 1964 had in the succeeding period been accompanied by economic
stability and the achievement of impressive development goals. The tourist
boom, exports and expenditure from the British bases and United Nations
Force in Cyprus (UNFICYP) brought in significant levels of revenue. In
addition, agriculture, which together with the construction sector formed
the backbone of Cyprus' economy, had grown rapidly. Meanwhile, foreign
development aid and post-independence British grants provided important
stimulus for the development of the island.[2]

The scene within the enclaves was entirely different. The Turkish-Cypriot
leadership had to manage severe structural problems and practical hardships
in addition to the housing problem of the displaced Turkish-Cypriots. The
more extreme wing of leadership, as in the case of Rauf Denktash, was
calling for Turkey's military intervention on the island and partition at
every opportunity. Conversely, the official Turkish-Cypriot line called for
firm adherence to the 1960 Constitution unless forced by Greek-Cypriots
to act differently. In the meantime, Ankara constituted the main financial

and military contributor for Turkish-Cypriots in order to help them endure isolation for as long as necessary.

Inevitably, the economic policies of the Cyprus Government crucially affected the development of the Cyprus problem as a whole. Low unemployment, the steady increase of Cyprus' gross domestic product (GDP) and the gradual improvement in Greek-Cypriots' standard of living had a significant impact on society's psychology and people's perceptions about both their Turkish-Cypriot 'opponents' and the solution of the national question; while the independence mentality was gradually being cultivated over the *Enosis* dream among Greek-Cypriots, the schism between the two communities was further aggravated. The combination of these two tendencies was to define Cypriot politics.

The aim of this chapter is to present the economic policies and development of both communities in the aftermath of the 1963 crisis up to 1967, as well as their wider significance. First, however, it is essential to make a brief reference to the economic indicators and intrinsic weaknesses of the Republic of Cyprus during the first three years of independence. Hypothetically, after the signing of the Zurich–London Agreements, the development of an integrated economy within the Republic of Cyprus should have been the chief priority for both communities. One substantial challenge existed, however: how to balance the aim of an integrated, prosperous economy with the divergent aims stemming from the national aspirations of the two communities, especially given the mutual suspicions surrounding the independence settlement itself.

1960–1963: First years of independence

Setting the foundations

Even before the official declaration of independence, the Cyprus authorities acknowledged that one of its first priorities was the establishment of the necessary mechanisms for economic growth. On 1 February 1960 the transitional Government of Cyprus, therefore, requested from the United Nations (UN) to 'undertake an intensive economic survey of the island and provide the Government with a report with recommendations for future action'.[3] After a thorough examination of each productive sector of Cyprus' economy, the UN Technical Assistance Board, under Willard Thorp, published a report indicating the island's handicaps as well as its most promising prospects for growth. Thorp's report marked the starting point of the island's development. The Cyprus Government integrated its suggestions into a structured five-year development programme published on 21 August 1961.[4]

According to Thorp, the Cyprus economy in 1960 'seemed to be running along a downhill and rather bumpy road.'[5] Paradoxically however, Cyprus had attained the second highest per capita income in the Mediterranean area, at a time when internal political conditions were distinctly troubled.[6] Because of several exogenous circumstances, such as the increased British military expenditure and the favourable world market prices of its main exports (cooper and citrus), Cyprus had enjoyed an unexpected economic boom in the period 1950–1957. Nonetheless, this reality did not change the fact that the island's economy struggled with multiple structural problems, limited inter-sectoral linkage or coordination, excessive dependence on unstable factors and a lack of diversity in its revenue sources.[7] Agriculture was the largest sector of employment but had a very low productivity rate – almost 44 per cent of the population was employed in this sector, producing only 16 per cent of the country's GDP.[8] Modern technologies in agriculture and land farming had yet to be introduced. Agriculture production was thus largely dependent on weather conditions.[9] The mining industry, an important contributor to the island's GDP, was also troubled by problems, including the reckless exploitation of natural resources during the previous years and the ensuing reduction of the island's reserves. The tourist industry was still only fledgling, mainly consisting of mountain resorts, while the lack of proper infrastructure such as roads, ports and airports exacerbated the problem.[10] Additionally, the economic stagnation that followed in 1958–1959, due to the emergency situation on the island, the gradual removal of the British troops from the region, and the adverse climate conditions that reduced agricultural production, led to a sharp decline of the island's income and a spike in unemployment and emigration, particularly to the UK. Moreover, instability led also to significant flight of capital from the local banks.[11]

The aim of the first post-independence development plan, therefore, was to address these challenges by stimulating agriculture, creating conditions for the encouragement of private industrial development, improving the country's infrastructure and promoting Cyprus as an attractive tourist destination. To achieve this aim, the establishment of new agencies and state bodies that would coordinate government actions, along with the enactment of relevant legislation, was of utmost importance.[12] It should also be stressed that Thorp drew attention to the need for effective cooperation between all the various arms of the government.[13] This was especially imperative in Cyprus, since the government was the primary investor in development and efficient management of scarce resources was essential.[14]

The first plan provided £62 million for development over the next five years. According to a prominent expert, Dr Renos Theocharis, there were two options for the government in order to mobilize such a sum for investment: first, foreign aid and outside borrowing; and second and most importantly, its own budgetary resources.[15] The latter option, as Theocharis explained, had two dimensions: important cuts in public spending with savings allocated to productive uses on the island and additional revenue derived from direct and indirect taxes. Theocharis lauded the government's early record in reducing its expenses and transferring substantial resources towards development. Equally important, the government's decision to remain in the sterling area, by keeping its currency at par with the British pound and its membership in the Commonwealth in 1961, brought significant trade benefits and critical indirect taxes to the government's funds.[16] As we shall emphasize, however, a continuing blockage was created in direct taxation policy leading to difficulties on fiscal collection.[17]

In addition to local resources, the government was also able to secure substantial outside contributions. First, the Treaty of Establishment of 1960 of the newly independent state envisaged that Britain would provide substantial aid to the state over five years. Second, the government applied for membership in the International Monetary Fund and the International Bank for Reconstruction and Development. In June 1961 membership was granted, and in 1961 and 1967 the government requested loans to fund major development programmes.[18] Foreign aid was also granted in the form of technical assistance through the UN and other international organizations.[19]

Intrinsic weaknesses of the new state

Although both Thorp's study and the first development plan analysed economic and structural deficiencies, there remained another important challenge that had not been taken into serious account; this was the gap between the economic situation of the two communities. Both the per capita income of Turkish-Cypriots and their share in the country's GDP were much less than those of Greek-Cypriots and less than their demographic, or indeed constitutional, status might have indicated.[20] Nevertheless, this reality did not necessarily mean that by comparing their daily lives Turkish-Cypriots were poorer than Greek-Cypriots.[21] Both communities were largely employed in the agriculture sector. However, the Greek-Cypriot community was better educated and included a sizeable number of businessmen and professionals, whereas Turkish-Cypriots traditionally 'had a disdain towards private business'.[22] In fact, Turkish-Cypriots were largely depended on Greek-Cypriots in several professions such as in trade, health, law, while the banking sector was largely in Greek-Cypriot hands.[23] In practical terms, this economic disparity meant that more subsidies from the state's budget had to be geared towards the Turkish-Cypriot community, in order to address the socio-economic and educational discrepancies; otherwise, economic assistance was going to be sought in Ankara.[24]

Although this particular gap has often been overlooked in the political and historical literature, the Turkish-Cypriot Professor Ozay Mehmet argues that it represented one of the main underlying factors in the later division. 'The fear of economic insecurity via domination by the more powerful Greek-Cypriots has always driven the desire of Turkish-Cypriots to be masters of their own destiny.'[25] Such insecurity had led in the 1950s to the formulation of a new movement aiming to consolidate a separate economy on the island, one dimension of which was the notorious 'from Turk to Turk' initiative launched in 1958.[26] Among the movement's aims was the promotion of self-reliance and support of Turkish-Cypriot trades and industries. To expedite this, the Turkish-Cypriot Chamber of Commerce was instituted, and this fed into the drive for separate municipalities after 1958.[27]

The 'from Turk to Turk' policy, although officially terminated by the Turkish-Cypriot leadership, was unofficially continued even after the declaration of independence. Nevertheless, until 1963, it had only made fitful progress with limited results.[28] This was due mainly to two realities. First, both communities shared a long history, especially during the Ottoman period, of economic co-existence. Attalides specifically argues that the two communities had created over time 'inextricably interdependent patterns of economic relations which survived until just before the invasion in 1974'.[29] Second, Mehmet contends that two schools of thought were current among Turkish-Cypriot economists and leaders regarding the most effective strategy for the economic development of their community within the newly founded Republic[30]: the first in support of the integrated economy and development spending to achieve economic parity between the two communities and the second which advocated '*etatism*' (statism), as then applied in Turkey as one of the core characteristics of Kemalism, that is, state intervention and public control of the economy.[31] In Cyprus' case, the second option was translated into channelling financial and technical assistance directly from Turkey to the Turkish Communal Chamber. The latter reached its peak mainly after the *de facto* separatism of 1964.

Beyond such economic discrepancies, the rigidity of the 1960 Constitution produced certain limitations in the economic development of the island. First and foremost was the divisive nature of the Constitution itself. The communities' political antagonism was further intensified by the Zurich–London Agreements mainly with regard to the state apparatus. Resulting differences distracted attention from the economic problems of the island. According to Nicholas Lanitis, a prominent Greek-Cypriot businessman, two of the most crucial problems of the Constitution were the existence of two autonomous communal chambers and the controversy over municipalities.[32] He specifically reported that 'they prevent unity, an essential provision for progress and impose on a small country an expensive governmental superstructure that sooner or later will become abortive both to the Greeks and to the Turks'.[33] First, separate municipalities for the five main towns of an island of 600,000 people constituted a heavy financial burden both for the municipalities themselves and for the taxpayers.[34] Second, the existence of two autonomous communal chambers with limited financial resources had severe implications for the educational policies of each community.[35] As Clerides explains, the programming and policies of each chamber depended mainly on its ability to cover its financial needs. This inevitably had a great impact on the social development of the Cypriot population as a whole.[36]

Similarly, further obstacles emerged in 1961 due to the failure to obtain the constitutionally mandatory separate majority in the Parliament for the extension of the taxation legislation. Although the Turkish-Cypriot leadership had no objections on the relevant legislation, they exercised their veto right against this crucial legislation in order to force action on other pending issues and laws they perceived as crucial.[37] This action, however, left the island without a critical piece of legislation for the collection of the Republic's revenue. After several months of negotiations, an interim agreement was reached which provided that, until there was final political solution, the two communal chambers would be responsible for collecting the direct taxes from their respective communities.[38]

Not surprisingly, the new system for the collection of taxes was complex and distinctly problematic. The most pivotal implication, according to Lanitis, was that this new system inevitably led to heavy costs, losses of revenue and the imposition of more indirect taxes and import duties on several products.[39] None of this encouraged Cyprus attractiveness as a place for international investment.[40] Statistical data confirmed that public revenue from direct taxes was reduced from 24.2 per cent in 1960 to 14.5 per cent in 1963, while the revenue from indirect taxes increased from 42.9 per cent to 50 per cent respectively.[41]

All of these problems derived from both the political realities and the Constitution, thus reinforcing an underlying instability prejudicial to the government's development plans. However, the achievements of the first three years of independence seemed indeed encouraging. It was also true that the Turkish-Cypriot leaders upon independence came to realize that the economic development of the state, and of their community, was far more important than promoting communal separatism.[42] Meanwhile there were promising signs of inter-communal collaboration within the Parliament on elements that concerned economic modernization of the state.[43] Essential institutions such as the Planning Bureau, the Central Bank of Cyprus, the Cyprus Development Bank and the Agriculture Research Institute were established, and foundations were successfully set in place for the further implementation of the plan. Private sector activity revived and the country's GDP gradually increased.[44] Exports of Cypriot agricultural products and wines also increased. Progress in tourism activity continued so that in 1963 Cyprus saw the highest percentage of increase in tourist arrivals of all European and Middle Eastern countries.[45] Despite this important beginning, there was still considerable concern from abroad regarding the pace of the development programme's implementation and the issue of underlying communal antagonism. The British had warned the Cypriot ministers that decisive actions were urgently needed to ensure the successful implementation of the five-year plan on schedule since 'there was a delicate balance that would be upset either by a loss of confidence following an outburst of violence or failure to check the growth of the communist influence'.[46] Events were soon to justify this pessimism.

The watershed of December 1963

The strong upward development trend of the Republic of Cyprus was shattered by the inter-communal clash of December 1963. The ensuing Turkish-Cypriot withdrawal from the state apparatus and their isolation created a volatile situation which led to economic stagnation and a deterioration of economic activity throughout the island. The most promising industry of the state, tourism, entered the doldrums in 1964. Statistical data showed that during the first six months of 1964, 7,722 foreign visitors came to Cyprus, whereas in the same period in 1963 the figure was as high as 49,585.[47] Both imports and exports were reduced, depleting state revenue. Up to 1963, the import duty had yielded one-third of the government's revenue[48]; thus, the radical decline of imports created a substantial fiscal deficit.[49] Insecurity in the towns and uncertainty in the villages located close to the enclaves paralysed economic activity in the main commercial hubs and the countryside. The factories situated within the 'Green Line' in Nicosia closed down. Inevitably unemployment had dramatically increased. Moreover, during the first months of 1964, the mining industry remained virtually inactive due to the proximity of the mines to high-risk areas as well as their reliance on mixed Greek/Turkish-Cypriot labour.[50] Additionally, many foreign experts providing technical assistance for the implementation of development programmes left the island.[51]

During the first half of 1964 the economic and political outlook of Cyprus was bleak. Some observers argued that without a political settlement the perpetuation of the economic crisis was inevitable, while others claimed that 'it seems whistling in the dark to expect prosperity to follow in the wake of a political solution. And anyway a political solution looks extremely remote.'[52]

Unexpectedly, however, the Cyprus economy recovered from what proved a brief period of stagnation, yet without any solution to the national problem. This seemingly confirmed the Greek-Cypriot leadership's arguments that previous constitutional provisions had hampered the economic and broader development of the island. More specifically, government officials argued,

> A political settlement which gave a simple majority control over the economic policy would encourage the Greek-Cypriot community – as the dynamic element of the Cyprus economy – to devote all of its energy and resources to repairing the ravages of the present disturbances and regaining momentum on the development programme.[53]

By the end of 1965, with all the 'Thirteen Points' of Makarios in place either *de facto* or via the Doctrine of Necessity, such a majority control had been assumed by the Greek-Cypriot leadership; consequently, the pace of development was augmented perceptibly. The question was whether such a pattern of economic growth – that is, one driven by Greek-Cypriot dynamism – would help or hinder better understanding at the political level.

The recovery: 1965–1967

The years after the Second World War, 1950–1973, Western Europe had experienced what is now characterized as the Golden Age of economic growth. In the case of Cyprus, it was only after independence that solid foundations for economic development were gradually established. As explained in the following section, however, a great boost to this growth had been given after the 1964 crisis.

Although it was true that by 1965 the economic situation on the island had improved, the viability of the government's financial planning was still at stake. The Finance Minister, Renos Solomides, had privately admitted that 'he had doubts about the viability of the Government's budgetary position after the end of this year [1965] unless there is a change for the better in the political situation.'[54] Publicly, however, the government presented a different image of the situation, a tactic that proved to be successful. Its main policy was to formally minimize the difficulties of the situation in order to present a brave front to the public.[55] This tactic subsequently justified the fact that Greek-Cypriots and the private sector in particular remained confident of the viability and growth prospects of the economy. It was also reported that several Greek-Cypriots had even appeared indifferent to the economic consequences of political divisions.[56] In July 1965 the British high commissioner admitted 'this pig-headed optimism [of Greek-Cypriots] has been a major reason for the resilience shown by the economy during the last eighteen months'.[57] This sanguine stance on Cyprus' economic prospects also had a positive effect on the island's banking sector. Unlike the emergency period of 1958–1959, there was no significant flight of capital from the Cypriot banks. The minister of finance praised his community's attitude by announcing,

> Indicative of the confidence of the Cypriots in the future of the country's economy and the ability of the Government to protect the Cyprus pound, even under conditions of rebellion and war, is the fact that no measure has been taken to prevent the transfer of capital outside of Cyprus. I must admit that the Cyprus Government has relied not only on the patriotism of the agents of the commercial and industrial activity, but also on their good sense as to what their true interests are; and as a matter of fact no panic has been noticed amongst them and they have not sent their capital abroad.[58]

One of the main challenges faced by the government in 1965, which remained the main investor in the development programme, was finding ways to shore up state revenue. Furthermore, the government now had another financial burden to tackle: the urgent need for financing the security forces of the island. These new realities inevitably created further delays in the implementation of the government's overall programme. The government admitted both in 1965 and 1966 that certain scheduled development programmes had to be deferred because of the extraordinary military spending.[59]

Nevertheless, the foundations that had been established up to that point, together with the Greek-Cypriot takeover of the state apparatus, surprisingly led to a remarkable degree of social stability on the island, facilitating steady progress in every sector of the economy. Neither the occasional small-scale inter-communal tensions nor the internal Greek-Cypriot and Athens-Nicosia rivalries were able to reverse the upward economic trend of the period 1965–1967. It should be clarified, however, that when there is a reference in the book about the 'island's economy', this corresponds only to the economy of the government-controlled sector. The economy of the Sovereign Base Areas and the economic situation within the enclaves were entirely different. The latter point in particular will be treated in the following paragraphs.

It is noteworthy that the Ministry of Labour and Social Insurance had proved to be the most active ministry of Makarios' Government, thus contributing a great deal to the island's impressive economic growth of this period.[60] Tassos Papadopoulos had confirmed in 1964 that his ministry 'within three years of its existence has covered all of the objectives set for it by the Development Plan'.[61] The problem of unemployment immediately after the 1963–1964 crisis was very quickly addressed by effective strategies for the growth of jobs and productivity in Cyprus. First of all, new services responsible for conducting surveys and studies regarding the labour demand in several sectors of the economy were established. In collaboration with the Ministry of Commerce, Industry and Tourism and the Greek Communal Chamber – and later the Ministry of Education – the results of these studies were transformed into new training courses or apprentice schemes. Consequently, the problem of unemployment was largely contained while industrial growth was in the same turns promoted.[62] Simultaneously, special attention was devoted to tourism education. By the end of 1964, with the financial aid of the UN Development Programme and the technical assistance of the International Labour Organization, the newly established Productivity Centre was nearly in full operation. This new institution organized seminars and conferences, addressed to both employers and employees, aiming at the increase of productivity and the promotion of private initiative and the industrial sector of Cyprus.[63]

By the end of 1965, the government's statistical data indicated the lowest unemployment rate on the island for seven years.[64] Further increase in productivity was reported in almost every sector with industrial growth steady and promising.[65] Government efforts to foster private initiative, both local and foreign, also bore fruit.[66] Many new enterprises were established in Cyprus, a reality characterized as 'a small industrial revolution'.[67] One of the most important new investments on the island, beginning in 1965, was the construction of an oil refinery in Larnaca by a consortium of the British petroleum companies Shell and Mobil. Indicative of the promising prospects of the Cyprus economy was the fact that this consortium acknowledged that the prospects for profitability were quite sufficient to outweigh the element of political uncertainty.[68]

Undoubtedly, tourism was one of the sectors that experienced the biggest blow in 1964. Nevertheless, it took only two years for recovery to set in. In 1966 tourist arrivals had exceeded the government's goal of 50,000 foreign visitors.[69] How was this possible given the lack of a permanent political solution to the Cyprus problem along with the sporadic increase of inter-communal tension on the island? From the outset of 1965 the government decided to renew its promotion campaign and to invest in the hotel industry and education.[70] Particularly, in the 1965–1966 development budget significant funding was allocated for the establishment of the Central Hotel Training School, the advancement of local tourism through attractive loan packages for hotel constructions and renovations through the Cyprus Development Corporation funding and the government-funded project of the Nicosia Hilton Hotel's construction.[71] Additionally, negotiations were initiated with the British Government for the release of the Golden Sands area in Famagusta, which was a property of the War Department of Britain before 1960.[72] There was also a degree of good fortune that Cyprus as a venue was well placed to benefit from the large increase in British tourism to the Mediterranean that occurred in the mid-1960s.

A significant upswing was also reported in the foreign trade of Cyprus. Britain remained the major trade partner of Cyprus, but a series of new trade agreements had also been signed with countries of the Soviet bloc.[73] Both imports and exports increased on this front, although the former continued to represent nearly double the value of the latter. Meanwhile, the current deficit in the total balance of payment was narrowed by two other sources. The UN force expenditure, along with the British bases' spending and the increase of Turkish and Greek troops on the island, had brought in a large amount of foreign exchange.[74] Additionally, Cyprus had a very small external debt while the island's financial management was broadly considered to be conservative.[75] The general policy of the government held that both ordinary and development spending should derive mainly from local revenue, in accordance with the government's broader practice of avoiding external borrowing. According to the finance minister,

We are in a position to lay down not only our non-aligned foreign policy, but also our economic policy free from foreign influences and pressures and from the need to resort exclusively to this or that country [...] Cyprus, whose borrowing ability is sound, cannot adopt the easy policy of over-borrowing and thus, be indirectly reduced to a political dependency or an economic dominion of another state. Moreover, under the present emergency conditions, our capability for external borrowing must, for national reasons not be used up; but, like a safety-valve, it must remain available for securing resources to meet a possible increase in the defence expenses, which may be needed for the preservation of the freedom of Cyprus.[76]

It was thus true that the government-controlled part of the island enjoyed remarkable prosperity. The end of the first five-year development plan indicated an average annual rate of growth 6.8 per cent (and 5.9 per cent at compound rate), which meant that it was 0.6 per cent more growth than the initial provision of the plan.[77] The UN Development Programme's resident representative in Cyprus, Dr Earl Hald, asserted that Cyprus might have little experience in governing itself but that it certainly was no longer the under-developed country as it had been in 1960.[78] The government was determined to continue this successful effort and adopt further measures to accelerate the level of growth. When the second five-year development plan was drafted, it decided to focus on a more complete coverage of all the sectors of economy with a particular emphasis on social and welfare aspects.[79] Additionally, it aimed to foster further consultation and cooperation between the public and private sectors and intended to involve both in the process of development planning.[80] By the end of this second plan, the government had successfully achieved a further acceleration of the growth rate. Moreover, after the milestone of November 1967 and the creation of new momentum in political discussions of the Cyprus problem, a moderate economic integration process began for the two communities. Although after 1968 the number of Turkish-Cypriots employed by Greek-Cypriots was gradually increasing, Christodoulou's assessment that 'the reunification of the Cyprus economy was very nearly realized on the eve of the Greek coup and the Turkish invasion' is certainly rather optimistic.[81] Nonetheless, by 1973, the government had achieved a remarkable level of welfare, with almost zero unemployment. Although the aim of diversification of the economy and the reduction of the over-dependence on exogenous sources was not achieved, the government implemented important steps that gradually increased productivity of sectors other than agriculture, such as industry services, construction and tourism.[82]

The economy in the enclaves

Despite this prosperity in the government-controlled sector, matters were by no means so 'rosy' for the Turkish-Cypriots who remained in the enclaves. Long before 1963 economic discrepancies existed between the two communities, but these were further widened when the inter-communal separation got underway. This increased social instability within its own share and thus had implications on the political aspects of the Cyprus problem. Although some studies argue that real economic integration between Greek-Cypriots and Turkish-Cypriots always remained superficial, most have agreed that there was at least before 1963 a peaceful commercial and trade co-existence.[83] December 1963, however, constituted a critical juncture that radically transformed the socio-economic realities of the Turkish-Cypriot community. This section provides a brief analysis of the economic status and employment of Turkish-Cypriots in and outside the enclaves in the period 1964–1967.

Mainly for propaganda purposes, both communities have deployed several arguments to ascribe blame for the political and economic separation and the relative economic stagnation of the Turkish-Cypriot community. The Turkish-Cypriot leadership for example contended that after 1963 its community lived in poverty while Greek-Cypriots enjoyed an unexpected economic boom owing largely to their separation. They claimed that all the funds that were constitutionally allocated to Turkish-Cypriots were now spent on the Greek-Cypriot programme. The same occurred with the benefits from the UN expenditure and external financial and technical assistance.[84] The Greek-Cypriots, however, retorted that Turkish-Cypriots had voluntarily abandoned their posts and that if they wished to return, or recognize the government's legitimacy and everything that had been conducted in their absence, they could also benefit from the island's economic development.[85] Regardless of who was right or wrong, the crucial element for our analysis is the outcome of this separation and its side effects regarding both the development of the Cyprus problem and the political and socio-economic realities for Turkish-Cypriots.

One of the main challenges for any contemporary scholar who studies the economic situation of the Turkish-Cypriot community is that there are no official data for the situation in the enclaves for the period 1963–1974 or for the actual extent of the economic involvement of the Turkish-Cypriots residing outside the enclaves to the Republic's development. According to several interviews conducted by Paul Strong, before the summer of 1974 the Turkish-Cypriot administrators were instructed to destroy various economic documentations in their possession.[86] Moreover, as Patrick observes, the government's statistics for Turkish-Cypriot employment in the government-controlled sector, especially after 1968, were most likely exaggerated.[87]

As already examined, immediately after the separation, the Turkish-Cypriot leadership had sought to improvise its own administrative structures and to form separate economic units within the enclaves. The most important consideration for the viability of the separate administration at this stage was financing. The Financial Department of the Turkish Communal Chamber became the main economic authority responsible for the collection and management of the 'General Committee's' funds.[88] Additionally, the Turkish Communal Chamber had imposed its own custom duties on several products entering the enclaves, such as cigarettes, fruits and vegetables. As a consequence, however, the Turkish-Cypriots often paid two sets of revenue taxes – one to the government authorities and another to the administration of the enclaves.[89]

Building a separate economy was disastrous for a minority with a very limited territorial control over certain areas of Cyprus. Lacking any substantial sources of income, or any productive services within the enclaves and not being internationally recognized as a separate authority on the island, the Turkish-Cypriot leadership inevitably had to turn to Turkey for financial aid. As we have seen, after 1964, 'etatism', the Turkish ideology of economic development, was fully applied in the Turkish-Cypriot embryonic administration, later to be consolidated into the post-1983 pseudostate.[90] In particular, Mehmet observes that 'the Turkish financial aid was modelled and channelled to Turkish-Cypriots to institutionalize statism within a top-heavy, uncompetitive and centralized framework'.[91] This policy was further strengthened in 1968 when Turkey financed the creation of the Turkish-Cypriot Planning Bureau responsible for the development planning of the enclaves.[92]

Ankara was thus now able to further infiltrate into the economic affairs – and by corollary all political and social affairs – of the Turkish-Cypriot community, by providing large grants for defence purposes, salaries for civil servants and fighters, and subsidies for the refugees.[93] For Turkish-Cypriots, turning towards their own 'motherland' was unavoidable by mid-1964 when the Cyprus Government imposed economic sanctions on the enclaves. Makarios' Government made a list of prohibited materials with which the Turkish-Cypriots in the enclaves could have built further fortifications and ammunitions.[94] This embargo, together with the restriction of movement imposed by the Turkish-Cypriot leadership, created enormous difficulties in the daily lives of the Turkish-Cypriots.

Turkey's financing and the Red Crescent relief shipments directed to the enclaves were effective for the dual purposes of the Turkish-Cypriot leadership: namely, to survive until Turkey was finally driven to intervene, which the Turkish-Cypriot leaders believed and hoped it will happen soon, and to convince the international community that Turkish-Cypriots were the victims of a Greek-Cypriot policy to destroy their capacity to resist. The latter was to some extent successful. As one observer at the time pointed out, although Greek-Cypriots might attract political sympathies, 'one's human sympathies are with the Turks (not because they are more virtuous, simply because they need it more)'.[95] Indeed, especially during 1964, the living conditions of the enclaved Turkish-Cypriots declined progressively. Although the data remains obscure – and there was often significant distortion of the actual situation experienced by Turkish-Cypriots – the number of 'refugees' swelled, inciting a housing problem.[96] The government, however, stood firm by its embargo policy. The minister of labour further invoked the argument that permitting any construction activity in the enclaves would obstruct UNFICYP's mandate.[97] Specifically, the UN force was responsible for the return to the *status quo ante* 1963; thus if houses were built within the enclaves, the artificial 'refugee' problem would be perpetuated.

Moreover, the increase in displaced persons concentrated in small areas of the island exacerbated unemployment. Jobs in the public service and agriculture were the main source of income for Turkish-Cypriots before 1963.[98] Thus, abandonment of their posts in the public service and their farmlands in the government-controlled areas inevitably resulted in a precipitous reduction of their standard of living. According to research conducted in 1971 by the Statistics and Research Department of the Ministry of Finance of the Government of Cyprus, the GDP of the Turkish-Cypriot community in 1964 was £60.[99] With the gradual diminishment of tension and the relaxation of strict measures by both communities, in 1967 it was raised to £101. However, the GDP of the Greek-Cypriot community during the same period was £215 and £292, respectively.[100]

The lack of other available job opportunities inside the enclaves had driven the majority of able-bodied males to enlist in the 'Turkish-Cypriot fighters'. Interestingly, women also contributed to the strengthening of the fighters' corps through several supportive activities.[101] In addition, military conscription became obligatory for all male secondary school students and graduates.[102] The whole community was actively engaged with the security mechanisms of this 'embryonic' administration. The fact, however, that well-educated Turkish-Cypriots were forced to abandon their studies for joining the fighters' corps, without any other productive employment opportunities, was gradually becoming a severe source of contention within the enclaves. Further discontent was brewing among Turkish-Cypriots, who claimed that the military commanders and the political leadership itself were appropriating Ankara's subventions for their personal benefit.[103] This situation gradually strengthened an opposition movement within the Turkish-Cypriot community, one which heavily criticized both the military's actions and their leadership's financial management, persistently demanding public legislative debates for the budget planning and spending.[104]

The fighters' corps soon became the largest source of employment within the enclaves. In growing so exponentially, it outweighed any military effectiveness. Patrick in particular emphasizes that the main responsibility of the majority of the fighters was to distribute Ankara's financial aid and food supplies from the Red Crescent, while it 'masked the unemployment and under-employment problem of the Turkish-Cypriot community'.[105] There was another truth about the fighters: once enlisted they could not voluntarily resign.[106] That however meant that the biggest source of employment had also created a 'hypertrophy of unproductive labour' within the enclaves.[107] This fact exacerbated the already grave financial problems of the enclaved administration. The great financial problems, the excessive dependence on Ankara, the power struggle between the Turkish-Cypriot political leadership and military commanders and the growing dissatisfaction of an important segment of the enclaved Turkish-Cypriots were constantly leading to a severe economic and political crisis within the enclaves during the period 1964–1967.

Nearly one year after the clashes, the Cyprus government followed a new policy designing to sever the moderate from the extremist elements of the Turkish-Cypriot community. By mid-1965 it finally relaxed the economic blockade and announced measures to persuade displaced Turkish-Cypriot to return to their villages. Makarios promulgated an official government agency aiming to settle the displaced in rebuilding homes in their original areas and to find employment for them.[108] Naturally, the Turkish-Cypriot authorities made every effort to deter any impulse to return to homes, or indeed any fraternization between Greek-Cypriots and Turkish-Cypriots, in order to prevent possibilities of inter-communal integration. In this they were largely successful.[109] Nevertheless, there were cases of Turkish-Cypriots escaping from the supervision of the enclaves, which the Greek-Cypriot press fastened upon for its own purposes. The Ministry of Labour also made a limited attempt to attract younger Turkish-Cypriots by expanding several of its training scheme programmes for various crafts trades inside the Nicosia enclave after 1968, when the strict bans of movement in and outside the enclaves were eased.[110]

Despite the serious problem of unemployment within the enclaves, it is also possible to identify certain indicators, derived from various studies and personal accounts, relating to employment of Turkish-Cypriots outside the enclaves. For example, employment in agriculture and agricultural production for Turkish-Cypriots farmers who did not abandon their farmlands after 1963 were not substantially affected.[111] Suggestively, inter-communal cooperation in agriculture was not curtailed.[112] It should also be stressed that although many Turkish-Cypriot businessmen were substantially affected by the 1963 crisis, many had continued to cooperate smoothly with their Greek-Cypriot partners. By October 1965 Greek and Turkish owners of factories situated inside the Nicosia Green Line, which had closed due to the inter-communal clashes, initiated negotiations for their re-opening under the auspices of the UN Political Liaison Committee.[113] Nonetheless, political complexities and considerations limited the scope here on both sides. Such cooperation also continued in another way. The Cyprus Development Bank, a mixed government–private institute established in 1963 to mobilize foreign and local capital along with the human resources for the industrial development of Cyprus, continued to operate with representation by members of both communities. The respected previous President of the Turkish-Cypriot Chamber of Commerce, Kemal Rustem, along with many other Turkish-Cypriot stockholders, remained members of the Board of the Development Bank.[114] According to the government's spokesman in September 1966, 506 Turkish-Cypriots were still employed within the government, in sectors such as the Post Offices, Port, Agriculture Services and the Diplomatic Corps.[115] In these ways, at least a residual cross-communal network of economic contacts continued to exist, however much against the grain of other tendencies.

Conclusion

Before leaving Cyprus in 1969, the British High Commissioner, Sir Norman Costar, interestingly concluded, 'Cyprus is the only country I know which has flourished economically on a civil war […] One might almost say that Cyprus has put all of its nonsense into politics and kept it out of economics.'[116] Ironic as this assessment might be, this was most certainly the case.

According to Strong's study, the events that occurred in 1963–1964 opened the way to an entirely differentiated boost to the Greek-Cypriot economy.[117] The scope this afforded subsequently brought considerable pressure to bear on the Turkish-Cypriot enclaves and, as Patrick's field research at the time described, had the benefit of offering limited justification for Turkey's direct intervention.[118] More retrospectively one leading historian, Paschalis Kitromilides, has contended that a much more subtle, calibrated economic policy might have evolved in the Republic, one which, while including certain embargoes, could have used to its advantage the large number of Turkish-Cypriots continuing to live outside the enclaves, encompassing a variety of actions and incentives to resume integration between the two communities.[119] While recognizing the role played by Turkish-Cypriot obstructiveness at the leadership level, Kitromilides remarks that 'one cannot escape the thought that more persistence and more imaginative policies might have been more effective'.[120] This perception is shared by other scholars who argue that a lasting solution could have eventually been reached through economic and social strategies, given that economic sphere and market place traditionally were the only sites in which both communities smoothly interacted.[121] Nonetheless, it was not until April 1967 that Tassos Papadopoulos admitted that the government's efforts needed to focus on assisting the 40 per cent of Turkish-Cypriots residing outside the enclaves.[122] Yet there was still no tangible evidence of real progress on this front. Had the Cyprus Government made progress in building a relationship with this significant segment of the Turkish-Cypriot community, it might have gained a firmer leverage on the overall situation while promoting social stability and peaceful co-existence. Instead, the economic development of the government-controlled sectors only intensified the disparities between the two communities, making the political dimensions of the Cyprus problem even more complex.

It should be stressed that Strong's study also argues that, had it not been for the separation of 1963, over the next few years the Turkish-Cypriots as a community would have experienced growth amounting to 18 per cent of the national income.[123] That is, their economic weight would have caught up with their proportionate share of the island's population and as such precluded any need for external subversion from Turkey. Such a trajectory, in the context of the sustained growth within the Republic as a whole, perhaps would have been able to lay the foundations for a common Cypriot consciousness and identity.[124] Nonetheless, by applying economic 'sticks' instead of carrots and by avoiding any genuine rapprochement and return to normality, the Cyprus Government had adopted a dangerous strategy for achieving its goals. As Clerides had explained, squeezing the Turkish-Cypriots, if truly effective, would have caused Turkish intervention and, if ineffective, as was the case, would have been played into the hands of Turkish-Cypriot extremists for their own gains.[125]

In conclusion, one crucial element was brought to the surface by the quick economic recovery and social stability: This was the new reality and cultivation of independence mentality which disproved Tassos Papadopoulos' initial argument that *Enosis* was essential for the stable and economic development of the Republic of Cyprus. By March 1967 Costar concluded that for a variety of reasons support for *Enosis* within the Greek-Cypriot community had been reduced from 40 per cent in 1965 to 20 per cent in 1967.[126] First, the acute political instability in Greece and the Athens–Nicosia rivalry together with the implications created by the presence of the Greek officers on the island tended to weaken rather than strengthen Hellenic sympathy. Most importantly, Costar explained that from 1964 to 1966 a series of practical studies analysed the real implications of *Enosis* for Cyprus in several fields, such as the banking sector, trade, industrial organization, civil service structure and taxation. These studies identified that if *Enosis* were achieved, many uncomfortable adjustments would take place to the overall disadvantage to Cypriots as a whole. Even Makarios admitted that 'while Cyprus remained prosperous in comparison with Greece, most

[Greek-Cypriots] were not really interested in *Enosis* though no one can openly say so. If there was an economic boom in Greece, the situation could change'.[127] However, economic prosperity was not the only issue at stake in the case of *Enosis*. Many Greek-Cypriots realized that achieving this national aim and keeping Turkey off the island were two highly contrasting aims.[128] The latter will become particularly evident in Chapter 4. Our analysis will focus on the diplomacy inside and outside of Cyprus aimed at breaking the internal blockage in the peacemaking efforts. Bearing in mind the internal restructuring and economic development underway, it emerges that the Cyprus Government tried skilfully to avoid any type of *Enosis* that would have countervailed Greek-Cypriot interests as well as any peacemaking effort that could have offset their advantages vis-à-vis the Turkish-Cypriots.

1965–1967: A 'Convenient' Negotiating Stalemate

The current historiography of the efforts to settle the Cyprus problem during the period of 1965–1967 is usually preoccupied with the negotiations between Greece and Turkey, without close attention to the underlying reasons for the United Nation's (UN's) inability to alleviate the blockage created after Galo Plaza. In particular, form the publication of the UN mediator's report on 26 March 1965 up to the turning point of November 1967, it proved impossible for the UN secretary-general to undertake any promising initiatives. What did occur was a fruitless Greco-Turkish exchange constantly interrupted by political developments in Greece. As already implied, this merely consolidated a mutually convenient stalemate for both communities' decision makers. After the mediator's conclusions were published, Makarios was convinced that time was working in favour of his community. Such an assumption gave him little incentive and no sense of urgency for any genuine conciliatory gestures. Although small signs of potential moderation coming from the Turkish-Cypriot sector could have been further exploited, the primary approach of the Turkish-Cypriot leadership remained the same: restoration of the 1960 Constitution followed by a new settlement on the basis of federation.

This chapter aims to explain the negotiating strategies and objectives of the two communities regarding the internal stalemate, especially those of the Cyprus Government which held the 'upper hand' on the island, as well as to ascertain the reasons for the UN secretary-general's inability to recapture any initiative for settling the problem. First, however, it is important to clarify why the contending parties had agreed to a dialogue between the Greek and Turkish Governments despite its very slim chances of success. Although the specific details of this external dialogue are beyond the scope of this study, a brief presentation of its dynamics is required in order to identify its impact on the consolidation of the internal impasse. This discussion begins by sketching the aims and calculations of various protagonists immediately after the rejection of the mediator's report in April 1965.

The immediate aftermath of Plaza's report

The most negative aspect of the UN mediation in 1965 was that its outcome was the precise opposite of what was originally planned. Plaza overestimated the permissiveness of the parties to accept a compromise solution at that stage. He was disillusioned when he claimed in February 1965 that his findings would be the face-saving device needed for the adoption of more flexible positions by the parties.[1] Instead, his report was used as a pretext for adopting the intransigent positions they instinctively favoured. At the same time, it created a diplomatic vacuum which brought the Cyprus problem back to the initial blockage, rekindling the question of whether the issue was to be adjudicated primarily between Greece and Turkey or between the two communities who actually lived on the island.

As discussed in Chapter 1, after the forthright Turkish and Turkish-Cypriot rejection of Plaza's report, the UN mediation came to a standstill. Ankara insisted that if mediation was to continue, Plaza should not be a part of it.[2] The truth, however, was that the Turkish side, long before the submission of this report, had repeatedly attempted to undermine the role of the UN. It aimed instead, 'behind the scenes', to involve either the North Atlantic Treaty Organization (NATO) or the Council of Europe as more appropriate fora to address what was mainly perceived as a dispute between Greece and Turkey than an internal problem of an independent sovereign state.[3] Thus, Plaza's report gave to the Turkish Government one more reason to undermine the continuation of the UN peacemaking efforts on the island.

Conversely, the mediator's conclusions diplomatically strengthened the Cyprus Government's position and arguments. Although the report triggered intense public debates because of Plaza's suggestion for the future of *Enosis*, it was unanimously agreed abroad that this particular suggestion suited Makarios' objectives. In early April 1965, the newly appointed British High Commissioner in Cyprus, Sir David Hunt, reported after his first meeting with Makarios that the president seemed very pleased with the mediator's report and 'scarcely bothered to conceal his delight'.[4] Meanwhile, upon discussing *Enosis*, Makarios commented that:

> if Greeks after weighing Turkish views and their other policy commitments decided that *Enosis* is off the table, well and good, the Cypriots will accept that. If they said it was on, it would be necessary to consult Cypriot people about [the] modalities.[5]

Clearly, Makarios and many members of his government were not at great pains to achieve *Enosis*. Conversely, Makarios' main aim since 1964 was independence in practice with minority rights for Turkish-Cypriots and *Enosis* in theory.[6] Plaza's conclusions gave further legitimacy to this plan which, if it was to eventually succeed, would require Makarios to remain adamant that no other basis for talks on the island would be acceptable.[7]

In order to avoid the imminent deadlock, UN officials along with Britain and the United States attempted to convince all interested parties to revive the earlier momentum in order to find an agreeable procedure for discussions on the Cyprus problem. This was very important for several reasons. First and most importantly, tension was gradually increasing in Cyprus not only because of Plaza's recommendations but also due to the earlier missile crisis and the outburst of new inter-communal friction near the buffer zone in Nicosia.[8] Because of the latter incident, the Cyprus Government issued a new blockade for the Nicosia enclave. The Turkish Government was constantly threatening that unless the missile issue was permanently settled and the living conditions of the Turkish-Cypriots within the enclaves immediately improved, it would be forced to militarily intervene on the island.[9] As a result, tension increased between Greece and Turkey, and the latter threatened to retaliate by expelling the Greek nationals and the Greek Orthodox Patriarchate in Istanbul.[10] Finally, a Security Council meeting for the renewal of United Nations Force in Cyprus' (UNFICYP's) mandate was due, and for this concrete evidence of progress on the Cyprus issue was required. The future of the peacekeeping force in Cyprus was uncertain due to its growing financial deficiencies and the contributing countries' resentment about continuing to offer their services on the island voluntarily.[11] Calm, therefore, had to be urgently restored and negotiations of any kind had to be initiated.[12]

Under these circumstances, three options existed: initiation of a dialogue between the two communities, as the mediator had suggested; negotiations between Athens and Ankara; or a combination of those approaches. The United States and United Kingdom along with the secretary-general of NATO attempted to convince the interested parties that integration of all processes was of crucial importance.[13] First of all, the inter-communal dialogue in Cyprus stood to contribute to a relaxing of the combustible atmosphere on the island. Meanwhile, it was suggested that a bilateral meeting after the forthcoming meeting of foreign ministers of NATO countries in May offered an appropriate occasion for an initial rapprochement between Greece and Turkey and perhaps for a preliminary round of contacts on Cyprus.[14]

Nonetheless, agreement regarding direct contacts on the island remained very unlikely. Makarios was only open to discussions on the basis of Plaza's report and particularly a new constitution with strictly minority rights for Turkish-Cypriots.[15] Conversely, Kuchuk insisted that the starting point of any talks would be the 1960 Constitution, which for him meant that discussions would have been held on equal political status. Both parties held a maximalist approach on the highly contested question on the basis of any potential talks between them, thus making it impossible for UN officials to find common ground.[16]

It seemed that the only viable option left was the bilateral dialogue of Greece and Turkey. It should be noted that the Greek Government was concerned by Makarios' prevarication over *Enosis*. Athens was neither ready nor willing to accept the disguised abandonment of *Enosis* through the consolidation of independence. The British ambassador in Athens explained that the Greek foreign and defence ministers appeared 'pretty sure that Makarios will consider this report as favouring his purposes and will therefore try to accept the renunciation of *Enosis* unless they can stop him; they propose to try'.[17] The danger of a permanent negotiating impasse together with Plaza's recommendation for supplementary talks between the motherlands provided to the Greek Government with the necessary excuse to accept the direct dialogue with Turkey in order to pursue *Enosis*.[18]

A way out of the impasse, interestingly, came from Makarios only a few days after the mediator's report. More specifically, Makarios gave an interview to the British newspaper *The Observer* avowing that he accepted, in principle, the possibility of a Greco-Turkish dialogue for the Cyprus problem provided that it was only about *Enosis*.[19] However, he emphasized that he would never agree to a type of *Enosis* with territorial exchanges or a Turkish base in Cyprus. Furthermore, he clarified that any bilateral talks between Greece and Turkey should not, under any circumstances, involve the domestic affairs of the sovereign State of Cyprus.[20]

Off-loading the responsibility for dialogue onto the two motherlands constituted the line of least resistance within both communities. Primarily, for the Cyprus Government, this dialogue had limited chances of success. Even if Turkey eventually agreed to *Enosis*, which was very unlikely at the time, significant territorial concessions would be needed in return. Makarios would never agree to such concessions in Cyprus, and the Greek Government was both unwilling and in any case too weak to 'sell' the acceptance of significant exchanges on its own national territory. The dialogue would have sooner or later collapsed, *Enosis* would have been unattainable and Makarios would have escaped internal criticism for the failure of achieving *Enosis*. Thus, by grudgingly consenting to this process, he would have continued pursuing his own vision for a unitary independent state without obstacles or the responsibility to negotiate and offer any concessions.

Determining the future of Cyprus through negotiations between Greece and Turkey was the most promising option for the Turkish-Cypriot leadership, ensuring what they wanted the most: security and effective guarantees for their position in any settlement. Indeed, the Turkish-Cypriots had long insisted that the Cyprus problem was an issue created by Greek territorial expansionism, and for that reason it had to be solved in the wider context of Greco-Turkish relations.[21]

Before final agreement on any new bilateral dialogue, Greece and Turkey at least shared one underlying motivation concerning Cyprus: a desire to push aside a problem that carried unwanted financial and political costs, and focus again on their own respective domestic challenges. Somehow, however, they needed to find a way to reconcile their deeply opposed perceptions on the issue, to allow a mutually desirable escape. Greece was only able to discuss *Enosis*, while this new procedure required the blessing of the UN.[22] For Turkey things were more complex. As a matter of principle the Turkish Government insisted on an assumed return to the 1960 Constitution, which meant that both *Enosis* and partition should be ruled out and a solution should be sought on the basis of federation. *Enosis* for Ankara would have meant disturbance of the territorial equilibrium in the area of the eastern Mediterranean, set in 1923 between the two countries by the Lausanne Treaty, and this marked their red line.[23] Meanwhile, an effective way out of the UN procedures had to be achieved; thus, Turkey had to convince Greece of the merits of holding discussions under NATO auspices.[24] It should also be borne in mind that the Turkish Government was in a difficult position domestically: The elections scheduled in October 1965 gave Ankara little room to manoeuvre in any prospective talks. The Turkish-Cypriot press and leadership as well as Turkish public opinion pushed for drastic actions in Cyprus, indicating that a solution on the basis of *Enosis* would not be tolerated.[25] However, Ankara had a good reason to urgently comply with the American and British suggestions for a quick initiation of bilateral talks. Both had warned the Turkish Government that if it continued publicly to insist that the mediator's task had come to a decisive end and no other procedure was agreed upon, then a Security Council debate on the situation would have been certain.[26] In such a debate, Turkey would have been isolated, the government would have been heavily criticized internally and Makarios would have achieved another diplomatic victory. Turkey, therefore, had to take into consideration all of the above in order to prevent any further setbacks over the Cyprus issue.[27]

After the shuttle diplomacy of Britain and the United States throughout April 1965, both Turkey and Greece agreed to discuss the problem without pre-conditions at the margins of the NATO ministerial conference in May 1965 and expressed their strong commitment to finding a functional settlement for Cyprus as soon as possible. Despite Turkey's attempt to actively implicate the NATO secretary-general in the bilateral talks,[28] this new initiative was carefully designed in order to be publicly translated as the realization of Plaza's suggestion for talks between not only the two communities but all of the parties concerned as well.[29]

Dynamics of the Greco-Turkish dialogue

On 12 May 1965 the Greek and Turkish foreign ministers met in London and initiated a new process, hoping to reach a mutually satisfactory settlement for Cyprus. Both ministers appeared cautiously optimistic about the continuation of this initiative and agreed to set up a suitable mechanism for the continuation of discussions between the two governments.[30] They also agreed that it was of utmost importance to maintain secrecy of the substance of the talks in order to avoid any complications issuing from the internal politics of each country. In spite of this secrecy, Athens had to be extremely careful not to appear that it was side-stepping the Cyprus Government, since that would have strengthened the anti-*Enosis* movement among Greek-Cypriots, a phenomenon that was beginning to present a real challenge to Athens.

The only element agreed on by both countries and the starting point of their talks was their willingness to settle the Cyprus problem as soon as possible. This was indeed a propitious omen. Another important factor was that both the United States and the United Kingdom, although privately admitting that any type of *Enosis*, with Turkey's agreement, would better suit their own and Western interests in general – since this would have established definitive harmony in the Southern flank of NATO – nonetheless stated that they would remain neutral towards the efforts of the parties to settle the Cyprus problem.[31] The British Foreign Office concluded that: 'we must keep on the right side of Turkey and avoid annoying Ankara, but otherwise we should equally avoid unnecessary disputes with Makarios'.[32] Above all, both America and Britain wanted a stable and permanent settlement which was acceptable to all contested parties. They were consequently bent on assisting the parties maintain the momentum created by the London meeting that in the long term could provide a settlement and in the short term deflect the possibility of another crisis on the island.[33] Contrary to what was usually reported in the Greek-Cypriot press, neither the British nor the Americans had any intention of imposing any particular solution on Cyprus.[34]

Although the Cyprus Government had accepted this bilateral and external process, the different perceptions of Nicosia and Athens over the specifics of this dialogue seemed unbridgeable from the very beginning. In order to fully apprehend this substantial gap and the limited chances of success of this process, we must take note of the background meeting of the Cyprus and Greek governments on the eve of the ministerial conference in London. George Papandreou, the Greek prime-minister, invited Makarios to Athens in order to exchange views.[35] The ultimate aim of the Greek Government was to commit Makarios to a common policy of achieving *Enosis*.[36] Although at the end of this meeting a joint communiqué was published announcing the common views of the two governments, there was no true convergence of their positions. Papandreou initially explained that the aim of his government was first to find out whether Ankara indeed sought to 'consolidate peace' on the island by accepting *Enosis* and what they might ask in exchange.[37] Then, he explained, if there was a preliminary agreement on such a solution, they intended to propose for a summit conference under the aegis of the UN to solidify the details. Makarios replied that he agreed primarily to the Greco-Turkish dialogue, as long as this was justified on the grounds of Plaza's report. He added that his government's chief aim in the long term was *Enosis* but without any *quid pro quo* for Turkey that affected the situation within Cyprus itself.[38] Cyprus had nothing to offer in exchange for *Enosis*. Makarios and his entourage were surprised when they were asked by Papandreou about the option of a Turkish base in Cyprus in the area of Cape Greco, and it came as a further shock when the Defence Minister, Petros Garoufalias, added that Grivas had already agreed to the suggestion.[39] Naturally, Makarios reacted negatively emphasizing once again that there would be no territorial concessions of any kind from the Cyprus Government. Although Grivas' exact views have not been fully clarified, it was true that he had accepted some territorial concessions in Cyprus albeit of 'minor importance', as he characterized them.[40] Besides, it was a widely known secret that if such an agreement was eventually reached with Turkey, the Greek Government would seriously consider of deploying the Greek army stationed in Cyprus, led by Grivas, to impose the solution on Makarios.[41]

According to Stavros Costopoulos, the Greek foreign minister, the nature and extent of concessions was the particular point of contention between the two governments and eventually a source of misinterpretation – perhaps deliberately – in the final outcome of the meeting in Athens.[42] Costopoulos stated that during their stormy discussions, his government told Makarios that *Enosis* was possible through either negotiations or war. The latter was not an option. However, if negotiations were held, inevitably that meant that compensations had to be given. When Makarios told them that he would not object if Greece wanted to make territorial compensations in its own territory, Papandreou responded that 'he had no mandate to surrender parts of Greek territory which had been Greek for decades, when Cyprus had not even reached the stage of being a Greek territory'.[43] After a long debate Costopoulos stated that Makarios had agreed that *Enosis* would require certain exchanges but without clarifying what he really meant. Although vague, his agreement on the principle of concessions to Turkey was perceived for the time being as quite sufficient for the Greek Government. Nonetheless, the latter was still afraid that this would not prevent Makarios from torpedoing the bilateral dialogue at any stage. In fact, what Makarios for his own part meant by concessions was probably a Charter of Minority Rights for Turkish-Cypriots, as Plaza recommended, and as he recurrently asserted publicly and privately after his return from Athens. This Charter, however, was 'off the table' for Turkey and thus not a useful negotiating card for the Greek diplomats. The gulf between the two governments was still wide open.

Despite their differences, on 9 May their joint communiqué confirmed their agreement to continue working in order to secure the right of self-determination in Cyprus in accordance with the UN Charter.[44] At a press conference when he returned to Cyprus, Makarios stated that he not only gave his consent for talks on *Enosis* between Greece and Turkey but also diverged from the sanguine statements of the Greek and Turkish foreign ministers in London. When asked whether he shared the general optimism embodied by Greece and Turkey after the London meeting, Makarios answered, 'It is a fact that I am optimistic but I think there are others who are more optimistic than me.'[45]

Indeed, the other parties, especially Greece, seemed to believe that with certain moderate concessions to Turkey, *Enosis* was within reach. In reality, in spite of the willingness of the two motherlands for a quick Cyprus settlement, this dialogue faced long odds from the start and these eventually proved insurmountable. In addition to the Athens–Nicosia rivalry and mistrust, the intensifying split within the Greek political arena and the constant change of weak governments during the period of 1965–1967 undermined the progress of negotiations, leaving little room to manoeuvre or to maintain leverage for Athens. Greece, therefore, was entering 'hamstrung' into this dialogue.

Ankara had privately agreed to consider *Enosis* with territorial concessions. Nevertheless, in order to appease Turkish public opinion and the Turkish-Cypriot fighters, the Turkish Government emphatically insisted, publicly, that discussions should be based on the existing 1960 Treaties.[46] Publicly committing itself to the latter meant that the Turkish Government would have required significant territorial gains in order to avoid domestic criticism for presenting a future solution based on *Enosis*. Finally, the key to any solution agreed between Athens and Ankara was Makarios' compliance, and he consistently attempted to sabotage the Greco-Turkish dialogue in order to ensure that he would not be confronted with an unacceptable Acheson-type solution. In September 1967, the meeting of the Greek and Turkish prime ministers, which became known as the 'Evros fiasco', effectively terminated this bilateral dialogue without even minimum agreement over the outline of a final solution to the Cyprus problem. It seemed that things were heading to the same dead end as in April 1965. Nonetheless, circumstances on the island had in the meantime undergone a considerable transformation, and it is to shifts at the internal level of Cypriot affairs – including the UN's efforts – that we must now turn.

Political realities in Cyprus at the outset of the Greco-Turkish negotiations

Following upon an intense and combustible atmosphere in March and April 1965, the initiation of the Greco-Turkish dialogue admittedly brought about a general relaxation of tension in Cyprus. This helped to freeze the *status quo* while the two communities adopted a policy of 'wait and see'. Makarios had agreed to the external dialogue for the future of Cyprus on the basis of *Enosis*, but his own agenda for the island was different. Internally he was planning to implement the 'positive elements' of Plaza's report, that is, consolidating the unitary character of the state and presenting a formula for guaranteeing minority rights while glossing over *Enosis*. Additionally, the 'salami-slice' strategy towards Turkish-Cypriots had to be maintained but this time combined with periodical relaxation of the embargoes. His public and private equivocation on the issue of local talks reflected his reluctance to accept them until the time was 'ripe'; until they were likely to bring to fruition his own long-term aims, murky though they might appear to others.

Conversely, Kuchuk had welcomed the external dialogue since internally he had limited room for manoeuvre. His role as a community leader was itself constrained by subordination to the rest of the Turkish-Cypriot leadership, military officers from Turkey and Ankara's policies. Although in principle the Turkish-Cypriot leaders disagreed with the inter-communal talks unless these were under the strict basis of the 1960 Constitution, several moderate leaders privately expressed their openness to have direct talks that would deal with daily problems and normalization measures. Nonetheless, even then certain pre-conditions were set. Kuchuk had also to tackle the ever-deepening split within his community and persistent criticism from both the moderate camp, which requested a return to normality, and the extreme factions, mainly motivated by their political antagonism.

This section further explores these political realities at the outset of the externally driven negotiating attempt, giving particular emphasis to the future of *Enosis* in Greek-Cypriot minds. The aftermath of the first joint communiqué of the Greek and Cypriot governments in May 1965 will be our starting point.

After several tense meetings in Athens during Makarios' visit in May, except from the bilateral dialogue between Greece and Turkey, the two governments came to agreement on four priorities: (1) to ensure that the Cyprus issue would remain under the UN aegis, (2) to use all the 'positive' elements of Plaza's report and request the mediator's return to lead the way for inter-communal talks, (3) to relax the restriction measures against the Turkish-Cypriots and (4) to avoid sources of friction on the island.[47] Despite this ostensible agreement, Makarios knew that the Greek Government would still enter negotiations by offering unacceptable compromises to Turkey in exchange for *Enosis*. The British high commissioner reported that after that meeting 'Makarios was much shaken by this threat to remove by bribery his Turkish safeguard [he had previously characterized the Turkish-Cypriots as his safeguard against *Enosis*]. I was very struck to see him so depressed and somber when he came back from Athens.'[48]

In order to avoid being confronted with *a fait accompli* and unacceptable territorial concessions from Cyprus' territory, Makarios' first goal was to strengthen his government's position. He aimed to improve Cyprus' Republic leverage, both diplomatically and economically, to gain influence in the international arena. Moreover, he attempted to send several messages, internally and abroad, about his own stance on the internal problem and the unacceptability of any imposed solutions. Additionally, Makarios had to ensure that the UN remained the only forum responsible for the Cyprus issue. Simultaneously, he needed to prepare his people for the possibility that even if *Enosis* was agreed upon in the Athens–Ankara talks, this would probably be at the expense of Greek-Cypriot interests. Thus, the main themes of Makarios' and his ministers' speeches during this period were about 'unadulterated *Enosis*' and a condemnation of foreign involvement that sought to impose solutions against the will of Greek-Cypriots.

Given the deterioration of relations between Nicosia and Athens, mainly due to the issue of the Cyprus army's control, there was also intense suspicion in the press about the ulterior motives of the Greek Government for entering into a dialogue with Turkey. Criticism of the Greco-Turkish talks and the possibility of NATO involvement were constant during the period. Furthermore, only a few days after the Nicosia–Athens communiqué, it was allegedly leaked through official channels to the Greek-Cypriot press that the government had discussed the possibility of holding a referendum if forced to agree on a solution for *Enosis* with unacceptable concessions. The government was planning to put to a public vote the alternatives of '*Enosis* plus NATO and Turkish sovereign bases on the island' or 'Full Independence'. The newspaper *Alitheia* observed that in such a case it was almost certain that independence would have been supported firmly by 90 per cent of the Greek-Cypriots.[49] The Minister of the Interior, Polykarpos Yorkadjis, confirmed to some British officials the validity of this article by remarking that although Grivas wanted union with Greece, he and President Makarios preferred complete independence.[50] By the end of June 1965, Makarios managed again to rally a large percentage of the Greek-Cypriot population in major demonstrations that were organized in many towns of the island. The Greek-Cypriot crowd had protested against the threat of imposed solutions and strongly supported their government's policies on their national question. The slogan of these demonstrations was 'Independence, Self-Determination, *Enosis* without any territorial exchanges'.[51]

The dominance of Makarios in Greek-Cypriot politics was indeed remarkable. This, however, led to the creation of a minority, at that point quite small, of fanatic enemies who accused him not only of abandoning *Enosis* but of continuously frustrating the efforts of Mother Greece for unification. This minority and the threat of a coup now began to hang over the 'undisputed' authority of Makarios like a Sword of Damocles. Until this stage, however, strong criticism of Makarios and his government was still confined to the extreme right-wing Cypriot and Greek press, as well as certain sectors of the Cyprus Army under Grivas' guidance and with the support of the some circles in Athens.

In July 1965, Sir David Hunt, three months after his appointment as Britain's high commissioner in Cyprus, provided his superiors in London with an acute analysis of the Greek-Cypriot and Turkish-Cypriot politics, including Makarios' moves after the Athens meeting and the prospect of *Enosis*. Like most who personally knew Makarios, Hunt was greatly impressed by his personality, his shrewdness and what he called his surprising frankness.[52] He also admitted,

> The strongest impression left on me by the three months I have been here is indeed the dominance of Makarios [...] There is no rival anywhere near the throne. As a result he is in the happy position of having almost complete freedom of movement in the certainty of faithful and enthusiastic obedience from his people. Only one condition is imposed: he [Makarios] must from time to time pay the appropriate lip-service to *Enosis*.[53]

Hunt also came to the conclusion that Makarios was indeed opposed to *Enosis,* at least at that stage, and that although he reluctantly agreed to the

Greco-Turkish dialogue with the ostensible goal of *Enosis*, 'he made his own hopes obvious by repeatedly proclaiming that it was bound to fail'. Through his dominance among Greek-Cypriots and the control he exerted on most Greek-Cypriot newspapers, Hunt believed that 'he inspired in the press a tearing campaign against the Greek Government'. Additionally, he explained that Makarios' timing – June 1965 – in appointing to the directorate of the Press and Information Office and the Cyprus News Agency individuals well-disposed to the Communist Party was not irrelevant to present developments on the island. In the meantime, Cyprus' foreign policy further emphasized on enhancing its bilateral relations with countries that were principally opposed to *Enosis*, such as the Non-Aligned states. Lastly and most importantly, Hunt had gone to some lengths to explain whether or not the Greek-Cypriots were still in favour of *Enosis*. The following abstract is indeed insightful:

> I think this question may not be entirely relevant to the current situation because part of Makarios' tactics is to reduce them to a thoroughly confused state. He probably hopes that he has by now convinced them that *Enosis* cannot come by way of the Athens-Ankara dialogue so that even if in fact agreement was reached in the course of the dialogue he could dupe public opinion into believing that *Enosis* was not really *Enosis*. It is not easy therefore to form an objective judgment but I will risk the view that if they are not too confused and misled, the vast majority of the Cyprus population still desires *Enosis*. I am not overlooking either the selfish interests of the politicians or the serious economic suffering which would result from union with Greece with the loss of the advantages of Commonwealth membership. But I hold that Greeks are not essentially, as so many people think, a money-loving nation of shop-keepers but enthusiasts who will always let their heart rule their head [...] It is, after all, noteworthy that A.K.E.L, whose leaders are even more opposed to *Enosis* than Makarios, and with good reason, are obliged to pay lip-service to it.[54]

The situation within the Turkish-Cypriot sector was different. They were entirely dependent on Ankara, and, according to Hunt's assessment, Turkey was prepared to accept *Enosis* and 'sell them down the river' at a certain price.[55] The official position of the Turkish-Cypriot leadership was that no other substantial initiative should take place on the island at the moment apart from the motherlands' dialogue. Additionally, Hunt commented that, unfortunately for Turkish-Cypriots, their leaders – especially Kuchuk – were totally ineffective, while Osman Orek, the minister of defence, who was the most effective, was also one of the most extreme and thus an obstacle to an inter-communal compromise.[56] Generally, the Turkish-Cypriot leaders were characterized as inept, petty minded and inflexible.[57] At that point, however, Kuchuk was for Ankara the best available option for the leadership of the Turkish-Cypriot community since 'he is an elected Vice-President and it is important for the Turkish formal position that his status should not be challenged until his term comes to an end and a new election according to the Constitution can be held'.[58] Nevertheless, Hunt reported that there were moderate and well-respected voices among the Turkish-Cypriot community, such as the President of the Supreme Court, Judge Zekia; the businessman and Chairman of the Turkish Chamber of Commerce, Kemal Rustem; Vasif Ali, and the chairman of the IS Bank; or Fuad Bey, a prominent lawyer. However, these voices were neither politically powerful nor consolidated into an effective organization.[59] By the summer of 1965, however, the disappointment triggered by the rejection of Plaza's report and the lack of any substantial efforts towards a solution led certain moderates to make their first tentative steps towards the creation of two political organizations: the Turkish-Cypriot Union formed in London and the Organization of the Turkish Patriots in Nicosia.[60] These were perceived to have Communist affiliations and to favour peaceful co-existence between Greek-Cypriots and Turkish-Cypriots. The Turkish-Cypriot leadership, however, was not for the moment greatly alarmed by bodies they saw as poorly supported and unlikely to survive. 'It is a silly season for the formation of Patriotic Fronts', Kuchuk declared, but the truth was that the opposition movements, and especially student opposition movements, would gain ground during the following decade, becoming a major nuisance for both the Turkish-Cypriot leadership and Ankara.[61]

Hunt's assessment represents one of the few documents of that period analysing the politics of each community. It accurately reflected the dominance of Makarios in Greek-Cypriot politics and his ability to influence the overwhelming majority of his community towards the solution he preferred, in contrast to the situation within the Turkish-Cypriot political arena. This meant that the dynamics of any prospective inter-communal negotiations were bound to favour the Greek-Cypriots. The Turkish and Turkish-Cypriot sides were well aware of this and instinctively fell back on the threat of a Turkish invasion. Nevertheless, especially after October 1965, the new government of Suleiman Demirel in Ankara wanted to avoid such drastic action.[62]

Equally, therefore, Makarios and the Turkish-Cypriot leaders did not seek a substantial inter-communal dialogue at that stage, leaving to the motherlands the primary responsibility of finding a settlement for the Cyprus problem. However, behind the scenes there had been an intense diplomatic activity, led mainly by the Cyprus Government and the UN, which considered various alternatives and scenarios. Whether expressed for tactical or for other reasons, all of these were eventually shelved and to these our analysis will now turn.

Reluctance to upset the status quo

1965: Diplomatic manoeuvres for gaining time and securing tactical advantage

It was unanimously believed abroad that in order for the bilateral Greco-Turkish dialogue to have any viable outcome, a period of calm had to ensue and most importantly to last. Thus, the UN, along with the British and Americans, believed that the only way forward was to find ways to convince the two communities of the necessity of direct contacts at any level possible.

The Cyprus Government publicly appeared willing to accept inter-communal talks, but Makarios reiterated that such talks should only be conducted on the basis of the mediator's report.[63] As soon as Makarios came back from Athens, therefore, he requested Plaza's return in order to prepare the two communities for talks about guarantees for the Turkish-Cypriot minority rights.[64] Makarios was well aware, however, that it was impossible for the UN secretary-general to initiate such a process when one of the contesting parties vehemently opposed it. Therefore, by insisting on a dialogue on these terms, Makarios skilfully insulated himself from the blame for the internal stalemate.

In spite of this, Makarios recognized that it was time to offer an olive branch to Turkish-Cypriots, a move that would have further enhanced his government's position diplomatically. The first signs of this approach surfaced quickly, on 31 March, with a speech by the President of the House of Representatives, Glafkos Clerides. As already commented in Chapter 1, the latter first admitted that '*Enosis* is not round the corner' and second he underscored the good intentions and determination of his government to guarantee Turkish-Cypriot rights through a Charter of minority rights in religious, language and cultural affairs.[65] Although all these measures were unacceptable to Turkish-Cypriots, it was perceived that Makarios himself wished to encourage Clerides as the Greek-Cypriot politician capable of negotiating directly with the Turkish-Cypriots, when the moment came, with some chance of success.[66] It should be noted that throughout the decade 1964–1974 the British had observed that Clerides was usually assigned to express any moderate views by the Cyprus Government, views that neither Makarios nor his ministers could afford to express.[67] Clerides had been accused of being pro-Western precisely because of such moderate observations. In retrospect, we can discern that he was one of the few, perhaps the only, leading contemporary politicians with a practical grasp on how to find a path towards a viable settlement, especially in the period before the 1974 invasion. This was something that the bulk of opinion could not readily grasp, and such views expressed by any politician without the prestige of Clerides' family name could easily mean political suicide. Throughout his political career Clerides was characterized by many Greek-Cypriots as a 'dove' who made unacceptable concessions, as was to be keenly illustrated in the view of many at a much later point, when he came to support the UN Annan Plan in 2004. Nevertheless, he was undoubtedly a pragmatic politician in his understanding of the costs of any agreement and the fact that international considerations and regional balances of power could not be excluded. In Greek-Cypriot political culture in the immediate wake of independence, such predilections did not come easily to the great majority.

As a second, more substantial good-will gesture, on 21 April 1965 Makarios announced that all roadblocks and fortifications were to be removed from all main towns, except Nicosia and the well-fortified and armed Kokkina enclave.[68] Moreover, he complied with the Turkish request for the extension of the list of supplies imported through the Turkish Red Crescent to Cyprus without paying extra duty.[69] In the prevailing logic, these measures were not well received by the Turkish-Cypriot leadership, which perceived them as mere propaganda since they provided no real relief. Instead, they claimed that the previous fixed check points were now replaced with mobile and erratic patrols further eroding their freedom and security of movement.[70]

It is interesting in this context to note *The Observer* correspondent's assessment of Makarios' 'peace offensive'. He stressed that Makarios was now adopting techniques similar to those used by Field Marshal Harding against National Organization of Cypriot Fighters (EOKA) in the mid-1950s.[71] Specifically, Makarios was switching between an attrition policy and a more moderate approach towards the Turkish-Cypriot community and then back again. The correspondent commented that those measures aimed at breaking the Turkish-Cypriot front, but to no avail. Although this proved accurate enough, at least it did help in practice to alleviate some tensions, a very important prerequisite for the initiation of the Athens–Ankara dialogue a few weeks later.

Although the Turkish-Cypriots in general rejected Plaza's recommendation for inter-communal talks, only a few days after the submission of the report moderate Turkish-Cypriot leaders showed genuine interest in the initiation of joint meetings with moderate Greek-Cypriot leaders under the supervision of UNFICYP during the Political Liaison Committee's meetings.[72] The Committee had been established on the island in the aftermath of the December 1963 crisis and it was the only forum then available in which officials from both communities could jointly discuss – in 1963 under the chairmanship of a British official – daily problems arising from the *de facto* separation.[73] Because of the ineffectiveness of the Committee, however, when UNFICYP arrived in Cyprus it decided to meet separately with the liaison officers of each community.[74] Nonetheless, by 1965 it was evident that this procedure was equally ineffective and time consuming. Since certain moderate voices within the Turkish-Cypriot leadership floated the option of the resumption of joint meetings, and since any type of high-level direct contacts between the communities was not forthcoming, both the UN and the Anglo-Americans believed that the former should be further pursued. Any approach to normalization, however, would certainly have stabilized conditions for the Turkish-Cypriot community and reduced the pressure on the Turkish-Cypriot leadership. Needless to say, it would also have enhanced Kuchuk's waning political standing within his community.[75]

Although in theory not opposed to the joint meetings of the Liaison Committee, the Cyprus Government was unenthusiastic at best.[76] The government was privately dissatisfied by the Committee's work because it was constantly reacting to Turkish-Cypriot requests.[77] The Committee's primary aim, after all, was to promote normalization which *ipso facto* benefitted the Turkish-Cypriots in the enclaves, and this undermined the government's aim to force the Turkish-Cypriots to capitulate. Against any radical relaxation of the pressure on the Turkish-Cypriots, the Cyprus president gave strict orders that his representatives should not attend any meeting of the Liaison Committee at which a Turkish-Cypriot representative was present.[78] Carlos Bernardes, the political advisor of UNFICYP who unofficially undertook to fill the vacuum after Plaza's withdrawal in April 1965, tried to convince both communities to have direct contacts through this Committee without any pre-conditions; that was inevitably an uphill task.

While on the local front Bernardes tried continuously to bring the two communities together, from May until December 1965 the Cyprus Government's attention to the national question was directed elsewhere. First of all, as soon as the Athens–Ankara dialogue had been initiated, Cyprus Government was at pains to stress that only Nicosia was the centre for determining the right course to the Cyprus problem and that no final solutions would be implemented over its head. Nonetheless, the government's policies and actions at times contradicted its own principles and were perceived as acutely in variance with the Greco-Turkish discussions. Second, a UN General Assembly meeting on Cyprus was in the offing, with the mediator's report on the agenda, and thus further lobbying missions had to be initiated.

One of the first diplomatic moves of the Cypriot Ministry of Foreign Affairs was to approach both Britain and the United States, to try to convince them of the futility of the Greco-Turkish dialogue and to induce them towards active involvement in finding a settlement along the lines favoured by the Cyprus Government. In London, Greek-Cypriot officials requested Britain's help to convince Turkey to accept the negotiations on the basis of minority rights.[79] At the same time, Cyprus' diplomats in Washington tried to test the waters for different approaches. Initially, Kyprianou suggested to the American Secretary of State, Dean Rusk, that since the current negotiations on *Enosis* had little chance of success, an informal US–Cyprus dialogue for *Enosis* held possibilities.[80] Believing, however, in the importance of the Greco-Turkish contacts, Rusk avoided encouraging Kyprianou's ideas. It should be noted that the latter was one of the closest advisors of Makarios and one of the hawks of his Cabinet. In contrast to the moderate influence that Clerides tried to exert on the Cypriot President, Kyprianou, according to Hunt, was convinced that *Enosis* was inevitable and for that reason he sought to achieve '*Enosis* at the earliest moment possible', based on the principles laid down by Makarios.[81] Through this policy, however, Hunt believed that Kyprianou pursued his own political ambition, which was to carve out a role for himself in Greek-Cypriot politics.

Meanwhile, other Greek-Cypriot diplomats were sending mixed messages concerning the next moves and perceptions of their own government. Despite previous disagreement over having any direct contacts with the Turkish Government, it was reported that certain Greek-Cypriot diplomats were putting out feelers, especially towards the United States, for the possibility of direct talks between Nicosia and Ankara probably on the basis of independence.[82] Nonetheless, this was perceived as another tactical move by the Cyprus Government for disrupting chances for any substantial progress through the Athens–Ankara talks.[83] However, rumours of a Nicosia–Ankara dialogue intensified after the collapse of the bilateral dialogue in July 1965 and the appointment of Ozdemir Benler, the new moderate *Chargé d'Affaires* in the Turkish Embassy in Nicosia in September 1965. Unlike his predecessor, Benler was willing to have contacts with moderate Greek-Cypriot leaders.[84]

According to several reports coming from the Foreign Office and the British ambassadors in Ankara and Athens, the option of a Nicosia–Ankara dialogue might not be totally opposed by the Turkish Government, as it had been previously reported. Nonetheless, this process might be further explored only if Makarios were to initially make a gesture towards acknowledging the validity of the 1960 Constitution, such as recognizing

Kuhcuk as the vice-president of the Republic, and provided that these talks would discuss some form of federation.[85] That option still faced one great challenge. Turan Tuluy, the Turkish ambassador in Athens, was convinced that the key barrier to such a procedure was the Greeks who 'were much more heavily pledged to *Enosis* than the Cypriots'.[86] Thus, a solution on independence would probably not be a lasting one, unless Greece agreed in advance. From another perspective, the Canadian high commissioner in Cyprus assessed that a Makarios–Ankara dialogue, perhaps without pre-conditions, would have been much more effective than any other alternative, especially that of talks between the two communities.[87] He explained first, that although Ankara did not recognize the Cyprus Government, it accepted that Makarios had *de facto* authority on the island. Second, contrary to the imbalance between Greek-Cypriots and Turkish-Cypriots, the two governments were evenly matched due to the fact that first they both had a fearsome instrument of war – the air superiority of Turkey and ground superiority of Greek-Cypriots – that could be used anytime they decided and, second, they both possessed the political power to implement their decisions on their people.[88]

All these, however, proved to be mere diplomatic brainstorming, first for undermining the Athens–Ankara negotiations and second for gaining time until the next UN General Assembly debate. After September 1965 the Cyprus Government sought to secure a diplomatic victory in the forthcoming UN debate. The timing was indeed propitious. As already discussed, by August 1965, the Cyprus Government had secured an anodyne Security Council Resolution concerning its new electoral law that had previously brought significant political tension. Meanwhile, the Greco-Turkish dialogue had been interrupted after the fall of Papandreou's Government in July, and there were not at the moment any realistic prospects for its quick resumption. By the beginning of September there was still no stable government in Greece while Turkey was concentrating on its general elections in October. With no other process ongoing, Nicosia calculated that it would be easier for Turkish-Cypriots to accept the dialogue that Makarios was offering without setting any pre-conditions. Still, the best time to initiate such a dialogue would certainly have been after a favourable outcome for the Greek-Cypriot position in the General Assembly, thus further enhancing the government's position vis-à-vis the Turkish-Cypriots. It is noteworthy that moderate voices within the Turkish-Cypriot leadership also opined that the period after the UN debate would likely be propitious for preliminary discussions with the Cyprus Government for a genuine relaxation of tension on the island, provided the General Assembly resolution was not an outright victory of the Greek-Cypriot position.[89]

In order to achieve this victory, therefore, Nicosia needed once again to appear more flexible towards the Turkish-Cypriots. The first move of the Cyprus Government was to present a 'Declaration of Intention and a Memorandum' with measures for the safeguarding of minority rights, and second to establish a Committee responsible for the rehabilitation of the displaced Turkish-Cypriots.[90] According to Makarios,

> the Government, following the recommendations of the Mediator of the UN, is prepared to accept the presence in Cyprus of a UN Commissioner with an adequate staff of observers and advisers who will observe on such terms as Your Excellency may direct, the adherence to all rights referred to in the Declaration and Memorandum.[91]

Trying, however, to prevent the ghosts of the past, such as his 'Thirteen Points' proposal and all the constitutional amendments since 1964, from haunting his new initiative, Makarios presented this memorandum not as a *fait accompli* but in the form of a declaration of intention to be discussed with the Turkish-Cypriots.[92] Meanwhile, the wording had to reflect the benevolent intentions of the government: because not only was this to be its main lobbying 'tool' before the General Assembly debate, but it was also to be officially presented during the proceedings of the debate.[93]

Naturally, both the Memorandum and the proposal for the Committee for the Displaced Rehabilitation were rejected by the Turkish-Cypriot leadership as nothing but more Greek-Cypriot propaganda. With regard to the formalities of the Memorandum itself, Kuchuk repeated their long-standing argument; the Zurich–London Agreements recognized that their community did not consist of a mere minority and that the Greek-Cypriots were trying to deprive them of their legal and political rights as granted by the 1960 Constitution.[94] Since there was no Cypriot nation, Kuchuk continued, the two communities were equal.[95] His counter-proposal was based on the long-standing Turkish-Cypriot argument that the two communities cannot live peacefully together and a voluntary population exchange must thus transpire under the supervision of UN.[96] Privately, however, several Turkish-Cypriot leaders appeared more conciliatory. They explained that it would not have been so difficult to accept Makarios' proposals if only they could be assured that the Greek-Cypriots could keep their word. For the Turkish-Cypriot MP Umit Suleiman, it was a question of confidence and the Turkish-Cypriots did not trust Makarios whatsoever.[97] Having in mind that Makarios' proposal came in the aftermath of the electoral law saga exacerbated their mistrust. Therefore, the fundamental reason for rejecting this proposal was that neither the judicial proceedings proposed in the Memorandum nor the system of the UN observer were adequate guarantees for their personal security in case of any attack on their position.[98]

Nonetheless, the preparations for the General Assembly debate brought a short period of calmness in Cyprus. Indicative of this was the fact that for the first time since 1963, on 29 October 1965, three Greek-Cypriot ministers met with Kuchuk and other Turkish-Cypriot leaders during a reception organized by the Turkish Embassy inside the Nicosia enclave for the celebrations of Turkish National Day.[99] This invitation was also one of the first promising moves of the Turkish Government of Suleiman Demirel. Nonetheless, this peaceful atmosphere proved to be the calm before the storm that followed – because of the Famagusta crisis of November and the General Assembly resolution of December. On 2 November heavy firing broke out between the National Guard and the Turkish-Cypriot fighters in Famagusta due to the former's decision to extend coastal fortifications, contrary to the previous recommendations of the UNFICYP to avoid such actions. The UN force managed to bring about an agreement a month later.[100] The Turkish and Turkish-Cypriot sides were greatly frustrated by this recent crisis; thus, when the General Assembly resolution of 18 December 1965 was adopted, they were further embittered. This resolution not only made reference to Plaza's report, which the Turkish delegation to the UN tried to prevent, but also made reference to Makarios' 'Declaration of Intention' and lastly to the declaration of the Non-Aligned Conference of October 1964, which reaffirmed the Cyprus right to unfettered independence.[101] Before the UN debate, Turkey emphatically urged the Americans, British and all other member-states to vote for a non-substantial, procedural resolution without any reference to the mediator's report.[102] This resolution was perceived as a major diplomatic defeat for Demirel and his Foreign Minister, Ihsan Sabri Caglayangil, who had once again to appease Turkish opinion, the press and their opposition. Hence, their next steps and decisions on the Cyprus problem had to be very thoroughly considered.[103] By the end of 1965 it was evident that there would be no radical development on the ground; the resumption of the Greco-Turkish dialogue was still ambivalent while agreement to any type of direct contacts on the island was distinctly unlikely.

1966: Consolidation of the stalemate

The aftermath of the General Assembly resolution provided an additional bargaining chip to the Cyprus Government which continued to insist on inter-communal talks for minority rights. As was the case with the Security Council Resolution of August 1965, publicly this resolution was presented as another great diplomatic success, especially for the Cypriot foreign minister.[104] On 30 December, Makarios again called the Turkish-Cypriot leaders to negotiate on the basis of the recently adopted UN resolution, while this time added that consultations of the Turkish-Cypriot leaders with the Turkish Government were also welcome.[105] Kuchuk rejected this proposal, reiterating that the 1960 Treaties were still valid and called for five-party discussions.[106] Turkey had one more reason to reject Makarios' offer as well as simultaneous offers of the Greek Government to resume their previous dialogue.[107] On 2 February 1966, a new Athens–Nicosia *communiqué* reaffirmed that any solution which excluded *Enosis* was unacceptable.[108] Although this communiqué was produced for internal consumption, since the relations of the Cyprus and Greek governments were on a tightrope, it triggered a strong reply by Turkey, bellicose statements against Greece, the recalling of the Turkish ambassador from Athens and a brusque communication with the UN secretary-general.[109] Inevitably these developments had also reduced the prospects for a quick resumption of the previous bilateral dialogue with the Greek Government. At the beginning of 1966, therefore, there was a complete impasse over the Cyprus problem, both inside and outside of the island.

The main problem for the UN secretary-general surfaced when Galo Plaza officially submitted his resignation on 22 December 1965. The *status quo* had to unfreeze and thus some new initiatives needed to be undertaken. U Thant decided in February 1966 to appoint his Under-Secretary for Special Political Affairs, Jose Rölz-Bennett, to a fact-finding mission to all concerned parties inside and outside of Cyprus along with visits to countries contributing to UNFICYP. Rölz-Bennett explained that his aim was to listen to the views of the parties, especially regarding the future of the mediation, in order to advise the UN secretary-general on his next moves after Plaza's resignation.[110] Meanwhile, he was about to examine the role of the UNFICYP for finding ways to remedy its substantial financial problems.

Rölz-Bennett's mission proved abortive. There was no way to bridge the gap between the divergent positions over the prospect of mediation. U Thant in his subsequent report summarized that:

> it needs to be said of Cyprus, in full frankness, I believe, that it remains still to be demonstrated that there is a genuine will to peace among the leaders of the two communities of sufficient earnestness and intensity to lead them towards those mutual accommodations in viewpoint and position which are essential to a pacific settlement [...] The key to a settlement, however, lies in the last analysis with the parties. Unless they are prepared to move towards resolving their basic differences, the prospects of an early solution are dim indeed.[111]

The only option left to the UN secretary-general was to expand Bernardes' mandate. In order to explore whether direct discussions under the Political Liaison Committee or even any indirect exchanges between the two communities were possible, U Thant in March 1966 instructed Bernardes to use his good offices to achieve 'in the first instance discussions at any level of problems and issues of either a purely local or a broader nature'.[112] This was another attempt that soon reached a dead end. Nevertheless, it may be interesting to investigate the parties' perceptions at that point.

Justified by its recent diplomatic victory, the Cyprus Government's position was now presented in a stricter tone. In particular, it appeared ready to contemplate direct talks but not under the Political Liaison Committee and only if there were indications that at least some common ground existed for those talks. For the Cyprus president the latter element was a *sine qua non;* otherwise, 'they would have no value and might even be harmful if they served only to emphasize differences and no common ground could be found'.[113] Since Makarios believed that time was on his side and no form of mediation was possible, 'the common ground' was not going to be achieved through bilateral discussions or concessions but only through total agreement of the Turkish-Cypriots to his own terms. Makarios, furthermore, clarified that neither the 1960 Constitution nor his previous 'Thirteen Points' were acceptable as a basis for discussions.[114] He explained,

> I proposed those Thirteen Points for the amendment of the constitution as a first step and not as a final solution of the problem. Their rejection by the Turkish community and the rebellion which followed have created a situation which goes beyond the Thirteen points and calls for a radical and final solution of the problem.[115]

On the other hand, Kuchuk reiterated that his community was ready for joint meetings to discuss daily affairs through the Political Liaison Committee and any other broader contacts to be held under the basis of the 1960 Constitution.[116] Nevertheless, a necessary pre-condition was to see several goodwill and effective unilateral gestures from the Greek-Cypriots.[117] It should be emphasized, however, that by the spring of 1966 Ankara had extended its financial assistance towards the Turkish-Cypriot enclaves, further reducing the Turkish-Cypriot sense of urgency to have any inter-communal talks.[118]

With very slim chances for any substantial progress, a few months later Bernardes returned to his original tasks, focusing on the technical issues of the daily affairs of the two communities. It was evident that the UN special representative was at his wit's end. As a last resort he turned to the UK and offered his services to Britain in case the latter wanted to offer any substantial approach or suggestion towards the Cyprus problem.[119] It seemed as if the UN were trying desperately to find an alternative route for achieving some progress, and Britain seemed to be the only way out. In light of the complete deadlock, Britain by this point had decided to re-examine its non-active involvement policy in Cyprus. Nonetheless, London eventually concluded that it was wiser to retain its neutral posture.

Subsequently, the UN secretary-general decided that since efforts were being made for the resumption of the Greco-Turkish dialogue, it was best to avoid interfering with another active initiative on the island until new circumstances arose.[120] Still, however, UN officials were greatly concerned with the situation in Cyprus and continued to seek fresh ideas that they could have injected to the parties at a later point. Interestingly, Bernardes privately admitted that he believed that the practical solution for the Cyprus problem was *Enosis* with federation.[121] He explained that since the Turkish-Cypriots were ready to accept federation with Makarios, a federated solution with the Greek Government was probably much better for them. Agreeing to a federal union of Cyprus with Greece, local autonomy for the Turkish-Cypriots and perhaps a port on the island under their control, for Bernardes, seemed an adequate guarantee for their safety.[122] Both the United States and the UK found merits in this proposal adding that this solution could have been a non-federation/federation, that is, a solution designed in such a way in order to be presented as federation to the Turkish-Cypriots and as a local autonomy for Turkish-Cypriots to the Greeks.[123] At the same time, the UN secretary-general was considering proposing to the parties his new idea of an Independent Cyprus under joint guarantees by the four of the permanent members of the Security Council, that is, United States, Britain, France and the Soviet Union.[124] According to him, the major flaw of the Zurich–London Agreements was the right of unilateral intervention.[125] If this provision was replaced with a collective intervention of the four members of the Security Council, then it might be acceptable to all parties.[126] This option was discouraged by the United States and Britain, since it seemed bound to introduce officially a Soviet foothold on or stake in the island. This proposal was rejected by Greece and Turkey as well.[127] Since neither enosis nor independence was at that stage possible, Bernardes proposed to seek for a provisional settlement for three to five years on the existing situation with certain guarantees for all the parties involved.[128] In other words, 'kicking the can down the road'. This alternative was, however, rejected by Greece and Turkey, which preferred to focus on the prospect of their own dialogue, soon to be resumed.

By early summer 1966 there was still no breakthrough. The *status quo* had been further consolidated, tension on the island had been reduced and the living conditions of the Turkish-Cypriots had been modestly improved. The Cyprus Government had internally focused on the deterioration of its relations with Athens and on the issue of command over the National Guard. It was not until June, when the Greco-Turkish dialogue was revived, that there were again some diplomatic activity coming from the island.

With the initiation of these talks, Makarios tried once again to upset the applecart with a new tactical move. He revealed to several Western diplomats that he planned to promote another process when the Athens–Ankara negotiations collapsed. He estimated that quite soon, and not later than August, the current exchange would founder due to Ankara's rejection of unconditional *Enosis*.[129] In these circumstances, he suggested that the issue of *Enosis* should be set aside and a new basis of independence found as a workable, if interim, solution. For that purpose he proposed that local talks should begin and that sometime in autumn 1966 a conference should be held in New York with the Cyprus Government, Greece, Turkey and probably Britain, under the aegis of U Thant. From New York, the US Government could also provide assistance and influence for arriving at an agreement. At the initial stages of this conference Makarios stressed that the Turkish-Cypriots should not be present, although he did not reject their participation at a later stage. This proposal seems to have been put forward by the president without any consultation or agreement among his own ministers. It is noteworthy that only a few days before floating this proposal, Kyprianou showed no awareness of it when indicating that the Cyprus Government has no intention to initiate any dialogue for the time being.[130] This represented an example of Makarios' usual tactic of taking important decisions without consulting or even informing his closest associates. It is clear, however, from the British archives that this idea did not gain any traction in other quarters, and in British and Canadian official circles it was perceived as yet another means of fostering a general pessimism about the Athens–Ankara process. From London it was stated,

> He [Makarios] is doubtless feeling some sense of isolation and perhaps wishes to recapture the initiative. If the dialogue ends in deadlock, he might be expected to gain some kudos by adopting the 'statesman-like' pose of calling for a conference which he knew would either be rejected by the Turks or, if held, would be open to Afro-Asian influence at New York.[131]

Contrary to Makarios' estimations, not only had the Greco-Turkish talks not collapsed by autumn 1966 but rumours about *Enosis* in exchange for either a Turkish or a NATO base had intensified. In light of these rumours, before the most crucial meeting of the Greek and Turkish foreign ministers in December 1966 in Paris, the Cyprus Government and this time the Turkish-Cypriot military leadership as well tried to ensure that the two motherlands would not neglect their own security and political concerns.[132]

On the one hand, within the enclaves there was a strained situation between the political and military leadership. Kuchuk and his entourage were under criticism from the extremists and the fighters for getting 'soft' towards the Greek-Cypriots. Meanwhile, the Turkish-Cypriot fighters bypassed their official leadership and informed Ankara that they deeply opposed any solution that did not guarantee their safety through physical separation of the two communities.[133] However, the British high commissioner asserted that although some tension existed among the fighters and the politicians within the enclaves, this was not as serious as the Greek-Cypriots believed or wished it was.[134] Nonetheless, the Greek-Cypriot press initiated an active propaganda campaign overstating all the convulsions within the Turkish-Cypriot leadership and highlighting all the cases of defection from the enclaves, in order to prove that the attrition policy of the government was gradually bearing fruit.

On the other hand, Denktash from Ankara declared that neither a form of *Enosis* with a Turkish base on Cyprus nor an independent demilitarized Cyprus with administrative autonomy and proportional representation of the Turkish-Cypriots would guarantee his community's safety.[135] He also added that the Greco-Turkish process was 'quite unnecessary' since Greece has no authority to determine the future of Cyprus. Instead, he claimed that this must be accomplished through the Greek-Cypriots' and Turkish-Cypriots' exercise of their right for self-determination.[136] Clearly, this also entailed the physical separation of the two communities. Nevertheless, the irony in this element was that both Makarios and Denktash agreed on the futility of the dialogue between Greece and Turkey and the importance of letting the people in Cyprus decide about their own future. This reflects the old truth that however deep their differences may run, Cypriots of whatever kind do not like having decisions taken for them.

Meanwhile, Makarios constantly emphasized that he would never agree to a Turkish base on the island. However, by late November he appeared amenable towards two particular proposals as a basis for discussions. The first was the idea of a NATO base on the island and Turkish participation in it under certain conditions.[137] The second was the idea of a federation between Greece and Cyprus.[138] Nonetheless, the possibility of a NATO base was unacceptable to Turkey and certainly not satisfactory to the Non-Aligned bloc. The latter argument was emphasized by Turkish diplomats during their efforts to approach the Non-Aligned countries in 1967.[139] In spite of the initial Turkish reactions, for the Greek Government these two new developments boded well for the eventual success of the bilateral dialogue. Indeed, by December, there apparently had been a mini-breakthrough in Paris between the Turkish and Greek foreign ministers. Nonetheless, this was very quickly offset by two other new developments on the ground: the fall of the Stephanopoulos Government in Greece, which again interrupted the negotiations, and the crisis sparked by the importation of Czechoslovakian arms in Cyprus. In addition, Carlos Bernardes resigned a few days later for personal reasons, thus creating another headache for the UN secretary-general.

1967: Ripe time for local talks?

The suspension of the Athens–Ankara dialogue at the beginning of 1967 and the political uncertainty in Greece had probably produced the new circumstances that U Thant anticipated for promoting a new UN active initiative. Indeed, the temporary successor of Carlos Bernardes, Signor Pier Spinelli, after a round of contacts on the island in January 1967, commented that he had found both Makarios and Kuchuk more responsive to the issue of direct local talks.[140] Makarios had also privately admitted to several foreign officials that he was ready to negotiate with Kuchuk if there was concurrence from Greece and Turkey.[141] This was his way to seize initiative of the Cyprus problem outside the framework of the Athens–Ankara process. However, unless definitive agreement on this procedure could be obtained in advance, Makarios could not afford to be seen as taking the initiative in approaching Kuchuk.[142] Likewise, Kuchuk was under a great internal pressure from the extremists of his own community; yet, he was not adamantly opposed to direct talks.[143] But to proceed in this way he had to gain something in advance, such as recognition that they were talking on equal terms. From January 1967 until the crisis of that November, the possibility of inter-communal negotiations was constantly discussed in diplomatic circles as the most appropriate remaining option, but the leaders of the two communities were still very reluctant to pursue this further. It should be borne in mind that, due to the *coup d'etat* and the imposition of an ultranationalist military regime in Greece in April 1967, the worsening of Nicosia–Athens relations, the constant rumours of a coup to overthrow Makarios and the internal strains among the Turkish-Cypriot leadership, neither community's leaders were in a position to appear conciliatory towards the other. Perhaps what was needed to encourage the parties to talk to each other was the 'green light' from Greece and Turkey.

However, Athens and Ankara were pouring cold water on the prospect of local talks mainly due to the ambivalent future of their own dialogue. Ankara insisted that unless Kuchuk and Makarios were treated on equal terms, it would never agree to local talks.[144] For Greece, there were much more at stake, if such a process was initiated. First, it would have meant the Greco-Turkish talks had failed, and second that talks on *Enosis* had ceased for good. Nevertheless, the diplomatic crisis generated by the importation of Czech arms in December 1966 increased again suspicion of the Greek Government over the ulterior motives of Makarios. Athens, therefore, did not want, for the moment at least, to give the 'go-ahead' to Makarios for taking full control over any negotiations about the future of Cyprus.[145]

On 20 February the new special representative of U Thant, Dr Bibiano Osorio-Tafall, came to Cyprus and was determined to work for at least the implementation of certain normalization measures. This could have produced fertile ground for any later talks on the island. Osorio-Tafall's first proposal for the relaxation of tension came on 10 April 1967 when he suggested the easing of the restrictions of movement of persons and goods by both sides.[146] This initiative, however, had the same fate as all the previous ones. Kuchuk replied that his community had nothing to offer.[147] Instead, he asked Greek-Cypriots first to make certain unilateral good-will actions that could then be reciprocated.[148] Additionally, Kuchuk decided to grasp this opportunity to diplomatically enhance his community's position. Thus, he informed all the foreign diplomatic missions in Cyprus about his views on the matter in order to show them that the ball was now in Makarios' court.[149] Although Makarios had the same negative response, this time he seemed different: It appeared that he was indeed considering displaying some genuine moderation but probably some more push was still needed.[150] That push came from Osorio-Tafall, who eventually convinced him a few months later, on 2 September, to announce a new 'Peace Plan' with several normalization measures affecting mainly Limassol and Paphos.[151] Although these measures were characterized as 'not altogether insignificant', as was the case with previously adopted normalization measures, the main barrier to their implementation was Grivas, who did not appear willing to proceed with a substantial disengagement plan.[152]

It seemed as if by 1967 the Cyprus Government indeed started to believe that time was ripe for talks; yet, an outside boost was needed in order to change Grivas' mood and move Makarios 'from words to action'. By 10 September 1967 and after the Greco-Turkish meeting at Evros, the bilateral dialogue of the motherlands collapsed definitively and a new process now had to fill the vacuum. The chief goal of Makarios was henceforth to ensure that an externally driven process would not be repeated and thus to seize the prime role in determining the next steps. Nonetheless, events did not unfold entirely the way Makarios had planned. After Denktash's clandestine return to Cyprus at the end of October and the well-known crisis of Ayios Theodoros/ Kophinou in November 1967, the previous momentum was rudely shattered. This crisis constituted an important turning point of the Cyprus problem. Subsequently, there was no other option available beyond the immediate initiation of inter-communal talks, not on Makarios' terms but on the basis of the new state of affairs that was created after the November crisis.

Conclusion

The rationale of the Greek-Cypriot policy towards the Cyprus problem may be summarized in Makarios' own words: 'The Cyprus struggle is a question of stamina and the party that shows the greater stamina will win.'[153] Since March 1964 the Cyprus Government had already held the sway over the island, while Plaza's report and the UN General Assembly resolution of December 1965 gave further legitimacy to the Greek-Cypriot negotiating position. The Greek-Cypriots, therefore, possessed all the vital tools to demonstrate the 'greater stamina' and then to pursue the following threefold strategy: (a) let time pass by abjuring any substantial initiative while constantly rejecting UN initiatives towards rapprochement with the Turkish-Cypriots; (b) focus on lobbying missions and mechanisms to secure diplomatic victories during the UN debates; and (c) simultaneously undermine the very shaky chances of progress of the Greco-Turkish talks every time their momentum seemed to be revived. Interestingly, Cyprus' high commissioner in London explained that the reasons for Makarios' acceptance of the Athens–Ankara negotiations despite his own lack of faith were, first, because he did not wish to be accused of intransigence and, second, because such an approach had in any event been suggested by Plaza.[154] In fact, the most important benefit of this externally driven peacemaking process was that it allowed Makarios to shape his foreign policy according to the above-mentioned three directions and these would have eventually facilitated the implementation of his internal vision for Cyprus: the transformation of the Republic of Cyprus into a stable and economically prosperous unitary state. Upon this achievement, this state would be effectively positioned to incorporate the Turkish-Cypriot minority.

The Turkish-Cypriot leadership had welcomed the negotiations between the two motherlands, although it acknowledged that this dialogue would not immediately alleviate the difficulties of their self-imposed isolation. Kuchuk was under fire from two fronts within his community, the moderates and the Turkish Resistance Organization (TMT). For this reason, he was ready to accept the moderates' voices for direct talks under the UN Political Liaison Committee, but at the same time had to appease the extremist interests by insisting on returning to the 1960 Agreements and on certain unilateral goodwill gestures from the Greek-Cypriots.

Makarios' policy of letting time do its job in practice served to ratchet up the tensions until the crisis erupted in November, introducing an even more dangerous phase. It was evident that the Cyprus Government had underestimated two important internal challenges. First, throughout 1967 the Turkish-Cypriot fighters had been attempting to extend their control outside the enclaves with the clear threat of sparking of local tension.[155] Grivas' military provocations against the Turkish-Cypriot's positions were adding further fuel to the fire. Second, as Costar explained, by 1967 Makarios had to tackle the following situation:

In fact the Turkish-Cypriot community, supplied and paid by the Turkish Government and the Turkish Red Crescent Society, shows little signs of cracking. Most of its members have by now adjusted themselves to a reduced standard of living and having, as they believe, already faced the worst, contemplate an indefinite period of ghetto life with comparative equanimity. Their administrative services work quite efficiently nowadays, and thanks to U.N. efforts, they even get their mail. When shortages become impossible they resort to clandestine deals with Greek-Cypriots across the Green Line. In face of this tenacity there is little the Archbishop can do. If he agrees to formalize matters as they now stand he would be giving *de jure* recognition to *de facto* partition. If he heeds the frequent admonitions which I and my colleagues deliver to 'kill the Turks with kindness', he fears that he will merely confirm them in intransigence. So he may well judge it best to allow affairs to continue as at present, taking opportunities to advance the Cyprus Government's position whenever they occur, but otherwise avoiding initiatives.[156]

While Makarios was waiting for Turkish-Cypriots to capitulate, there was also one new reality that had been cultivated within the Greek-Cypriot community. The ultimate unfeasibility of *Enosis* was gradually becoming more obvious for most (but not all) Greek-Cypriots. Makarios repeatedly emphasized that he would accept *Enosis,* only if it came without any territorial compromises in Cyprus. In practice, however, *Enosis* without territorial exchanges on the island was extremely difficult to achieve, as Makarios fully understood. The president acknowledged that independence was currently the best solution for Cyprus and since it was still not possible to admit that openly, Hunt explained that 'by skilful propaganda he [Makarios] hopes to reduce the Greek-Cypriots to such a state of confusion that they will reject *Enosis* in the name of *Enosis*.[157] This policy – however subtle and ambiguous – appeared to strike a chord with the majority of the Greek-Cypriots, but with one important side effect. Ironically, Makarios was repeating the old British tactic of firstly paying lip-service to *Enosis* as the ideal solution for the Cyprus problem, while at the same time skilfully rejecting it for being inappropriate to the complicated circumstances as they stood. Just as the British did during their colonial rule in Cyprus, so Makarios in the 1960s strove to retain ultimate control over the island for as long as he was holding the reins and leave everything else to be decided at some later point. It is noteworthy that it was spread as gossip outside the island that Makarios preferred 'deathbed *Enosis*': unification to be achieved after his death but his name to remain in history as the one who led the island towards its national destiny.[158] Such a strategy to some extent explains the intense hatred that was gradually cultivated during that period among nationalist right-wing circles on the island against Makarios. It seemed as if the nationalists, from their perspective, once again were being 'deceived' about the realization of *Enosis* in the same way that they had been 'deceived' earlier by the colonial rulers. Eventually their growing dissatisfaction over Makarios' prevarication towards *Enosis* found its expression in the paramilitary organizations formed in 1969–1971.

In retrospect, then, we might conclude that the last months of 1965 would have been the most propitious period for Makarios to have taken some decisive initiative. By then the Cyprus Government had managed to implement all the necessary changes to the 1960 Constitution, had economically managed to recover from the losses of the 1963–1964 crisis and the Athens–Ankara negotiations were still at a convenient standstill. Therefore, the Greek-Cypriot leadership could have used their economic and political leverage to move quickly to bring about a negotiated agreement. As Clerides admitted many years later, the denial of the pressing reality for direct contacts between the two communities both by the president and by all of the other political leaders was one of their most serious mistakes.[159] When Bernardes asked Makarios in May 1966 if the latter had truly been considering the prospect of local talks, as he often claimed, his answer suggestively was 'to discuss what?'[160] For Makarios, there was no sufficient common ground for substantial talks. However, in order to achieve such ground, at least some type of contact between the parties, either direct or through a UN intermediary, was essential. This was what both the UN and the Americans and British constantly highlighted in their meetings with Greek-Cypriot officials from 1964 until 1967.[161] Fatally, Makarios' conception of common ground at this stage was in effect the submission of the Turkish-Cypriot leadership to his terms after years of the latter's isolation in the enclaves. Given this assumption, in Makarios' eyes, 'progress' did not equate to any easing of the circumstances in the enclaves or indeed anything that brought the parties together prematurely.

There were several elements indicating that the initiation of direct contacts would have gained the sympathy of moderate Turkish-Cypriots and potentially created a fruitful dynamic to settle the problem. According to Kemal Rustem, a well-respected figure among Turkish-Cypriots,

> even moderate Turkish-Cypriots would accept nothing less than an international guarantee for Turkish-Cypriot rights which must be so phrased as to appear to them as constituting community rights [...] the essential thing was to give the Turkish-Cypriots an effective political voice, for example, by ensuring they had adequate representation in the House of Representatives. Although they might not have a veto on legislation, they wanted to be able to bring their point of view to bear and not be at the unchecked mercy of Greek-Cypriots. If this were assured [...] other matters would be fairly easily negotiated.[162]

Certainly, Rustem was not the only important figure within the Turkish-Cypriot elite that held such moderate views. It is central to the argument of this study that, in the ways already described, Makarios' strategy – while having its own logic grounded in the Cypriot history of its times – carried a very costly burden in failing to mobilize the sort of opinion represented by Kemal Rustem.

The key element, therefore, to prevent the freezing of the stalemate during the period 1965–1967 in Cyprus was the initiation of some meaningful contact, direct or not, between the two communities. Something, however, was still needed to push the Cyprus Government into this logic. The 'incentive' needed for realizing the importance of inter-communal talks came with the November 1967 crisis. Part Two of the book will concentrate on this change in the course of the Cyprus problem, after the island was brought again to the brink of war. Chapter 5 aims to identify the reasons why the impulse to talk became more pressing than ever and how the logjam to such an effort was finally cleared.

Part Two

1968–1974

November 1967 Crisis: A Turning Point

From 1965 to 1967, discussions on the Cyprus problem were taking place outside the island, ostensibly on the basis of *Enosis*. Although never publicly admitted, Turkey accepted this basis, while the British and Americans believed that *Enosis* was still the best possible solution for their own interests. Nonetheless, by autumn 1967, all of them had to revise their foreign policies vis-à-vis the Cyprus problem. When the clouds of war gathered around Cyprus in November 1967, it was clear that a permanent settlement had to be achieved as soon as possible if some disaster was to be averted. It should also be kept in mind that a few months earlier, in June 1967, a serious Arab–Israeli war had threatened the region's stability. Therefore, the West, especially the Americans, wanted to avoid any other source of friction that could have led to a catastrophic war in the same area.

If a solution on independence was to be sought, the main protagonists in any negotiations would have to be the two communities themselves. Indeed, in June 1968, for the first time in four years, the two communities agreed to sit at the same negotiating table and discuss for a solution on the basis of independence. These discussions were to last until 1974. What was about to change that would have made both communities' leaders to accept a process that they were constantly rejecting since 1964? The aim of this chapter is to analyse the transformation of the political landscape in Cyprus and how the new dynamics of the problem triggered inter-communal talks. Our analysis will focus on the aftermath of the November 1967 crisis, the new realities it created and the ensuing approach to inter-communal talks. We shall then explore the objectives of the parties, their negotiating tactics and the position of each interlocutor on the eve of the local negotiations.

Background of the crisis

By mid-1967 it appeared that the failure of the Greco-Turkish negotiations on Cyprus was imminent and thus a new strategy had to be invented both inside and outside the island to fill the vacuum. As stated earlier, Makarios decided to implement a new peace plan entailing a degree of normalization while diplomatically floating the idea of negotiations within the island between the two communities. Up until 1967, therefore, it appeared that things were slowly going as Makarios wished and that he was gradually regaining the advantage over the handling of the Cyprus issue. The factors that nonetheless circumscribed his control over the situation, according to the British ambassador in Ankara, were Grivas' activities, the Turkish threat of invasion, the Turkish-Cypriot resistance and the United Nations Peacekeeping Force in Cyprus (UNFICYP).[1] Soon enough, the first two factors would 'get out of hand', leading to a severe crisis. Only a few days later, however, both problems would be eliminated, at least temporarily.

Simultaneously, a diplomatic 'brainstorming' was taking place in London, Washington and Ottawa on how to make progress after the collapse of the bilateral Athens–Ankara dialogue.[2] After September 1967 it was at last clear to all parties involved that *Enosis* was off the table for good and that it was time to align their foreign policy interests, given that the only practical solution remained some sort of independence.[3] Additionally, the new Special Representative of the UN Secretary-General in Cyprus, Bibiano Osorio-Tafall, by October 1967 had managed to achieve something on the ground. The British high commissioner had commented

Those of us here who see Osorio-Tafall at work think that he is doing a first-class job. His methods are slightly unorthodox and one may not always agree with his views. But where all the previous Special Representatives of the Secretary-General have made minimal progress, he has in a matter of six months at least succeeded in pushing the Archbishop (and pushing is the word) into his 'peace offensive'. If only the obstacle of General Grivas can be overcome this is to my mind at least the beginning of the beginning in solving the Cyprus problem.[4]

The most important success of UNFICYP throughout 1966 and early 1967 was that it managed to reduce the petty violent incidents between the Turkish-Cypriot fighters and the National Guard. However, the construction of fortifications by the National Guard and the effort of the Turkish fighters to gradually extend their control in other areas beyond their enclaves remained a constant source of concern. This was to become the underlying cause of the most serious crisis after three years, near the area of the Turkish-Cypriot village of Kophinou and the mixed village of Ayios Theodoros. Throughout 1967, it was evident that the Turkish-Cypriot fighters had been trying to create tension in that area in order to establish another enclave in a very strategic location of the island, as Brigadier Michael Harbottle, chief of staff of UNFICYP during 1966–1968, explains.[5]

These accumulating frictions in the area eventually led to a very serious confrontation between the National Guard and the Turkish-Cypriot fighters on 15–16 November 1967. The events over these two days, along with the crisis diplomacy that followed and the American effort to prevent a wider Greco-Turkish war, are very well known and, having been analysed in several other studies, are not repeated in this book. Nevertheless, hitherto there has been little clarity as to who might have instigated the operation and for what reasons the National Guard unleashed heavy weaponry against Kophinou. Whatever might have led to this serious inter-communal clash, its outcomes were to be crucial for the concerns of our analysis.

Counting 'gains and losses'

The events of November 1967 have generally been considered an important turning point for the Cyprus problem. The death of 28 Turkish-Cypriots and the extensive damage in both Kophinou and Ayios Theodoros, along with the recall of Grivas to Athens, were only the beginning of wider effects. A Greco-Turkish war and an international crisis were averted only after the United States decided to send Cyrus Vance to convince Athens and Ankara to show restraint and avoid a catastrophic war. Vance's shuttle diplomacy between the two motherlands led a few days later to a four-point understanding. The core of this agreement referred to the immediate withdrawal of surplus military forces within their national contingents stationed on the island.[6] The Greek Government had almost immediately accepted Turkey's demands for the withdrawal of its excessive military personnel from Cyprus within 45 days, almost 7,000 troops, thus returning to the 1960 levels of 950 military personnel. In exchange, Turkey's military forces stood down and did not invade in Cyprus.

Although it seemed that the crisis had been contained from having the most extreme effects, matters were further destabilized when the US envoy went to Cyprus on 29 November to seek President Makarios' approval for the four points. When he was informed about the last of these, Makarios recoiled. This concerned the Greco-Turkish agreement for the extension of UNFICYP's role which was going to assume responsibility to supervise the subsequent disbanding of all military forces established on the island after 1963, above all the Cyprus National Guard. Makarios explained that disarmament was a purely domestic affair of the Cyprus Government. Any implementation of such a plan, he insisted, would have to include both the Greek and Turkish contingents, something that for Makarios would have the advantage of chipping away at the 1960 Treaties.[7] Ankara was never likely to accept Makarios' conditions and thus Vance tried repeatedly to exert moderate influence on the Archbishop who 'dug in his toes, despite the danger of invasion'.[8] It was finally U Thant's appeal of 3 December that managed to cut the Gordian knot. This appeal incorporated an amended version of the four-point agreement with wording acceptable to all three governments. Meanwhile, he proposed to offer his own good offices.[9] After almost a month of uncertainty over the peace of the eastern Mediterranean, war was ultimately prevented.

The way that the crisis burst open, heightened and then 'evaporated' illustrated many important elements about the Cyprus problem up to that point and of the altered context that was taking shape. First of all, it proved beyond any doubt that peace in Cyprus was in fact highly precarious and that any small outbreak of violence could lead to a wider Greco-Turkish clash. Second, it also made clear, especially outside the island, that Turkey was determined to use its right take action in order to protect the Turkish-Cypriots and to go further to protect its own interests on the island. Although in the past protecting Turkish-Cypriot well-being arguably had not been a priority for the Turkish Governments, now it was gradually becoming an important issue within Turkish domestic politics. Upon the eruption of the crisis in November 1967 the Turkish Government came under fire at home. Both the political opposition and the public opinion demanded Ankara to take a forceful action in Cyprus.[10] The American ambassador in Ankara recollects that '[the Turks] warned me that if we intervened again as in 1964, to prevent Turkey from rescuing its ethnic brothers in Cyprus, we would never be forgiven'.[11] Although Cyrus Vance's mission came successful after most of Ankara's demands were accepted by Greece and Cyprus, in the event of an analogous situation in the future in Cyprus, Roger Allen, the British ambassador in Ankara, concluded that it would be extremely difficult for Turkey not to invade the island.[12] To this extent the dangers of the situation had taken a very ominous turn.

Meanwhile, it became equally manifest that for Greece, led by the Greek military regime, maintaining peace with Turkey was much more important than risking a catastrophic war over Cyprus with very limited chances of winning such a conflict.[13] From this arose the eventual disengagement of Greece from the Cyprus problem. It was generally expressed that the existence of a military regime in Athens made the quick accommodation of this matter with Turkey much easier. If there were a democratically elected regime and no censorship of the press, public opinion would have never accepted such a rapid disengagement.[14]

Conversely, the Cyprus Government and Greek-Cypriots remained surprisingly calm over the entire period of this crisis. Harbottle specifically reports,

Despite the gloomy prospect ahead there was no visible panic or alarm but rather a remarkable sang-froid among the Greek-Cypriots, many of whom appeared confident and assured that Turkey would not invade. It was difficult to understand why they should be so confident when all around them and in their newspapers they could witness and read about the imminence of war.[15]

The calm and confidence of Cyprus' president derived mainly from two elements: Soviet assurances that Turkey's threat for invasion was a bluff and Makarios' perception that in any case the Americans would prevent the war as they had done in June 1964.[16] Although this was like walking a tightrope, Costar remarked that Makarios in fact won the contest in competitive brinkmanship with Ankara.[17] As he acknowledged,

> Makarios never lost his nerve: even under great pressure he refused to do more than acknowledge the Greco-Turkish agreement on the first three of Vance's four points while reserving his position on the question of the dissolution of the Cyprus National Guard and the future role of UNFICYP, thus avoiding any diminution of the sovereignty of the Cyprus Government.[18]

Meanwhile the Turkish-Cypriots and the political opposition in Ankara were greatly disappointed because for the first time they had confidently anticipated that Turkey was about to militarily intervene, first in order to rescue them and second to settle the Cyprus problem permanently.[19] Their disappointment was palpable. Although Demirel's Government was criticized for not securing the dismantling of the National Guard in Cyprus, Ankara's diplomatic success in securing the withdrawal of the Greek troops from the island was exploited as a counter-weight to appease Turkish-Cypriot public opinion.[20]

Ironically, all three governments – in Ankara, Nicosia and Athens – gained something important from this crisis. Primarily, Turkey succeeded in removing the Greek division from Cyprus and, although not explicitly stated in U Thant's appeal, this had been achieved on the basis of the 1960 Treaties.[21] Furthermore, according to Michael Stewart, the British ambassador in Athens, the Greek military regime was in a state of euphoria.[22] Greece was now able to withdraw its thousands of troops from Cyprus and so alleviate a heavy political and financial burden. Nonetheless, substantial disengagement did not mean that it was in a position to admit that *Enosis* was shelved.[23] It should also be clarified that there remained a pending issue for Turkey in relation to Greek military personnel serving in the National Guard. Ankara insisted that their agreement implied that these personnel had to be recalled as well.[24] While Greece responded that this was not the case, Stewart explained that the Greek Government 'did not actually want to keep those troops a day longer than necessary in Cyprus, but they wanted to reach agreement with the Turks over long-term issues'.[25] After all, for Makarios as for the Greek Government, this was one of the last remaining bargaining cards for any negotiations over the issue of the complete demilitarization. As proved with the 1974 *coup d'état* however, this element was to cast a long shadow.

The Cyprus Government managed to prevent any reference within a United Nations (UN) Security Council Resolution implying the downgrading of the sovereignty of the Republic of Cyprus. By not accepting the fourth paragraph of the Greco-Turkish agreement for disarmament of all forces constituted after 1963, and thus the dissolution of the National Guard, Makarios eschewed the creation of a precedent that might be used against the sovereignty of Cyprus at a later stage. When Makarios, however, stood firm on this issue he did not imagine that it would prove a double-edged sword since the National Guard and the Greek officers employed therein would eventually emerge as the driving force behind the *coup d'état* of 1974.[26] Nonetheless, Grivas' recalling to Athens, Greece's gradual disengagement from the Cyprus problem and the withdrawal of the Greek division from the island meant that Makarios managed, at least temporarily, to negate factors constantly undermining his own authority and stoking internal unrest within his community. The question of *Enosis* was ineluctably being ruled out, and in that sense Makarios was now able to determine the course of the Cyprus problem in the way that he really wished: a solution through UN channels on the basis of an independent unitary state under the effective rule of the Greek-Cypriot majority.

December 1967, therefore, brought very significant developments on the island. A few days after U Thant's appeal, on 8 December, the first shipload of Greek military personnel left the harbour of Famagusta back to Greece. Calm was again restored on the island, while on 22 December a new Security Council Resolution was issued which endorsed U Thant's offer of his good offices to the parties. This endowed peacemaking efforts with a fresh momentum.

Although the Security Council Resolution was accepted in principle by all parties concerned, there were still several conditions set by Ankara and Nicosia that had to be clarified. For instance, Nicosia insisted on complete demilitarization but this was unacceptable to Turkey, which sought to ensure the removal of all the Greek officers, including those employed in the National Guard.[27] Without losing time, U Thant called all parties to hold a series of discussions in New York. Contacts were immediately initiated in January 1968, in both New York and Cyprus, between UN officials and Greek-Cypriot and Turkish-Cypriot representatives in order to iron out all of their differences and reach an agreement on how to use U Thant's good offices effectively towards a stable and lasting settlement.

New realities: January–June 1968

Turkish-Cypriot Provisional Administration

Back in Cyprus, a few days after the Security Council Resolution, Makarios decided to take the first positive step towards reconciliation by announcing on 24 December 1967 that a new series of peace measures would be put into effect very soon. Although everything looked to be on track for a smooth reconciliation process, five days later a new development came from the enclaves, creating an important setback: the establishment of the Turkish-Cypriot Provisional Administration ('TCPA'). Although at first this move was perceived as ill timed and provocative by everyone outside the island, the reaction and the duration of the measures taken by the Cyprus Government ended up causing even greater frustration, not least to Western powers. The skilful way that it was handled by the Turkish and Turkish-Cypriot side, along with the ineffective reaction of Nicosia and the brinkmanship of Makarios, led to a diplomatic defeat of the latter on an issue that he had hoped to exploit to his own advantage.

On 29 December the Turkish-Cypriot leadership, in the presence of high-profile Turkish officials, declared that the 'TCPA' would henceforth operate within the Turkish-Cypriot-controlled areas. This 'TCPA' was essentially an embryonic government with executive, legislative and judicial functions. The official justification of the Turkish side was that this development was necessary in order to reorganize and make the existing mechanisms operative since 1964, more efficient in administering the population residing in the enclaves.[28] According to the Turkish-Cypriot leadership, this act did not practically change anything beyond merely institutionalizing on a temporary basis the arrangements already in place.[29] They underscored that they did not aim to set up a new government and that in no way did this new formation infringe upon the 1960 Constitution.

The first pillar of this administration was the 'Executive Council', composed of nine members with almost the same portfolios as those of the ministries provided by the Constitution, with Kuchuk as its president and Denktash as its vice-president.[30] A 'Legislative Assembly' was also set in place to operate under the basis of the 1960 provisions, composed of fifteen Turkish-Cypriot members of the Parliament and an equivalent number drawn from the Communal Chamber.[31] The third pillar was the 'Judiciary', constituted by the independent Turkish Courts. Finally, a 'Public Service Commission' was also established, similar to that prescribed by the Constitution.[32]

Both the Turkish-Cypriot leadership and the Turkish Government explained that internal problems and lack of coordination, especially between the Turkish-Cypriot leadership and the fighters in the enclaves, made this reorganization essential.[33] In particular, they claimed that this move had been scheduled for some time but had been delayed due to the November crisis. The Turkish foreign minister commented that the unrest created by the announcement was due to a misunderstanding, explaining,

> Turkish-Cypriots had been compelled by events [of 1963] to set up the General Committee of the Turkish Community. In time the division of powers within the Committee had become confused and as a result certain defects had appeared. In addition, confusion had arisen because neither those who had been officials in the joint administration nor the officials of the Community Chamber knew to whom they were responsible [...] Recently, in order to solve these problems which had become acute, the General Committee was reorganised. The object of this new and provisional arrangement is to provide a unified administration for the community and to put an end to the confusion and conflict of the past. It consists of measures which have no connection with the search for a final solution to the Cyprus problem.[34]

Quite provocatively, the Turkish-Cypriot leadership asserted that the Greek-Cypriots should welcome this move since it would improve their own internal organization and 'will allow intermediaries and at a later stage the Greek-Cypriots themselves to deal with a properly constituted body which can take decisions'.[35]

Inevitably, the announcement for the 'TCPA' served to inflame once more the inter-communal relations on the island. The Cyprus Government characterized this decision as highly provocative and inconsistent with the recent UN Security Council Resolution. Additionally, the fact that it was announced in the presence of top-ranking officials of the Turkish Foreign Ministry was considered an inadmissible interference of Ankara in the internal affairs of the Republic of Cyprus.[36] 'If what they say is true, all they need is a Committee and not an Administration including Foreign Affairs, Commerce, Defence etc.', Kyprianou asserted in New York, adding that 'the Turkish Government refers to the Cypriot Government as the "Greek-Cypriot Administration" and to the "T.C.P.A" as the "Turkish-Cypriot

Administration", so trying to equate their roles'.[37] The Cyprus Government, therefore, decided to issue a ban on contacts with the Turkish-Cypriot leadership and to inform all heads of missions in Cyprus that any visits or contacts with members of the so-called TCPA would be contrary to their accreditation to the Republic of Cyprus.[38]

The establishment of the 'TCPA' was essentially a gimmick for maximizing the Turkish-Cypriot bargaining position for any reconciliation procedure in the offing. Two months later, and after the long debate over this move had run out of steam, Denktash explained that 'the only way to make Makarios see the need for a Cyprus settlement was for Turkish-Cypriots to establish progressively their identity as a separate entity. The announcement of the "T.C.P.A" was a step in this direction, and others were being considered'.[39] The Turkish-Cypriot side believed that by forcing this reality on Greek-Cypriots, they would sooner or later make their case loud and clear; the previous stalemate created a *de facto* reality that would not be accommodated merely with a Charter of Minority Rights in a Greek-led state.

This new development caused a new headache abroad, especially for Britain and the United States. There had been no prior consultation or any diplomatic indication as to what the Turkish-Cypriots were planning and the announcement came as a shock to the British and Americans.[40] The latter blandly indicated to the Turkish Government the regrettable nature of this action, while they made clear to Nicosia that they did not under any circumstances recognize any political status or legality of the so-called TCPA.[41] It is noteworthy, however, that Turkey tried to convince its Western partners that the Turkish-Cypriot motives were sincere.[42] For some time Ankara attempted to play down the issue by avoiding any public statements that referred specifically to the 'TCPA', justifying their claims that the establishment of the 'TCPA' was merely for internal organizational purposes.[43]

The British acknowledged that the 'TCPA' was indeed contrary to the provisions of the constitution, but they still decided that it was better not to press Turkey on issues of legality. They believed that to do so would simply trigger yet more unconstructive exchanges about the legality of the Cyprus Government's actions since 1964.[44] The British decided, therefore, merely to express regret for a development at odds with the spirit of the December Security Council Resolution.

Although it was generally believed that the Cyprus Government indeed felt legitimate anxiety about the Turkish-Cypriot initiative, both the United States and Britain along with France, Canada and Italy agreed that Nicosia's reaction and the ban of ambassadorial contacts with the Turkish-Cypriot leaders was contrary to diplomatic custom.[45] Soon enough, therefore, the attention of the West fixed on how to convince Makarios to lift this ban. The British and US archives indicate a strenuous effort to move Makarios from his intransigent position. For two and a half months they unsuccessfully pushed compromise formulas. Sir Norman Costar advised Makarios that despite the actual Turkish-Cypriot motives 'the Cyprus Government would be unwise from their point of view to attribute to it [the "T.C.P.A"] a governmental status which the Turks themselves consistently and privately denied'.[46] He continued that the ban on contacts prevented foreign representatives from exerting conciliatory influence on the Turkish-Cypriot leadership or even communicating the illegality of their own actions. Most importantly, he stressed that Western ambassadors were irritated at being involved in inter-communal manoeuvring.[47] Both the Americans and the British were under Turkish pressure to resume their contacts with Kuchuk, since his position as vice-president of the Republic of Cyprus was never challenged, except by Greek-Cypriots.[48] Having official contacts with the Turkish-Cypriot leader became even more pressing after the elections of February, when Kuchuk's mandate was renewed. It was evident to the British that behind Makarios' natural aim to get the Western powers to condemn the establishment of the 'TCPA' there lay another purpose: to erode Kuchuk's acceptance as vice-president, and so drive another nail into the coffin of the 1960 Treaties.[49]

By March, after many unsuccessful attempts British and American diplomats, supported by other Western countries as well, agreed that their 'excuses for not calling Kuchuk were running thin'.[50] In any case, contacts with the Turkish-Cypriot leadership had to be resumed before the forthcoming Security Council debate concerning the renewal of UNFICYP's mandate of mid-March. Instructions were, therefore, issued both to Costar and Toby Belcher, the American ambassador, to defy the ban.[51] It was reckoned that the retaliatory actions that the Cyprus Government might impose were worth a risk, since safeguarding good relations with Turkey was more vital.[52] However, before setting a definite date for contacting Kuchuk, both diplomats tried twice to change Makarios' mind. The latter, however, refused, offering evasive excuses. At the eleventh hour, even after arranging their appointments with Kuchuk, the two diplomats still tried to placate matters by approaching Clerides and asking him to influence Makarios. It was only then that Makarios realized that the Americans and British were indeed determined to defy his ban. In order to avoid an open diplomatic defeat before the initiation of the inter-communal talks (which was about to be agreed in New York), he finally complied with their intended action.[53]

The British high commissioner stressed that after Makarios' statement on the lifting of this ban, the latter tried publicly to claim credit for this concession to the Turks. At this stage Costar explained that the Turkish-

Cypriot leadership had proved rather helpful since 'they kept their promise to us not to reveal the true story of the Archbishop's climb-down, which the Archbishop's own obstinacy compelled us to reveal to them, and they have allowed him to make public virtue of the necessity for withdrawal'.[54] For Costar this seemingly petty saga was perceived as 'an unimportant but irritating episode' from which many interesting conclusions could be drawn.[55] Makarios had confronted a Turkish-Cypriot *fait accompli* by using the same tactic as in 1964: imposing isolation on the Turkish-Cypriot leadership believing erroneously that it would force them to retreat. It had failed yet again.

Costar's dispatch, suggestively entitled 'An exercise of Archiepiscopal brinkmanship', dealt insightfully with the aftermath of this development.[56] Costar indicated that in practical terms Nicosia did not gain any benefits, while by 'rejecting every avenue of retreat which was offered to them, they invited a direct clash with three Permanent Members of the Security Council and Italy, which could only have benefited the Turks and indirectly the Russians'. Moreover, he explained that the Russians had played an important role in Makarios' obstinacy. The Russians along with the Arabs had accepted Makarios' ban immediately, and after the elections of February, the Russians 'attempted to provoke further trouble for us by suggesting that it would be appropriate for all Heads of Mission to present fresh credentials to the Archbishop'. Costar's striking analysis continued,

The Archbishop's judgment succumbed to the taste for brinkmanship which had served him well so often in his past [...] Mr. Kyprianou must bear much of the responsibility for allowing Archbishop Makarios to get himself into an untenable position. The indications are clear that he encouraged the Archbishop to maintain his stand and advised him that we and the other Governments involved would not defy him. He himself implied a counter threat of declaring any Head of Mission who did so *persona non grata*. His error has probably not sufficed to induce the Archbishop to replace Mr. Kyprianou in his promised ministerial re-shuffle. But it may have usefully increased the influence of Mr. Clerides [...] [who] favours a realistic compromise with the Turks to settle the Cyprus problem [...]

Nevertheless, the Archbishop is unlikely to be tempted by his reverse into any major change of policy [...] This latest reverse has emphasised his isolation and, if an open clash with four Western Governments had materialised, it might well have increased the Archbishop's dependence on Russia's support. It may be that the consequence has been to push him a little closer to the Russians. But on the whole I am more inclined to think that the shock of a minor defeat may have brought home to the Archbishop the realities of the balance of power here without precipitating any major change in his international position. There is therefore, some hope that the most significant outcome of the episode will be a greater sense of realism on the Greek-Cypriot side in the search for a solution or a modus vivendi in Cyprus.[57]

Although perhaps accurate as to operations of Makarios' mind, Costar's final hope was not fulfilled. During the initial stages of the inter-communal negotiations Makarios used the same brinkmanship, believing that if he 'dragged things out a little bit longer he could have gained a better deal'.[58] Significantly, Clerides has already been seen striking out a position very different from the rest of the Greek-Cypriot leadership, seeking thereafter to exert a more pragmatic influence on Makarios. Besides, the Greek-Cypriot side had a great deal at stake, the consolidation of the separation, that was already well-advanced, being the most important of all. Three years later, when negotiations were to be at an impasse, the Turkish-Cypriot leaders decided to drop the word 'Provisional' from the 'TCPA' abbreviation, in the same skilful and cunning way as in 1968.[59]

Policy of the 'feasible' and Elections, 1968

The first month of 1968 brought significant changes indeed to the island's affairs. Even though the 'TCPA' was established, the November crisis brought a striking wind of change. By 18 January almost all Greek troops had returned to Greece, and despite the announcement for the 'TCPA', Makarios decided to implement the peace plan that he had previously announced on 24 December. Full freedom of movement and all other restrictions from 12 January were lifted from the Turkish-Cypriot-controlled areas, except Nicosia, which was the centre of the 'TCPA', and the Kokkina enclave.[60] On 12 January the president made the following famous declaration, 'Courageous decisions and important initiatives are required if we are to break the present deadlock. A solution, by necessity, must be sought within the limits of what is feasible, which does not always coincide with the limits of what is desirable.'[61] Presenting it as his own personal decision, this was the first time that Makarios implied openly that *Enosis* was no longer attainable and that his government would seek a solution on the basis of an independent, unitary state with a Charter of Rights for the Turkish Community. At the same time he declared that this new official direction of the government required a fresh mandate and thus presidential elections were to be held on 25 February 1968. Through these elections, Makarios sought to gain a clear and stronger mandate to use against those rivals who persisted in accusing him of mishandling the Cyprus problem and the *Enosis* goal. Consistent with his usual tactics, Makarios had not previously informed anyone about his decision to hold elections. The statement came as shock once again to his ministers and closest advisors who revealed that they knew nothing about this plan.[62]

This speech was perceived as marking a new, more conciliatory era for Cyprus not only because of this new direction but also because Makarios avoided using the term 'minority' when referring to the Turkish-Cypriot rights. At this point it is worth noting the different approaches of the various ministers in Makarios' Cabinet, as reflected through their private discussions with foreign officials. The Foreign Minister Kyprianou, as we have already seen, had been one of the hardliners of the government and tried to minimize the importance of characterizing the Turkish-Cypriots as a 'community', denying that it had any particular significance.[63] Conversely, the Acting Foreign Minister, and Minister of Commerce, Andreas Araouzos, maintained that this reference was 'deliberately conciliatory'.[64]

Likewise, mixed messages were also coming from the Cyprus Government about the electoral law to be used in the forthcoming elections. Initially, Makarios was determined to implement the new legislation adopted in 1965, but Osorio-Tafall advised him that this would have been a dangerous development.[65] The main concern was that if the new law was implemented, it would increase tension. Kyprianou, however, insisted that if the 1965 electoral legislation was not implemented, the Cyprus Government would be publicly humiliated by the fact that it was not consistent with its declarations of the last four years about removing all seeds of division incorporated in the constitution.[66] Conversely, Clerides, other Greek-Cypriot diplomats and the Attorney-General, Criton G. Tornaritis QC, stressed that in order to avoid any increase of tension the 1959/1963 laws should be enacted in the forthcoming elections.[67] Eventually, the elections took place on 25 February under the 1959 legislation.[68] Makarios achieved his aim of gaining a strengthened mandate by winning with an overwhelming majority of 95.45 per cent over his opponent, Takis Evdokas,[69] who was supported by the 'immediate-*Enosis*' front.

These two examples are indicative of the mixed hawkish-dovish trends present among Makarios' advisors and within his Cabinet. In the British archives there is much repetition of Kyprianou's intransigence, and his role in encouraging the Archbishop's inclination towards brinkmanship and implacability. On several occasions, Western representatives in Cyprus preferred to bypass Kyprianou when attempting to exert direct influence on Makarios, or to hold meetings with more moderate members of the government instead. 'We live in hope' was the British remark when commenting about the rumour of Kyprianou's replacement from his ministry in January 1968.[70]

Makarios' speech of 12 January was met with a guarded reaction by Turkish-Cypriots, and many expressed suspicion over the true motives of the Greek-Cypriot side.[71] However, Kuchuk responded that a settlement must be reached and that the 1960 Constitution indeed required some amendments.[72] A few days later he stated that vice-presidential elections would also be held on 25 February. Nevertheless, due to the growing dissatisfaction over Kuchuk's leadership among both the moderate and extremist camp, the chances for the renewal of Kuchuk's mandate were in the balance. On 23 January, the Judge Mehmed Zekia announced his candidacy and, paradoxically, he gained immediate and widespread support.[73] His nomination sparked some enthusiasm within the Greek-Cypriot community, while the West believed that Zekia's pragmatic approach provided carve for optimism.[74] Nevertheless, four days later Ankara forced Zekia to withdraw his nomination. The Turkish Government wanted to present a united front within the Turkish-Cypriot community and insisted Kuchuk remain at his post. Denktash was also advised that before returning back to Cyprus he should cooperate with Kuchuk and not let their disagreements damage the Turkish-Cypriot cause.[75] It was also reported that the Turkish Government tried to appease Zekia's supporters by promising that as soon as a solution was in sight, Kuchuk would step down.[76] Ankara thus managed for the moment to paper over the cracks within the Turkish-Cypriot leadership's ranks and Kuchuk was indeed re-elected unopposed on 25 February. Nonetheless, the latter's authority had diminished sharply within his community. Both the vice-president and his old clique were progressively losing ground within their community's politics, leaving the door open to the later 'omnipotence' of Denktash.

Consultations of the UN secretary-general in New York

The Security Council Resolution of 22 December 1967 gave a rather ambiguous 'go-ahead' to U Thant to use his good offices with the interested parties in order to find a way to reach a settlement. More specifically, the resolution invited the parties 'to avail themselves of the good offices proffered by the Secretary-General'.[77] As was the case with Resolution 186, however, this did not clarify the extent of the UN secretary-general's new mandate. The resolution's wording was characterized as quite disappointing by U Thant himself since it did not give him clear guidelines and he warned the Security Council members that his task would be very difficult.[78] Although Cyprus, Greece and Turkey accepted in principle the secretary-general's good offices, it was very soon realized that the different interpretation given by the various parties would lead to another deadlock. It took almost six months of discussions between Nicosia, Ankara and New York in order to reach a final solution on the scope of this process. Indicative of the difficulty is also the fact that even after the inter-communal talks began, the parties still maintained different views of the discussions' aims. Since early indications were so poor, during January and February 1968 the British, Americans and Canadians were intensively discussing contingency plans in case U Thant's efforts ran into the sand.[79] After the 1967 crisis a momentum was inevitably created that should have been maintained at any cost. Moreover, the UN secretary-general noted that Cyprus had not been so quiet since December 1963,[80] while for the first time Makarios' Government agreed to talk with the Turkish-Cypriots and Kuchuk accepted modifications to the 1960 Constitution.[81] There seemed at last to be a genuine opportunity to move forward in a constructive direction.

Because of their distrust of UN peacemaking efforts, after Plaza's mediation and subsequent reverberations, the Turkish side was determined to ensure that any good offices should be an extension of the discussions held during the November crisis and confined to the internal security issues on the island, such as the future of the National Guard, the Greek officers in Cyprus and pacification.[82] Conversely, for a long-term solution Turkey preferred a forum wholly outside UN auspices. It is noteworthy that by February both Turkey and Greece agreed to a Canadian formula for a secret four-party conference with the Canadians taking the chair.[83] This option, however, was shelved a month later when the UN secretary-general proposed inter-communal talks under his chairmanship.[84] Although the Turkish and Turkish-Cypriot side initially insisted that the political aspects of the problem should be addressed on a quadripartite basis without the UN's presence, they eventually changed their mind.[85] By April 1968 the Turkish side agreed to talks between representatives of the two communities on constitutional issues, while insisting on the purely administrative involvement of the UN. Such talks, they argued, should also be held outside Cyprus.[86]

The Cyprus Government initially wanted the agenda to cover all aspects of the problem, from constitutional to political and other daily problem questions. For that purpose, on 14 March 1968 Makarios transmitted to the UN secretary-general a series of proposals that could have been used as a basis for further talks between the two communities.[87] Although these proposals were drafted in a moderate tone, they still reflected the majority of Plaza's recommendations of 1965.[88] Besides, the lifting of all the remaining restrictions by the Cyprus Government on 8 March placed the ball firmly in the Turkish-Cypriot court, since the remaining restrictions were only those imposed by the Turkish-Cypriot leadership on the Greek-Cypriots. On the issue of inter-communal talks, the Cyprus Government insisted that they should definitely take place on the island under the aegis of the UN secretary-general and the oversight of his representatives.[89] Nevertheless, Makarios left the door open for some later discussion with all interested parties for the future of the Treaties of Guarantee and Alliance.[90]

After several discussions and informal meetings in New York, it was finally agreed that the representatives of the two communities, Rauf Denktash for Turkish-Cypriots and Glafkos Clerides for Greek-Cypriots, would initiate a round of informal exploratory talks, without any pre-agreed basis on which they would discuss a constitutional solution of the Cyprus issue that envisaged an independent and unitary state.[91] Regarding the highly contested issue of the venue of the talks, it was decided that they would take place in Nicosia, beginning on 24 June 1968 without the presence of any UN representative, although a preliminary meeting was about to be held in Beirut on 3 June 1968 under the auspices of the Special Representative of the UN Secretary-General, Osorio-Tafall.[92] It is important to stress for our purposes that the rival parties interpreted the source of the ensuing inter-communal contacts very differently. For Greek-Cypriots this fell under the personal responsibility of the secretary-general and of his good offices, on the basis of the Security Council Resolution of December 1967. For Turkish-Cypriots, the engagement of the secretary-general stemmed directly from the November crisis and the recognized need for pacification; for them, the recent Security Council Resolution had nothing to do with the talks. These interpretations were an indication of the wider underlying differences in the parties' perceptions of the UN involvement in Cyprus.[93]

Before local talks: Objectives of the parties and limitations of the two interlocutors

Before analysing the development of the first round of inter-communal talks which lasted until the end of 1971, it is necessary to have a brief outline of each party's objectives, the internal political situation in each community in 1968 and their priorities in any putative final settlement of the Cyprus problem. In addition, an understanding of the position occupied by the interlocutors within their own communities is required to grasp the role they played.

The most important reality of all was that for the first time both communities' leaderships openly acknowledged that they were ready to settle the problem through negotiations rather than war. Moreover, the Greek and

Turkish governments clarified that they did not want a Greco-Turkish war over Cyprus and expressed their determination to urge the parties to reach a settlement as soon as possible on the basis of an independent, unitary state through inter-communal talks. Although they remained strictly neutral, Britain and the United States both favoured this new process of the inter-communal talks for reaching a final settlement to the Cyprus problem.[94] All these elements, therefore, seemed to bode well for the prospect of successful negotiations. In this light, it would be interesting to investigate why the two communities accepted the direct talks in 1968 without posing unacceptable pre-conditions, as had been the case from 1964 until 1967.

Greek-Cypriot objectives

As remarked in previous chapters, the Cyprus Government throughout 1964–1967 controlled a well-functioning state apparatus and an economically prospering state. By imposing on the enclaves several restrictions, it erroneously believed that sooner or later the Turkish-Cypriot leadership would be compelled to capitulate and accept the minority rights on offer. Until 1967, the Cyprus Government was not genuinely in favour of any inter-communal contacts except under its own terms. Besides, Makarios was convinced that the policy of attrition was likely to lead to a swifter and more decisive outcome than negotiations.

Nonetheless, the collapse of the Greco-Turkish dialogue and the November crisis in autumn 1967 forced Makarios to modify and adopt an ostensibly flexible strategy vis-à-vis the Turkish-Cypriots. He agreed to informal talks between representatives of the two communities, abandoning his previous conditions that discussions could only be held on the basis of minority rights and only after the Turkish-Cypriot leadership endorsed all the modifications of the Constitution as passed by the Cyprus Government during its absence. Additionally, and most importantly, the president realized that the attrition policy of the last four years against the enclaves had not borne the expected fruit. Instead of buckling, the Turkish-Cypriot cadre had become more hardened against the notion of a unitary Greek-led state that Makarios wished to consolidate. Acutely conscious that something had to be done to head off such a reaction, Makarios had decided to remove all the restrictions without first securing any concession in exchange.

This urgent and tactical *volte-face,* however, did not mean alteration of the ultimate objective of the Cyprus Government for a Greek-led unitary state with minority rights for Turkish-Cypriots. If the lifting of restrictions and the partial normalization of the island were shrewdly exploited by the government, it could conceivably strengthen the unity of the *de facto* Greek-

Cypriot state through the gradual economic integration of the Turkish-Cypriots to the relatively prosperous Republic and thus undermine the Turkish-Cypriot leadership's authority within the enclaves. Establishment of genuine inter-communal links, especially after 1968, was a policy that was favoured and promoted by Progressive Party of Working People (AKEL) in particular.[95] Nonetheless, AKEL's power was overshadowed by Makarios' political dominance, and its purely subordinate role in shaping what happened was to impose limits on the process. The British high commissioner in Nicosia, in 1970 commenting on the presence of a pro-communist Turkish-Cypriot student movement, suggests that

> A.K.E.L has failed to make any discernible response to the student suggestions about mutual cooperation. The dilemma A.K.E.L faced in choosing between a sufficiently Greek line to appeal to its membership and avoid accusations from other parties of being pro-Turkish and sufficiently universalist line to match its ideology has clearly been resolved in favour of the former.[96]

The official Greek-Cypriot negotiating position revolved around the degree of participation – meaning proportional representation – of the two communities in the state machinery as well as complete autonomy on religious, educational, cultural and personal status affairs, along with a degree of local autonomy compatible with the concept of the unitary state for Turkish-Cypriots.[97] How far could autonomy be taken while remaining compatible with a unitary state, and at what point did it drift into a federation proper? That proved to be the crucial moot-point for the two communities. The most important obstacle for a genuinely unitary state was the gradual consolidation of the administrative autonomy enjoyed by Turkish-Cypriots since 1964. Nevertheless, in strictly legal terms, a compromise could have been reached, but it had for some time become clear that the problem was not legal but intensely political. Makarios had even explained to his negotiator that although certain arguments for compromise might have been legally valid, 'if our objective is to reduce the excessive rights which the Zurich Agreements gave to the Turkish-Cypriots and make the constitution workable, we should not add other rights in place of those we subtracted and thus create again an unworkable constitution.'[98] This was indeed the Greek-Cypriot approach throughout the inter-communal talks: to reverse the imbalance set by the Zurich–London Agreements.

As Clerides explains, Makarios' guidelines for the process of the talks were: to insist on a unitary state under a presidential system and to try to reduce the political status of the Turkish-Cypriot community to that of a minority with autonomy on the above-mentioned affairs.[99] Moreover, it was of utmost importance for their side to avoid making any commitments and keep all subjects open until there was clear understanding on all pending issues.[100] This meant that the Greek-Cypriot side should avoid making any proposals and, if forced to do so, they should be such as to extract as many concessions as possible from the other side. This naturally displayed a maximalist logic.

Erroneously, Makarios believed that since there was no further danger of Turkish invasion and a Greco-Turkish war, time was working in favour of his community.[101] Interestingly, Costar, explaining the current situation among Greek-Cypriots, reported,

> The Archbishop is known to have said in private that the Greek-Cypriots do not find the current situation in Cyprus intolerable for them, and that if the Turks wish to remain second-class citizens living in their ghettos he is content to wait until they change their minds i.e. virtually surrender to his terms.[102]

That negotiating policy, as would later be shown, inevitably led to damaging delays that allowed the political realities of each community to feed into their negotiating positions. The result, as the British High Commissioner, Peter Ramsbotham, concluded in 1971, was to make Makarios 'offer too little too late'.[103]

According to Costar, however, there was another underlying reason for this dilatory negotiating policy and the rigid line of certain Greek-Cypriot politicians. A solution would have radically changed the *status quo* and upset the apple cart within Greek-Cypriot politics in general. He explained,

> Some of the present Ministers and others in positions of power, have few qualifications for office beyond their identification first with the E.O.K.A movement and subsequently with the struggle against Turkish Cypriots […] The majority of the present generation of leaders have been in power since independence, have no tradition to reconcile them to the loss of office and few opportunities for alternative employment.[104]

Costar's interesting analysis went on to explore the underlying impulse of Makarios' position within the Greek-Cypriot political world, and how it would be affected by a political solution. This hinged on his relations with AKEL. Although he always appeared confident of 'riding this tiger', Costar felt that the Archbishop must be aware that once Cypriot politics ceased to be entirely dominated by the inter-communal question, his relations with AKEL would automatically become far more problematic. He continued:

The problem of the Archbishop would be made more acute because it would coincide with the resurgence of political rivalry and pressure within his own loosely-knit Patriotic Front, and in other sectors of the population, including trade unions. He would also [...] be obliged to take account of the Turkish Cypriot views, both within the Council of Ministers and outside it, and, if he were to avoid a further inter-communal breakdown, he might have to give more weight to these than would be justified by the constitutional position and voting strengths of the Turks[...] [He] would face a situation that is unprecedented for him, in that he would no longer enjoy automatically the overwhelming popular support of the Greek Cypriots that has since 1965, and would be subject to overt criticism from Greek-Cypriots for the first time [...] It is questionable whether his commitment to an independent unified Cyprus is strong enough to lead him to accept, say, criticisms from the Bishops of his own church in defending Turkish Cypriot interests. His task would be made harder by the fact that Turkish Cypriot community would, for the first time since independence, be led by a man [Denktash] who was a worthy opponent.[105]

Those elements were characterized by Costar as the 'invisible' price to be paid by the Greek-Cypriot leadership, and the prospects involved would certainly have an impact on its decision-making processes as the talks evolved. These views were definitely perceived as a taboo subject that none could openly admit. These implications and dynamics were indeed to prove lasting and arguably still exist in Cyprus today.

Turkish-Cypriot objectives

After the 1967 crisis and the establishment of the Turkish-Cypriot Provisional Administration ('TCPA'), the Turkish-Cypriot side gained additional leverage at the negotiating table. The Turkish-Cypriot leadership, therefore, realized that given the new realities a complete return to the 1960 Constitution was not in their community's best interest any more. Despite their arguments that the formation of the 'TCPA' solely aimed to fill the gaps in their own administrative and organizational affairs, the truth was that it created an embryonic state within a state. If that formation was further consolidated, it could have strengthened their *de facto* separation and, thus, purport to justify their later demands for *a de jure* recognition of this separatism through a federal structure of the state.

Nevertheless, while the 'TCPA' was still in its early stages, there were signs that the Turkish-Cypriot side was at least going to be flexible on certain constitutional aspects. Its main concern was the immediate economic challenges of its community and it initially believed that this could only be fully achieved after a solution.[106] Such thinking, however, did not undermine the determination of the Turkish-Cypriot political leaders to maintain the separate administration that they had spent four years building, or their intention to see it strengthened in the approach to a settlement. Therefore, in June 1968 they decided to establish the Turkish-Cypriot 'Economic Development Committee' under the personal supervision of Denktash.[107]

Their official negotiating policy remained that the Turkish-Cypriot community was as a co-founder of the Cyprus Republic, not a minority, and that the inter-communal balance established with the 1960 Constitution should be reflected in any new settlement.[108] According to Denktash's proposals during the initial stages of the talks, his side was aiming to accommodate the Greek-Cypriot demand for amendment of the 1960 constitutional rights of the Turkish-Cypriots by re-arranging them in such a way that the unity of the state could be maintained. This meant they were ready to accept proportional participation in the core structure of the state, but in order to prevent the downgrading of their political status into that of a Greek-controlled minority, they asked in exchange for genuine local autonomy with limited state supervision.[109] Particular importance should be attributed to the use of the term 'unity of the state' by the Turkish-Cypriot side. As we shall see, the interpretation given to it by Denktash in the beginning of the talks was different, and certainly closer to the Greek-Cypriot line, from the one that was later given in 1970–1971, when he argued that even federation is compatible with the concept of a unitary state.

Although the Turkish-Cypriot side had gained some credit in world opinion due to its ostensibly flexible stand on the constitutional aspects, it was also 'losing points' in the blame game due to a much more negative approach over normalization. It was a fact that the Greek-Cypriot side provided complete freedom of movement throughout the island by lifting all the remaining restrictions. The Turkish-Cypriots had not reciprocated. Despite the continuous efforts of Osorio-Tafall, UNFICYP and the British and American representatives in Cyprus, the Turkish-Cypriots stubbornly rejected any suggestions that allowed freedom of movement for Greek-Cypriots through their areas, arguing that the continuous provocative statements and actions by the Greek-Cypriot side did not dispel their doubts about the latter's sinister motives. They claimed that they had intended to respond to Makarios' normalization measures, but when it became known that heavy Czech arms were distributed for the National Organization of Cypriot Fighters (EOKA) military parade of 1 April 1968, they suspended this plan.[110] Since then any effort to convince them to reciprocate ran into the sand. Denktash, however, admitted that this was the only bargaining chip left to them and one that could only be played when a substantive settlement was close.[111] It should be borne in mind that the normalization process was an issue mainly directed by the militias and the hardliners of the community's leadership, such as Orek.[112] It was a fact that the Turkish-Cypriot fighters and military officers from Turkey were constantly causing difficulties for pacification.[113] By taking advantage of the freedom of movement established by the Cyprus Government, they constantly sought to extend their areas of their control. Although on the political front it seemed that by 1968 Denktash had convinced them about his own will for a settlement through negotiations, Osorio-Tafall and other Western diplomats were expressing doubts and suspicion over the real motives of the Turkish-Cypriot fighters and the other hardliners who stood behind them.[114]

As with certain Greek-Cypriot politicians, many of their counterparts in the Turkish-Cypriot side were by no means sincerely committed to a radical alteration to the existing circumstances. It was a fact that life within the enclaves was a constant struggle, but the existing situation suited its leadership well enough. Costar explained,

> The present Turkish Cypriot leaders, with the exception of Denktash, are so closely identified with the 'siege' policy of the Turkish Cypriot community and, in some cases so discredited by their personal financial dealings over the past four years, that is seems doubtful whether many of them could continue in office following an inter-communal settlement.[115]

As we shall see, Denktash had much to gain from an inter-communal settlement or at least getting talks off the ground. This is why Ankara entrusted him as the negotiator, granting him almost complete freedom of manoeuvre.[116] But like Makarios, Denktash also needed to satisfy both his friends and the opposition, and ultimately he had to secure a settlement that he could 'sell' to his community at large.

Denktash's position

During the first round of the inter-communal talks, the internal politics of each community played an important role in both the formation of the two communities' positions and the eventual progress of the talks. However, one of the most important variables was the personal standing of each leading negotiator and their political impact on the decision-making process of their constituencies.

In 1964 Denktash was perceived as an extremist politician who was fighting for partition. When he returned in April 1968, things were different. After four years in Ankara, Denktash acknowledged that, unlike Inonu's Government of 1964 favouring federation, the current Turkish Government sought a peaceful solution of the Cyprus problem as soon as possible, on the basis of an independent unitary state.[117] Denktash returned to Cyprus, realizing that Turkey would not risk a war with Greece over Cyprus and accepting that the Greek-Cypriots themselves no longer wanted *Enosis,* making partition no longer feasible.[118] He had, however, to convince the hawks of the Turkish-Cypriot leadership along with the other extremist factions and the military officers from Turkey who were still bent on federation, about the shift in Ankara's policy. His own personal gain from fulfilling Ankara's wishes was that he would have been able to build a mutually trusting relationship with the Turkish Government, which would later have enabled him to receive Ankara's green light to at last replace Kuchuk.[119]

Being abroad during the first four years of the *de facto* separation, Denktash as a political figure did not link his name with the misfortunes and disappointment endured by Turkish-Cypriots and to a large extent caused by the old clique around Kuchuk.[120] Therefore, Denktash returned to Cyprus as the beacon of hope for many Turkish-Cypriots, receiving a hero's welcome in Nicosia.[121] As Denktash explained, the Turkish-Cypriots expected him to solve both their economic and political problems.[122] However, this was by no means easy. Despite their efforts to paper over their rivalry through public statements, Denktash's relations with the existing political leadership and certain military officers were strained.[123] After his re-establishment in Turkish-Cypriot politics, Kuchuk's entourage tried to reduce Denktash's political influence by constantly undermining his efforts to settle the community's practical problems and his attempts at compromise on the negotiating table.[124] In the early stages of the inter-communal talks, Denktash had confessed to Clerides about the reasons for his previous insistence on holding the inter-communal talks outside the island. He stressed that if there was any constructive common ground between the two sides, he would have been able to bypass the rest of the Turkish-Cypriot leadership and to directly consult and formulate an agreement with Ankara.[125] Now that the talks were held in Cyprus, this was impossible. In the event that the Turkish-Cypriot leadership took an unhelpful stand on a matter of substance, Ankara would not have been able to ignore their disagreement.[126] Although Denktash had Ankara's support on the inter-communal talks, the latter also wished to retain, at least for the time being, an equal balance of power between the current leadership and Denktash.[127] From the aspect of a constitutional settlement, Ankara had warned Denktash that it would support any solution he reached in talks, on the basis of a unitary state with adequate local autonomy for Turkish-Cypriots, as long as he managed to convince the rest of the Turkish-Cypriot leadership.[128] Therefore, Denktash had to work discreetly in order to achieve two goals. First, in the short term he had to replace the old ineffective leadership of the 'TCPA' through the promotion of his own people within the rungs of the administration. This would give him the ability to implement any decisions he reached in the inter-communal talks within the 'TCPA'. Second, if he could achieve this, he would need to assume the reins of his community from Kuchuk in close association with Ankara.

The greatest challenge for both Denktash and Ankara was to reach a constitutional settlement as soon as possible. Otherwise, if negotiations wore on, there was a lurking danger that the opponents of the negotiated settlement, that is, the Turkish-Cypriot fighters and the hawks within the local political leadership, would take advantage of the delay to regroup and reduce the chances for a viable and lasting settlement.[129] Both the Turkish Government and several moderate Turkish-Cypriots attempted repeatedly to warn the Greek-Cypriot leaders of this critical danger.[130]

Clerides' position

Unlike Denktash, whom Turkey initially granted an almost free hand to negotiate, Clerides enjoyed no such flexibility. The latter had to strictly follow Makarios' guidelines even on the simplest questions.[131] Conversely with Makarios, Clerides believed that a moderate approach in the negotiations would yield greater benefits. The truth was that although Makarios trusted him, Clerides had very limited personal influence over the president and indeed very few supporters in Makarios' immediate circle willing to help him push the Archbishop towards a more flexible stance. Although within the Cabinet there existed a fine balance between the doves and the hawks, the latter group had much more direct influence on Makarios. Clerides admitted that he had insisted that talks should take place in Cyprus in order to ensure that he would be able to discuss all the proposals with Makarios in person. Otherwise, he explained he had 'little chance of keeping Makarios on the right light lines [...] and lead the doves in the Cabinet'.[132] Ironically, both interlocutors insisted on the different venues for the talks for the same reason: to prevent the hawks of their leaderships from having a damaging effect on their negotiations.

Moreover, the Greek-Cypriot interlocutor disagreed with Makarios, both on negotiating techniques and on the handling of political problems that had an important impact on the inter-communal talks, such as the growth of extremist illegal activities throughout 1969. His only tactical 'weapon' for convincing Makarios to adopt a less intransigent line was the threat of his resignation. Moreover, his only important 'allies' on the decision-making procedure for the talks were the Greek Government and, more specifically, the Greek Foreign Minister, Panayiotis Pipinelis. Nonetheless, the latter, who favoured a quick and peaceful solution to the problem and was thus open to certain concessions to Turkish-Cypriots, had two important limitations. First, Athens had, as always, a very fragile grip over Makarios. Second, Pipinelis needed to ensure that his own role was perceived as entirely secondary in order to avoid being accused by Makarios of interfering in the internal affairs of the island. Therefore, he avoided making – at least in writing – any specific suggestions for concessions to Makarios.[133]

If Clerides wanted to gain more room for manoeuvre in negotiations, he needed to increase his own influence over Makarios. He could only achieve this by bringing to bear his own increased standing within the Greek-Cypriot community. By autumn 1968, therefore, as soon as he realized that the inter-communal talks were heading into a deadlock mainly due to his side's rigid line, he tried to convince Makarios to accept parliamentary elections followed by a ministerial reshuffle as soon as possible. When Clerides realized that for various reasons elections in the near future were not possible, he decided to form a political party of his own. Had the elections been conducted and had he won an absolute majority, he might have constituted an important counter-balance to Makarios' power and increased his own influence on policy.[134] Although parliamentary elections took place in 1970, Clerides, as we shall see, failed to achieve such a tactical position.

Throughout mid-1969 and into 1970 Clerides had to tackle another great difficulty: the gradual increase of extremist organizations' actions against the government and the increasing proliferation of accusations that the national goal of *Enosis* had been 'betrayed'. This reactivated a sterile public debate over *Enosis* and instigated the rise of a national right wing polarizing yet further the Greek-Cypriot community. 'Makarios' Achilles heel was his sensitivity to the accusations of treachery', Clerides admitted to the British high commissioner in 1969.[135] Inevitably, Makarios fell into the trap of making successive public statements about the unfinished struggle for *Enosis* and of tolerating such statements by some of his own ministers. All these undermined Clerides' authority in negotiations, infuriated the Turkish-Cypriot leadership and bogged down the already 'snail-like' pace of the talks.

The president himself took a rather softer line on the rising of the extremist elements within his community. In this he failed to realize the importance of taking certain pre-emptive measures for their suppression. Conversely, he once again deployed his characteristically Byzantine tactics, convinced that due to his personal status and the undeniably great impact of his speeches on the majority of Greek-Cypriots he could safely ignore this threat.[136] This assumption was to prove fatally flawed.

Conclusion

Neither Plaza's report, the subsequent efforts of the UN secretary-general, nor the Greco-Turkish dialogue had managed to achieve what the 1967 crisis finally brought about. It made both communities get to grips with their problem through inter-communal talks, creating for the first time some sort of credible momentum. At first it seemed that there was room for compromise and that both Clerides and Denktash could have led their communities towards a lasting compromise. They were characterized in particular as the ablest and most dovelike leaders at this juncture, and indeed if a solution had been up to them they would probably have reached a satisfactory settlement in the initial two rounds of the talks. Nevertheless, constant delays and mutual mistrust over the ulterior motives of each party came to haunt any chance for progress. This caused everyone to realize that each party's objectives were hardly different than in 1964–1967: iron-clad guarantees on the internal security elements for the Turkish-Cypriots, meaning in essence an enhanced degree of local autonomy amounting to disguised federation, versus the complete unity of the state under Greek-Cypriot control. Eventually, the prevailing context irrevocably widened the gap between the parties, pulling the two interlocutors down.

6

Inter-Communal Negotiations, 1968–1971

On 3 June 1968, Denktash and Clerides duly held their first meeting in Beirut, thus marking the beginning of a new chapter in the Cyprus problem. For the first time, representatives of the two communities were entrusted with a very delicate task: to work together in search of a settlement. Time appeared ripe for mutual concessions. But was that the case? The Cyprus issue is usually characterized as 'a problem of missed opportunities'. If we accept this characterization, then the first round of inter-communal talks was indeed one great, yet missed, opportunity, as this chapter intends to illustrate.

From the very first meeting, the two interlocutors clarified the views of each community in relation to the problems derived from the 1960 Constitution. They acknowledged that certain problematic provisions existed for both communities, but their mistrust and fear concerning the ulterior motives of each side, *Enosis* and partition respectively, prevented them from working peacefully together.[1] Henceforth, they both established that their common goal was to find a constitutional settlement, although without explicitly agreeing on any terms of reference for their discussions, and 'to talk frankly to each other during the course of the talks'.[2] This procedure, however, would only be the first step towards a settlement. All other interested parties would then have to endorse any agreement reached between the two communities and then decide about the international aspects of the solution.[3]

Believing and genuinely wanting to reach a quick settlement, the two interlocutors decided to hold meetings twice and, if necessary, three times a week. Despite their qualified optimism, they had few illusions about the difficulties ahead. According to Clerides, the greatest challenge faced by the negotiators was selling their tentative agreements to their superiors.[4] In the event, these exchanges were to last until July 1974, when they were terminated abruptly after the *coup d'état* and the Turkish invasion. They were conducted in two rounds: the first begun in June 1968 and was unsuccessfully terminated at the end of 1971 and the second was initiated in June 1972 and lasted until July 1974.

This chapter examines in chronological order the four phases of the first round of the inter-communal discussions, between 1968 and 1971, focusing on the negotiating practices of each side and the proposals made. Throughout we are especially concerned with the internal developments in each community in order to understand their impact on the negotiations. In doing so, the focus is not on arcane legal matters, although these were often argued about, but on the political roots of a failure that was to shape the later evolution of the Cyprus problem.

The first phase: June–August 1968

The exploratory phase of the talks raised hopes that the negotiations might swiftly prove successful. The two interlocutors exchanged views, establishing that there was sufficient common ground on a variety of subjects. The main reason for a prevailing optimism was the fact that Denktash was more flexible than ever while he seemed open to concessions and suggestions. He certainly appeared to be responsible for giving the talks an early boost.

As shown by Clerides' personal records, containing reports and correspondence drafted after his meetings with Denktash, the two interlocutors had decided that their purely personal discussions should proceed *ad referendum*, meaning that they would not be bound by any decision without explicit agreement. Additionally, in order to avoid further complications, Clerides proposed that when they did disagree on a matter of importance, they should refrain from reporting every minor detail to their principals.[5] In that way, it would be easier to 'sell' a later compromise to their superiors.

Among the preliminary concessions made by Denktash during this short first phase of talks were several from Makarios' original 'Thirteen Points'. First and foremost, he accepted the proportional representation of each community in state institutions. Equally importantly, he concurred with the abolition of the veto powers of the vice-president and his right to promulgate laws along with the president. Regarding legislative matters, Denktash agreed to the abolition of the separate majorities and to the principle that the president and vice-president of the House would be elected by all members of Parliament, ensuring that if the former is Greek, the latter would be Turkish and vice versa. Likewise, Denktash conceded to the unification of courts for the two communities and the option of the litigant to be tried by a judge competent in his own language.[6]

It appeared, therefore, that in the executive, legislative and judicial spheres there was a common ground in principle between the two sides. It is also noteworthy that Clerides accepted Denktash's request that Turkish-Cypriot education would be financed by the state.[7] Despite this initial ostensible consensus on the core structure of the state, the Greek-Cypriots wished to secure two more elements that were 'red flags' for Turkish-Cypriots: the unification of electoral rolls and the complete abolition of the vice-presidency. It should be stressed that the retention of the latter office, even without the majority of the powers envisaged in the 1960 Constitution, highlighted the bi-communal character of the state. Denktash had intimated that insisting on the abolition of this post was a waste of time because his community would not retreat.[8] Conversely, he did not completely shut the door on a later compromise regarding common electoral rolls, although this was perceived as an important safeguard of the Constitution for his community. The Turkish *Chargé d'Affairs* in Nicosia explained that this provision was a guarantee that genuine representatives of the Turkish-Cypriot community were elected and not mere stooges. He gave the example of the Turkish-Cypriot politician Ihsan Ali, a supporter of Makarios but regarded as a quisling by the Turkish-Cypriot leadership.[9]

The Turkish-Cypriot negotiator had indeed made far-reaching concessions, but on one condition. The Greek-Cypriots would concede to a substantial degree of local autonomy for his community, not subject to amendments by the Greek-Cypriot majority of the Parliament. Genuine local autonomy was, for Turkish-Cypriots, the key to any prospective solution of the Cyprus problem. Concluding this phase, Clerides explained to Makarios that although this issue was indeed difficult, the most promising element was the overlap between the two parties on the responsibilities of the local administration.[10] Conversely, their main disagreements had centred upon the areas that this local autonomy would cover and the degree of state supervision on it. Regarding the former, Denktash proposed a local administration based on communal criteria and more specifically a grouping of Turkish and Greek villages, irrespective of whether they formed geographically cohesive areas.[11] The Greek-Cypriot negotiator objected that this was unacceptable because such a grouping could lead to the cantonization of the island. The Greek-Cypriot side propounded a form of decentralization which gave more say to the inhabitants of a certain village, rather than setting up a new layer of local government for a group of villages lacking geographical proximity.[12] Clerides proposed that such 'lower' administration would exist only at the village level, without any grouping of villages, under the complete control of the minister of interior. Denktash rejected this proposal on the grounds that it did not provide the Turkish-Cypriots genuine autonomy. Meanwhile, he argued that if he were indeed aiming at a disguised federation through local autonomy, he would have insisted on special executive, legislative and judicial powers for the local governance, with a separate police force, but he did not do this.[13]

This first phase of talks was indeed critical since the Turkish-Cypriot concessions seemed to have produced a real opportunity for progress. At first glance, it was evident that most of the points of the 1960 Constitution that hindered the smooth functioning and unified character of the state were among Denktash's concessions. Although Denktash was negotiating in good faith, a more thorough examination of his preliminary concessions indicates that they did not compromise his side's ultimate goals. The same applied to Clerides' position as well. At this stage, therefore, we must summarize certain elements regarding the negotiating tactics of the two interlocutors.

As emerges from Clerides' records, Denktash appeared transparent and flexible on issues of lower importance for his community, with the aim of securing more critical demands. Indeed, Denktash's acceptance of several of the 'Thirteen Points' did not extract a heavy price for his own community. First, these were not in contrast to the concept of local autonomy that he wanted to secure from these talks. Second, as he had admitted, the provisions of the 1960 Constitution that he was ready to forego were in any case against the best interests of his community.[14] It should be stressed that Denktash avoided making any reference to normalization and the question of freedom of movement throughout the enclaves. Had he done so, compromises from his side would have been expected, and his community was not prepared to give in. The Turkish-Cypriot interlocutor explained to Clerides that the majority of the concessions he made were not yet accepted by the rest of the Turkish-Cypriot leadership and, if made public, might lead to his own dismissal. However, Denktash was optimistic that if Greek-Cypriots were flexible about local autonomy, he could prevail upon Turkish-Cypriot public opinion to move forward on this basis.[15] That, however, had to be done as quickly as possible. Denktash confessed that the prolongation of negotiations would inevitably strengthen his less moderate political opponents within the Turkish-Cypriot public opinion, making it even more difficult to 'sell' a compomise.[16] The same degree of urgency had been consistently expressed by the Turkish Foreign Minister, Caglayangil, to his counterparts in Greece, Cyprus and Britain.[17]

Strictly following Makarios' guidelines, the Greek-Cypriot interlocutor tried to elicit information regarding Denktash's intentions for all constitutional issues, but without revealing his own side's goals or hinting at any substantial concessions.[18] The only exception to this strategy was his very early acceptance of the proposal that the state would finance Turkish-Cypriot education. Even that, however, not only provided material benefits to the Turkish-Cypriots but aimed essentially to the strengthening of the unitary character of the state. Makarios believed that, due to economic pressure and the sense of urgency for a settlement stressed repeatedly by both Ankara and Denktash in private, the Greek-Cypriot side could afford to maintain an inflexible position on all other constitutional issues, at least for the moment.

By the end of July, after exchanging their personal suggestions, the two negotiators decided to recommence their talks in September with a more thorough exchange of proposals on all issues. Both parties were also receptive to examining the option of implementing tentative agreements as soon as they were reached without waiting for an overall settlement.[19] The Turkish-Cypriot negotiator then visited Ankara along with other members of the Turkish-Cypriot leadership to discuss their next steps. Similarly, Clerides met with Makarios and Pipinelis. Both in Cyprus and abroad, hopes were rising that a constitutional settlement might soon prove possible. However, such expectations would before long be checked by a marked hardening of the Turkish-Cypriot position.

The second phase: August–December 1968

Because of the initial optimism, Clerides harboured hopes that this phase would be concluded successfully and swiftly. It seemed that the main disagreements revolved around the formation of the local administration areas, the issue of the common/separate electoral rolls and the vice-president's post. Nevertheless, Denktash had returned from Ankara with more strict guidelines. A few days before the resumption of negotiations, Denktash said to Costar that he was disappointed by the Greek-Cypriot position thus far and that, unlike during the first phase, he 'would be getting down to bargaining and it was to be hoped that the Greek Cypriots might then prove flexible'.[20] He was not alone, however, in taking a rigid line. It was acknowledged by United Nations Force in Cyprus (UNFICYP) officials that aside from the constitutional aspects, Turkish-Cypriots were now taking a tougher line on various normalization issues.[21] Although the setback in the talks flowed mainly from the 'backsliding' of the Turkish-Cypriot side, the Greek-Cypriot negotiating tactic of holding back from substantial and realistic proposals also contributed to this phase's disappointing end. Manoeuvring instead to make a decisive gesture at some future climax had simply reduced Dektash's capacity to persuade his own community along the way.

Progress of the negotiations

After a month's adjournment and after each side's consultation with its motherland, Clerides and Denktash opened the second phase of the talks on 29 August, lasting until the end of the year. As soon as the meetings began, it became apparent that Denktash's views had been entirely modified on all constitutional issues. Before the exchange of written proposals, he explained that on the legislature and the judiciary, on which it was believed that agreement was within reach, he had to retract many of his previous personal suggestions. He argued that the rest of the Turkish-Cypriot leadership held a sterner approach on legislative issues; at the same time he insisted on the principle of communal separation in the judiciary, including the preservation of the litigants' right to be tried by a judge of their own community and not merely someone who spoke their language.[22] Regarding the vice-presidency, Denktash repeated that its retention was non-negotiable, but its powers were open to discussion. The only point on which he seemed willing to negotiate was the unified electoral rolls, but even here a mutually acceptable arrangement was more complex than expected.[23]

The major issue of contention, however, remained the structure of local government. On 16 September Denktash decided to table the first list of written proposals for the local government which reflected a stricter approach than the one he expressed during the exploratory phase. Unlike in Denktash's previous indications, the Turkish-Cypriot side was asking for a local government formation with executive, legislative and judicial functions as well as a separate police force. In essence, this entailed a two-level administration on the island, consisting of a central government and an autonomous local administration.[24] This local administration was to be organized under communal criteria with groupings of Turkish-Cypriot and Greek-Cypriot villages. Each group – there being about seventy in all for the Turkish-Cypriot villages – would be represented on a central body. There would be two central bodies, one for the Turkish-Cypriot and one for the Greek-Cypriot entities; these would be responsible for the coordination and exercise of the local government powers. The Turkish central authority would have links with the Turkish Communal Chamber and be responsible to a Turkish-Cypriot minister of Turkish affairs. Additionally, it was suggested that the local authority organs would enjoy wider functions than those agreed upon in the previous phase, including legislative powers and their own communal courts. Finally, all these provisions would be entrenched in the Constitution.[25] Needless to say, Clerides rejected this package immediately on the grounds that it was in effect a proposal for a cantonal system. Both Osorio-Tafall and the American ambassador agreed that the Turkish-Cypriot proposals were proposing a federal system of governance.[26]

Despite the early tabling of the Turkish-Cypriot proposals for local administration, the Greek-Cypriot side decided not to make any counter-proposals as yet. The negotiators, therefore, decided to exchange proposals on two issues on which they believed, despite the hardening of the Turkish-

Cypriot views, concrete progress could quickly be achieved: the judiciary and the police. Had this proved possible, these agreements would have been implemented, affording a fresh impetus and better prospects for tackling later the difficult problem of local government. Soon enough the negotiators were disillusioned. A final compromise was again impossible as it emerged that these subjects were closely related with the local administration arrangements. As Costar explained, 'neither side was prepared to prejudice its position or to place any confidence in the good faith of the other by operating a partial agreement in advance of a wider constitutional settlement'.[27] In this way, the various issues converged simply to frame the underlying deadlock in new terms.

After this impasse and in response to consistent pressure from Greece, on 9 December the Cyprus Government decided to present its counter-proposals on local administration.[28] According to these, the Greek-Cypriot side adhered to the line that there should be no grouping of villages whatsoever and suggested instead that each village or town should constitute the basic unit of local administration. These units would be supervised by the District officers appointed by the government.[29] Moreover, it rejected both the concept of central local authority organs and the assertion that the functions of the local administration should be embedded in the Constitution. As expected, these positions were repudiated by Denktash, who argued that they were not acceptable even as a basis for further discussions. A few weeks later, this phase of the negotiations ended with a complete deadlock on almost all pending issues.

Clerides admitted that both negotiators privately acknowledged that their proposals for the local government were not realistic and should be merged into a new proposal. Nevertheless, whatever practical or legally satisfactory arrangement for local government was agreed solely between Clerides and Denktash had very limited chances of wider acceptance. This represented a very sensitive issue, and each community was intent on securing an optimal arrangement for itself. Nevertheless, there remained a possibility that if the two interlocutors presented an integrated package of proposals in which concessions on local government were compensated by other elements, then it might be possible to 'sell' it to the respective lobbies.[30]

Background of the second phase

In order to clearly understand why by December 1968 the inter-communal talks were heading into a blind alley, focus must shift to internal political developments within each community and the associated diplomatic activity which determined negotiating techniques. Unlike the Greek-Cypriot side, which until December followed essentially the same tactic, Denktash adopted a new, more complex approach.

This second phase of the talks was bound to be crucial since it would clearly indicate what the two communities were really striving to achieve. Despite the fact that the two negotiators appeared to be discussing in good faith, both communities' opening offers, especially on the most important element of local administration, were boxed into maximalist programmes. Both the Turkish-Cypriot proposals of 16 September and the Greek-Cypriot proposals of 9 December were totally unacceptable to the other party, leading to a very damaging hiatus.

Although Denktash, other moderate leaders and Ankara clearly were pursuing a quick solution, disagreements within the Turkish-Cypriot leadership created several difficulties at this point. Moreover, the Greek-Cypriot position during the previous phase of refraining from any substantial concession had further compromised Denktash's leverage on his colleagues.[31] In an attempt to try and formulate a common position within the Turkish-Cypriot leadership, Denktash was accompanied during his visit to Ankara by the hardliners Orek and Kuchuk.[32] Upon their return, the Turkish-Cypriot position had stiffened further, as reflected in their public statements that highlighted the need for watertight guarantees for the security of Turkish-Cypriots. As before, this tendency soon affected the negotiation itself. On these grounds the Turkish-Cypriot leadership justified its insistence on rejecting any normalization or allowing total freedom of movement throughout the Turkish-Cypriot areas. Concerning the constitutional proposals, Denktash argued that his side did not endorse several of his personal suggestions which, therefore, had to be retracted.[33] This was particularly evident on his 16 September proposals. The Turkish *Chargé d'Affairs* in Nicosia admitted that those proposals did not fully reflect Turkish-Cypriot views and were presented mainly for internal purposes.[34] He explained that although Denktash strongly disagreed, several circles among the Turkish-Cypriot leaders insisted on them. Denktash, however, strove to avoid an open rift with the rest of the leadership and did not want to take responsibility for rejecting them. Hence, he tabled them although he knew that they would be rejected *in toto* by Greek-Cypriots.[35]

During the third meeting of this phase Denktash had also explained to Clerides his reasons for withdrawing their previously agreed points on the judiciary and legislature. More specifically, Denktash complained that unlike Greek-Cypriots, his side had returned with certain proposals both on issues on which common ground already existed and on those on which there was great gap.[36] Conversely, Clerides' instructions entailed continuing to sound out the Turkish-Cypriot views, without making any proposals or commitments. Denktash, however, explained that before the resumption of the negotiations in August, he had with difficulty persuaded some of his colleagues to allow certain flexible proposals to be put to the Greek-Cypriot side on judicial and legislative matters, on the grounds that they would elicit corresponding concessions. By the third meeting of this phase, however, this had not happened and there was a danger of the Turkish-Cypriot line reverting boomerang style in the opposite direction. Therefore, Denktash stated that he was now forced to perceive his side's previous flexible proposals as no longer binding.[37]

Meanwhile, on the Turkish-Cypriot political front several members of the leadership and many extremists and military officials took advantage of this Greek-Cypriot rigidity to spread rumours that the Greek-Cypriots were still bent on *Enosis* and did not genuinely want a solution.[38] Moreover, by exploiting the Greek-Cypriot stand they contended that Denktash's 'soft' tactics during the first phase of the talks had failed.[39] By the end of December, after the Greek-Cypriot proposals on local administration were tabled, the Turkish-Cypriot Provisional Administration ('TCPA') instructed Denktash to inform the Turkish Government that the Turkish-Cypriots recommend the immediate break-off of the inter-communal talks, allowing a new round of discussions between the Greek and the Turkish governments.[40] Denktash had reluctantly transmitted this decision to Ankara, where it was flatly rejected. Nonetheless, the Turkish Government warned Denktash that it would not be able to support him in the event of a final agreement with Clerides if the majority of the Turkish-Cypriot leadership had not endorsed it in advance.

It is also noteworthy that while Denktash was in Ankara in December 1968, rumours circulated that Denktash had proposed to the Turkish Government to use certain provocative tactics, such as the proclamation of the 'TCPA' into a separate government in Cyprus, in order to make Makarios realize the urgent need for concessions. According to these rumours, Ankara rejected this scenario.[41] Although widely spread in the Turkish press, these rumours, it was believed, were likely generated by Denktash himself for two reasons. First, they were directed towards his own critics within the Turkish-Cypriot community in order to prove that Denktash was not as 'soft' as alleged. Second, they were formulated as an indirect threat towards the Greek-Cypriot leadership in order to expose the dangers of the delay in finding a solution.[42]

It was not, however, only the Turkish-Cypriot side that accused the Cyprus Government of causing delays and being unconstructive. Since summer 1968, the Greek foreign minister had persistently warned as to the perceived flaws in the Greek-Cypriot tactic of merely listening to Turkish-Cypriot proposals and rejecting them without advancing counter-proposals. This strategy, he argued, only enabled the Turkish-Cypriots to hold the initiative in shaping proposals and so control the agenda of the talks. It also meant that in the event of an early collapse of the talks, the Greek-Cypriot side would lose the blame game. It was already evident to several outside parties that the Cyprus Government seemed unwilling to provide anything else than minority rights to Turkish-Cypriots.[43] Moreover, by leaving all matters open it already proved that it gave the option to the Turkish-Cypriot side to retract its previous concessions.[44]

Contrary to Pipinelis' suggestions, both Makarios and Kyprianou believed that it was still too soon for them to make binding proposals on any aspect and especially on local administration.[45] By avoiding taking firm positions, Kyprianou explained that they also prevented an early impasse to the talks.[46] Regarding the local administration Makarios argued that since there were substantial points of disagreement on other constitutional elements, the Greek-Cypriot side should not commit itself on an element that was not part of the Zurich–London Agreements.[47] Kyprianou was also confident that the Turkish-Cypriot maximalist proposals of September were likely to be withdrawn soon.[48] Although this technique was widely supported within Makarios' Ministerial Council, it created difficulties in negotiations and dissatisfaction to Clerides, who believed that his community should have taken a more positive and flexible line. Disillusioned, by October 1968 he announced his intention to resign from his post but retracted this once he realized that he would thereby lose any influence over Makarios and the Cabinet.[49]

Despite the admonitions of the Greek foreign minister and the warnings of several moderate members of the Turkish-Cypriot community, it was not until the end of November that the Greek-Cypriot side decided to prepare its counter-proposals. Clerides had by then visited Athens, where Pipinelis gave him a rather strictly worded memorandum for Makarios in which he warned about the dangers of the delay in agreeing on a settlement.[50] This memorandum eventually pinned Makarios down on the highly contentious issue of local administration, and on 9 December 1968 Clerides presented the Greek-Cypriot proposals.

Nevertheless, these were advanced again only for tactical purposes since it was certain that Turkish-Cypriots would immediately reject them. Interestingly, the British High Commission reported that the committee that prepared them consisted of 'two rather ineffectual doves' – the Minister of Justice, Stella Soulioti, and the Director-General of the Ministry of Foreign Affairs, Christodoulos Benjiamin – as well as 'two very effective hawks' – the Minister of Labour, Tassos Papadopoulos, and the Director-General of the Ministry of Interior, Antonakis Anastasiou.[51] The main reasoning behind the maximalist proposals was Makarios' estimation that time was still working in his favour. In order to make Makarios realize the mistake of this approach, Clerides again offered his resignation. Makarios rejected this but agreed that if in the end it proved necessary, some substantial concession to the Turkish-Cypriots might be made.[52]

Another factor that justified the Cyprus Government's continuing inflexibility was a most likely misleading report by the American ambassador in Cyprus. According to Belcher, the main reason behind the hardening of Turkish-Cypriot views during the second phase was Turkey's desire to stall any progress of the negotiations until after the Turkish general elections in autumn 1969.[53] This view, according to the British ambassador in Ankara, was flawed as Belcher had probably misunderstood Ankara's intentions, since the latter was still in favour of a quick settlement of the Cyprus problem.[54] Nonetheless, Belcher's view was disseminated by the Cyprus Government. The British High Commission in Nicosia reported that Belcher's assessment was exploited by the hardliners of the Cyprus Government, who convinced the president that 'it is no good for the Greek-Cypriots to be forthcoming over the local government issue because the Turks will merely pocket any concession which is offered and find some other excuse for delaying actual progress until after next October'.[55] In fact, however, the Turkish elections seemed to have lacked any impact on the formulation of the Turkish-Cypriot proposals for local administration. Both political opponents in Turkey, the then Prime Minister Suleiman Demirel and his opponent, Ismet Inonu, had agreed first that the Cyprus issue should not be used by either party in this electoral campaign and second that whoever was elected would pursue the same policy regarding the degree of Turkish-Cypriot local autonomy.[56] In retrospect, Makarios admitted that his side's estimation had indeed been erroneous.[57] This unanimity in foreign policy matters within Turkish politics (government's and opposition's) was – and still is – not very common within the Greek and Greek-Cypriot political culture.

By this stage the odds of the negotiations having a fruitful outcome were progressively declining. Denktash and Clerides were exhausted and disappointed by their respective leaderships. The delays were causing increasing frustration among both communities and especially among Turkish-Cypriots. Both the Turkish-Cypriot press and various elements of the Turkish-Cypriot leadership accused the Greek-Cypriots of not genuinely seeking a solution. Matters were further complicated when Makarios decided on 30 December to hold a press conference in which he admitted that talks were in 'a state of stagnation' due to the unreasonable Turkish-Cypriot demands aiming at partition or federation.[58] This infuriated the

Turkish-Cypriot leadership, which believed that Makarios had breached the confidential character of the inter-communal talks and was publicly rejecting the Turkish-Cypriot proposals, indicating that he did not intend to compromise.[59] The Turkish *Chargé d'Affairs* in Nicosia explained to Costar,

> It was understood between Clerides and Denktash that they came to the conference table with no pre-conditions on either side. The majority of the Turkish-Cypriot leadership were reasonably happy so long as this remained the basis on which the two negotiators were working. Denktash constantly assured them that Clerides understood and accepted this position. But now they were able to say to Denktash that the Archbishop had in effect imposed conditions by ruling out a particular solution, which was moreover the only sort of solution which they were likely to regard as acceptable. This made life very difficult for Denktash.[60]

With this press conference and the strong reactions of the Turkish-Cypriot side, the second phase of the inter-communal talks ended. Unlike at the end of the first phase, this time there was general disillusionment over the future of the negotiations.

The third phase: January 1969–September 1970

In spite of the difficulties and the 'state of stagnation' at the negotiating table, the local discussions had at least produced a peaceful atmosphere between the two communities. That 'benign stalemate', as the British characterized it, however, was a double-edged sword.[61] The two communities were meanwhile evolving in separate directions and undermining any genuine wish or impulse to replace the existing stalemate with an authentically fresh start.

Sir Norman Costar, before leaving Cyprus in April 1969, commented that the Cypriot people 'are too narrowly concerned with their own political problem whose solution is not made easier by their love of bargaining for its own sake and their tendency to reach firmly held convictions on inadequate and unverified premises often emotional in genesis'.[62] The third phase of the talks had dragged on for a year and a half under three different processes, but none had borne any fruit, mainly due to what Costar explained as 'inadequate and unverified premises' from both sides. Makarios continued to operate under the premise that his side was best advised to wait for two reasons: there was no danger of a Turkish invasion, and the Turkish-Cypriot economy was likely to implode.[63] Nonetheless, the situation on the island was changing, and one of the biggest challenges for the Cyprus Government was to realize the consequences of this transformation. Various political developments were soon to have an even more detrimental impact both on the pace and progress of the inter-communal negotiations.

Progress of the negotiations

The establishment of sub-committees, January–March 1969

As soon as the new phase began, the two interlocutors exchanged proposals about the executive when it again became apparent that the gap on this issue was still wide. On the local administration issue there was yet to be found a suitable basis for discussions, and in order to avoid the deadlock, the two interlocutors decided to add a new procedure. On 3 February 1969 they announced that sub-committees would be established examining technical issues on which there already existed some common ground.

Reaching agreement, however, on the specific mandates of these sub-committees was more difficult than expected. It took almost a month to decide their portfolio and almost two months to initiate actual discussions. Eventually, it was agreed to establish two: one for the legislature dealing with the electoral system and the other to examine Turkish-Cypriot reintegration in parastatal organizations.[64] This development initially afforded some hope that the inter-communal talks were indeed making some progress. Soon disillusionment came. Mistrust and ulterior motives made it again impossible to produce any tangible progress before an *over-all* settlement of the Cyprus problem.

Their initial point of contention concerned the sub-committees' terms of reference. Denktash requested a sub-committee responsible for elements of the parastastal organizations that would have provided substantial benefits to Turkish-Cypriots, such as their gradual reintegration on the basis of 20 per cent representation and the re-activation of normal services in the enclaves.[65] Nonetheless, the Cyprus Government rejected this proposal on the grounds that this was not a constitutional matter. It was a normalization measure that could have been discussed under the existing Political Liaison Committee.[66] For Makarios the Turkish-Cypriot motives were clear,

> Turkish policy was not at present aimed at achieving a constitutional settlement. The Turkish-Cypriots wanted to secure more measures of normalization, improving their economic and social lot at the expense of the Cyprus Government, without making any concessions which would materially affect the separateness of the Turkish-Cypriot community

[…] [He] was very much in favour of normalization but concessions had to be made by both sides and he could not go on indefinitely agreeing to measures of normalization which benefit the Turkish-Cypriots only.[67]

Nonetheless, the Greek-Cypriot tactic had another, deeper meaning. Although Makarios had adopted normalization measures that mainly concerned freedom of movement, he was reluctant to accept genuine normalization and reintegration of the Turkish-Cypriot factor in the state machinery. He still wanted time to force the Turkish-Cypriots to their knees while any real normalization would only serve to put off the implosion that he intended. Needless to say, the reluctance of the Turkish-Cypriots to reciprocate with genuine normalization measures suited Makarios' interests. That reality, however, could hardly be admitted outside a very narrow circle.

In order to avoid another impasse, the two interlocutors agreed that at a first stage this sub-committee would examine only the possibility of the Turkish-Cypriot reintegration in the parastatal organizations while any agreement on the technical aspects would only be implemented given a wider constitutional settlement. Nonetheless, their very strict terms of reference made any substantial progress impossible.

New proposals for local administration, March 1969–August 1969

While discussions on the sub-committees were still ongoing, outside the island there was an increasing concern about the lack of results so far. Pipinelis from Athens was trying through diplomatic channels and public speeches to urge the Cyprus Government to work for an overall settlement before the Turkish elections of October 1969.[68] Afraid about the possibility of an early deadlock in Cyprus, Britain and Greece along with the United States and Canada decided to convince U Thant to exert pressure on the parties and request swift progress.[69] After intense diplomatic activity throughout March in New York and Nicosia, it was finally decided that, in order to avoid prejudicing renewed substantial negotiations, the UN secretary-general would merely send a personal appeal to the Cypriot and Turkish governments expressing concern.[70] Interestingly, the Turkish Foreign Minister, Caglayangil, criticized U Thant's appeal, explaining that it was misdirected because Denktash was receiving instructions from the Turkish-Cypriot leadership and not from Ankara.[71] Thus, this appeal had to be sent to Kuchuk instead.

In March 1969, while seeking to produce fresh momentum to the local discussions, both Osorio-Tafall and the American Ambassador, Belcher, produced draft papers that gave informally to the parties with ideas on a compromise solution for the local administration. Although both sets of proposals were similar, Osorio-Tafall's ideas, on the one hand, were closer to the Turkish-Cypriot requests because, in general, they provided a Turkish minister of interior responsible for the central local authorities.[72] The US ideas, on the other hand, were more balanced, providing a Greek minister of interior and a Turkish deputy-minister, each responsible for the respective Greek and Turkish central local authorities.[73] Both suggestions, however, were rejected by the parties.

Almost simultaneously and mainly due to Pipinelis, Makarios decided to instruct Clerides to prepare new proposals on local autonomy. These proposals were slightly more flexible than those of 9 December, and the Greek foreign minister seemed to be satisfied, explaining that he would do his best to convince his counterpart in Turkey to endorse them.[74] Nevertheless, due to the previous hostile reaction of Turkey to the substance of the US proposals – which were definitely more flexible – Clerides expressed his concern to Pipinelis that presenting them now was most likely premature.[75] The latter, however, explained that after the four-month hiatus, the Greek-Cypriot side should now take the lead and get things moving again. This would provide an important tactical advantage, for if the inter-communal talks ended in deadlock, as was generally feared, the burden of the failure would fall on the Turkish-Cypriot side.[76] Hence, this element was of the utmost importance to Pipinelis.

According to the new Greek-Cypriot proposals, presented on 24 April, local government was still formulated based on administrative rather than political criteria.[77] Each village remained the basic unit and the first tier of local government. Nevertheless, it was now accepted that in the second tier there would be a grouping of villages, not based on racial criteria, as the Turkish-Cypriots suggested, but rather on the principle of geographical proximity, embracing a similarity of administrative, economic and social problems. Finally, the Districts would constitute the third tier while all three levels would be supervised by the State through a District commissioner.[78] When informing Denktash about these new proposals, Clerides asserted,

> I don't wish to mislead you and, therefore, I want to emphasize that as far as the proposed structure is concerned, this is the last step which the Government is willing to take. Of course, the question of the functions and the delineation of the areas is a matter on which some flexibility may be shown.[79]

Indeed, when the new proposals were submitted, Pipinelis explained to Caglayangil that it was an achievement for the Greeks to convince Makarios to make such concessions and that if the Turkish-Cypriot side failed to respond, there would be no further chances to convince Makarios to make any more concessions.[80] Not only were the revised proposals rejected by the Turkish-Cypriot leadership,[81] but they once again led to a new debate over the immediate break-off of the talks.[82] Although the Turkish Government agreed that the proposals were unacceptable, it urged the Turkish-Cypriots to advance counter-proposals in order to prevent deadlock.[83]

Denktash had first to defuse aroused public opinion and the extremists before making counter-proposals.[84] Second, he admitted that some members of the 'TCPA' were infiltrating the press with unhelpful comments and statements, thus complicating his task. For that reason, Denktash decided that henceforth only he would claim authority to make public statements on the negotiations' progress. Meanwhile, he believed that the best procedure for the moment was merely to seek further clarifications from Clerides. The new counter-proposals were eventually presented a few months later, on 11 August.

The new Turkish-Cypriot counter-offer repeated its previous views over the structure, functions and state supervision of local governance.[85] Clerides admitted that there was one positive element within Denktash's response: His proposals, for the first time, talked of a 'gradualist approach' to the Cyprus problem. Denktash explained that the Turkish-Cypriots wanted iron-clad guarantees regarding the new settlement because they feared absorption by the Greek majority. However, he added that if a solution was agreed upon and implemented, after some years fair play and justice would be restored, dispelling the fears and suspicion of both communities.[86] When such a point was reached, all contentions could be resolved once and for all. According to Clerides, this suggested that in some distant future his community would get the type of state they wanted.[87] He recognized, however, that such a scenario was not yet available because

> Makarios would never again sign a constitutional document which looked as though it gave the Turkish-Cypriots such a privileged position that the unitary nature of the state was endangered. The Archbishop was concerned with the opinions of ordinary Greek-Cypriots, and particularly with the opinions of a vociferous minority of them, who did not appreciate arguments about 'evolutionary growth'. And the Archbishop took formal documents literally: he saw things as the text described them and a text based on anything like Denktash's proposals would not look good [to him].[88]

After this set of proposals the inter-communal talks were again at a standstill. Clerides and Denktash decided to resume their confidential discussions on a personal basis only.[89] But the danger of the discussions running completely into the sand was now real. For that reason, the Greek-Cypriot interlocutor decided on 1 September to officially restate his side's proposals on local government, in order to produce a clear-cut proof that his side had indeed been aiming for a compromise.[90] When Denktash received this letter, he realized that it was a 'grandstand play' directed to public opinion and he feared that this might mean that the two negotiators were 'reaching the end of the line.'[91]

Seeking a fresh approach

By October 1969, the two interlocutors came to the conclusion that they had exhausted every margin for discussion regarding local administration and that there was no more room for concessions. The talks remained at a standstill for two months. Notably, Clerides and Denktash had already managed to agree on the functions of the local authorities while the remaining stumbling blocks were the local administration's structure and the degree of the state control.[92] In truth, after the one small step ahead made by the Greek-Cypriot proposals of 24 April, the ball was now in the Turkish-Cypriot court. Meanwhile, both Pipinelis and the re-elected Government of Demirel were urging the parties to continue the inter-communal dialogue and try to avoid deadlock at all costs.

Osorio-Tafall in September unofficially intervened and suggested a new approach, discussing all other elements *except* local government.[93] Moreover, he proposed that elements of an administrative and economic nature should now be discussed in order to practically enhance inter-communal cooperation. Although the chances of this approach succeeding were limited, it was the only viable alternative. Pipinelis also suggested to the Cyprus Government that it ought to use its economic muscle to foster inter-communal cooperation in the administrative and economic sectors in order to produce a practical incentive for Turkish-Cypriots.[94] Even though the Turkish-Cypriot leadership had been extremely cautious, opening up the 'tap' of the Cyprus Government's money or technical help to the enclaves would have gradually brought the Turkish-Cypriots closer to the idea of a quick settlement. There were already encouraging signs, coming especially from the agricultural and private sectors where inter-communal cooperation since 1968 had been enhanced, that a coordinated government policy targeting normalization in economic and administrative sectors could have indeed proved fruitful.[95] Nonetheless, this tactic would have meant further normalization and this still had little appeal to most Greek-Cypriot leaders and especially to Makarios. Moreover, for Turkish-Cypriots it would have meant a practical delay of their plans for separate economic development. As expected, neither community took genuine measures towards that end.

After a two-month break, the two negotiators met again on 1 December 1969. Denktash proposed that the issue of local administration should be set aside, as Osorio-Tafall suggested, and try instead to work on two parallel exercises: (1) the re-examination of all constitutional issues, except local government, on the assumption that an agreement could not be reached on the latter and (2) all constitutional elements on the presumption that the 1960 system of local government would be maintained – that is, at a village level – with the difference that the local councils would be elected and not appointed by the interior minister.[96]

While both negotiators started to work on this fresh idea, they were soon forced to abandon it. Denktash came under strong criticism from the Turkish-Cypriot leadership for making an unacceptable concession by accepting this procedure, while Ankara was concerned about the marginalization of the local government question. When he was notified of Denktash's internal difficulties and the implications that these might cause for the discussions, Makarios instructed Clerides to inform Denktash that the first exercise – to discuss all issues except local government – was unacceptable because Turkish-Cypriots would try to wring several concessions from Greek-Cypriots and then renew their unacceptable local government demands. Conversely, the only acceptable basis for Makarios was for local government to remain on the 1959–1960 basis, provided that all the concessions made by Denktash on the other constitutional issues were still valid.[97] This was naturally rejected by the Turkish-Cypriot side. In order to avoid the new deadlock, the two interlocutors tried to work again for a compromise on the judiciary, believing still that it was the only element that was easier to accommodate.[98] If they could reach an agreement on this, they could finally present some concrete results to the public opinion, thus giving another kiss of life to the faltering negotiations.

Throughout March 1970 there were serious developments within the Greek-Cypriot community which inevitably led to the slower pace of the inter-communal talks. The growth of the extreme nationalist movement and its underground activities led to the assassination attempt against Makarios and a week later to the assassination of Yorkadjis. This book will not analyse the events that led to these two developments, since these are studied elsewhere.[99] Nevertheless, what is illustrated in our study is that the internal developments created a new challenge for the two sides regarding the inter-communal talks: The Turkish-Cypriot side was going to increase its public demands for further guarantees on security aspects while the Greek-Cypriots were not in a position to appear weak by making concessions.

After the assassination attempt, Makarios announced that parliamentary elections would take place in July 1970. This was bound to hamper the negotiators from having any substantial exchanges; thus, Clerides and Denktash decided instead to focus on a stock-taking exercise. In May 1970 they agreed to draft a joint paper presenting their points of agreement and disagreement hitherto on all constitutional aspects. This was necessary for two reasons: first, to summarize what had been achieved so far, and second, to provide the basis for a subsequent package deal. According to Clerides the two sides 'would have looked into the five items in the joint document as a whole, to see whether concessions on one could be balanced by gains on another.'[100] This long, joint paper, prepared by mid-August 1970, covered the five main topics, of the judiciary, police, legislature, executive and local government. The different approach and philosophies on all aspects were evident throughout, but local government was clearly the most complex.[101] The two sides did not even agree on the title of this section. With the presentation of this paper the third phase of the local talks dragged to an end.

Preparing for the next phase

Before the official closing of the longest phase of the negotiations, there was an unfortunate development. The architect of the moderate policy of Greece towards Cyprus and the one who had established a very friendly and constructive cooperation with his counterpart in Ankara, Panayiotis Pipinelis, died in July 1970. The British ambassador in Athens ominously commented in 1968, 'I am quite confident that as long as Papadopoulos and Pipinelis are in control of Greek domestic foreign policy, the question of *Enosis* can be considered dead.'[102] That was indeed a very important reality both for the initiation and for the development of the talks. Since his appointment in November 1967 until his death, Pipinelis believed in a pragmatic approach towards the Cyprus problem and tried to convince the Greek and Greek-Cypriot leadership about its necessity.

By August 1970, Makarios decided to follow one of the suggestions that Pipinelis made long before he died. The latter suggested that the Greek-Cypriot side should prepare a 'concessions paper' in which it would clearly state the maximum number of concessions it could offer in various negotiating contingencies.[103] In that way, Clerides would have clear instructions on what he could offer in a possible package deal and so quicken the pace of the talks.

Makarios, therefore, prepared this document, which covered all constitutional aspects except local government. This was to be completed by Clerides.[104] Surprisingly, however, Makarios drafted this memorandum in a notably moderate fashion.[105] Nonetheless, the guidelines he gave to Clerides about the local government still had traces of intransigence. The main Turkish-Cypriot demand for a central local authority organ was flatly rejected. Clerides explained that Makarios would have never accepted the latter point while he also knew that equally Turkish-Cypriots would have never waived from this. For tactical reasons, therefore, Makarios was willing to appear flexible on all other issues, 'since he was pretty sure that he would never be called upon to honour the bargain'.[106]

Unlike Makarios, Denktash was not willing to make any concessions at the opening of the next phase.[107] According to the Cyprus Government's intelligence, the Turkish-Cypriots decided to take a hard line because of the internal turmoil within the Greek-Cypriot community. They overestimated the Archbishop's insecurity due to the growing split within the Greek-Cypriot community, the gradual regrouping of pro-*Enosis* forces and the erroneous belief that Athens was now considering displacing Makarios.[108] However, Caglayangil had again warned Denktash to keep the negotiations alive at all costs. The Greco-Turkish understanding was that as long as there was no other alternative, negotiations should not break down no matter the difficulties.

Internal developments

The third phase of the inter-communal talks coincided with one of the most eventful periods of the Cyprus problem: the birth of four new political parties along with the emergence of several extremist organizations, the first democratic parliamentary elections for ten years and the gradual consolidation of the 'TCPA' along with the primacy of Denktash within his community. In dealing with this period it will be important to connect developments at the negotiating table with those on the ground.

Formation of Greek-Cypriot political parties

In February 1969 the political scenery of Cyprus changed overnight with the more or less simultaneous creation of four new political parties. Although there were from time to time efforts to create political parties, for nine years Progressive Party of Working People (AKEL) had remained the only coherent political party. Despite its electoral strength, however, it had always operated in Makarios' shadow. Most importantly, this was due to the 'stifling' effect of Makarios' and the Church's role on the island. Makarios' political predominance along with his posture that he was above politics essentially undermined the orthodox cultivation of the political consciousness within his constituency.[109] By 1969, however, things had changed. As will be explained below, this modest politicization was to a degree instigated by Makarios himself in order to avoid losing total control over the island's politics.

First, on 5 February Glafkos Clerides along with Polikarpos Yorkadjis announced their intention to establish the Unified Party, a centre-right wing party which belonged in the pro-government camp and favoured an independent unitary state and supported the inter-communal talks. Second, on the same day, Vassos Lyssarides announced the formation of his own socialist party, Unified Democratic Union of the Centre (EDEK), again a supporter of Makarios' policies. Two days later, Nikos Sampson announced the creation of the Progressive Party, which held a pro-*Enosis* line but simultaneously supported the continuation of the current constitutional talks.[110] Meanwhile, Andreas Azinas, the leader of PEK (Pancyprian Farmers Association) (*Παναγροτική Ένωση Κύπρου*), the Farmer's Union, and the governor of the cooperative movement, with Makarios' encouragement, worked on the sidelines to establish the fourth party, the Progressive Front. The official leader of the party was the Mayor of Nicosia, Odysseas Ioannides. Similar in aims to Sampson's party, the Progressive Front was nonetheless under Makarios' total control. There were several ideological and political differences between all these parties but they all supported Makarios' Government, since this was a prerequisite for popular support.[111] Indicative was the fact that during the elections of 1970, each party competed to prove itself the most devoted supporter of Makarios.[112]

The main questions deriving from the formation of these political parties concerned their timing, Makarios' reaction and their effect on inter-communal talks. Also relevant here are the repercussions of Yorkadjis' resignation from his post as minister of interior in November 1968 due to his alleged involvement in the assassination attempt of Colonel George Papadopoulos in Greece. After the turmoil following this event, Belcher accurately remarked that 'the net result of the Yorkadjis affair in the domestic political arena will probably be to make political life much more "political".[113] Although Yorkadjis was disappointed that Makarios had sacrificed him then, it was nonetheless reported that there had been an understanding between them, with Makarios declaring Parliamentary elections after which Yorkadjis would return to Greek-Cypriot politics. Belcher believed that Yorkadjis would grasp the opportunity to form an anti-Communist party, as he had long since intended to do.[114]

Clerides admitted that he also favoured a counter-weight of AKEL and a consequent reduction of the church's involvement in politics. Moreover, it was no secret that he was discouraged about the progress of the inter-communal talks and disillusioned by the short-sighted strategy of President Makarios. He believed that a right-wing party with wide popular support would be the only way to increase his own standing among Greek-Cypriots and his influence on Makarios.[115] It was already apparent that the various forces formed in Parliament since independence, and now seemingly unified under the Patriotic Front, were actually in disarray. Their common denominator, Makarios, who had brought them together in 1959, was no longer able to keep them under the same roof. Therefore, the Clerides-Yorkadjis collaboration, although peculiar due to their very different political personalities, was 'a marriage of convenience'.[116] Yorkadjis had influence throughout the island, while his 'rural organization of village groups was strong enough to provide a skeletal electoral machine, something which Clerides completely lacked'.[117] Despite Turkish-Cypriot concerns over Yorkadjis' past military record on the national issue, Clerides had assured Denktash that Yorkadjis was fully supportive of Clerides' views and aims.[118]

The announcement of the Clerides–Yorkadjis' initiative was arguably crucial in sparking the formation of all the other parties. There was little doubt that Makarios was opposed to this development. He reluctantly accepted Clerides–Yorkadjis decision but worked discreetly in order to prevent them from gaining enough political power that could have circumscribed his, hitherto unchallenged political authority. This most likely was among the reasons that Makarios encouraged Azinas to work for the creation of another right-wing party.[119] Several diplomatic circles also reported that Clerides had tried unsuccessfully to convince Azinas to join forces with him.[120]

Makarios, at least publicly, welcomed these developments within his community. Nonetheless, he instructed his ministers not to participate in any party as such. The Greek Government and Pipinelis were likewise concerned. They believed that such formations would hinder Makarios' position in his community, reduce Clerides' standing as Greek-Cypriot negotiator and divide the Greek-Cypriot community. All of these could have undermined progress of the talks. This fear, however, did not come to fruition. In spite of this feverish political activity in February 1969, the basic political stasis remained until the end of 1969, when it was finally decided that elections would take place sometime in 1970.

The National Front and the government's stance

Although the creation of the parties was a move towards the modernization and potential democratization of the Greek-Cypriot politics, a major setback to that goal, detrimentally impacting the peacemaking process, occurred almost simultaneously. Makarios' declaration of support for a 'feasible policy' of independence in January 1968, the initiation of inter-communal negotiations on that basis, the forthcoming parliamentary elections and the formation of political parties could only mean that an independence mentality was being further consolidated within the Greek-Cypriot community. By the same token, it appeared that the goal of *Enosis* was being shelved for good. Yet, various segments of the Greek-Cypriot population failed to grasp the futility of the *Enosis* aim and decided to force the government to restore this national goal through extremist organizations.[121] In March 1969 these underground formations made their first appearance. Their aims were mainly to terrorize, punish and politically eliminate those who were not working towards *Enosis* and who sought to cultivate a 'Cypriot consciousness'.[122] Throughout spring and summer 1969 they distributed pamphlets and instigated physical attacks against various high-profile members of the government, while bombs were left outside government buildings. There were several small terrorist groups behind those actions but the most important of them all was the so-called National Front.[123]

By the summer of 1969, the inter-communal negotiations ground to a halt and a renewal of violence in the name of *Enosis* had been initiated among the Greek-Cypriot community. *The Guardian* particularly commented that 'the long lull in progress towards a Cyprus settlement is producing the Greek-Cypriot factionalism that the moderate politicians feared. Underground groups, recapturing the heady days of their struggle against Britain, are proliferating and turning to violence'.[124] Nonetheless, the Cyprus Government underestimated this threat and its implications on the negotiations. Likewise, President Makarios overestimated his ability to convince the extremists to dissolve through mere exhortation and the use of his own personal prestige as the *Ethnarch* of the Greeks of Cyprus.[125] 'The more his secular legitimacy was questioned, the more he relied on his religious role as representative of all Greek-Cypriots', Sant Cassia explains.[126] Nonetheless, Makarios' reliance upon his ethnaric role, 'his once powerful weapon for his imposition as an undisputable President, was by now the Achilles' heel of the presidential role'.[127]

Both Denktash and several foreign representatives in Cyprus were constantly expressing to the Greek-Cypriot leaders their intense concern and warned them about the negative repercussions of this situation. Although on 28 August the National Front was declared illegal and in December certain actions were taken to confront this threat, these were ineffective. By January 1970 the British High Commissioner, Peter Ramsbotham, commented,

> It is clear that the National Front is not the fragmented collection of thugs, on whom the Cyprus Government were liable to crack down at any moment, which the Archbishop tried to lead me to suppose [was the case] during various conversations last year. The implications for

the Cyprus internal situation, and more widely the Cyprus problem, are disturbing.[128]

The National Front was dissolved after an armed raid on the Police Headquarters in Limassol in May 1970 and the ensuing trial of several of its members.[129] It was a fact, however, that although short-lived, the National Front actions had a further impact. By mid-1970 it had disrupted internal security, opened the door for the exiled Grivas' return to the island's politics and spread the seeds for the formation of National Organization of Cypriot Fighters (EOKA) B a year later. The troubles created among the majority community on the island inevitably led a few years later to a decline in inter-communal relations which rudely shattered the peaceful efforts for settlement.

The Turkish-Cypriots did not lose time, attempting to capitalize on this unstable situation within the Greek-Cypriot community by holding that their demands for increased local autonomy within their own areas with a separate police force were entirely justified. They claimed that the Greek-Cypriot authorities had failed to maintain law and order within their own areas and thus would also be unable to exert effective control on the Turkish-Cypriot areas in the event of any settlement. As time was passing and the situation among the Greek-Cypriot community was deteriorating, the Turkish-Cypriot stance was becoming more and more inflexible, while the Cyprus Government's ability to make any concessions was undermined by its own internal problems.

Additionally, the government's indecisiveness concerning these extremist movements proved to be a significant mistake with one severe long-term side effect. The *Enosis* drum was beating again among Greek-Cypriots and seeds of division were spreading. Various segments of the Greek-Cypriot community, especially the unsophisticated villagers, appeared to be sympathetic, if not to the actions of the National Front, then to its aims and goals. Ramsbotham observed that 'no-one ever appears to witness who distributes National Front leaflets in the villages although everyone has copies, very much what happened over E.O.K.A leaflets during the Emergency'.[130] The assassination attempt against Makarios on 8 March 1970 and the assassination of Yorkadjis ten days later, attended by rumours of the involvement of several Greek army officers, confirmed that the situation was getting out of hand.

The rise of nationalistic feeling, still controllable at the moment, constrained Makarios' room for manoeuvre, making him even keener to avoid accusations from the extreme right. As Clerides was later to emphasize repeatedly, Makarios was not willing to move in any direction unless he was sure of public support.[131] Makarios' tendency to avoid swimming against the current led him to give speeches to arouse nationalistic sentiments within his community. In several of his speeches he still highlighted the undying national goal of *Enosis* while helping to inflame Greek-Cypriot public opinion by making references to what he depicted as devious Turkish-Cypriot plans to divide the island. Above all, he consistently referred to the bleak prospects of the inter-communal talks due to Turkey's inflexible position, re-assuring his audience that he would not make any more concessions since these would entail national dangers for Greek-Cypriots.[132] Both the Turkish and Greek governments, therefore, pressed Makarios to tone down his own rhetoric.[133] Meanwhile, similar provocative statements were also made by the Cabinet's hawks, such as the new Minister of Interior, Epaminondas Komodromos, and the Minister of Education, Constantinos Spyridakis. Clerides told the British high commissioner that although he intended to protest about these statements to the Ministerial Council, Makarios more likely was not going to support him since the latter preferred to allow his ministers to say whatever they wanted in order to test out public reactions.[134] The rekindling of the *Enosis* rhetoric inevitably sabotaged Clerides' constant efforts to dispel Turkish-Cypriot doubts about the good intentions of his side and the prospect that a unitary settlement could indeed guarantee their rights without being at the mercy of Greek-Cypriots.

Nationalistic sentiment was further aroused by a series of press reports throughout the summer of 1969 concerning increased military preparations within the Turkish-Cypriot sector. It was indeed true that a crisis sparked in Turkey in late May 1969 had encouraged Turkish-Cypriot hawks of taking a more aggressive posture within the 'TCPA'.[135] Information about partition plans had been transmitted from the Intelligence Service of Cyprus to the Presidential Palace. This intelligence, based on a 'reliable Turkish-Cypriot source', asserted that Turkish-Cypriots were preparing the ground for military partition.[136] Irrespective of whether those reports were indeed reliable or not (and they probably were not), it seemed that Makarios was convinced of their validity and this inevitably affected his decision making.

In closing this section, we may reflect on Denktash's outburst to the British high commissioner about Makarios' speech on 24 August 1969, which brought Denktash, as he stated, into a very difficult situation. As the high commissioner reported, Denktash was particularly furious because

> Makarios again accused the Turkish-Cypriot leaders [...] of pursuing 'federation and partition plans'. Denktash said that the Archbishop's statements and the most recent one in particular had exposed him to considerable pressure from the hard-liners on his own side. Already this week he had received nine delegations which had come to congratulate

him on his reconversion to the idea of partition and to seek his approval
for their plans for increasing the separation of the Turkish community
from the Greek Cypriots in the particular fields in which they operated.
[...] [Makarios'] statements continuously undermined the basis [of the
talks] on which Denktash conducted them and gave encouragement to
extremists of both sides. It was essential that the Archbishop should, at
least in public, accept the official statements of the Turkish Government
policy and the views of the Turkish-Cypriot leadership at their face
value.[137]

Interestingly, during this period both Ankara and Turkish-Cypriot leaders
were praised by the British for their moderate and 'statesmanlike reaction'
on all the provocations issuing from the Greek-Cypriot leaders and press.[138]
If there was indeed a blame game in motion, the Turkish-Cypriot side had
scored once again.

Elections 1970

Against this background, both Makarios and the Greek Government accepted
that parliamentary elections should no longer be postponed; thus, they were
scheduled for 5 July 1970. Extremely worried, however, that an electoral
campaign would increase tension among his community, Makarios tried to
sound out whether he could convince all parties that supported him to enter a
pact over seats, similar to the 1960 understanding with AKEL and the Patriotic
Front. Although he acknowledged that it was undemocratic, Makarios believed
that under the current circumstances, such a pre-arrangement would prevent
any further division among his community. Especially after the assassination
attempt against his life, Makarios was at pains to convince Clerides above all
to accept a number of seats that would give his party a narrow majority in
Parliament.[139] It was evident that Makarios wanted to achieve a distribution
of seats that would enable him to retain his complete control. AKEL initially
accepted Makarios' offer of five seats; this did not represent its public support,
but was in line with the party's desire at the moment to avoid responsibility.
Makarios also retained close contacts with Ioannides' Progressive Front, the
only serious rival of Clerides' Unified Party in the forthcoming elections.

Although Yorkadjis' death in March 1970 and the scandal over his
involvement in the assassination attempt on Makarios had affected the
electoral strength of the Unified Party, Clerides rejected Makarios' offer.
His aim since 1968 had been to rival Makarios' absolute control within
Parliament.[140] Therefore, Clerides insisted on rejecting any pact if that did

not give a clear majority to one party.[141] Therefore, Makarios' attempts to secure a wide pre-electoral agreement failed. It should be noted, however, that almost on the eve of the elections, Sampson's apparently weak party merged with Ioannides' Progressive Front. It is noteworthy that Clerides revealed to the British high commissioner that although he had tried before the elections to form between his party and the Progressive Front 'a solid bulwark against the communists', it was Makarios that undermined his efforts. Clerides explained,

> He had recently access to the minutes of the post-mortem meeting of the Progressive Front from which it was clear that the Archbishop had not really encouraged their close cooperation with Clerides' party against both the communists and the extreme right-wing forces. On the contrary, the Archbishop had made certain half promises which had not been fulfilled and which were now causing much resentment in the Progressive Front. Some of Clerides' own UP followers were also feeling bitterness against the Archbishop.[142]

Despite Makarios' concerns and Grivas' messages from Athens to Greek-Cypriots to boycott them, on 5 July 1970 elections did take place uneventfully. Clerides' Unified Party (UP) gained fifteen of thirty-five seats, the Progressive Front seven, EDEK two, AKEL nine and two independent candidates were also elected. The most significant part of these elections was first that AKEL won the majority of the votes and managed to elect all of its nine candidates and second that EDEK's candidates benefitted by the way that AKEL was represented in these elections.[143] Although Clerides' party won the majority of the Parliaments seats, he still failed to establish UP as an effective political counter-balance to Makarios' dominance.

Just a week before the elections, Makarios decided on a major ministerial reshuffle. He retained only the Foreign Minister, Kyprianou; Interior Minister, Komodromos; and the Finance Minister, Andreas Patsalides. It was reported that Makarios initially intended to appoint another minister of interior since Komodromos had already caused several problems for the government with his public speeches, but the Abbot of Kykko Monastery, who exerted significant influence on Makarios, urged the president to retain Komodromos.[144] The balance between the hawks and the doves in the Cabinet remained the same, while Makarios decided to appoint Dr Ihsan Ali as his personal advisor. This infuriated the Turkish-Cypriots and gave further credence to their demand for separate electoral rolls for the parliamentary elections.

Turkish-Cypriot internal developments

The most important characteristic of this period for the Turkish-Cypriot side was a gradual diminution of the previous urgency for a settlement. The 'TCPA' had focused on the strengthening of its administrative structures, trying to find ways to finance its needs. By 1970 it managed to extend its control over the 12–13 per cent of the island in which the Turkish-Cypriot community, according to Denktash, had 'independent administration, security forces, courts, taxation system and everything else'.[145] In spite of this structural development, Turkish-Cypriots still had enormous economic and social problems and were inevitably dependent on Ankara.

Throughout 1968–1969, dissatisfaction steadily increased among the Turkish-Cypriot community regarding the continuation of economic hardships and unemployment. The Turkish-Cypriot student movement and the graduates returning from Ankara, along with the strikes of the school teachers, were only some of the problems of the 'TCPA'. The press reports and public debates about economic and political scandals within the 'TPCA' also inflamed public debate concerning the ineffectiveness of the old Turkish-Cypriot leadership.[146] In their effort to tackle these problems, the 'TCPA' along with Ankara tried to promote the economic development of the enclaves by increased financial support from Turkey and the establishment of various new economic and administrative structures.[147] As already seen in May 1968, the 'TCPA' decided to establish a committee for economic development, later constituted as an Economic Planning Bureau. This was designed to produce a plan for industrial development and improvements in the agricultural sector. Moreover, a five-year development plan for the period 1969–1974 was drafted along with a separate 'TCPA' development budget of £500,000 per annum.[148] There were also reports that the 'TCPA' approached several countries and organizations in order to gain technical and economic support for its development plan. Meanwhile, it intended to issue its own bonds that would have been mainly available to wealthy Turkish-Cypriots abroad, as another measure to cover its financial needs.[149] Turkey also instructed that there should be reductions in military expenditure with the savings directed to other sectors of the administration.[150] It is also noteworthy that the size of the Executive Council of the 'TCPA' was reduced from nine to eight members to reduce its administrative cost.[151]

Ramsbotham's report on the economic planning of the Turkish-Cypriot leadership explained that the Turkish-Cypriot leaders had to realize that only economic reintegration could have saved them from permanently being second-class citizens in Cyprus.[152] Unfortunately, however, 'there have been disturbing signs that what the leadership desire is not economic parity for their community but economic separateness for its own sake'.[153] Such an impulse became clearer by the end of 1969 and into 1970, when a discussion took place between the two negotiators regarding the increase of inter-communal cooperation in economic and administrative sectors of the island. Although the Greek-Cypriot side was not willing to make any generous proposals, the Turkish-Cypriot leaders were now also reluctant to take any radical action that would mean freezing their own economic and development plans. Their official justification was that the proposals or efforts made by the Greek-Cypriot side to increase the economic inter-communal cooperation were aiming at absorbing them into the majority.[154]

Preserving their separateness for security reasons, therefore, was an intensifying theme of the public speeches of Turkish-Cypriot leaders. When UNFICYP officials and Osorio-Tafall himself tried to convince Turkish-Cypriots to allow some freedom of movement in their areas, they stubbornly refused to do so on such grounds. By the end of 1969, Osorio-Tafall, greatly discouraged by the situation, started to question whether the presence of UNFICYP on the island was doing more harm than good. As he pessimistically noted to the American, Canadian and British diplomats, he had serious doubts about the real Turkish motives in Cyprus explaining,

> He had made his contribution to the extraction of various concessions from the Greek Cypriot side. The lot of the Turkish-Cypriots had been improved and, incidentally, their military situation had benefited. But the Turks had given nothing in return and had not even bothered to answer UNFICYP's recent proposals in the field of military deconfrontation. Things had got to the stage where it could be argued that his activities favoured the Turkish side.[155]

Their only concession came in August 1969 when Turkish-Cypriots offered Greek-Cypriots, for tactical reasons, limited use of the Kyrenia-Nicosia road that they controlled.

In July 1970, simultaneous elections took place within the enclaves for the fifteen seats in the Parliament and the fifteen seats in the Communal Chamber. Like Makarios, Ankara wanted a pre-electoral pact in order to prevent the emergence of any political rivals to Denktash. For this reason, it prohibited the formation of political parties under the pretext of maintaining the unity of the community. Ahmet Berberoglu, in particular, tried twice before the elections to establish his own opposition left-wing Republican Turkish Party and at both times Ankara stopped him.[156] Although not re-elected, he was able to formally establish this party after the elections. Denktash was the key figure of the electoral campaign and all candidates had to sign up under his electoral manifesto: the National Solidary Programme.[157] All these candidates formed a loose political grouping, like the 1960 Patriotic Front, designated the National Formation. This Formation's manifesto was wide enough to be accepted by the majority of the Turkish-Cypriot community, except for some extreme voices. Naturally, the main key in his programme was the importance of their economic development, while it also highlighted the need for a solution that would permanently close the door to *Enosis*.[158]

As expected, Denktash managed to gain an overwhelming majority, making him from this point on the unchallenged leader within his community. Nonetheless, due to the way the inter-communal talks had evolved and the revival of the *Enosis* campaign among Greek-Cypriots, Denktash was not about to express any signs of moderation thereafter. Indeed, a high-ranking Turkish diplomat who visited Cyprus in June 1970 reported that 'he had found the Turkish-Cypriots much less impatient [for settlement] than in the past'.[159]

The fourth phase: September 1970–September 1971

The fourth phase of talks will open on 21 September. The omens for success are not good. *A hesitant Greek Government, a weak Turkish Government, an embattled Turkish-Cypriot community and an obstinate and ingenious Archbishop, are not the right ingredients for settlement.* Even so, the next round will have more substance than seemed possible a few months ago, and the deliberations in and between Athens and Ankara may give them some added impetus. It is at least encouraging that 'package deal' is now becoming part of the accepted vocabulary.[160]

With these words, Peter Ramsbotham set the background of the last phase of this first round of talks, which was to end unsuccessfully a year later. The pace of the talks was now further reduced; the two interlocutors decided to have their meetings once a fortnight. The discussions on the constitutional elements were also reduced, as Denktash tried to focus on other elements such as the resettlement of the displaced Turkish-Cypriots and civil servants' compensation. One of the most important characteristics of this phase was the intensification of unhelpful public statements from both sides. The terms *Enosis* and 'functional federal administrative system' were now on Denktash's agenda. Turkey's domestic problems led to a tougher posture of the Turkish-Cypriot side in general, while Makarios had to focus on two internal fronts: the worsening Athens–Nicosia relations and the internal division of his community.

Progress of the negotiations

Package deal

The new formula that would be used by the Greek-Cypriot side was the so-called package solution. A few days before the re-activation of the negotiations, Makarios visited Athens and both governments seemingly agreed on their next steps and the concessions they would make in order to avoid the early break-off of the talks. They agreed, among other considerations, to the retaining of the Vice-President's office without veto powers, and to an examination of: (a) the grouping of villages on ethnic criteria; (b) which of the functions proposed by the Turkish-Cypriots for the central local government authority were not in conflict with the concept of the unitary state; and (c) whether the Turkish communal chamber could be used as a coordinating body.[161] Nonetheless, Clerides stated that when Makarios returned to Cyprus, members of his Cabinet and his entourage disagreed with the Athens–Nicosia understanding, especially on the latter three points.[162]

Although this disagreement caused delay, Clerides prepared this package deal on the basis of this Athens–Nicosia understanding and handed it over to Denktash on 30 November 1970. From this new set of proposals, the Greek-Cypriot side for the first time conceded to three points about which it had hitherto been intransigent: the retention of the vice-presidency; separate electoral rolls and the grouping of villages based on communal criteria. All these concessions hinged on certain concessions by the Turkish-Cypriot side. This, however, constituted a genuine effort on the part of the Greek-Cypriot negotiator to produce a promising basis for further negotiations.[163]

Paradoxically, this was the only set of proposals that the Greek-Cypriot side had 'protected' from the press, while the government officially had insisted that it was not intending to make any new proposals anytime soon.[164] These proposals represented the Greek-Cypriot negotiator's most constructive effort to place the talks on the right track; perhaps by avoiding any early leakage, Clerides aimed to avoid any public statements or unnecessary debates that would have destroyed this advantage. It was not until 17 January 1971 that Clerides admitted publicly that his side tabled proposals but without giving any details.[165] According to Clerides' explanation to Ramsbotham, he had not yet received permission from Makarios to submit these proposals. Nevertheless, he believed that Denktash seemed in a position to respond positively, and he thus decided to 'chance his arm'.[166]

Two weeks later Denktash offered his personal thoughts on Clerides' proposals. The former acknowledged that his community's demand for a central authority organ would have never been accepted by the Greek-Cypriot side. However, a compromise reflecting two politically equal communities in Cyprus was needed and the new settlement must clearly illustrate this partnership status.[167] To this end, Denktash made two suggestions following, however, the same intransigent path. These were naturally rejected by the Greek-Cypriot side.[168] Nevertheless, the most important element to be highlighted in his response was his remark that 'the aim of his side was to achieve a functional federal administrative system, since geographical federation does not seem possible'.[169] For the first time, Denktash was openly manipulating the term of the 'unitary state', used during the previous three rounds of the talks, in order to justify his side's now open demand for a functional federation.

Denktash, however, confirmed that he would discuss with the rest of the Turkish-Cypriot leadership and Ankara in order to formulate a comprehensive response to the 30 November proposals. Notwithstanding that, before leaving to Ankara he explained that he had held meetings with various sections of his community in order to 'elicit some indication of a wish for settlement [...] and it was only the hawkish elements who had spoken up'.[170] The usefulness of the continuation of this dialogue again became a matter for debate among the Turkish-Cypriot leadership. It was also apparent that the serious internal problems of the Demirel Government had started to affect negatively Turkey's public perception of the inter-communal negotiations. The official response of the Turkish-Cypriot side, presented on 27 April 1971, was inevitably shaped within this context. These proposals are discussed in the following section.

The rehabilitation of the displaced Turkish-Cypriots

From January until April 1971 there were no important discussions on constitutional elements. The Turkish-Cypriot side was deliberately delaying its response to the Greek-Cypriot proposals. Clerides acknowledged that although talks should continue, unless there was a Turkish-Cypriot response to the latest constitutional proposals, 'topics for discussion were running out'.[171] Although several normalization and practical issues were still pending, Clerides believed that if the balance of the talks was shifted onto them, then it would seem as if the talks were a high-level liaison committee between two separate communities for solving practical problems.[172] But for the moment the focus remained on displaced persons.

Since the end of the second phase of the talks in 1968, Denktash had proposed the discussion of a scheme that would allow Turkish-Cypriots to return to their villages. Although there were not any substantial negotiations, Denktash brought this matter up throughout 1969–1970. The

Cyprus Government initially appeared receptive and agreed to undertake responsibility for the reconstruction of destroyed houses, and despite the return of some families to their homes there was still not a coordinated policy to deal decisively with this issue. Clerides explains in his memoirs that 'Makarios accepted the views of the hawks that such a development was premature, and that it would ease the economic problem the Turkish-Cypriots were facing'.[173] It was indeed true that if almost 25,000 displaced Turkish-Cypriots returned to their abandoned houses, and to their previous jobs, and begin again to contribute to the economy, the 'TCPA' would have been relieved of the huge financial burden of subsidies for 'refugees'. Likewise, the benefits of this to the Turkish-Cypriot economy and sectors would have been evident.

Makarios constantly reiterated the purely practical reason for delay on this issue. Ramsbotham recollected from his discussion with Makarios that the latter explained,

> The Government's policy was genuinely in favour of progress in this matter. But they suffered from the incompetence of their own agents. There were endless formalities to be gone through and there was a chronic shortage of skilled labour in the building trade. There was also the question of priorities: he [Makarios] had guaranteed to the inhabitants of two Greek-Cypriot villages badly damaged in the 1968/9 floods that their villages would be restored before winter; despite this direction nothing had so far been done; if he now gave priority to Turkish villages, he would lay himself open to severe criticism by his own community.[174]

For the Greek-Cypriot side the displaced persons' rehabilitation was a very delicate issue. It had to find a suitable way to achieve the return of as many displaced Turkish-Cypriots as possible under government control but in the meantime not give the possibility to the Turkish-Cypriots to build up their own numbers and thus potentially challenge the *status quo* in the areas controlled by the government. This meant that it was willing to allow only the return of those who lived in villages where the Turkish-Cypriots constituted a minority. For their part, the Turkish-Cypriot leadership was not prepared to allow displaced Turkish-Cypriots to accept rehabilitation in villages where they would be once more integrated into a Greek majority. In this way the freeze on any genuine resettlement policy only became more pronounced.[175]

The delay of the Cyprus Government to propose a concrete plan for the mass return of the 'refugees' was usually exploited for propaganda reasons by the Turkish-Cypriot leadership. Finally, on 25 February 1971, Clerides presented a two-phased plan for their gradual return, first in areas that were not marked as sensitive and of strategic importance and then to the rest of the island.[176] That plan, however, set several unacceptable conditions for Denktash, and it was not fully accepted. Once again on this very critical element, the talks ended in deadlock.

Heading for a deadlock

Since the submission of the 30 November proposals renewed debates among the Turkish-Cypriot leadership considered whether the inter-communal talks should indeed be continued. Nonetheless, Makarios' speech on 14 March 1971 in Yallousa was the straw that broke the camel's back. In a very intense and emotional speech, Makarios spoke extempore:

> Cyprus is a Greek island. It was Greek from the dawn of history and it shall remain Greek forever. We have taken it over as a wholly Greek island and we shall preserve it as an undivided Greek island until we hand it over to mother Greece.[177]

The Greek Government tried diplomatically to play down this incident and to convince Ankara that it should not be given wider significance.[178] Nevertheless, this speech coincided with the military coup and the fall of Demirel's Government in Ankara. The new government, therefore, inevitably adopted a tougher line on the Cyprus issue. The Turkish-Cypriot reaction was strong. The press and the Turkish-Cypriot leadership exploited this development in order to justify their insistence for a federal solution and for the imperative need of preserving partnership status in any new settlement. Suggestively, within the main propagandist publications issued by the Turkish-Cypriot authorities, this particular speech was usually highlighted as revealing of the 'true' intentions of the Greek-Cypriot side.[179]

Denktash explained that although, personally, he did not believe that such rhetoric was of any significance since it was so endemic on both sides, this particular outburst 'reinforced Turkish-Cypriot belief that Greek-Cypriots were aiming at unification and independence simply as a prelude to *Enosis*'.[180] Against this background, Denktash along with Ankara prepared and tabled the long-awaited Turkish-Cypriot response on 27 April in a toughly worded letter. On matters of substance there was not any real advance of the Turkish-Cypriot position and nothing that could give a real momentum to the foundering process of the inter-communal negotiations. Alarmed by the *Enosis* statements, however, Denktash requested from Clerides a statement clarifying that the current discussions still aimed at a constitutional settlement on the basis of independence and that the international status of the Republic would later be agreed upon by all the interested parties.[181] It should be stated that before the submission of the new counter-proposals, Clerides was informed by various diplomatic sources that the Turkish-Cypriot decision as to whether or not to continue the current negotiations would hinge on Makarios' reaction to the impending communication.[182]

Notwithstanding the above, the reply of the Greek-Cypriot side on 26 June did not satisfy the Turkish-Cypriot demands. According to the instructions he received from Makarios, and despite the urge of the Greek Government to make substantial concessions in order to avoid the break-off of the talks, Clerides made concessions on elements of reduced importance merely to keep the talks going but without any substantial progress. According to the high commissioner,

> This letter was an ingenious document, well drafted for presentational purposes, particularly at the UN [...] If published, it could be used as evidence that the Greek and Turkish Governments would be unreasonable if they tried to impose a solution on the pretext that the Cyprus Government were being very stubborn. Nevertheless, the letter rejected both the Turkish-Cypriot and Greek proposals for local government [...] It was as much a snub to Athens, as to Ankara and the Turkish-Cypriots.[183]

As will later be explained, the background to this particular answer was the one that led to a crucial crisis between Nicosia and Athens.

By the end of June it was clear that the talks were heading towards deadlock and both parties wanted to avoid the blame by a 'sterile point-scoring exchange'.[184] Another set of letters was exchanged throughout August, especially focused on the issue of local government. The last letter was transmitted by Denktash to Clerides on 20 September and marked the end of the fourth phase of the inter-communal negotiations.

Internal developments

While on the inter-communal front 'a negative stability' was gradually consolidated,[185] the same did not occur in the internal politics of the two communities and in their relations with their respective motherlands. Makarios was trying to re-establish both his authority and the unity among his community, while Denktash was constantly strengthening his side's position in negotiations with *de facto* realities. All these developments led the two parties to an unconstructive 'double soliloquy'. Both parties were exchanging letters just for the sake of discussion, eventually leading to the termination of the first round of talks in September 1971.

Makarios' desperate need for unity and further consolidation of the 'TCPA'

Throughout 1969–1970, Makarios came to realize that the rise of the *Enosis* movement was gradually undermining his popularity. For that reason, after the parliamentary elections, the arrest of certain members of the National Front and the standstill in negotiations, Makarios had the time to focus on his own internal problems and try to find a way to settle them. Moreover, after the heated exchanges between Pipinelis and Makarios in the spring of 1970, the meeting of Makarios and Papadopoulos in Athens on September 1970 seemed to have managed to put Nicosia–Athens relations back on track. According to the Cypriot ambassador in Greece, the two leaders came to a complete agreement over the next steps in the talks, adding that 'he had never during his ten years in Athens known such a good general understanding between them as now'.[186]

One of Makarios' first goals in order to regain popularity was to find a way to reconcile with the extreme-right wing and bring the centre-right wing under his own complete control. The latter was helped by the fact that Clerides had no intention himself of playing an independent hand in the centre henceforth.[187] Conversely, any rapprochement with the extreme right was difficult but still crucial for securing the internal unity within his community. His first move, despite public assurances to the contrary, was to release on parole the thirty-one members of the National Front a month after their conviction.[188] The president was afraid that keeping the convicts in prison any longer would give the National Front a chance to retaliate against the government. If this happened a permanent schism might open up within the Greek-Cypriot community. Nevertheless, several voices within the government argued that this was a mistake which in the long term might disappoint other sections of the population. For example, Clerides believed that this move risked making the extreme-right respectable again and might negatively influence the morale of the police or the civil servants who still remained loyal to the government.[189] Furthermore, this could have been a useful tool for exploitation in Turkish-Cypriot hands when arguing for stronger security guarantees. It should be stressed that after the release, the National Front did abstain from the use of violence and was transformed into a political pressure group under the guidance of the nationalist Bishop of Kitium.[190]

Additionally, on 27 January Makarios decided for the first time to invite seventy-eight political figures, old and new ministers and members of Parliament, along with political leaders from all parties, to discuss the national issue. Makarios wanted first and foremost to clear up the rumours that he was working for a solution in a way that might fatally compromise the future of Greek-Cypriots as a community. Second, he had in mind that in case of a settlement, certain concessions would have to be made. To avoid a serious confrontation when this moment came, he decided to repeat a tactic from the past. As was the case in February 1959 when he invited all the main political forces to Lancaster House in London, it was now equally vital 'to involve all shades of political opinion with his own position'.[191] Several reports indicated that this meeting was a success. Although the extreme-right voices that attended wanted to press the president to take a more nationalistic approach, eventually, by emphasizing the need for internal solidarity, Makarios 'had imposed, [at least temporarily], on the Greek Cypriot political leaders the onus of moderating their more extreme factionalism and uniting in support of his policy'.[192]

Although the nationalist camp did not abandon the *Enosis* goal and the danger of further violent incidents was not fully averted, by March 1971 it seemed that Makarios had managed to establish a precarious calm on his own side. Moreover, the constitutional proposals tabled on 30 November 1970 placed the Greek-Cypriots in an advantageous positions vis-à-vis the Turkish side. Nevertheless, Makarios on 14 March made a serious tactical mistake. His feverish reference to *Enosis* in his speech in Yallousa was exploited by Turkey and the Turkish-Cypriot side to justify two important developments. First, this speech afforded a further excuse to the new coalition government of Nihat Erim to take a more rigid line on the Cyprus issue.[193] Stronger guarantees would be needed against *Enosis,* and the beginning was made with Denktash's 27 April proposals when asking Clerides to confirm the direction of the talks. A few months later, however, the Turkish side demanded a clear-cut statement against *Enosis.* On 9 August Denktash stated,

> The question of guarantees never came up in our talks because that was a matter for later consideration [...] Now, why did it come up all of a sudden? It came up because of certain statements by Archbishop Makarios to the effect that he will never sign any agreement which bars the way to *Enosis.* This immediately made this issue a fundamental one for us.[194]

Second, a few days after this speech, Denktash issued a *communiqué* which he signed as the 'Vice-President of the Executive Council of the Turkish-

Cypriot Administration', dropping the word 'Provisional' from the 'TCPA'.[195]
The secretary-general of the Turkish Foreign Ministry argued that although
this move changed nothing, Makarios was responsible for this development.
He warned that

> if he [Makarios] persisted as he had done for the past two and a half
> years in frustrating every advance in the inter-communal talks, he
> would himself bring about the situation which he claimed most to fear
> and crystallise the two communities into a *de facto* partition.[196]

This move was the culmination of actions over the preceding two years by
the Turkish-Cypriot leadership which aimed at forcing their *de facto* realities
onto the negotiating table. The Turkish-Cypriots were now focused on
increasing rapidly their economic and administrative separatism as *a fait
accompli*. Part of that plan was probably the reason for the four-month delay
in drafting a reply to the first flexible proposals of the Greek-Cypriot side.
Meanwhile, the public statements of several Greek-Cypriot leaders about
Enosis, although directed at unifying the Greek-Cypriot front, only served to
assist Turkish-Cypriot goals.

Throughout 1971 the so-called Turkish-Cypriot Administration adopted
new measures which went further than merely providing the essential
services for a deprived community, as it initially argued.[197] It was reported
that the most striking change in the outward appearance of the Turkish-
Cypriot sectors was 'the transformation of the fighters from ragged, poorly-
armed irregulars of 1963 to the trained and efficient units', as they sought to
establish their control of Turkish-Cypriot areas outside the enclaves.[198]

Moreover, Turkish-Cypriot political leaders no longer pretended that
they were operating in accordance with the 1960 Constitution. Kuchuk
and his entourage did not hesitate to openly call their 'administration' a
'government', while the 'members' of the 'Executive Council' operated as
full-fledged Ministers with organized and structured development plans for
each portfolio.[199] The community which since 1960 argued in favour of the
full implementation of the Constitution until there was a new settlement was
now openly disregarding it. It is also noteworthy that at the beginning of
the local talks, the Turkish-Cypriot side believed that its economic problems
could substantially be solved only after a settlement. Four years later they
believed that they should organize and consolidate the economic structures
of their side and only then reach a solution according to the new realities.
In negotiations they no longer used the term 'unitary state' with the same
meaning as in 1968. Denktash explained that 'when we say unitary state we
mean one single state [...] A federal system, a cantonal administration which

the Greek-Cypriot regarded as unacceptable, does not alter the concept of a unitary state'.[200] The British high commissioner stressed that the Turkish-Cypriots 'are now denying that they ever accepted the concept of a unitary state. Denktash's agility has produced the concept of functional federalism and back-dated it to the 1960 Agreements, which he claims enshrined this idea'.[201]

All of these led to an important boost to the morale of both the Turkish-Cypriot leadership and fighters. They still continued to resist the freedom of movement of the Greek-Cypriots throughout the enclaves, while their provocative attitude and obstructiveness in their relations with UNFICYP was placing the latter in a predicament. Certain UNFICYP officials admitted,

> This [normalization] was not too difficult when Turkish-Cypriots were on the defensive and had to be protected from the Greek Cypriots; but now that both communities are asserting themselves, UNFICYP are finding that they are being ground between two millstones.[202]

By means of this stance, therefore, the Turkish-Cypriot fighters steadily extended their *de facto* control of their enclaves, and UNFICYP was unable to prevent them.

The Athens–Nicosia crisis

Pipinelis, for his part, had repeatedly tried to convince the Cyprus Government to recognize the necessity of a quick settlement without specifying actual concessions. After his death, that changed. By 1971, the danger of the collapse of the talks was evident and this risked severely affecting Greco-Turkish relations as well. Both the new coalition government of Nihat Erim and the Greek Government wished to avert these scenarios. Erim had admitted that the Cyprus problem was insignificant compared with the importance of Greco-Turkish relations.[203] Therefore, the two governments decided to hold an informal parallel dialogue while stressing, however, that it would be no substitute for inter-communal talks and hoping that some general agreement on Cyprus could be reached between them first.[204] Meanwhile, when Denktash's letter of 27 April 1971 was handed over to Clerides, Athens decided to formulate specific suggestions for the Cyprus Government.[205] This Greek-Cypriot response would probably have been critical to the whole future of the inter-communal negotiations and thus the Greek Government decided to intervene. Nonetheless, the submission of these Greek proposals on 11 June 1971 sparked a serious crisis between the two governments.

The Greek suggestions had attempted to accommodate several Turkish-Cypriot demands on local government in a way perceived by Makarios as damaging for the Greek-Cypriot cause.[206] Specifically, responding to the Turkish-Cypriot demand for the consolidation of the local government functions within the new constitution, Athens proposed that these provisions of the settlement be incorporated in a streamlined law liable to amendment with the same strict procedures as the constitution itself. Additionally, regarding the concept of the two separate central organs for local government, it was suggested: (a) to accept either a Turkish-Cypriot minister or deputy minister responsible for the local government or (b) to establish a Ministry of Local Government with a Greek-Cypriot minister and a Turkish-Cypriot deputy minister.[207]

According to Clerides, the rejection of these Greek suggestions was one of the gravest Greek-Cypriot mistakes because they would not have hindered the unitary type of state that their side wanted to secure.[208] Although Osorio-Tafall tried to exert some moderate influence on Makarios for a genuine form of local government to Turkish-Cypriots, the Cyprus president cut no ice.[209] Clerides was notified by several diplomatic sources that if Cyprus had adopted Greece's proposals, the Turkish side would have accepted them.[210]

Several people of Makarios' entourage henceforth openly accused Greece of colluding with the Turkish Government in the previous North Atlantic Treaty Organization (NATO) meeting in Lisbon in early June to impose a partitionist solution in Cyprus. Although this is a theory given credibility in several studies, there is little evidence of it from British archives.[211] The most important point of the Lisbon meeting agreement between the Greek and the Turkish foreign ministers was that 'there would be a final effort by both Governments to secure an agreement in the inter-communal talks'. The parties rather vaguely agreed – without specifying any particular solution – that a further meeting would be held in September to review the situation and 'if there is still no headway perhaps consider other ways of achieving a settlement'.[212] Claude Nicolet is probably correct in asserting that the later repetition of conspiracy theories surrounding the Lisbon meeting was mainly useful for 'propaganda and justification purposes'.[213]

Constantinos Panayiotacos, the Greek ambassador in Cyprus, explained that the leaks of the Greek letter to the Greek-Cypriot press and the accusations against the sinister plans of Athens infuriated Colonel Papadopoulos in Greece.[214] The Greek dictator, therefore, decided to grasp the nettle and wrote a fierce letter to Makarios in which he explained once again the Greek proposals, while adding an indirect threat if the latter against did not comply. This was the straw that broke the camel's back between the two governments.[215] Relations between the two capitals were further strained after August 1971 when it was reported that General Grivas left Athens, where he had been since December 1967, and returned to Cyprus. Although the Greek Government reported that it was unaware of Grivas' plans, several Junta officials were certainly behind it.[216] From that point onwards, the relations between the two capitals progressively deteriorated. Grivas' presence in Cyprus undermined Makarios' authority while the former secretly started to build an anti-Makarios underground organization dedicated to sabotaging the 'feasible solution' and to leading the island back to the *Enosis* track.[217] The consequences of these developments were to prove fatal.

It was not until mid-1972 that the relations between the two governments tentatively returned to fruitful cooperation. Nevertheless, the June 1971 crisis and the inherent mistrust of Nicosia over Athens' intentions was the main factor behind Cyprus' reluctance to accept U Thant's later proposal to save the process of the inter-communal talks, as we shall now see.

Time for a new approach: September–December 1971

The only variable that could have saved the inter-communal talks after September 1971 was an outside intervention and injection of fresh ideas. In early autumn, Kyprianou travelled to New York with several proposals. He sought the reactions mainly of countries of the Western bloc regarding the direct involvement of the UN secretary-general with his good offices as well as a parallel discussion in New York with the three governments on the international aspects of the Cyprus problem.[218] Simultaneously, Makarios in Nicosia was testing the waters in regard to a new process of a seven-power enlargement of talks, with members of the Security Council.[219] The latter proposition, however, was rejected by the West since it would have enabled the Soviet Union's active involvement in the Cyprus problem.

A fresh idea with some potential came in late September from Greece and was adopted, with certain modifications, by the UN secretary-general. In particular, U Thant on 18 October proposed the broadening of the inter-communal talks, with the participation of his Special Representative Osorio-Tafall and two constitutional experts, a Greek and a Turk, having a purely advisory role. Initially both Ankara and Nicosia had strong reservations about this new process. The Turkish Government was uncomfortable with the idea of a UN appointed member participating in the local talks. This would have led to an increased UN role in the process, which Ankara had traditionally tried to prevent.

Conversely, the main reason for Nicosia's reserved position was the proposal for participation of the constitutional experts from Greece and Turkey. On account of the previous Athens–Nicosia crisis, Makarios wanted to prevent Athens' active involvement in the negotiations. He was convinced that a Greco-Turkish presence would assist the implementation of the unacceptable Greek suggestions of 11 June.[220] Kyprianou explained that Nicosia did not want 'expert' advice since the Cyprus problem was essentially political.[221] He was also convinced that the new UN proposal for the enlarged talks was 'cooked up' in a NATO meeting between Greece and Turkey and that Turkey's reluctance to accept it was not genuine.[222]

Several reports claim that while Kyprianou was in New York and until he finally accepted U Thant's proposal, he had caused resentment in several diplomatic circles due to his strong accusations that plans were being drafted behind his government's back.[223] The Cyprus foreign minister had openly accused his Greek counterpart in the hallways of the UN building, while Osorio-Tafall alleged that Kyprianou's behaviour in New York was 'that of an unbalanced man'.[224] It was believed among foreign diplomats that Makarios' reluctance to accept U Thant's proposal was mainly due to Kyprianou's strong position and his erroneous assessments that U Thant would eventually either drop his proposal or at least modify it to something more favourable for them.[225]

After the increased diplomatic activity both by UN officials and other foreign diplomats, two months later, on 13 December, U Thant's proposal was accepted in principle by Nicosia. Ankara, however, still had certain reservations, and a UN emissary had been sent to convince the Turkish Government to unconditionally accept the new formula.[226] The danger of a complete collapse of the inter-communal talks was averted by February 1972, but there were still several pending procedural issues to be settled before their re-activation. The differences between Nicosia and Ankara over the exact terms of reference of the three extra participants and the scope of the negotiations had firstly to be ironed out.

By summer 1972 all differences were settled; thus, the new phase of the enlarged inter-communal talks began on 8 June in Nicosia with the presence of the new UN Secretary-General Kurt Waldheim; the Greek constitutional expert, Michael Dekleris; the Turkish expert, Orhan Aldikacti; and the two negotiators, Glafkos Clerides and Rauf Denktash. As will be seen in Chapter 7, the aftermath of the previous crisis between the Greek and Cyprus governments formed the main underlying obstacle to the quick resumption of the new round of inter-communal talks. Despite the fact that this new UN formula proved to be effective indeed, the problems at the outset of the talks suggested that it was perhaps already too late for a viable settlement by June 1972. This will be more clearly indicated in the final chapter of this book.

Conclusion

> The Cyprus problem could be solved by an act of statesmanship rather
> than by violence or time; but statesmanship still looks the least likely
> way of solving it, even though the conditions in Greece and Turkey may
> never have been so favourable.[227]

That was the ominous conclusion of a British diplomat in 1972 for the
Cyprus problem. He was surely right. The first round of the inter-communal
talks that it was so closely explored had proved as one lost opportunity for
Cyprus' future.

When Polyviou in 1980 identified the reasons that the inter-communal
talks failed (taking into account their whole duration from 1968–1974), he
distinguished three factors: (a) reluctance and insufficient motivation of
the parties; (b) the policies of Greece and Turkey, which were inimical to
a speedy agreement; and (c) insufficient international support, particularly
from the Western powers and the UN.[228] Although after 1972 these three
reasons were valid to some extent, the first prolonged round of the talks
indicates something rather different.

It is probably true that the Western powers during 1968–1971 did not
actively interfere with the Cyprus problem and decided to take an ostensibly
neutral line between the two sides. They were constantly trying through
diplomatic channels to influence the parties towards moderation, while
avoiding direct involvement. Both for the United States and Britain, a peaceful
and lasting solution on whatever the parties together might agree upon was
regarded as the best possible scenario for their own security interests in
the eastern Mediterranean. Until this permanent settlement was achieved,
however, the situation in Cyprus was characterized as a 'benign stalemate'
which served their interests well enough.[229] The only danger was the
transformation of the benign to a malignant stalemate if the situation on the
ground deteriorated. However, until the latter prospect occurred and forced
them to recalculate, it was perceived that 'this is a moment in the history
of the Cyprus dispute when we should stand apart from it'.[230] Presumably,
London and Washington not only recognized that the gap was still wide,
but were not prepared as well to risk their relations with the various parties
by pressing them in any direction.[231] The two negotiators also admitted in
private that they did not favour any outside interference yet.[232] Besides,
the United States had already tried unsuccessfully in March 1969 to assist
the parties by presenting some unofficial ideas that had immediately been
rejected. Although Britain and the United States were reluctant to attempt
to convince either of the parties of the need for particular concessions, we

may remark that by the end of 1968, the Americans were indeed thinking about various ways that they might cajole Makarios to show some flexibility. It was widely believed that the key to a settlement was Makarios himself, since at that point he was the only one who could afford to appear flexible. According to the US State Department, although making direct suggestions was not an option, perhaps 'playing upon his vanity' might work.[233] In particular, the Americans suggested that 'we should point out to him that the world recognized the peculiar importance of the personal role which he could play'.[234] This possibility, however, was abandoned because the British believed it might prove counter-productive and be condemned as an effort to interfere in Cypriot politics.[235] It was only at the outset of the talks that the Commonwealth Secretary, George Thomson, intimated to Kyprianou that more concessions were primarily expected by the Greek-Cypriot side. 'In dealing with their internal problems the Cyprus Government might remember it was always easier in such situations for the majority to take risks'. Kyprianou said that 'this might be true of an internal situation [...] but within the whole area affected by this conflict, the Greek-Cypriots were a minority'.[236] The British in general were wary of trying to suggest to Makarios anything more than the above perception. Costar had commented in 1968 that 'anyone who tried to mediate or to be impartial with the Cyprus Government was seen as being opposed to it'.[237] This is probably one of the most important considerations of British foreign policy towards Cyprus during this period. Therefore, the neutral posture of London and Washington was primarily intended to serve their interests and avoid being drawn into the details of the inter-communal talks, endangering their relations with the three players in the Cyprus problem: Cyprus, Greece and Turkey.

The second dimension for our purposes, and the one identified by Polyviou, refers to the position of the two motherlands. Certainly throughout this period, the argument that they were inimical to a speedy agreement is problematic. As already seen, both governments wanted genuinely and urgently to settle the problem on the basis of independence. In all their meetings with the communities' representatives their main advice was always to continue negotiating, even if there was nothing substantial to discuss. Otherwise, the danger of deadlock without any other visible alternative would endanger the peace on the island.

During this period, the bilateral, but unofficial, Greco-Turkish meetings over the Cyprus problem continued and the only thing that they always agreed on was the need to exert moderate influence upon the parties in order to make concessions. Notwithstanding that, there was one main difference between the two governments. Athens tried repeatedly to put pressure on Makarios for more concessions, and this eventually led to a serious rift between the two. Conversely, Turkey was by no means keeping its own part of the bargain, making little effort to convince the Turkish-Cypriot leadership for concessions either on constitutional or on normalization issues. Initially, Demirel had instructed Denktash that although he supported his efforts, it was up to the latter to convince the rest of the Turkish-Cypriot leadership of the specifics of the negotiations. After 1969 it seemed that the Turkish Government was not in a mood to actively urge the Turkish-Cypriots towards moderation. This, according to the British, was for two main reasons. First, both before and after the elections, the Demirel Government was in a very difficult position internally. Even though it had won the October 1969 elections, it still had serious domestic problems and pressure towards Turkish-Cypriots for concessions could have sparked further criticism from the political opposition and the military. Especially by the end of 1970 the situation inside Turkey was deteriorating, and by March 1971 Demirel's Government fell. In order to avoid similar criticism as its predecessor, the new government was not in a position to be constructive over Cyprus. Second, it was reported that Ankara remained erroneously convinced that it could sit back and do nothing because Athens would in any case be driven to force Makarios to make concessions, even if this involved the use of extreme measures against him.[238] Ankara's reluctance to urge Turkish-Cypriots towards flexibility, at least on freedom of movement, was definitely an unhelpful factor for the development of the talks, and it gave Makarios an excuse for not actively pursuing measures that could have enhanced inter-communal cooperation.

Lastly and most importantly, a factor that definitely influenced the lack of any positive development of the talks was the attitude of the two communities in Cyprus. Both communities' leaders were reluctant to upset the *status quo* without first securing significant gains for their community. Certainly, the gains that each community sought were incompatible with each other: a Greek-Cypriot-led state and a minority status for Turkish-Cypriots versus strong local autonomy with limited state supervision which would guarantee their partnership status. As already stated, the problem was always inherently political rather than legal. Thus, the compromise would not arise through constitutional negotiations but through the realities taking shape on the ground.

Above all, there were two determining aspects of the problem: constitutional divergences and normalization/freedom of movement throughout the enclaves. Both leaderships adopted the same negotiating tactic in relation to these topics; they chose to appear flexible on the matters least existential to their own perceived interests and wholly unconstructive on the others. The Greek-Cypriots made certain concessions on normalization by removing the embargo policy, which in any case proved ineffective, but were totally inflexible on constitutional aspects. Likewise, the Turkish-Cypriots made certain concessions on the constitutional aspects, which did not compromise their aim for local autonomy, but were totally rigid on normalization and on freedom of movement.

Makarios, on the one hand, believed that initially taking this rigid line on the constitutional problem and letting Denktash lay his own negotiating cards on the table openly was the best strategy. The former acknowledged that the key to the settlement was the bad economic situation within the enclaves. This undoubtedly had some validity. However, his passive policy of waiting for the latter to surrender was ineffective. Since 1968 the *de facto* separation of the Turkish-Cypriots was strengthening and these new realities were used as a bargaining chip by the other side. The Cyprus Government was aware of that danger since Denktash, Turkish diplomats and Pipinelis had many times warned the Greek-Cypriot politicians about the risky policy of 'wait and see'.

Denktash, on the other hand, during the initial stages of the talks held the most moderate posture perhaps of his whole political career. The economic development of his community was one of the top priorities for him. First, he believed that this might have been possible through a quick settlement of the Cyprus problem. That, however, completely changed by the third phase of the talks. Public statements of the Turkish-Cypriot leadership after 1970 were highlighting the need to preserve their separateness until a settlement was reached. That was a consequence of the realities developed within the 'TCPA'.

> Vested interests have grown up which cannot be ignored. There is, for example the personal position not only of politicians but of civil servants who depend on the Administration. It is hard to imagine many Turkish-Cypriot institutions being abandoned once they have been set up with so much difficulty [...] In short if the inter-communal talks succeed, the practical problem of reintegration will still remain.[239]

Those according to the British High Commissioner, Robert Edmonds, were the harsh realities prevailing by 1972.

However, the Turkish-Cypriot reintegration in the state apparatus and the economic life of the island, along with the mass return of displaced persons in the government-controlled areas were perhaps the elements over which progress might have been achieved during the first two years of the talks. It should be noted that applying the 'return to homes' policy is perhaps the most important element for restoring normalcy in cases like Cyprus, where breakdowns had triggered physical movement. Had both sides realized the importance of that element and had they chosen to grasp this nettle, much goodwill might been gained all round.

Except from settling the displaced persons' problem, the chairman of the Turkish Chamber of Commerce, Kemal Rustem, explained that any 'carrot' given by the Cyprus Government to Turkish-Cypriots for improving their economic situation would have positively affected Turkish-Cypriot public opinion.[240] Nevertheless, Makarios and other hawkish members of his Cabinet believed that if such a policy was pursued it would have eased the economic problems of Turkish-Cypriots, negatively affecting their willingness for settlement. The truth, however, was that in 1968 it was the Greek-Cypriot side which was in the position to make substantial proposals, to appear more generous or to try to re-enforce Turkish-Cypriot integration in order to promote trust and stop the further consolidation of the *de facto* realities that would have purportedly justified a federal solution.

By early 1970 the situation within the Greek-Cypriot community was deteriorating and this crucially reduced Makarios' possibility of taking a constructive approach on the Cyprus problem. The mishandling of the National Front affair and the growing reflorescence of the *Enosis* sentiment were factors that hindered any chance of progress on the inter-communal front. Doubts over the ulterior motives of the two communities were, therefore, gradually increasing.

In 1968, which was one of the most peaceful years of the decade,[241] there was definitely important momentum with at least some hope of a real settlement. Later developments, however, disillusioned everybody. The 30 November 1970 Greek-Cypriot proposals seemed to be a beacon of hope but they came too late. The truth was that by 1971 the chances of a settlement were running thin mainly due to the internal developments within each community. The British high commissioner in August 1971 concluded,

> Had President Makarios been a statesman, rather than a highly skilful politician, he might have seized the opportunity which then [in 1968] presented itself to negotiate a constitutional settlement on which it might have been possible to build a peaceful Cyprus. He missed it, deliberately, because he is convinced that time is on his side and because, for him the lesson of 1967 was not that war in the Eastern Mediterranean had only just been averted, but that his personal brinkmanship had paid off once again.[242]

Makarios, as he himself admitted, had always used brinkmanship believing that he knew how far to take it.[243] If this approach had succeeded in the past, at this juncture it failed precisely because it underestimated the capabilities of his 'opponent'.

Although the new negotiating procedure after 1972 initially seemed capable of breaking this vicious circle, by the end of 1972 the developments on the ground had transformed the inter-communal talks into little more than a safety-valve which had to be maintained in order to forestall for as long as possible some kind of denouncement feared by everybody. Chapter 7 will explore – in relation to the now staggering phenomenon of inter-communal dialogue – how this eventually happened.

The Final Attempt, 1972–1974

By 1972, all previous efforts to find a settlement to the post-1960 Cyprus problem had run into the sand. Neither Plaza in 1964–1965, nor Greece and Turkey in 1965–1967, nor finally the two communities themselves in 1968–1971, had been able to find acceptable common ground. It was clearly time to try a new 'recipe': bring all the parties collectively around the same negotiating table, including representatives of the two communities, the special representative of the UN secretary-general and constitutional experts from Greece and Turkey. Although this new formula came as a 'kiss of life' to the foundering process of inter-communal negotiations, it was generally believed that on matters of substance little could be achieved. The prior four-year experience inevitably had produced polarization and public commitments from which it was difficult to escape. Nevertheless, on 8 June 1972 under the aegis of the new UN Secretary-General, Kurt Waldheim, the new round of the expanded inter-communal talks commenced.

Surprisingly, this new recipe proved to be the most effective of all. For the first time in ten years, in July 1974, there existed a comprehensive formula for the revision of the 1960 Constitution that could have accommodated the concerns and interests of both communities. However, the crucial moment for the implementation of a compromise solution on the basis of an independent, unitary state, with adequate local government for Turkish-Cypriots, had slipped away since the end of 1971. At that critical point, all parties were distracted by their own severe and intensifying internal problems, which made the need for meaningful progress through inter-communal talks less important. The internal problems that eventually led to the 15 July 1974 *coup d'état* and the Turkish invasion five days later are beyond the scope of this book. However, it is essential to highlight in brief how the internal developments and the political problems within each party condemned this new effort to futility. Particular focus will be given to three important junctures of the new round of the expanded negotiations: February 1972, January 1973 and April 1974. In each of these three junctures, talks were interrupted but when resumed, the deterioration of the prevailing context made the prospects for a viable settlement progressively more bleak. By exploring the successive junctures, it will become clear that in any rounded and admittedly retrospective analysis, the real 'lost opportunity' had been in the inter-communal nexus in 1968–1969.

February 1972: The second Czech arms crisis

The first important hiatus in the fresh process came in February 1972, almost simultaneously with Ankara's unconditional acceptance of the initiation of the inter-communal talks, on the lines expressed in U Thant's formula of 18 October 1971. As already noted, Greece had immediately gone along with U Thant's proposal. Additionally, by December 1971, Nicosia conceded the participation of the Greek and Turkish constitutional experts in the inter-communal dialogue, provided these would have a purely advisory role. Conversely, Turkey was wholly negative, due to its desire to avoid a more active UN involvement in negotiations. The Turkish Government wanted to minimize the UN role at the outset, but simultaneously to upgrade the role of the two constitutional experts.[1] Meanwhile, it sought to ensure that the new initiative would constitute a fresh approach for a settlement, and not just the continuation of the previous discussions.[2] This was also favoured by Nicosia, since it believed that it could have injected the Treaty of Alliance question into this new phase.[3] It was not until 5 February that the new UN secretary-general managed to convince Ankara to withdraw its reservations by offering a formula securing that the new round of talks would not compromise the positions and principles of the parties.[4] With Turkey's final concurrence, the chances of Nicosia blocking the initiative was much reduced.[5] In February 1972, therefore, almost three months after U Thant's proposal for the expanded talks, everything seemed ready for their activation. Developments on the island, however, altered the calculations involved.

Early in February, the discovery by Grivas' supporters that Makarios had secretly imported a large quantity of Czech arms, to be distributed to his loyal followers, led to a new crisis and to a serious diplomatic clash between Nicosia and Athens.[6] Hence, the resumption of inter-communal talks had to be put in cold storage. Although the details need not concern us here, it is important to state why Makarios decided to make such a move and to identify its immediate consequences.

It should be kept in mind that since June 1971 there had been increased rumours that Greece and Turkey were planning to impose a settlement on Cyprus over Makarios' head. In September 1971, Makarios visited Athens, where he was warned that if the situation in Cyprus deteriorated to such an extent that could lead to a Greco-Turkish confrontation, Athens would actively collude with Ankara in order to settle the Cyprus problem.[7] The situation was further complicated by the clandestine return of Grivas on the island on 31 August. Grivas' aim was to organize a new *Enosis* movement against Makarios' 'feasible' policy. This movement, National Organization of Cypriot Fighters (EOKA) B, would be under his own leadership, while it would also be supported and funded by various groups within the shadowy penumbra of the military junta in Athens. These developments had caused great concern to Makarios, whose dependence on his loyal left-wing groups steadily grew as a consequence.[8]

On 11 February 1972, upon discovery of the arms shipment, the Greek Government gave an ultimatum to Makarios, asking first to place the arms be placed under United Nations Force in Cyprus's (UNFICYP's) custody and, secondly, to form a government of 'national unity', but without the Communist elements.[9] Meanwhile, it was privately suggested that Makarios and Grivas should both withdraw from the island's politics. It was evident that Athens was seeking ways to get rid of Makarios; thus, by 14 February it became known that the Greek Government was preparing a *coup d'état* in order to force Makarios' replacement. This dangerous action was prevented through American pressure on Athens.[10] Amidst this storm, another crisis developed. In order to increase pressure against Makarios, in a meeting of the Holy Synod three *enotist* Bishops, with Athens' support, called on Makarios to resign from the presidency, on the grounds that his political office was incompatible with his archiepiscopal position.[11]

It took almost three months for the most serious – up to that point – Athens–Nicosia crisis to temporarily damp down and to bypass the arms issue. Eventually, Athens dropped its insistence upon Makarios' resignation and distanced itself from the *enotist* Bishops.[12] However, the damaging effect of this crisis on the inter-communal talks was evident; it stalled the resumption of talks for almost three months and placed them in a still more combustible context.

With the fatal timing of this importation of arms, Makarios exposed his authority to criticism from three different directions: Athens, the Bishops and Grivas. The centre-right wing tried to keep a moderate stance throughout, while Makarios' dependence on the left-wing groups was more evident than ever.[13] Although the external threat against Makarios rallied Greek-Cypriot public opinion in his favour, the British high commissioner explained that Greek-Cypriots remained sharply divided:

The fact has not been lost on the Greek-Cypriot community that it was the Archbishop who got himself into this mess in the first place by ordering the arms. While most Greek-Cypriots care little about the continuance of the inter-communal dispute, and (incredible though it may seem) rarely give a thought to the potential threat from Turkey [...] they have been rattled by the crisis with Greece. Some members of the business community are already murmuring, somewhat helplessly, that if the crisis can be alleviated by the Archbishop's resignation, then he should go.[14]

Meanwhile, after the unsuccessful initiative of Makarios to meet with Grivas on 26 March 1972, and convince him of the dangers of *Enosis*, it became certain that Grivas would not be easily sidelined. Ankara predictably exploited this crisis for its own interests by solidifying its demands for further security guarantees.[15] As soon as the arms issue was completely settled, the Turkish Government decided to set six new pre-conditions for the initiation of enlarged talks, arguing that the suggested Makarios–Grivas meeting had increased their suspicions over the real motives of the Greek-Cypriot community.[16]

After the UN's involvement, on 18 May 1972, Kurt Waldheim made a new written request for the quick resumption of talks by using wording that satisfied all parties. Thus, on 8 June 1972, in Ledra Palace under the aegis of the UN Secretary-General, Clerides along with Denktash, and the two constitutional experts, Michael Dekleris and Orhan Aldikacti, alongside Osorio-Tafall, re-activated the inter-communal negotiations. Nevertheless, this ceremonial meeting was 'something of a cliff-hanger' because of the parties' disagreement up to the last moment over their opening statements.[17] Having this background in mind, it was evident that the inter-communal talks had the odds stacked against them from the outset.

February 1973: Presidential elections

Although the chances for a quick solution were perceived as slim, by December 1972 there was, nevertheless, a crucial breakthrough on the negotiating table. The facilitative role of Osorio-Tafall, along with the fruitful cooperation of Dekleris and Aldikacti, proved to be extremely helpful both towards bridging their differences on very important constitutional questions and avoiding counter-productive debates over the origins of the Cyprus problem and the guarantees' question.

In July 1972, as soon as the briefing stage of the talks began, Clerides decided to make a very important acknowledgement in order to dispel the Turkish-Cypriot doubts concerning the allegedly sinister Greek-Cypriot motives. He explicitly stated for the first time ever that his side considered the Zurich–London Agreements valid and made particular reference to the Article 185 of the Constitution, which excluded both *Enosis* and partition.[18] Although this temporarily satisfied the Turkish-Cypriots, the upsurge of the pro-*Enosis* campaign within the Greek-Cypriot community, along with the revelation of Grivas' surreptitious importation of arms in October 1972, made Clerides' previous acknowledgement ineffective. Therefore, by October the Turkish side demanded an agreement in advance between Turkey and Greece for the renunciation of *Enosis*.[19] After many attempts, the Greek Government and Clerides convinced their counterparts that if there was an open renunciation of *Enosis* before having a complete constitutional settlement, Grivas' supporters would definitely react violently and destroy any chance for progress.[20] For this reason, Turkey agreed to temporarily stop calling for some broad statement of the Greek-Cypriot long-term goals.

After this setback, all parties agreed that a new procedure should be employed to give emphasis to the legal, rather than political, nature of the problem.[21] More specifically, the inter-communal talks were about to be reconfigured in two ways: the five-party meetings and the bilateral meetings of the two constitutional experts. After the two negotiators set their basic political lines for each of the five constitutional issues, the two advisors would privately produce compromise legal formulas and then present them to the other three parties for discussion and validation.[22] This procedure proved to be very useful. Although the prevailing tension within the Greek-Cypriot community occasionally affected Ankara's and Turkish-Cypriot's demands, by the end of 1972 Dekleris and Aldikacti made significant progress on legislative, executive and judicial matters.[23] It was even asserted that by mid-1973 it would have been possible to reach an overall agreement.[24]

At this critical stage, the second and most severe halt in the negotiating process took place. The talks were interrupted because of the February 1973 presidential elections. Dekleris characterizes the end of 1972 as the golden missed opportunity for a settlement.[25] If elections were deferred, as had already happened in the period 1965–1967, momentum would not have been lost and settlement would have been in reach by 1973.

Both Clerides and Dekleris, along with Aldikacti, tried to warn Makarios that this was not the right time for elections, mainly for two reasons.[26] First and foremost, it was going to interrupt the impetus achieved after October's setback. Second, a pre-electoral campaign within the already sharply divided Greek-Cypriot community, where pro-Grivas and pro-Makarios factions were at loggerheads, further soured the fragile atmosphere. It should be stressed that it was already known that Grivas' supporters had penetrated the whole state apparatus, while only a third of the police remained loyal to Makarios.[27] In November 1972, Patroklos Stavrou, the president's under-secretary, reported that hardly a week passed without reports of plots against Makarios.[28] There was still, however, a third important reason for eschewing elections at that time. It was certain that Denktash would have been the absolute winner of the elections held within the enclaves. He would have definitely been elected as the vice-president of the Republic of Cyprus and, henceforth, he would be not only the Turkish-Cypriot negotiator but also the political leader of his community and a genuine rival to Makarios. Moreover, in this new capacity, Denktash's posture in negotiations was going to be susceptible to his own opposition and, finally, as the vice-president would have worked to secure as many privileges as possible in the new constitutional settlement.[29]

The final decision to hold or postpone the presidential elections depended on the Cyprus Government. The Turkish-Cypriots stated that if Greek-Cypriots decide to postpone elections, they would concur.[30] On 29 December 1972 Makarios announced that elections would be conducted on 18 February 1973. Had elections taken place, Makarios believed that he would have won the overwhelming majority of Greek-Cypriot votes, as in 1968, and, subsequently, would have strengthened his hand against all of his opponents inside and outside of the island.[31] Nevertheless, Makarios' and his entourage's assessment of the outcome of the elections was erroneous. His re-election was certain indeed and, in order to avoid an open humiliation that would have further delegitimized their plans, Grivas and EOKA B decided to abstain. Makarios was, therefore, re-elected unopposed after an intense campaign that saw constant attacks and bombings against the state authority by Grivas' faction. Consequently, Makarios failed to prove his predominance over the *Enosis* front through an electoral battle, while the pre-elections period afforded Grivas a live opportunity for fomenting violent opposition against Makarios.[32]

The damage was now severe; Greek-Cypriots were further divided, making the re-activation of inter-communal talks impossible before May 1973. Simultaneously, the Turkish-Cypriot negotiator's position had been upgraded to that of the vice-president of the Republic of Cyprus. The latter element was profoundly reflected in the subsequent proposals of Denktash in the inter-communal discussions. He was constantly increasing his demands both on the executive and local government issues.[33]

April 1974: A new political landscape in Ankara

The chaos created before and after the elections eliminated the chances for a successful implementation of any later constitutional settlement and brought the violent showdown closer. The Greek-Cypriot split and violence were getting worse. Indicative was the fact that in March 1973 an ecclesiastical coup took place by the enotist Bishops of the Holy Synod against Makarios. Moreover, by the summer of 1973 the underground struggle between Grivas and pro-Makarios factions was reaching its peak.[34] Inevitably, all these further inflamed the unstable atmosphere in Cyprus. Makarios was now completely distracted by these problems, giving no attention to what was happening on the negotiating table.[35] Denktash again took a tougher line, causing constant setbacks, while the Turkish diplomats more frequently than ever argued about the necessity of a federation.[36] Because of the strengthening of *Enosis* militancy in Greek-Cypriot ranks, Ankara was also preparing militarily to invade the island, should circumstances make this essential.[37] Being totally pre-occupied with their own internal problems, the Greek-Cypriots wholly missed the threats surrounding them. By early 1974, Stephen Olver, the new British high commissioner in Nicosia, characteristically reported,

> Behind a superficially business-as-usual atmosphere, both the Greek and Turkish sides have [...] lost interest in the talks. These are still regarded as a useful safety-valve, and I am sure neither side will readily accept the odium of causing them to collapse. But there is no longer [...] much real belief on either side – or for that matter on Osorio-Tafall's part either – that they can provide any real solution to the Cyprus problem.[38]

In spite of these realities, both Aldikacti and Dekleris continued their private meetings and produced compromise arrangements, especially on the most complex issue, that of local government. This had been the focus of their work since May 1973, and ironically, by the end of February 1974 they made significant progress.[39]

Nonetheless, the autumn of 1973 marked a politically unstable era not only for Cyprus, Greece and Turkey but also for the region as a whole. The severe Arab–Israeli Yom Kippur War of October 1973 had almost led to a US–Soviet confrontation. Moreover, the changes of the Greek and Turkish leaderships produced a new more poisonous dynamic to the Cyprus problem.[40] More specifically, Papadopoulos' regime in Greece was overthrown by Brigadier Demetrios Ioannides, on 25 November 1973. The new regime consisted of 'inexperienced and largely unsophisticated men with some xenophobic tendencies'.[41] Although the official line of the new leadership was the continuation of the inter-communal dialogue, through several other channels, the Greek regime set in motion a dangerous policy that culminated in the 15 July *coup d'état* which overthrew Makarios and opened the way to the Turkish invasion five days later. It should also be stressed that Grivas died in January 1974 and the leadership of EOKA B had passed to the new Athenian regime. Grivas' death, therefore, facilitated further the implementation of Ioannides' partitionist plans for Cyprus.

Circumstances had changed in Ankara as well. In January 1974, the new coalition government of Bulent Ecevit was formed. When in February Ecevit promulgated his government's political programme, he underscored that federation was the most appropriate type of settlement in Cyprus. This is when the third interruption of the inter-communal talks occurred. As expected, this statement infuriated the Greek-Cypriot side. During the negotiators' meeting on 2 April, Clerides explained that both the negotiators and the experts would suspend their meetings unless there was an explicit retraction of Ankara's statement.[42] Denktash publicly accused the Greek-Cypriot side of deliberately stalling the talks, while attempting to water down Ecevit's statement by stating vaguely that there was no change in his side's aims.[43] It was not until 14 June that all the parties agreed to an acceptable wording of a statement that would have enabled the continuation of the talks.[44]

Although Dekleris believes that this suspension was also fatal,[45] this third hiatus did not change anything practically. After the resumption of talks in 14 June, Makarios was absorbed in concern for the worsening of the Athens–Nicosia relations and was unable to deal with the inter-communal dialogue.[46] Therefore, the talks indeed served as a mere safety valve, because neither party was willing to take responsibility for their failure. When Olver reported in February 1974 on this reality, he also ominously predicted the inevitable eventual confrontation.[47] This is what in fact occurred on 15 July, when the inter-communal negotiations were forcibly terminated by developments on the ground.

Conclusion

We have already underlined the irony that despite the grave deterioration of the situation on the island by 1974, the two constitutional experts had found a comprehensive compromise that had seemed impossible during the previous Clerides–Denktash talks. Arguably, this came about because the experts focused completely on the legal nature of the problem, expressing both professionalism and moderation in doing so. While they followed the political guidelines and instructions of the two communities, they were still determined to find even *sui generis* legal formulas to settle all pending and unresolved issues. It was the case, therefore, that a settlement was indeed reached on paper on the eve of the tragic events of the summer of 1974. However, a real political settlement was not near, although this is often held to have been so in later Cypriot accounts. The compromise agreement that Aldikacti and Dekleris so skilfully prepared was essentially meaningless without authentic political endorsement by both the Greek-Cypriot and Turkish-Cypriot leaderships. Compromise on the negotiating table seemed much easier than actually saying it out loud, especially in the context that developed from 1972 until 1974. Despite the fact that there was a theoretical settlement which in principle accommodated the needs of the two communities, all too suggestive of the difficulties was the renewal of the 'statement-battle' for the semantics of this outcome in 1974. Was the solution that was being negotiated providing for a federal or a unitary state? Olver gave his own explanation by remarking,

> The original vague skeleton – an improved version of the 1960 Constitution, removing some of the obvious friction points (Makarios' 'thirteen points') and at the same time providing better safeguards for the Turks – looked attractive; but as more and more flesh was put on the bones by the two constitutional experts, it began to look more and more awkward by both sides. The closer they got – and over most issues, including local autonomy but not internal security, they are now very close – the more sharply focussed became the remaining sticking points. An act of faith could have jumped the gap – but neither side is in the mood for that.[48]

The train of a final settlement, which some people at least were ready to embark upon in 1972, had at last left the station and made a good deal of progress on its journey, but it was not clear that it still carried any real passengers on board. The Greek constitutional advisor believes that if the second interruption had been prevented, it would have been possible to reach a settlement by early 1973, and this would have subsequently been guaranteed in a five-party conference among the three guarantors and the two communities.[49] If that had been possible, Dekleris estimates that Grivas would have been neutralized and a solution successfully implemented on the island. Nevertheless, this is probably rather too optimistic. Grivas and the *Enosis* front, both in Cyprus and in Greece, seemed determined to disrupt any solution that would have excluded *Enosis*. It is ambivalent whether the extreme factions of the junta military regime in Athens, which eventually violently took the lead in Greece after November 1973, or Grivas' supporters on the island, would have allowed the new constitutional settlement to work. Since 1971, the political environment on the island was becoming more and more envenomed. The conditions in Cyprus would not easily have allowed an easy transition from the fragile *status quo* to a new state of affairs which would have definitively shelved *Enosis* and granted a large degree of autonomy to Turkish-Cypriots.

After six years and with an almost complete settlement drafted, the focus of the two communities' leaderships had shifted elsewhere. Simultaneously with the advisors' discussions, Denktash's concern was diverted to his own internal opposition problems and the constant upgrade of the Turkish-Cypriot Provisional Administration ('TCPA') to a full-fledged autonomous state.[50] Meanwhile, Makarios, greatly pre-occupied by his own violent opposition, declared that there would be 'neither partnerships, nor cantons, nor regional self-government, nor federation'.[51] The only factor that kept the negotiations alive was the reluctance of both parties to openly admit and accept blame for the failure and termination of the inter-communal talks. On the morning of 15 July 1974, the coup instigated by the military regime in Athens and executed by members of the National Guard against Makarios brought to an end the first prolonged and essentially deadlocked phase of Cyprus' post-independence history after 1960. Its effects were to usher in a new post Turkish invasion phase, with its *de facto* partition and a vicious circle of unsuccessful UN peacemaking efforts to settle the Cyprus problem for more than 40 years.

Conclusion

In a study conducted in 1979 on the dynamics of the Cyprus problem and the underlying reasons that led to the 1974 crisis, Paschalis Kitromilides arrived at the following conclusion:

> Foreign strategic interests dictated by the Cold War and power politics in the Middle East have been decisive factors in the development of ethnic conflict within Cyprus. In the context of all this, domestic conflict and the failures of local political leadership only *facilitated* the promotion of foreign interests at the expense of internal peace.[1]

Although the cultivation of mistrust and ethnic rivalry in Cyprus, especially in the 1950s, was indeed manipulated by external factors, and the Zurich-London Agreements had indeed brought to life an inherently divisive bi-communal state, the scope of this book illustrated how domestic policies and internal factors from 1964 until 1974 *determined* to a large extent – rather than merely 'facilitated' – the sequence of events that led up to 1974 crisis. The studies that usually give prominence to the great influence of the external factors into the evolution of the Cyprus problem tend to argue that the partition plans and actions of all interested parties, including the United States, Turkey and Greece, that were particularly evident during the December 1963–August 1964 crises, had been eventually brought to fruition in July 1974.[2] Nonetheless, what is generally downplayed in the literature of the Cyprus problem is the fact that the situation on the island from 1964 until 1974 had not been static. Likewise, the foreign policies of Greece and Turkey as well as of the United States and Britain vis-à-vis the Cyprus problem had passed through several stages and variations. Therefore, the aim of this study was to throw into sharp relief the fact that the internal dimension and the *de facto* divergent development of the two communities after 1963–1964, which was mainly domestically driven, had been decisive factors for the tragic ending of an important chapter in Cyprus history.

Since the signing of the Zurich-London Agreements in 1959, both communities firmly believed that independence was merely an interim path towards their long-term, but contradictory aims. First, Greek-

Cypriots felt confident that the recognition of unfettered independence and the implementation of the right of self-determination would eventually convince the international community that *Enosis* with Motherland Greece was inevitable. Conversely, Turkish-Cypriots, even though they had already gained significant political privileges, had evolved a further long-term goal of their own: a federation in Cyprus that would ultimately produce partition. The crisis in 1963–1964 was believed to be the first step towards the fulfilment of all these contradictory goals. Yet although a good deal of the reality forged in 1963–1964 was to remain in place, many of the variables surrounding the political conflict by no means remained static over the following decade.

The most significant 'gain' for the Turkish-Cypriot leadership from the crisis commencing in December 1963 was that events had fortuitously given them an opportunity to seize several strategic parts of the islands, make them into enclaves, encourage and even discipline parts of the minority population to move into these areas. Through these measures the Turkish-Cypriot leaders gradually forged a separate administrative structure of their own. This was the first step for generating the necessary pre-conditions for a federation in Cyprus. Despite their enormous financial difficulties, these separate structures, with Ankara's assistance and without any substantial peacemaking effort during the first years of the separation that could have seriously undermined the leadership's plans, had been consolidated, strengthened as well as expanded their reach to those Turkish-Cypriots who had remained outside the enclaves.

Although the Turkish-Cypriot long-term plans had indeed been ominous, their main pre-condition until 1967 for the initiation of a substantial dialogue between the two communities, that is the full return to the 1960 Constitution, had traces of legality. In 1968, however, they realized that the new realities up to that point were indeed pressing for substantial amendments to the constitution. The *de facto* separation had made them realize that accepting the majority of Makarios' previous 'Thirteen Points' was a small price to pay for securing the genuine local autonomy that they now favoured. This proved to be a unique window of opportunity through which both communities' goals could have been effectively bridged. Nonetheless, there was one critical factor that Greek-Cypriots failed to grasp. Although the three-year separation between 1964 and 1967, and especially Makarios' policies towards the enclaves, had indeed made the Turkish-Cypriots realize the benefit of accepting the 'Thirteen Points', the latter were still adamant on one essential consideration: the preservation of the bi-communal nature of the state and the rejection of the downgrading of their political status gained in 1960.

It is generally acknowledged that the most important victory of the Greek-Cypriot community came in March 1964, when UN Security Council

Resolution 186 confirmed the legitimacy of the Cyprus Government even without the Turkish-Cypriot participation. In this way, the Greek-Cypriots gained full control of the Cyprus state leading towards the creation of an economically and socially stable country. The Doctrine of Necessity proved to be the most vital tool in the government's hands in order to reverse the political injustices produced by the constitution and set the foundations for the unitary state under the majority's rule. By the same token, the Cyprus Government was confident that through the UN mechanisms and resolutions, either of the General Assembly or of the Security Council, it was possible to offset the remaining limitations set by the Treaties of Guarantee and Alliance. 'The Cyprus Government had schooled its public to expect important advantages from the deliberations of the Plenary Assembly of UN.'[3] Thus, the Greek-Cypriot leaders aligned their foreign policy towards securing what they saw as important and essential diplomatic victories within the UN. Finally, another important aspect of the Cyprus Government's policy was the embargo policy against the enclaves. Makarios believed that this strategy would eventually make the Turkish-Cypriots realize that the best interests of their community lay in returning to an economically thriving Republic of Cyprus, even if this meant doing so on terms determined by the stronger side.

Moreover, regarding the *Enosis* question, new realities had also emerged. Although *Enosis* was constantly repeated in public rhetoric, it was no longer feasible, or even desirable, for the majority of Greek-Cypriots. This fact even came to be acknowledged by President Makarios, even though it clashed with so much that he had sought to stand for in his own political and indeed ecclesiastical career. As Attalides suggests, however, the *Enosis* slogan had been manipulated by a dangerous minority within the Greek-Cypriot community in a way that in the end 'reduced politics to chaos.'[4] Attalides also explains that the Greek-Cypriot leaders decided to tackle this great challenge 'not by denouncing *Enosis* as an ultimate aim, but rather by arguing that in the long run they were in favour of pure *Enosis* (between 1963 and 1968), or that *Enosis* was the desirable aim, but it was impracticable (after 1968)'.[5]

All the above Greek-Cypriot policies, however, carried costs: They further alienated the Turkish-Cypriot community, giving them in that way more excuses for consolidating their new *de facto* realities. These realities placed the Cyprus problem onto a more complicated basis. Despite their advantages for the Greek-Cypriot cause, all three policies of the Cyprus Government – the application of the Doctrine of Necessity, the internationalization and the importance given to the UN resolutions along with the embargo policy towards the enclaves – had equally severe side effects for the Cyprus problem. First, all the changes made under the Doctrine of Necessity had fatally neglected the most fundamental aspect of the 1960 Constitution: the bi-communalism which was clearly evident throughout the whole of the rigid, detailed and complex constitution. Second, the UN resolutions provided merely moral support to the Greek-Cypriot cause and limited practical benefits. On the contrary, it could be argued that the diplomatic victories within the UN enhanced the Cyprus Government's intransigence over accepting nothing less than a unitary state under Greek-Cypriot control and minority rights for Turkish-Cypriots. That, as has already been seen, had led to an almost three-year stalemate in the UN peacemaking efforts on the island. Likewise, after the initiation of the inter-communal talks in 1968, the Greek-Cypriot negotiating tactics were still reflecting the same intransigence, leading to detrimental delays in the negotiating process. Finally, the embargo policy towards the enclaves had exacerbated the economic discrepancies between the two communities. In 1969, the British High Commissioner, Peter Ramsbotham commented,

> What is required of the Cyprus Government is to see that it is not in their interest to allow Turkish-Cypriots to fall irretrievably behind in the economic race and, consequently, not to insist on political concessions as a prerequisite for economic assistance. Turkish-Cypriot economic serfdom could only serve to accentuate inter-communal differences and perpetuate grievances with the consequent built-in risk of clashes after settlement.[6]

Bearing in mind all the above, the Greek-Cypriot aim to hold tight the reins of the Republic of Cyprus had to be sought *pari passu* with a substantial effort aiming at winning over the Turkish-Cypriot community, especially the part that continued to live outside the enclaves and the moderate leadership. That would have been an essential dynamic that could have produced a critical push towards inter-communal integration, thereby undermining the separatist plans of the Turkish-Cypriot leadership. This new internal dynamic was characterized by various diplomatic circles, especially after 1968, as a *sine qua non* for a settlement. Inter-communal integration along with substantial inter-communal negotiations could have eventually led towards a lasting political settlement.

In order to achieve integration, however, 'a modus vivendi' was needed; in other words, normalization enhancing inter-communal contacts and cooperation both in the private as in public sector and rehabilitation of refugees. Although both communities' leaders, and especially the Cyprus Government, accepted in theory the importance of normalization, modest efforts for inter-communal integration were promoted and this had been essentially driven from within the private sector, rather than by the Government's policies themselves.[7] Arguably, in passing over the opportunities for integration, the Greek-Cypriots, who were traditionally regarded as more entrepreneurial and dynamically commercial, missed a trick. Certainly, they critically failed to realize the dangers in alienating the Turkish-Cypriots. In 1971, before leaving Cyprus, Ramsbotham ominously concluded,

> if the Archbishop had handled the Turkish-Cypriots from the beginning with as much shrewdness as he has displayed in the United Nations, he might have been nearer to his objective of a Cyprus fully controlled by Greek-Cypriots. By his short-sighted policies towards the Turkish community he is, in effect, realizing his own worst fears – *de facto* partition of Cyprus.[8]

This critique touches on something quite basic in the political career of Makarios. Even back in the early 1950s he had set out to 'internationalize' the Cyprus question, and later as president he had sometimes skilfully presented himself as a leading figure of Non-Alignment. In other words, his acute sense of tactics and his taste for taking risks often led to apparent diplomatic successes. But the same sure touch seemed to desert him when it came to internal politics, and above all anything that concerned other communities than his own.

This study tried to shed some light on certain elements that until today have been considered taboo in Cyprus society: To admit that the impact of the domestic policies of the two communities, especially from mid-1964 until 1971, had a decisive effect on how the Cyprus problem evolved and derailed, leading to the July 1974 tragedy. The ways that the two communities separately developed on the island, coupled with the way that the UN peacemaking efforts produced limited results during this critical decade, were primarily the aftermath of internal policies and choices rather than the exclusive outcome of external manipulations, even though outside diplomacy clearly had a part to play.

However, a historical analysis of any past event is like watching a film you have seen before. When you already know the *finale*, by re-watching the movie you have a clearer perception of the context, the mistakes or the right decisions of the protagonists as well as the information and evidence that they 'failed' to grasp when it was absolutely necessary. Nonetheless, as the protagonists of a movie, the decision makers in politics do not always take decisions based on purely cynical and rational criteria. Political considerations, internal rivalries, psychological barriers, firm beliefs and personality traits inevitably have a critical effect on the decision making or the political planning processes. This is absolutely evident in the peculiar case of Cyprus' politics.

It is impossible at this stage not to see the recent history we have been discussing without resonances of where we are today, with all the inevitable differences this will raise. It has become common among some academics, and perhaps still more generally younger people, to see partition as an inevitable (and often by implication acceptable) destiny for the island.[9] Only time can tell. In some ways, 'formalising' partition – which was brought about by the Turkish invasion of 1974 – would bring about a 'solution' not involving the wrench of painful compromises, and which would give limited benefits to each community. However, in protracted problems in plural societies, of which Cyprus is certainly one, the most broadly based and sustainable solutions do need compromises that are less than optimal for various parties. 'Win-win' outcomes for the society as a whole in the long term can only be brought about by what might be seen as 'lose-lose' compromises along the way. If this remains the nub of things, it was undoubtedly the case in the decade we have examined in this book. Because it was the Greek-Cypriots who then dominated the foreground of political and administrative life in the island, this logic is one that applied most aptly to them. This study has, therefore, sought principally to highlight the driving forces of Greek-Cypriot political culture, since in the 1960s, as today, they are among the keys – though not of course the only ones – to regain a united island if this is indeed the ultimate objective of all the parties involved.

Appendix I

Thirteen Points of Makarios 1963

1. The right of veto of the president and vice-president of the republic to be abolished.
2. The vice-president of the republic to deputize for or replace the president of the republic in case of his temporary absence or incapacity to perform his duties. In consequence all the constitutional provisions in respect of joint action by the president and vice-president of the republic to be modified accordingly.
3. The Greek president of the HoR and its Turkish vice-president to be elected by the House as a whole and not the president by the Greek members of the House and the vice-president by the Turkish members of the House.
4. The vice-president of the HoR to deputize for or replace the president of the House in case of his temporary absence or incapacity to perform his duties.
5. The constitutional provisions regarding a separate majority for enactment of laws by the HoR to be abolished.
6. The separate municipalities in the five main towns to be abolished. Provisions should be made so that:
   a. The municipal council of each of the aforesaid five towns shall consist of Greek and Turkish councillors in proportion to the number of the Greek and Turkish inhabitants of such town by whom they shall be elected respectively.
   b. In the budget of each of such aforesaid towns, after deducting any expenditure required for common services, a percentage of the balance proportionate to the number of the Turkish inhabitants of such town shall be earmarked and disposed of in accordance with the wishes of the Turkish councillors.
7. The constitutional provision regarding courts consisting of Greek judges to try Greeks and of Turkish judges to try Turks and of mixed courts consisting of Greek and Turkish judges to try cases where the litigants are Greeks and Turks to be abolished.
8. The division of the security forces into police and gendarmerie to be abolished (provision to be made in case the head of the police is a Greek the deputy head to be a Turks and vice versa).
9. The numerical strength of the security forces and of the army to be determined by law and not by agreement between the president and vice-president of the republic.
10. The proportion of the participation of Greek-Cypriots and Turkish-Cypriots in the composition of the public service and of the forces of the

Republic, that is, the police and the army to be modified in proportion to the ration of the population of Greek-Cypriots and Turkish-Cypriots.

11. The number of the members of the Public Service Commission to be reduced from then to either five or seven.

12. All the decisions of the Public Service Commission to be taken by simple majority. If there is allegation of discrimination on the unanimous request either of the Greek or of the Turkish members of the Commission, its chairman to be bound to refer the matter to the Supreme Constitutional Court.

13. The Greek communal chamber to be abolished.

Notes

Introduction

1   Paul Sant Cassia, 'The Archbishop in the Beleaguered City: An Analysis of the Conflicting Roles and Political Oratory of Makarios', *Byzantine and Modern Greek Studies*, 8 (1982), p. 192.

2   For a study on UN involvement in Cyprus, see Oliver P. Richmond, *Mediating in Cyprus: The Cypriot Communities and the United* Nations (London: Frank Cass, 1998); James Ker-Lindsay, *The Origins of the United Nations Force in Cyprus (UNFICYP), International Politics on the Road to Security-Council Resolution 186 (1964)* (PhD Thesis, University of Kent at Canterbury, 1997); Oliver P. Richmond and James Ker-Lindsay (eds), *The Work of the UN in Cyprus: Promoting Peace and Development* (Basingstoke: Palgrave Macmillan, 2001).

3   Peter Ramsbotham (Nicosia) to Foreign Commonwealth Office (hereinafter FCO), 23 May 1969: FCO 9/781, The National Archives of the UK (hereinafter TNA).

4   Sir Norman Costar (Nicosia): *Valedictory Dispatch*, p. 2, 26 March 1969: FCO 9/785, TNA.

5   Claude Nicolet, *United States Policy towards Cyprus, 1954–1974, Removing the Greek-Turkish Bone of Contention* (Möhnesee: Bibliopolis, 2001), p. 304.

6   James E. Miller (ed), *Foreign Relations of the United States, 1964–1968, Volume XVI, Cyprus; Greece; Turkey* (Washington: United States Government Printing Office, 2000), http://history.state.gov/historicaldocuments/frus1964-68v16 [Accessed 2 December 2014].

7   *Άπαντα Αρχιεπισκόπου Κύπρου Μακαρίου Γ, Τόμοι Η-ΙΒ] [Collected Works of Archibshop Makarios III Vol. 8–13]* (Nicosia: Makarios III Foundation, 1997–2004).

8   http://www.glafkosclerides.com.cy/Archives.aspx [Accessed 1 December 2014 – Link no longer available].

9   Michael A. Attalides, *Cyprus: Nationalism and International Politics* (Möhnesse: Bibliopolis, 2005), p. 183.

10 Stathis Panagides, 'Communal Conflicts and Economic Considerations: The Case of Cyprus', *Journal of Peace Research*, 5/2 (1968), p. 134; Michael Attalides, 'The Turkish-Cypriots: Their Relations to the Greek-Cypriots in Perspective', in Michael A. Attalides (ed), *Cyprus Reviewed* (Nicosia: The Jus Cypri Association, 1977), pp. 74–76.

11 AKEL: The Communist Party of Cyprus, known as KKK, was founded in 1926. In 1941, evolved into a new political formation named as AKEL (*Ανορθωτικό Κόμμα Εργαζόμενου Λαού*). Information about the Left's

position on the Cyprus problem and *Enosis* in Loukas Kakoullis, *H Αριστερά και οι Τουρκοκύπριοι: το κυπριακό από μια άλλη σκοπιά [The Left and the Turkish-Cypriots: The Cyprus Problem from Another Angle]* (Nicosia: Kasoulides Printings, 1990).

12 Sia Anagnostopoulou, 'Makarios III, 1950–1977: Creating the Ethnarchic State', in Andrekos Varnava and Michalis N. Michael (eds), *The Archbishops of Cyprus in the Modern Age: The Changing Role of the Archbishop-Ethnarch, Their Identities and Politics* (Newcastle upon Tyne: Cambridge Scholars Publishing, 2013), p. 247.

13 Further information about Makarios' Ethnarchic role during this period: Demetris Assos, *Makarios: A Study of Anti-Colonial Nationalist Leadership, 1950–1959* (PhD Thesis, Institute of Commonwealth Studies, University of London, 2009); Anagnostopoulou, 'Makarios III, 1950–1977', pp. 240–290.

14 Anagnostopoulou, 'Makarios III, 1950–1977', pp. 245–247.

15 For helpful treatment of the EOKA struggle and its implications, see Robert Holland, *Britain and the Revolt in Cyprus 1954–1959* (Oxford: Oxford University Press, 1998); Nancy Crawshaw, *The Cyprus Revolt: An Account of the Struggle for Union with Greece* (London: Allen and Unwin, 1978).

16 Sant Cassia, 'The Archbishop in the Beleaguered City', p. 198.

17 Niyazi Kizilyurek, *H Κύπρος: Το αδιέξοδο των εθνικισμών [Cyprus: The Dead-End of Nationalisms]* (Athens: Black List, 1999), p. 35.

18 Altay Nevzat and Mete Hatay, 'Politics, Society and the Decline of Islam in Cyprus: From the Ottoman Era to the Twenty-First Century', *Middle Eastern Studies*, 45/6 (2009), p. 921.

19 Niyazi Kizilyurek, *Οι Τουρκοκύπριοι, η Τουρκία και το Κυπριακό [Turkish-Cypriots, Turkey and the Cyprus Problem]* (Athens: Papazisi Publications, 2009), pp. 45–50.

20 Hubert Faustmann, 'The Colonial Legacy of Division', in James Ker-Lindsay and Hubert Faustmann (eds), *The Government and Politics of Cyprus* (Oxford: Peter Lang, 2008), p. 53.

21 Ismail Tansu, *In Reality No One Was Asleep: A Secret Underground Organization with State Support … TMT* (Nicosia: Bolan Printing Limited, 2007), p. 27.

22 Ibid.

23 For an elaborative analysis on the theories of nationalism and their implementation on the Cyprus' case, consult Kizilyurek, *Το αδιέξοδο*.

24 Ibid., p. 37.

25 Evangelos Averoff-Tossizza, *Lost Opportunities: The Cyprus Question 1950–1964* (New Rochelle: Caratzas, 1986), pp. 305–362.

26 Diana Weston Markides, *Cyprus 1957–1963, From Colonial Conflict to Constitutional Crisis, The Key Role of the Municipal Issue* (Minnesota: Minnesota Mediterranean and East European Monographs, 2001), p. 44.

27 Stella Soulioti, *Fettered Independence, Cyprus, 1878–1964: The Narrative* (Minnesota: Minnesota Mediterranean and East European Monographs, 2006), pp. 101–102.

28 Averoff-Tossizza, *Lost Opportunities*, p. 387.
29 For the basic structure of the Republic of Cyprus, see Glafkos Clerides, *My Deposition, Vol. I* (Nicosia: Alitheia, 1989), pp. 416–432.
30 Kizilyurek, *Το αδιέξοδο*, pp. 41–42.
31 More information on the transition period: Soulioti, *Fettered Independence*, pp. 101–107; Weston Markides, *Cyprus 1957–1963*, pp. 43–69; Hubert Faustmann, 'Independence Postponed 1959–1960', in Emilios Solomou and Hubert Faustmann (eds), *Colonial Cyprus 1878–1960. Selected Readings from the Cyprus Review* (Nicosia: University of Nicosia Press, 2010), pp. 235–246.
32 Weston Markides, *Cyprus 1957–1963*, p. 69.
33 For an analysis of the first political formations and the first presidential and parliamentary elections, see Clerides, *My Deposition, Vol. I*, pp. 87–108.
34 Christophoros Christophorou, 'The Evolution of the Greek-Cypriot Party Politics', in James Ker-Lindsay and Hubert Faustmann (eds), *The Government and Politics of Cyprus* (Oxford: Peter Lang, 2008), p. 86.
35 Weston Markides, *Cyprus 1957–1963*, pp. 58–59.
36 Christophorou, 'The Evolution', p. 86.
37 Kyriakos C. Markides, *The Rise and the Fall of the Cyprus Republic* (London: Yale University Press, 1977), p. 82.
38 Faustmann, 'Independence Postponed', p. 234.
39 Arif Hasan Tahsin, *Η Άνοδος του Ντενκτάς στην Κορυφή [Denktash's Rise]* (Nicosia: Diafania, 2001), p. 130.
40 Kizilyurek, *Οι Τουρκοκύπριοι*, p. 82; Weston Markides, *Cyprus 1957–1963*, p. 49.
41 Robert Holland and Hubert Faustmann, 'Independence through the Colonial Eye: A View from the British Archive', *The Cyprus Review*, 22/2 (2010), p. 49.
42 Ibid., p. 50.
43 Ibid., p. 57.
44 Ibid., p. 51.
45 Ibid., p. 50.
46 Yiannis Papadakis, 'Reflections on the 1st October Commemoration of the Independence of Cyprus', *The Cyprus Review*, 22/2 (2010), p. 62.
47 Zaim M. Necatigil, *The Cyprus Question and the Turkish Position in International Law* (Oxford: Oxford University Press, 1989), p. 15.
48 Niyazi Kizilyurek, *Glafkos Clerides: The Path of a Country* (Nicosia: Rimal Publications, 2008), p. 97.
49 Clerides, *My Deposition, Vol. I*, p. 130.
50 Ibid., pp. 114–126. More about the main constitutional tension areas in Stanley Kyriakides, *Cyprus: Constitutionalism and Crisis Government* (Philadelphia: University of Pennsylvania Press, 1968), pp. 72–103.
51 Paul Sant Cassia. 'Patterns of Covert Politics in Post-Independence Cyprus.' *European Journal of Sociology*, 24/1 (1983), pp. 115–135, 122; Attalides, *Nationalism and International Politics*, p. 55.

52 Ismail Tansu, *In Reality No One Was Asleep: A Secret Underground Organization with State Support … TMT* (Nicosia: Bolan Printing Limited 2007), p. 27.
53 Ibid., p. 13.
54 See Appendix I.
55 Soulioti, *Fettered Independence*, p. 315.
56 Necati Münir Ertekün, *The Cyprus Dispute and the Birth of the Turkish Republic of Northern Cyprus* (Nicosia: K. Rustem, 1984), p. 13.
57 Soulioti, *Fettered Independence*, p. 368.
58 Ibid., p. 369.
59 James Ker-Lindsay, 'The Origins of the United Nations Force in Cyprus (UNFICYP): International Politics on the Road to United Nations Security Council Resolution 186 (1964)' (PhD Thesis, University of Kent at Canterbury, 1997), p. 123.
60 Further information about the Security-Council proceedings in Ker Lindsay, 'The origins of the UN Force in Cyprus'.
61 Security-Council Resolution 186, 4 March 1964 (S/5575).
62 Soulioti, *Fettered Independence*, p. 465.
63 Claude Nicolet, *United States Policy towards Cyprus, 1954–1974: Removing the Greek-Turkish Bone of Contention.* (Möhnesee: Bibliopolis, 2001), p. 293.
64 UN Security-Council, *Report by the Secretary-General on the UN Operation in Cyprus, 26 April–8 June 1964* (S/5764), 15 June 1964.
65 Nicolet, *US Policy,* pp. 236–246.
66 Ibid., p. 230.
67 Ibid., p. 231.
68 Ibid., p. 306.
69 Soulioti, *Fettered Independence*, p. 371.

Chapter 1

1 Press Release UNC88, Press Conference by Galo Plaza, Special Representative of the secretary-general on 17 September 1964: DO 220/121, TNA.
2 UN Security-Council, *Report of the UN Mediator on Cyprus to the Secretary-General,* 26 March 1965 (S/6253), paragraph 169.
3 Ibid., paragraph 170.
4 Sir Patrick Dean (New York) to Foreign Office (hereafter FO), 14 March 1964: DO 220/120, TNA.
5 Linda B. Miller, *World Order and Local Disorder: The United Nations and Internal Conflicts* (Princeton: Princeton University Press, 1967), p. 130; Derek Dodson (FO): *Visit of the UN Mediator,* 16 October 1964: FO 371/174770, TNA.

6   *The Morning Record*, 23 September 1964.
7   Ibid.
8   John Rennie (FO): *Cyprus, Appointment of a Mediator*, 14 September 1964: FO 371/174770, TNA.
9   Press Release UNC88, 17 September 1964: DO 220/121, TNA.
10 Dodson, *Visit of the UN Mediator*, 16 October 1964: FO 371/174770, TNA.
11 Memorandum of Conversation, US Department of State (hereafter DoS), 9 November 1964, Doc. 164: US Department of State (DoS): https://history.state.gov/historicaldocuments/frus1964-68v16.
12 Claude Nicolet, *United States Policy towards Cyprus, 1954–1974, Removing the Greek-Turkish Bone of Contention* (Möhnesee: Bibliopolis, 2001), pp. 306–312; Dodson, *Visit of the UN Mediator*, 16 October 1964: FO 371/174770, TNA.
13 Major-General Alec Bishop (Nicosia) to Commonwealth Relations Office (hereafter CRO), 21 September 1964: DO 220/121, TNA.
14 Memorandum of Conversation, DoS, 9 November 1964, Doc. 164: US DoS, https://history.state.gov/historicaldocuments/frus1964-68v16.
15 For more information, see Petros E. Garoufalias, *Ελλάς και Κύπρος: Τραγικά Σφάλματα, ευκαιρίες που χάθηκαν (19 Φεβρουαρίου 1964–15 Ιουλίου 1965) [Greece and Turkey: Tragic Mistakes, Lost Opportunities 19 February 1964–15 July 1965]* (Athens: Bergadi Publications, 1982); Spyros Papageorgiou, *Από την Ζυρίχη εις στον Αττίλα, Τόμος II [From Zurich to Attilas, Vol. II]* (Athens: Ladias, 1980).
16 Henry Labouisse (Athens) to DoS, 9 October 1964, Doc. 163: US DoS, https://history.state.gov/historicaldocuments/frus1964-68v16.
17 Michael A. Attalides, *Cyprus: Nationalism and International Politics* (Möhnesse: Bibliopolis, 2005), p. 8.
18 Ibid., p. 141.
19 Dean Rusk (DoS) to Ankara, 5 June 1964, Doc. 54: US DoS, https://history.state.gov/historicaldocuments/frus1964-68v16.
20 Raymond Hare (Ankara) to DoS, 8 September 1964, Doc. 156: US DoS, https://history.state.gov/historicaldocuments/frus1964-68v16; Tozun Bahceli, 'Cyprus in the Politics of Turkey since 1955', in Norma Salem (ed), *Cyprus: A Regional Conflict and Its Resolution* (London: Macmillan Press, 1992), p. 66; Suha Bolukbasi, *The Superpowers and the Third World: Turkish-American Relations and Cyprus* (Lanham: University Press of America, 1988), p. 89.
21 Bishop to CRO, 12 October 1964: FO 371/174770, TNA.
22 Press Release UNC88, 17 September 1964: DO 220/121, TNA.
23 Zenon Stavrinides, *The Cyprus Conflict: National Identity and Statehood* (Nicosia: Loris Stavrinides Press, 1976), pp. 57–60.
24 Hare to DoS, 30 November 1964, Doc. 166: US DoS, https://history.state.gov/historicaldocuments/frus1964-68v16.
25 Robert Stephens, *Cyprus: A Place of Arms. Power Politics and Ethnic Conflict in the Eastern Mediterranean* (London: Pall Mall Press, 1966), p. 202.

26 UN Security-Council, *Report of the UN Mediator* (S/6253), paragraph 67.
27 Memorandum of Conversation (DoS), 9 November 1964, Doc. 164: US DoS, https://history.state.gov/historicaldocuments/frus1964-68v16.
28 Ibid.; FO to UK Mission New York, 20 October 1964: DO 220/121, TNA.
29 Interview with Glafkos Clerides, Nicosia, 23 September 2011.
30 UN Security-Council, *Report by the Secretary-General on the UN Operations in Cyprus,* 10 September 1964 (S/5950), paragraphs 188–191; Richard A. Patrick, *Political Geography and the Cyprus Conflict, 1963–1971* (Waterloo: Department of Geography, Faculty of Environmental Studies, University of Waterloo, 1976), p. 106.
31 *Eleftheria,* 12 February 1965.
32 *Cyprus Mail,* 27 February 1965; Arthur Adair (Nicosia) to Christopher Diggines (CRO), 31 December 1965: DO 220/50, TNA.
33 *Cyprus Mail,* 2 January 1964.
34 FO to UK Mission, New York, 20 October 1964: DO 220/121, TNA; Sir David Hunt (Nicosia), *Reactions to the UN Mediator's Report,* 7 May 1965: DO 220/110, TNA.
35 Program of Visits of Foreign Office Officials in African and Asian countries, November 1964–January 1965: FA1/1840, Cyprus State Archive.
36 Nicolet, *US Policy,* p. 314; Hare to DoS, 1 October 1964, Doc. 161; Toby Belcher (Nicosia) to DoS, 10 February 1965, Doc. 176: US DoS, https://history.state.gov/historicaldocuments/frus1964-68v16.
37 Hare to DoS, 19 March 1965, Doc. 182: US DoS, https://history.state.gov/historicaldocuments/frus1964-68v16.
38 Record of Meeting: Cyril Pickard and Rauf Denktash at CRO, 7 December 1964: DO 220/178, TNA.
39 UN Security-Council, *Letter Dated 26 August 1964, from the Permanent Representatives of Turkey Addressed to the President of the Security-Council* (S/5916).
40 *Bozkurt,* 10 February 1965 cited in DO 220/65, TNA; UN Security-Council, *Report of the UN Mediator* (S/6253), paragraph 46.
41 Bishop to CRO, 12 October 1964: DO 220/121, TNA; Memorandum of Conversation (DoS), 9 November 1964, Doc.164: US DoS, https://history.state.gov/historicaldocuments/frus1964-68v16; Criton G. Tornaritis, *Cyprus and Federalism* (Nicosia: 1974), pp. 5–7.
42 UN Security-Council, *Report by the Secretary-General,* 10 September 1964 (S/5950), paragraph 103.
43 Intelligence Report No. 80, 20–28 October 1964, Intercommunal Affairs: WO 386/2, TNA.
44 Stavrinides, *The Cyprus Conflict,* p. 58.
45 Niyazi Kizilyurek, *Οι Τουρκοκύπριοι, η Τουρκία και το Κυπριακό* (Athens: Papazisi Publications, 2009), p. 57; Yael Navaro-Yashin, 'Affect in the Civil Service: A Study of a Modern State-System', *Postcolonial Studies,* 9/3 (2006), pp. 281–294 and 'Confinement and Imagination: Sovereignty and

Subjectivity in a Quasi State', in Thomas Blom Hansen and Finn Stepputat (eds), *Sovereign Bodies: Citizens, Migrants, and States in the Postcolonial World* (Princeton: Princeton University Press, 2005), pp. 103–119.

46 Bishop to CRO, 14 September 1964: DO 220/56, TNA.

47 Hare to DoS, 30 November 1964, Doc. 166: US DoS, https://history.state. gov/historicaldocuments/frus1964-68v16.

48 Intelligence Report No. 82, 3–10 November 1964, General: WO 386/2, TNA.

49 Research Department Memorandum, Soviet Policy towards the Middle East (January–October 1965), 19 July 1965: DO 220/11, TNA.

50 Hare to DoS, 30 November 1964, Doc. 166: US DoS, https://history.state. gov/historicaldocuments/frus1964-68v16.

51 Ibid; Memorandum of Conversation (DoS), 9 November 1964, Doc. 164: US DoS, https://history.state.gov/historicaldocuments/frus1964-68v16.

52 Interview with Glafkos Clerides, Nicosia, 23 September 2011.

53 Memorandum of Conversation, New York, 4 December 1964, Doc. 168: US DoS, https://history.state.gov/historicaldocuments/frus1964-68v16.

54 Ibid.

55 Reports from meetings of the Cypriot and Turkish foreign ministers in December 1969 reflect the same position. See John Edmonds (Ankara) to FCO, 20 December 1969: FCO 9/783, TNA; Peter Ramsbotham (Nicosia) to FCO, 31 December 1969: FCO 9/1147, TNA.

56 Bishop to CRO, 12 October 1964: DO 220/121, TNA.

57 Memorandum of Conversation (DoS), 9 November 1964, Doc. 164: US DoS, https://history.state.gov/historicaldocuments/frus1964-68v16. Record of Meeting of Commonwealth Secretary and Plaza, 20 October 1964: DO 220/121, TNA; Memo by Richard Parsons (FO), 27 November 1964: FO 371/174770, TNA.

58 Helpful treatment for Cyprus and Turkish politics within: Haralambos Kafkarides, *Τουρκία-Κύπρος 1923–1960: Η Τουρκική Πολιτική στο Κυπριακό από τον Ατατούρκ στον Μεντερές [Turkey-Cyprus 1923–1960: The Turkish Policy towards the Cyprus Problem from Ataturk to Menderes]* (Nicosia: Amorgos, 2010), pp. 137–157.

59 Ibid.

60 UN Security-Council, *Report of the UN Mediator* (S/6253), paragraph 8.

61 Michael Steward (FO) to Lord Caradon (UKMIS, New York), 5 March 1965: FO 371/179996, TNA; Bishop to CRO, 16 February 1965: DO 220/121,TNA.

62 Bishop to CRO, 16 February 1965: DO 220/121, TNA.

63 Bishop to CRO No. 289, 26 February 1965: DO 220/121, TNA.

64 Dodson: *Visit of the UN Mediator,* 16 October 1964: FO 371/174770, TNA.

65 Memorandum of Conversation (DoS), 9 November 1964, Doc. 164: US DoS, https://history.state.gov/historicaldocuments/frus1964-68v16.

66 Ibid.

67 Bishop, Nicosia to CRO, 17 November 1964: TNA, DO 220/121.

68 Record of Meeting: Commonwealth Secretary and Galo Plaza, London, 20 October 1964: DO 220/121, TNA; Memorandum of Conversation (DoS), 9 November 1964, Doc. 164: US DoS, https://history.state.gov/historicaldocuments/frus1964-68v16.

69 Steward to Lord Caradon, 5 March 1965: FO 371/179996, TNA.

70 Bishop to CRO, 17 November 1964: DO 220/121, TNA.

71 Memorandum of Conversation (DoS), 4 February 1965, Doc. 175: US DoS, https://history.state.gov/historicaldocuments/frus1964-68v16; Steward to Lord Caradon, 5 March 1965: FO 371/179996, TNA; Adair to Diggines, 31 December 1965: DO 220/50, TNA.

72 Rusk to Athens, 22 January 1965, Doc. 170: US DoS, https://history.state.gov/historicaldocuments/frus1964-68v16; Memorandum of Conversation, DoS, 4 February 1965, Doc. 175; Belcher to DoS, 1 February 1965, Doc. 174: US DoS, https://history.state.gov/historicaldocuments/frus1964-68v16; Record of Conversation, with Galo Plaza, DoS, 2 February 1965: DO 220/121, TNA.

73 Hunt, *Reactions to the UN Mediator's Report*, p. 2, 7 May 1965: DO 220/110, TNA.

74 Bishop to CRO, 26 February 1965: DO 220/121, TNA; Steward to Lord Caradon, 5 March 1965: FO 371/179996, TNA.

75 Steward to Lord Caradon, 5 March 1965: FO 371/179996, TNA.

76 Rachel Owen (Washington) to FO, 10 March 1965: FO 371/179996, TNA.

77 FO to Ankara, 25 February 1965: DO 220/121, TNA.

78 Hunt, *Reactions to the UN Mediator's Report*, p. 3, 7 May 1965: DO 220/110, TNA.

79 Ibid.

80 Dodson, *Talks in London with the UN Mediator*, 27 February 1965: FO 371/179996, TNA; Nicolet, *US Policy*, p. 316.

81 Steward to Lord Caradon, 5 March 1965: FO 371/179996, TNA.

82 UN, Security-Council, *Report of the UN Mediator*, 26 March 1965 (S/6253).

83 Ibid., paragraph 113.

84 Ibid., paragraphs 123–124.

85 Ibid., paragraphs 123, 147, 159–164.

86 Ibid., paragraphs 126–129.

87 Ibid., paragraph 146.

88 Ibid., paragraphs 156–157.

89 Dennis Allen (Ankara) to FO, 1 April 1965: DO 220/110, TNA.

90 Allen to FO No. 375 and No. 376, 2 April 1965: DO 220/110, TNA.

91 Ibid.

92 DoS to Secretary of State Rusk, 6 April 1965, Doc. 186: US DoS, https://history.state.gov/historicaldocuments/frus1964-68v16.

93 Ibid.

94 UN Security-Council, *Exchange of Letters between the Permanent Representative of Turkey and the Secretary-General, regarding the Report of the UN Mediator* (S/6267), 2 April 1965.

95 Ibid.

96   Hunt to CRO, 3 April 1965: DO 220/110, TNA.
97   Statement by the Turkish-Cypriot Leadership on the Report of the UN
     Mediator, 2 April 1965: DO 220/110, TNA.
98   Intelligence Report No. 14/65, 30 March–6 April 1965, General: WO 386/3, TNA.
99   FO to Washington, 1 April 1965: FO 371/179996, TNA.
100 *Machi*, 31 March 1965; *Patris*, 1–2 April 1965; Interview with Lellos
     Demetriades, Nicosia, 27 May 2014; *Private Papers of Major-General Sir
     Alec Bishop*, p. 292: Imperial War Museum.
101 UN Security-Council, *Report of the UN Mediator* (S/6253), paragraph 142.
102 *Eleftheria*, 1 April 1965.
103 Hunt to CRO, 23 April 1965: DO 220/49, TNA.
104 Intelligence Report No. 16/65, 13–21 April 1965, Views of General Grivas:
     CAB 191/10, TNA. Note: After the end of the EOKA struggle, Colonel
     Georgios Grivas returned to Athens where he was promoted to general.
105 *The Economist*, Foreign Report, 8 April 1965.
106 UN Security-Council, *Note Verbale Dated 12 April 1965 from the
     Permanent Representative of Cyprus Addressed to the Secretary-General*
     (S/6275/Add.1).
107 David Hunt, *On the Spot: An Ambassador Remembers* (London: Peter
     Davies, 1975), p. 157.
108 Ibid.
109 Plaza's Resignation, 5 January 1966, Doc. 83: FA1/1881, Cyprus State
     Archive.
110 Plaza's letter of resignation, 22 December 1965: DO 220/110, TNA.
111 Oliver Richmond, 'UN Mediation in Cyprus, 1964–65: Setting a Precedent
     for Peace-Making', in Oliver P. Richmond and James Ker-Lindsay (eds),
     The Work of the UN in Cyprus: Promoting Peace and Development
     (Basingstoke: Palgrave Macmillan, 2001), pp. 101–126 (p. 115).
112 Nicolet, *US policy*, p. 318.
113 Richmond, 'UN Mediation', p. 115.
114 Donald Tebbit (Copenhagen) to Dodson, 1 March 1966: DO 220/28, TNA.
115 Ibid.
116 Michael Brown (Ankara) to FCO, 7 December 1971: FCO 9/1357, TNA.
117 More on that aspect will be presented in chapters 4 and 6.
118 More on the differences between mediation-'good offices', in G. R.
     Berridge, *Diplomacy: Theory and Practice* (Basingstoke: Palgrave, 2005),
     pp. 194–195; Richmond, *Mediating in Cyprus*, pp. 25–31.
119 Interview with Galo Plaza Lasso, 28 March 1984: Dag Hammarskjold
     Library: United Nations Oral History, http://dag.un.org/
     handle/11176/89710 [Accessed 2 March 2017].
120 Ibid.
121 Richard Haas, 'Ripeness and the Settlement of International Disputes',
     Survival: Global Politics and Strategy, 30/3 (1988), p. 241.
122 Bishop to CRO, 27 February 1965: DO 220/121, TNA.

Chapter 2

1 Bishop to CRO, 2 February 1965: DO 220/132, TNA.
2 (1964) Cyprus Law Reports 195. http://www.uniset.ca/other/
cs2/1964CLR195.html [Accessed 2 December 2014].
3 *Eleftheria*, 24 March 1965.
4 Nicholas C. Lanitis, 'Cyprus Must Be United: Our Destiny', series of articles
in *Cyprus Mail*, 3–7 March 1963.
5 PIO, Press Release, Speech of the Minister of Education and Culture
Andreas Demetriou at the memorial service for Constantinos Spyridakis,
Nicosia, 17 January 2011.
6 Kyriakos C. Markides, *The Rise and the Fall of the Cyprus Republic*
(London: Yale University Press, 1977), p. 98; Andreas Kasoulides, *Πολιτική,
Εκπαιδευτική Πολιτική και Διδασκαλικός Συνδικαλισμός στην Κύπρο
(1960–1974) [Politics, Educational Politics and Teachers Unions]* (Nicosia:
Epifaniou Publishings, 2016), p. 165; *Agon*, 24 December 1968.
7 Sir Norman Costar (Nicosia), *Vested Interests and the Cyprus Problem*, p. 4,
11 September 1968: FCO 9/786, TNA.
8 Interview with Lellos Demetriades, Nicosia, 27 May 2014.
9 Ibid.
10 *Eleftheria*, 25 November 1964.
11 Demetris Christodoulou, *Inside the Cyprus Miracle: The Labours of an
Embattled Mini-Economy* (Minneapolis: University of Minnesota, 1992),
p. 10; Kasoulides, *Πολιτική*, pp. 505–508; *Eleutheria*, 17 March 1966.
12 Claude Nicolet, 'The Turkish Cypriot Failure to Return to Cypriot
Government in 1964: A View from the US Archives', in John
Charalambous, Alicia Chrysostomou et al. (eds), *Cyprus, 40 Years from
Independence: Proceedings from a Conference Held at the University of North
London 16–17 November 2000* (Möhnesee: Bibliopolis, 2002), p. 63.
13 Dean Rusk (DoS) to Nicosia, 28 March 1964, Doc. 28: US DoS, https://
history.state.gov/historicaldocuments/frus1964-68v16.
14 Ibid.
15 Nicolet, 'The Turkish Cypriot Failure', p. 64.
16 UN Security-Council, *Letter Dated 25 April 1966 from the Permanent
Representative of Turkey Addressed to the Secretary General* (S/7267),
26 April 1966 (see also UN documents S/7276 and S/7304).
17 William Peters (Nicosia) to Peter Lewis (CRO), 23 April 1966: FO
371/185620, TNA.
18 Ibid.
19 CRO to Nicosia, 4 May 1966: FO 371/185620, TNA; *Cyprus Mail*, 15 July
1967.
20 Diana Weston Markides, *Cyprus 1957–1963, From Colonial Conflict to
Constitutional Crisis, The Key Role of the Municipal Issue* (Minnesota:
Minnesota Mediterranean and East European Monographs, 2001), p. 178.

21 The Municipal Corporations Law 1964 cited in FCO 27/70, TNA;
Philelftheros, 29 December 1964.
22 Intelligence Report No. 86, 1–8 December 1964, Turkish-Cypriot Press:
WO 386/2, TNA.
23 Labour Report 1966–1967, Tel Aviv, 18 January 1968: LAB 13/2205, TNA.
24 Ο περί Επιτροπής Δημοσίας Υπηρεσίας (Προσωριναί Διατάξεις) Νόμος
του 1965 (Ν. 72/1965); Ο περί Δημοσίας Υπηρεσίας Νόμος του 1967 (Ν.
33/1967) [Legislation about Public Service Commission 1965 & 1967].
25 Peters to Lewis, 11 December 1965: DO 220/150, TNA.
26 UN Security-Council, *Letter Dated 13 December 1965 from the
Permanent Representative Turkey Addressed to Secretary-General* (S/7013),
14 December 1965; UN Security-Council, *Letter Dated 3 October 1966 from
Permanent Representative Turkey Addressed to Secretary-General* (S/7527),
4 October 1966.
27 Stathis Panagides, 'Communal Conflicts and Economic Considerations:
The Case of Cyprus', *Journal of Peace Research*, 5/2 (1968), pp. 142–144.
28 *Kipros*, 29 March 1965.
29 Rebecca Bryant and Mete Hatay, 'Guns and Guitars: Stimulating
Sovereignty in a State of Siege', *American Ethnologist*, 38/4 (2011), p. 634.
30 Richard A. Patrick, *Political Geography and the Cyprus Conflict, 1963–1971*
(Waterloo: Department of Geography, Faculty of Environmental Studies,
University of Waterloo, 1976), p. 112.
31 Zafer Ali Zihni to Cyril Pickard (Nicosia), 1 March 1964: DO 220/101, TNA.
32 Ibid.
33 Intelligence Report No. 45/65, 2–9 November 1965, Turkish-Cypriot
Affairs: WO 386/3, TNA; Bryant and Hatay, 'Guns and Guitars', p. 636;
Hakan Arslan, *The Political Economy of State–Building: The Case of Turkish-
Cypriots (1960–1967)* (PhD Thesis İstanbul Bilgi University, 2014), p. 615.
34 See reports from August–November 1964 in DO 220/117, TNA.
35 Peters to Tony Lennard (CRO), 30 November 1964: DO 220/117, TNA.
36 Bryant and Hatay, 'Guns and Guitars', p. 638.
37 Patrick, *Political Geography*, p. 75.
38 Arslan, *The political Economy*, p. 606.
39 Paul N. Strong, *The Economic Consequences of Ethnonational Conflict in
Cyprus: The Development of Two Siege Economies after 1963 and 1974* (PhD
Thesis, London School of Economics, 1999), p. 133; Navaro-Yashin, 'Affect
in the Civil Service', p. 287; Eleni Lyras and Charis Psaltis, *Formerly Mixed
Villages in Cyprus: Representation of the Past, Present and Future* (Cyprus:
PRIO, 2011), pp. 14–18.
40 Patrick, *Political Geography*, p. 78.
41 UN Security-Council, *Report by the Secretary-General on the UN
Operations in Cyprus,* 10 September 1964 (S/5950), paragraphs 180–183;
Bryant and Hatay, 'Guns and Guitars', p. 634.
42 Patrick, *Political Geography,* p. 336; UN Security-Council,
Report by the Secretary-General on the UN Operations in Cyprus,

10 September–12 December 1964 (S/6102), 12 December 1964, paragraph 143; Costar to Commonwealth Office (hereinafter CO), 6 April 1967: FCO 9/65, TNA. Note: According to the 1960 Demographic Report the Turkish-Cypriot population was approximately 104,000.

43 Ibid., p. 335.
44 Ibid., p. 82.
45 Ibid.
46 Bryant and Hatay, 'Guns and Guitars', p. 636.
47 Patrick, *Political Geography*, p. 82.
48 Ibid., p. 84; Arslan, *The Political Economy*, p. 618.
49 Peters to Lewis, 30 July 1965: DO 220/132, TNA.
50 Ayla Gürel, *Turkish-Cypriot Legal Framework, Displacement in Cyprus – Consequences of Civil and Military Strife, 4* (Nicosia: PRIO Cyprus Centre, 2012), p. 3.
51 *Special News Bulletin*, 11 May 1966: DO 220/65, TNA.
52 Shemsi Kiazim (Turkish Communal Chamber) to the Administrator of Sovereign Base Areas, 29 December 1964: DO 220/135, TNA; *Kipros*, 2 August 1965.
53 Bryant and Hatay, 'Guns and Guitars', p. 634.
54 Ibid., p. 635.
55 Patrick, *Political Geography*, p. 84. Note: There were five administrative levels: (a) village (or quarter of mixed villages) where the mukhtar or the fighter commander was responsible, (b) the group, where the police and fighter officers within the group's headquarters were responsible, (c) sub-region – it was the lowest level which a Turkish army officer was posted and there were full-time fighter units, (d) region (composed by two or more sub-regions) where the civil affairs were directed by District officers. There were also major police stations and Turkish army colonels, and (e) the Nicosia headquarters and headquarters of the 'General Committee'.
56 Yael Navaro-Yashin, 'Confinement and Imagination: Sovereignty and Subjectivity in a Quasi State', in Thomas Blom Hansen and Finn Stepputat (eds), *Sovereign Bodies: Citizens, Migrants, and States in the Postcolonial World* (Princeton: Princeton University Press, 2005), pp. 103–119 (p. 107).
57 Erol Kaymak, 'The Development of the Turkish-Cypriot Politics', in James Ker-Lindsay and Hubert Faustmann (eds), *The Government and Politics of Cyprus* (Bern: Peter Lang, 2009), pp. 231–256 (p. 233).
58 Arslan, *The Political Economy*, pp. 614–617.
59 Ibid., pp. 620–624.
60 *Cyprus Mail*, 26 January 1967; Tahsin, Η Άνοδος του Ντενκτάς, pp. 98–102; Oliver Miles (Nicosia) to FCO, 18 June 1971: FCO 9/1367, TNA. Note: In March 1966, the Cyprus Government accused Coshkun of being the mastermind behind the bomb explosions in the recently built oil refinery in Larnaca and he declared him as *persona non grata*: see file FCO 27/100, TNA.

61 Miles to FCO, 18 June 1971: FCO 9/1367, TNA.
62 Michael Dekleris, *Κυπριακό: Η Τελευταία Ευκαιρία 1972–1974 [The Cyprus Problem: The Last Chance 1972–1974]* (Athens: Sideris, 2003), p. 80.
63 *Eleftheria,* 2 February 1965.
64 Bishop to CRO, 6 February 1965: DO 220/49, TNA.
65 Ibid.
66 Christopher Makins (CRO), 20 July 1965: FO 371/179973, TNA; Hunt, *Cyprus at the Security-Council, August 1965*, p. 2, 20 August 1965: DO 220/133, TNA.
67 Glafkos Clerides, *My Deposition, Vol. II* (Nicosia: Alitheia, 1989), p. 150.
68 Richard Sykes (Athens) to FO, 3 February 1965: DO 220/132, TNA.
69 Clerides, *My Deposition, Vol. II*, p. 86.
70 *Phileleftheros,* 26 February 1965.
71 Lord Caradon to FO, 24 July 1965: DO 220/132, TNA.
72 Nigel Trench (Washington) to Derek Dodson (FO), 18 February 1965: DO 220/132, TNA.
73 Ibid.
74 Denis Allen (Ankara) to FO, 2 February 1965: DO 220/132, TNA.
75 Bishop to CRO, 2 February 1965: DO 220/132, TNA.
76 Ibid.
77 *Haravgi,* 10 February 1965.
78 *Eleftheria,* 21 July 1965.
79 PIO, Press Release, 22 July 1965.
80 PIO, Press Release, Statement by the President of the HoR, 22 July 1965.
81 Ibid.
82 Republic of Cyprus, *Πρακτικά της Βουλής των Αντιπροσώπων, Σύνοδος E [Minutes of House of Representatives, Session E]* (Nicosia: Government Printing Office-RoC, 1966), pp. 130–134.
83 Ibid.
84 *Eleftheria,* 24 July 1965.
85 PIO, Press Release, Statement by the President of the HoR, 22 July 1965.
86 *Eleftheria,* 24 July 1965.
87 Hunt to CRO No. 946, 28 July 1965: DO 220/132, TNA.
88 Ibid.
89 Peters to Lewis, 30 July 1965: DO 220/132, TNA.
90 FO to Athens, 23 July 1965: FO 371/179973, TNA.
91 Ralph Murray (Athens) to FO, 27 July 1965: DO 220/132, TNA.
92 Lord Caradon to FO, 24 July 1965: DO 220/132, TNA; Hunt, *Cyprus at the Security-Council, August 1965,* p. 4, 20 August 1965: DO 220/133, TNA.
93 Hunt to CRO, 28 July 1965: DO 220/132, TNA.
94 Hunt to CRO No. 938, 26 July 1965: FO 371/179973, TNA.
95 *Phileleftheros,* 3 August 1965.
96 Hunt, *Cyprus at the Security-Council, August 1965,* p. 4, 20 August 1965: DO 220/133, TNA.

97 Pemberton-Piggott to FO, 30 July 1965: DO 220/132, TNA.
98 FO to Ankara, 29 July 1965: FO 371/179973, TNA.
99 *Eleftheria,* 3 August 1965.
100 *The Times,* 19 August 1965; PIO, Press Release, *The Foreign Minister Returns,* 17 August 1965.
101 UN Security-Council Resolution 207 (1965), 10 August 1965, 1236th meeting.
102 Hunt, *Cyprus at the Security-Council, August 1965,* summary, 20 August 1965: DO 220/133, TNA.
103 Peter Goulden (Ankara) to Christopher Makins (FO), 13 August 1965: DO 220/41, TNA; Hunt to CRO, 11 August 1965: DO 220/133, TNA.
104 Intelligence Report No. 33/65, 10–17 August 1965, General: WO 386/4, TNA.
105 Costar to CO, 15 January 1968: FCO 27/79, TNA; PIO Press Release, 15 February 1968.
106 CRO to Nicosia, 18 August 1965: DO 220/133, TNA.
107 *Special News Bulletin,* Saturday, 31 July 1965: DO 220/65, TNA.
108 *Cyprus Mail,* 1 January 1967.
109 Bishop to CRO, 24 July 1964: DO 220/152, TNA.
110 Bulletin of the International Commission of Jurists, September 1966, Article: The Administration of Justice in Cyprus: DO 220/152, TNA.
111 PIO, Press Release, *A Law on the Administration of Justice,* 9 July 1964; Chief registrar to the director-general of the Ministry of Foreign Affairs (Nicosia), 16 July 1964: FA2/1027, Cyprus State Archive.
112 Statement by the President of the Republic of Cyprus, cited in Bishop to CRO, 21 July 1964: DO 220/152, TNA.
113 Arthur Adair (Nicosia), *Cyprus: The Supreme Court,* p. 3, 11 November 1966: DO 220/152, TNA.
114 Ibid.
115 Peter to Lewis, 10 June 1966: DO 220/152, TNA.
116 Adair, *Cyprus: The Supreme Court,* p. 3, 11 November 1966: DO 220/152, TNA.
117 'Cyprus Turkish Information Centre', Press Release, 3 June 1966, Turkish Judges: DO 220/152, TNA.
118 Ibid.
119 PIO, Press Release, *Statement by the President,* 14 June 1966.
120 Adair to CRO, 10 October 1966: DO 220/152, TNA.
121 Ibid.
122 Michael Edes (FO) to Lewis, 19 August 1966: DO 220/152, TNA.
123 PIO, Press Releases, *High Court Appointments,* 9 & 19 September 1966.
124 Peters to Lewis, 9 July 1966: DO 220/152, TNA.
125 For current perceptions of Turkish-Cypriot lawyers about the Doctrine of Necessity: Zaim Necatijil, *The Cyprus Question and the Turkish Position in International Law* (United States: Oxford University Press, 1993), p. 62;

Kudret Özersay, 'The Excuse of State Necessity and Its Implications on the Cyprus Conflict', *Perceptions*, IX (2004–2005), pp. 31–70.

126 Stella Soulioti, *Fettered Independence, Cyprus, 1878–1964: The Narrative* (Minnesota: Minnesota Mediterranean and East European Monographs, 2006), p. 167.

127 Petros E. Garoufalias, *Ελλάς και Κύπρος: Τραγικά Σφάλματα, ευκαιρίες που χάθηκαν (19 Φεβρουαρίου 1964–15 Ιουλίου 1965) [Greece and Turkey: Tragic Mistakes, Lost Opportunities 19 February 1964–15 July 1965]* (Athens: Bergadi Publications, 1982), p. 94; *Phileletheros*, 26 February 1964.

128 Michael A. Attalides, *Cyprus: Nationalism and International Politics* (Möhnesse: Bibliopolis, 2005), p. 69.

129 Garoufalias, *Ελλάς και Κύπρος*, p. 99.

130 Makarios Drousiotis, *The First Partition: Cyprus 1963–1964* (Nicosia: Alphadi, 2008), p. 180.

131 Attalides, *Nationalism and International Politics*, p. 69.

132 *Phileleftheros*, 1 August 1964.

133 Drousiotis, *The First Partition*, p. 204.

134 *Eleftheria*, 18 June 1965.

135 Nikos Kranidiotis, *Ανοχύρωτη Πολιτεία, Κύπρος 1960–1974, Τόμος Ι [The Unfortified State, Cyprus 1960–1974, Vol. I]* (Athens: Estia, 1985), p. 186.

136 Cited in *Eleftheria*, 24 June 1965.

137 Spyros Papageorgiou, Από Την Ζυρίχη Εις Στον Αττίλα. [From Zurich to Attila] 3 Vols. (Athens: G. Ladia, 1980), pp. 222–223.

138 Ibid., Vol. III, p. 75.

139 Ibid., Vol. II, p. 225.

140 Clerides, *My Deposition, Vol. II*, p. 88.

141 Ibid., p. 185.

142 Ibid., p. 96.

143 *Eleftheria*, 3 July 1965.

144 Clerides, *My Deposition, Vol. II*, p. 96.

145 *Phileleftheros*, 4 December 1965.

146 *Eleftheria*, 29 June 1965.

147 Kranidiotis, *Ανοχύρωτη Πολιτεία*, p. 359; Intelligence Report No. 11/66, 22 March 1966: WO 386/4, TNA.

148 Papageorgiou, *Από τη Ζυρίχη στον Αττίλα*, Vol. III, p. 69.

149 Kranidiotis, *Ανοχύρωτη Πολιτεία*, p. 390.

150 Note: The Second Czech arms crisis occurred in February 1972.

151 Clerides, *My Deposition, Vol. II*, pp. 180–181.

152 Brief for Rölz-Bennett's Calls on the Permanent Under-Secretary and Peter Hayman (FO), August 1967: FCO 9/67, TNA; Costar, *The Crisis of November 1967, 28 December 1967*: FCO 27/91, TNA.

153 UN Security-Council, *Report of the Secretary-General on the UN Operations in Cyprus, 13 June 1967* (S/7969), paragraph 27.

154 Ibid., paragraph 48.
155 David Hunt, *On the Spot: An Ambassador Remembers* (London: Peter Davies, 1975), pp. 164–165.
156 Kraniditions, *Ανοχύρωτη Πολιτεία*, p. 231.
157 *Eleftheria*, 30 March 1965.
158 Intelligence Report No. 21/65, 18–25 May 1965, Greek/Cypriot discussions on Missiles: CAB 191/10, TNA.
159 *Άπαντα Αρχιεπισκόπου Κύπρου Μακαρίου III, Τόμος Η' [Collected Works of Archbishop Makarios III, Vol. 8]* (Nicosia: Arch. Makarios III Foundation, 1997), p. 322.
160 Clerides, *My Deposition, Vol. II*, p. 185.
161 Dekleris, *Κυπριακό 1972–1974*, p. 106.
162 Suha Bolukbasi, *The Superpowers and the Third World: Turkish-American Relations and Cyprus* (Lanham: University Press of America, 1988), p. 131.

Chapter 3

1   *Cyprus Mail*, 7 December 1964.
2   Michael A. Attalides, *Cyprus: Nationalism and International Politics* (Möhnesse: Bibliopolis, 2005), p. 75.
3   Willard Thorp, *Cyprus: Suggestions for a Development Programme* (New York: United Nations, 1961), p. v.
4   Republic of Cyprus, *The First Five-Year Plan 1962–1966* (Nicosia: Printing Office of the Republic of Cyprus, 1961).
5   Thorp, *Cyprus*, p. 5.
6   Ibid., p. 3.
7   John Hudson and Marina Dymiotou-Jensen, *Modelling a Developing Country* (Avebury: Gower Publishing Company, 1989), p. 8.
8   Paul N. Strong, *The Economic Consequences of Ethnonational Conflict in Cyprus: The Development of Two Siege Economies after 1963 and 1974* (PhD Thesis, London School of Economics, 1999), p. 64.
9   Thorp, *Cyprus*, p. 4.
10 Hudson and Dymiotou-Jensen, *Modelling a Developing Country*, p. 9.
11 Ibid.
12 Demetris Christodoulou, *Inside the Cyprus Miracle: the Labours of an Embattled Mini-Economy* (Minneapolis: University of Minnesota, 1992), p. xxxi.
13 Thorp, *Cyprus*, p. 96.
14 Ibid., p. 95.
15 Renos Theocharis, 'A General Review of the Cyprus Economy', in Greek Communal Chamber, *Cyprus: A Handbook on the Island's Past and Present* (Nicosia: Publications Department, Greek Communal Chamber, 1964), p. 203.

16 Sir David Hunt, *Cyprus and the Commonwealth*, p. 1, 14 February 1966: DO 220/118, TNA.
17 Ibid.
18 Renos Solomides to Spyros Kyprianou, 26 June 1961: FA1/1270, Cyprus State Archive.
19 Statistics and Research Department, *Economic Review 1961* (Nicosia: Printing Office of the Republic of Cyprus, 1963), p. 12.
20 Ozay Mehmet, *Sustainability of Microstates: The Case of North Cyprus* (Salt Lake City: The University of Utah Press, 2010), p. 22; Stathis Panagides, 'Communal Conflicts and Economic Considerations: The Case of Cyprus', *Journal of Peace Research*, 5/2 (1968), p. 138.
21 Michael Attalides, 'The Turkish-Cypriots: Their Relations to the Greek-Cypriots in Perspective', in Michael A. Attalides (ed), *Cyprus Reviewed* (Nicosia: The Jus Cypri Association, 1977), p. 87.
22 Mehmet, *Sustainability of Microstates*, p. 35; Panagides, 'Communal Conflicts', p. 135.
23 Hakan Arslan, *The Political Economy of State–Building: The Case of Turkish-Cypriots (1960–1967)* (PhD Thesis, İstanbul Bilgi University, 2014); Niyazi Kizilyurek, *Η Κύπρος: Το αδιέξοδο των εθνικισμών [Cyprus: The Dead-End of Nationalisms]* (Athens: Black List, 1999), pp. 84–85.
24 Arslan, *The Political Economy*, p. 438.
25 Ibid., p. 23.
26 Kizilyurek, *Το αδιέξοδο*, p. 85.
27 Diana Weston Markides, *Cyprus 1957–1963, From Colonial Conflict to Constitutional Crisis, The Key Role of the Municipal Issue* (Minnesota: Minnesota Mediterranean and East European Monographs, 2001), p. 49.
28 Arslan, *The Political Economy*, pp. 469–473.
29 Attalides, 'The Turkish-Cypriots', p. 75; Arslan, *The Political Economy*, p. 426.
30 Mehmet, *Sustainability of Microstates*, pp. 37–38.
31 Ibid.
32 Nicholas C. Lanitis, 'Cyprus Must Be United: Our Destiny', series of articles in *Cyprus Mail*, 3–7 March 1963.
33 Ibid.
34 Weston Markides, *Cyprus 1957–1963*, p. 73.
35 Glafkos Clerides, *My Deposition, Vol. I* (Nicosia: Alitheia, 1989), p. 120.
36 Ibid.
37 Stella Soulioti, *Fettered Independence, Cyprus, 1878–1964: The Narrative* (Minnesota: Minnesota Mediterranean and East European Monographs, 2006), pp. 149–156.
38 Ibid.
39 Lanitis, 'Our Destiny'.
40 Ibid.
41 Theocharis, 'A General Review', p. 201.

42 Arslan, *The Political Economy,* p. 451.
43 Sia Anagnostopoulou, 'Η Κυπριακή Δημοκρατία, Καθρέφτης Πολλαπλών Ανακλάσεων: Τουρκία και Τουρκοκυπριακή Κοινότητα, 1960–1983' [The Cyprus Republic, Mirror of Many Reflections: Turkey and the Turkish-Cypriot Community], in Chrysostomos Pericleous (ed), *Κυπριακή Δημοκρατία 50 Χρόνια: Η επώδυνη Πορεία [Republic of Cyprus 50 Years: A Painful Course]* (Athens: Papazisi Publications, 2010), p. 317.
44 The Cyprus Economy since Independence, 1966 by Renos Solomides: DO 220/57, TNA.
45 *The Economist,* 7 March 1964.
46 *Economic Consequences by the Civil Disturbances in Cyprus:* Note by the Economic Advisor, Nicosia, 5 March 1964: DO 220/129, TNA.
47 Theocharis, 'A General Review', p. 205.
48 Hunt, *The Economic Situation in Cyprus,* p. 2, 10 July 1965: DO 220/129, TNA.
49 *Eleftheria,* 3 July 1965.
50 *Cyprus: Economic Situation,* Nicosia, 4 December 1964: DO 220/129, TNA.
51 *Economic Consequences by the Civil Disturbances in Cyprus:* Note by the Economic Advisor, Nicosia, 5 March 1964: DO 220/129, TNA.
52 *The Economist,* 7 March 1964; The Cyprus Development Corporation Ltd, *Second Annual Report, 1964* (Nicosia: 'Proodos' Print & Publ. Co Ltd, 1965).
53 *Economic Consequences by the Civil Disturbances in Cyprus:* Note by the Economic Advisor, Nicosia, 5 March 1964: DO 220/129, TNA.
54 Hunt, *The Economic Situation in Cyprus,* p. 3, 10 July 1965: DO 220/129, TNA.
55 *Cyprus: Economic Situation,* Nicosia, 4 December 1964: DO 220/129, TNA.
56 Ibid.
57 Hunt, *The Economic Situation in Cyprus,* p. 3, 10 July 1965: DO 220/129, TNA.
58 Address by the minister of finance at the Annual Meeting of Larnaca's Chamber of Commerce, 16 May 1965: DO 220/129, TNA.
59 *Cyprus Mail,* 1 January 1967.
60 Labour Report for Cyprus 1965: LAB 13/2205, TNA.
61 Tassos Papadopoulos, 'Labour and Social Insurance', in Greek Communal Chamber, *Cyprus: A Handbook on the Island's Past and Present* (Nicosia: Publications Department, Greek Communal Chamber, 1964), p. 210.
62 *Eleftheria,* 23 April 1965.
63 Cyprus Productivity Centre, Training Programme 1967, Welcome by the minister of labour and social insurance: FA2/972, Cyprus State Archive.
64 Cyprus: The effect of the Emergency on the Trading Conditions, Labour (Nicosia), December 1965: DO 220/129, TNA.
65 Ibid.
66 *Eletheria,* 26 May 1965.

67   *The Three-Pronged Drive*, by Andreas Araouzos 1966: DO 220/57, TNA;
      Also see The Cyprus Development Corporation, *Annual Reports 1964–1974*
      (Nicosia: 'Proodos' Print & Publ. Co Ltd., 1965–1976).
68   Future possibilities for British exports and private investment (Nicosia),
      June 1964: DO 220/38, TNA.
69   *Cyprus Mail*, 1 January 1967.
70   *Phileletheros*, 20 March 1965.
71   *Eleftheria*, 11 February 1965; The Cyprus Development Corporation,
      Annual Reports 1964–1974.
72   Draft Brief on Golden Sands (Nicosia), March 1967: FCO 27/156, TNA.
73   See Trade Agreements in DO 215/150, TNA: Sino-Soviet Economic
      Penetration of Cyprus 1965–1967.
74   Stuart Taylor (Beirut) to Sir Hugh Parry (Ministry of Overseas
      Development), 31 May 1966: DO 220/129, TNA.
75   Ibid.
76   Address by the minister of finance at the Annual Meeting of the Larnaca's
      Chamber of Commerce, 16 May 1965: DO 220/129, TNA.
77   Republic of Cyprus, *The Second Five-Year Plan (1967–1971)* (Nicosia:
      Planning Bureau, 1967), pp. 4–5.
78   *Cyprus Mail*, 22 October 1966.
79   Republic of Cyprus, *The Second Five-Year Plan*, p. 1; Republic of Cyprus,
      The Third Five-Year Plan (1972–1976) (Nicosia: Planning Bureau, 1972),
      p. 4.
80   Ibid.
81   Christodoulou, *Inside the Cyprus Miracle*, p. xiv; Richard A. Patrick,
      Political Geography and the Cyprus Conflict, 1963–1971 (Waterloo:
      Department of Geography, Faculty of Environmental Studies, University of
      Waterloo, 1976), p. 167.
82   Paul N. Strong, *The Economic Consequences of Ethnonational Conflict in
      Cyprus: The Development of Two Siege Economies after 1963 and 1974* (PhD
      Thesis, London School of Economics, 1999) p.76.
83   Paschalis Kitromilides, 'From Coexistence to Confrontation: The Dynamics
      of Ethnic Conflict in Cyprus', in Michael A. Attalides (ed), *Cyprus Reviewed*
      (Nicosia: The Jus Cypri Association, 1977), p. 37.
84   Patrick, *Political Geography*, p. 108.
85   Attalides, 'The Turkish-Cypriots', p. 88.
86   Strong, *The Economic Consequences*, pp. 125–126; Note: Strong cites the
      following abstract from David Barchard: 'Economic information about
      Northern (*sic*) Cyprus was regarded as a virtual military secret by the
      Turkish-Cypriot authorities' (D. Barchard, *Asil Nadir and the Rise and Fall
      of Polly Peck* (London: Victor Gollanc, 1992), p. 91).
87   Patrick, *Political Geography*, p. 167.
88   *Special News Bulletin* No. 417, 18 February 1965: DO 220/135, TNA.
89   Intelligence Report No. 3/65, 12–19 January 1965, Turkish-Cypriot Affairs:
      WO 386/3, TNA; *Eleftheria*, 21 July 1965.

90 In November 1983, Rauf Denktash declared the establishment of the 'TRNC'.
91 Mehmet, *Sustainability of Microstates*, p. 38.
92 Ibid.
93 Arslan, *The Political Economy*, p. 613.
94 Tassos Papadopoulos to Kythreotis (Political Liaison Officer to UNFICYP), 2 October 1965: FA1/1897, Cyprus State Archive.
95 George Mikes, Letter from Cyprus, *Encounter,* March 1965, pp. 87–92 (p. 92).
96 Bishop to Lennard, 14 September 1964: DO 220/56, TNA.
97 Tassos Papadopoulos to Kythreotis, Political Liaison Officer to UNFICYP, 2 October 1965: FA1/1897, Cyprus State Archive.
98 Strong, *The Economic Consequences,* p. 139.
99 Per Capita GDP for the Cypriot Ethnic Communities 1963–1968: In Patrick, *Political Geography*, p. 109.
100 Patrick, *Political Geography*, p. 109.
101 Rebecca Bryant and Mete Hatay, 'Guns and Guitars: Stimulating Sovereignty in a State of Siege', *American Ethnologist*, 38/4 (2011), p. 635.
102 Arslan, *The Political Economy*, p. 611.
103 *Eleftheria*, 11 March 1966.
104 Patrick, *Political Geography,* p. 162; Yael Navaro-Yashin, 'Affect in the Civil Service: A Study of a Modern State-System', *Postcolonial Studies*, 9/3 (2006), pp. 287–288; Peters to Lewis, 9 July 1965: DO 220/65, TNA.
105 Ibid., p.160.
106 Intelligence Report No. 3/65, 12–19 January 1965, Turkish-Cypriot Affairs: WO 386/3, TNA.
107 Arslan, *The Political Economy*, p. 633.
108 *Eleftheria*, 24 September 1965.
109 Intelligence Report No. 39/65, 21–28 September 1965, Turkish-Cypriot Affairs: WO 386/3, TNA.
110 Labour Report for Cyprus 1966–1967 (Tel Aviv), 18 January 1968: LAB 13/2205, TNA; UN Security-Council, *Report by the Secretary-General on the UN Operations in Cyprus*, 20 May 1971 (S/10199), paragraph 39.
111 Commonwealth Survey No. 18, Cyprus, Economic Situation 1965: DO 220/49, TNA; UN Security-Council, *Report by the Secretary-General on the UN Operations in Cyprus*, 10 June 1965 (S/6426), paragraph 117.
112 Strong, *The Economic Consequences*, p. 142.
113 Minutes of the 369th meeting of the Political Liaison Committee, 7 October 1965: FA1/1897, Cyprus State Archive.
114 Peters to Diggines, 26 June 1965: FO 371/179973, TNA; The Cyprus Development Corporation, Annual Reports 1963–1974.
115 *Eletheria,* 2 September 1966.
116 Costar to FCO, 26 March 1969: FCO 9/785, TNA.
117 Ibid.

118 Patrick, *Political Geography,* p. 106.
119 Kitromilides, 'From Coexistence to Confrontation', p. 53.
120 Ibid.
121 Panagides, 'Communal Conflicts', p. 137; Attalides, *Nationalism and International Politics,* p. 52.
122 PIO, Press Release, *Highlights of the Speech Made by Minister of Labour,* 16 April 1967.
123 Strong, *The Economic Consequences,* p. 298.
124 Anagnostopoulou, 'Η Κυπριακή Δημοκρατία', p. 315.
125 Interview with Glafkos Clerides, 23 September 2011, Nicosia.
126 Costar, *Prospects for a Solution to the Cyprus problem,* pp. 1–2, 9 March 1967: FCO 9/65, TNA.
127 Peter Ramsbotham (Nicosia) to Foreign Commonwealth Office (hereinafter FCO), 29 March 1971: FCO 9/1353, TNA.
128 Attalides, 'Turkish-Cypriots', p. 63.

Chapter 4

1   Bishop to CRO 16 February 1965: DO 220/121, TNA.
2   UN Security-Council, *Exchange of Letters between the Permanent Representative of Turkey and the Secretary-General regarding the Mediator's report* (S/6267/Add.1), 7 April 1965.
3   FO to Athens No. 679, 13 April 1965: DO 220/168, TNA; Note: Following the Security-Council Resolution 186, the secretary-general of the Council of Europe (CoE) commented that several of its member-states were disappointed of the fact that the interested parties to the Cyprus problem had shown preference to the UN without trying to settle their problem on a regional basis under the CoE, as it is provisioned under the Article 33 of the UN Charter (Porter (Strasburg) to FO, 17 April 1964: DO 220/87, TNA). Also: FA2/178, Cyprus State Archive: The Cyprus Government perceived that the CoE was traditionally holding a more pro-Turkish position; *Eleftheria,* 6 April 1965: President of the Political Committee of CoE: 'CoE more appropriate to provide guarantees to the Turkish-Cypriots than the UN'.
4   Hunt to CRO, 7 April 1965: DO 220/86, TNA.
5   Ibid.
6   Michael A. Attalides, *Nationalism and International Politics* (Möhnesse: Bibliopolis, 2005), p. 120.
7   PIO, Press Release, *Statement by a Government Spokesman,* 9 January 1966; Plaza's Resignation, 5 January 1966, Doc. 83: FA1/1881, Cyprus State Archive.
8   *Phileleftheros,* 16 April 1965.
9   Hunt to CRO, Turkish-Cypriot position, 23 April 1965: DO 220/49, TNA.

10 *Eleftheria,* 20 April 1965; *Phileleftheros,* 22 April 1965. Note: As in 1955 when the Istanbul pogrom took place. As Robert Holland explains, 'Their political purpose [of the riots] was to demonstrate unequivocally the seriousness of the Turkish claims over Cyprus'. In *Britain and the Revolt in Cyprus 1954-1959* (Oxford: Oxford University Press, 1998), pp. 75–78.

11 James A. Stegenga, *The United Nations Force in Cyprus* (Columbus: Ohio State University Press, 1968), pp. 165–176.

12 FO to Washington, 1 April 1965: FO 371/179996, TNA.

13 George Ball to Secretary of State Rusk at Tehran, 6 April 1965, Doc. 186; Martin Herz (Tehran) to DoS, 9 April 1965, Doc. 188: US DoS, https://history.state.gov/historicaldocuments/frus1964-68v16; Evelyn Shuckburgh (UK Delegation NATO) to FO, 28 April 1965: DO 220/168, TNA.

14 Record of a conversation: Foreign Secretary and Turkish Minister of Foreign Affairs (Tehran), 7 April 1965: DO 220/110, TNA.

15 Άπαντα Αρχιεπισκόπου Κύπρου Μακαρίου ΙΙΙ, Τόμος Η' [Collected Works or Archbishop Makarios III, Vol. 8] (Nicosia: Arch. Makarios III Foundation, 1997), p. 256.

16 UN Security-Council, *Report of the UN Mediator* (S/6253), paragraph 123.

17 Sir Ralph Murray (Athens) to FO, 2 April 1965: DO 220/110, TNA.

18 Claude Nicolet, *United States Policy towards Cyprus, 1954–1974, Removing the Greek-Turkish Bone of Contention* (Möhnesee: Bibliopolis, 2001), p. 318.

19 *The Observer,* 10 April 1965.

20 Άπαντα, Τόμος Η', p. 81.

21 UN Security-Council, *The Question of Cyprus, Note by the Secretary-General,* 9 April 1965 (S/6279).

22 Rusk from London to DoS, 13 April 1965, Doc. 190: US DoS, https://history.state.gov/historicaldocuments/frus1964-68v16.

23 Allen to FO, 26 April 1965: DO 220/41, TNA.

24 Record of Conversation: Secretary of State for Foreign Affairs and George Ball (London), 10 May 1965: PREM 13/792, TNA.

25 *Kipros,* 10 May 1965; See reports in DO 220/41, TNA. Indicative: Allen to Dodson, 9 August 1965.

26 Steward to FO, 5 April 1965: FO 371/179996, TNA.

27 Allen to Rennie, 23 April 1965: DO 220/168, TNA.

28 FO to Athens No. 679 & No. 680, 13 May 1965: DO 220/168, TNA.

29 UN Security-Council, *Report of the UN Mediator* (S/6253), paragraphs 120 & 170.

30 FO to Athens No. 679 & No. 680, 13 May 1965: DO 220/168, TNA.

31 Cyprus Policy Planning Paper, FO December 1967: FCO 9/74, TNA.

32 Diggines to Tyler, 24 January 1967: DO 220/86, TNA.

33 Cyprus Policy Planning Paper, FO, December 1967: FCO 9/74, TNA.

34 Hunt to CRO, 15 May 1965: DO 220/49, TNA; Intelligence Report No. 21/65, 18–25 May 1965, US Attitude: CAB 191/10, TNA; Lewis to Peters, 13 April 1966: DO 220/50, TNA; Note: During 1966 the United States

drafted four proposals to be used in case the Greco-Turkish dialogue collapsed. However, all of them were shelved because of the American reluctance to become actively involved and due to the change in circumstances. See Claude Nicolet, *United States Policy towards Cyprus, 1954–1974: Removing the Greek-Turkish Bone of Contention*. (Möhnesee: Bibliopolis, 2001), p. 335.

35 Άπαντα, Τόμος Η᾽, pp. 77–89.
36 Murray to Hunt, 18 May 1965: DO 220/168, TNA.
37 Intelligence Report No. 20/65, 11–18 May 1965, Arch. Makarios talks in Athens, 6–8 May 1965: CAB 191/10, TNA.
38 Ibid.
39 Intelligence Report No. 21/65, 18–25 May 1965, The Athens talks and after: CAB 191/10, TNA.
40 Intelligence Report No. 12/65, 18–15 May 1965, General: WO 386/3, TNA; Intelligence Report No. 41/65, 5–12 October 1965, Grivas' Visit to Athens: CAB 191/10, TNA.
41 Intelligence Report No. 18/65, 27 April–4 May 1965, Greek Relations with Makarios: CAB 191/10, TNA.
42 Murray to Hunt, 18 May 1965: DO 220/168, TNA.
43 Ibid.
44 Nikos Kranidiotis, Ανοχύρωτη Πολιτεία, Κύπρος 1960–1974, Τόμος Ι [The Unfortified State, Cyprus 1960–1974, Vol. I] (Athens: Estia, 1985), p. 359.
45 Murray to FO, 15 May 1965: DO 220/168, TNA.
46 News from Turkey, Turkish Embassy London, 20 May 1965: DO 220/41, TNA.
47 Kranidiotis, Ανοχύρωτη Πολιτεία, pp. 323–324.
48 Hunt, Dispatch: *First Impressions*, 8 July 1965: FO 371/179973, TNA.
49 *Alitheia*, 17 May 1965.
50 Intelligence Report No. 21/65, 18–25 May 1965, Greek-Cypriot Affairs: WO 386/3, TNA.
51 *Eleftheria*, 29 June 1965.
52 Hunt, Dispatch: *First Impressions*, 8 July 1965: FO 371/179973, TNA.
53 Ibid.
54 Ibid.
55 Hunt, *First Impressions*, Summary, 8 July 1965: FO 371/179973, TNA.
56 Ibid.
57 Brief for high commissioner's consultations in London (Nicosia), 16 September 1965: DO 220/164, TNA.
58 Alan Pemberton-Piggott (Ankara) to Dodson, 5 May 1965: DO 220/117, TNA.
59 Peters to Diggines, 10 July 1965: DO 220/49, TNA.
60 *Eleftheria*, 3 July 1965; Peter to Lewis, 9 July 1965: DO 220/65, TNA; Intelligence Report No. 30/65, 20–27 July 1965, Turkish-Cypriot Affairs: WO 386/3, TNA.

61 *Special News Bulletin* 6 July 1965: DO 220/54, TNA; About student movements, see FCO 9/1172, TNA.
62 Suha Bolukbasi, *The Superpowers and the Third World: Turkish-American Relations and Cyprus* (Lanham: University Press of America, 1988), pp. 128–154.
63 Glafkos Clerides, *My Deposition, Vol. II* (Nicosia: Alitheia, 1989), p. 173.
64 Ibid.
65 *Phileleftheros*, 1 April 1965.
66 Intelligence Report No. 15/65, 6–13 April 1965, Makarios' initial reaction to Plaza Report: CAB 191/10, TNA.
67 Timothy Daunt (Nicosia) to Tyler, 13 June 1967: FCO 27/83, TNA.
68 *Phileleftheros,* 22 April 1965.
69 Hunt: *Reactions to the Report of the UN Mediator*, p. 12, 7 May 1965: DO 220/110, TNA; *Eleftheria*, 18 April 1965.
70 Hunt to CRO, General, 1 May 1965: DO 220/49, TNA; *Eleftheria*, 30 April 1965.
71 From the correspondent of '*The Observer*' in Cyprus, cited in *Eleftheria,* 27 April 1965.
72 Hunt to CRO, Long Term Solution, 8 May 1965: DO 220/49, TNA.
73 Stella Soulioti, *Fettered Independence, Cyprus, 1878–1964: The Narrative* (Minnesota: Minnesota Mediterranean and East European Monographs, 2006), p. 373.
74 Stegenga, *The United Nations Force,* p. 127.
75 Secretariat British Forces Cyprus, Memorandum, Annex A, 21 April 1965: CAB 191/7, TNA.
76 FO to Washington, 25 February 1966: DO 220/214, TNA.
77 District Officer Nicosia/Kyrenia to all ministries, 8 December 1966: FA1/1898, Cyprus State Archive.
78 District Officer Nicosia/Kyrenia to president of the Republic, 29 July 1966: FA1/1900, Cyprus State Archive.
79 Note from Adair, 24 May 1965: DO 220/168, TNA.
80 Memorandum of Conversation (DoS), 10 June 1965, Doc. 193: US DoS, https://history.state.gov/historicaldocuments/frus1964-68v16.
81 Note for the Record, 18 February 1966: FO 371/185629, TNA.
82 Dean (Washington) to FO, 29 May 1965: PREM 13/792, TNA; Intelligence Report No. 23/65, 1–9 June 1965, General: WO 386/3, TNA.
83 Dean to FO, 29 May 1965: PREM 13/792, TNA.
84 Note for the Record, Nicosia, 16 October 1965: FO 371/179973, TNA; FO to Ankara, 8 December 1965: DO 220/50, TNA.
85 Allen to FO, 1 December 1965: DO 220/50; Murray to Dodson, 15 November 1965: DO 220/50, TNA.
86 Ibid.
87 Thomas Blake Burrill Wainman-Wood (Nicosia) to Ottawa, 13 December 1965: DO 220/50, TNA.

88 Ibid.
89 Peters to Lewis, 21 September 1965: DO 220/149, TNA.
90 PIO, Press Release, *Central Rehabilitation Committee*, 9 October 1965; Άπαντα, Τόμος Η', pp. 143–147.
91 PIO, Press Release, *Declaration on Minority Rights,* 12 October 1965.
92 Hunt to CRO, 12 October 1965: DO 220/149, TNA.
93 Peters to Lewis, 21 September 1965: DO 220/149, TNA.
94 *Special News Bulletin*, 26 September 1965: DO 220/65, TNA.
95 Ibid.
96 *Special News Bulletin*, 17 October 1965: DO 220/65, TNA.
97 Note for the Record (Nicosia), 13 October 1965: FO 371/179973, TNA.
98 Wainman-Wood to Ottawa, 12 October 1965: DO 220/149, TNA.
99 *Eleftheria*, 30 October 1965.
100 UN Security-Council, *Report by the Secretary-General on the Situation in Cyprus* (S/6881), 5 November 1965; *Report by the Secretary-General on the Situation in Cyprus* (S/7001), 10 December 1965.
101 UN General-Assembly No. 2077 (XX), *The Question of Cyprus,* 18 December 1965. This resolution was adopted with 47 votes in favour, mainly Afro-Asian; it received fifty-four abstentions – including Britain and Soviet Union – and five opposing votes – including the United States.
102 Parker Hart (Ankara) to DoS, 3 November 1965, Doc. 211: US DoS, https://history.state.gov/historicaldocuments/frus1964-68v16.
103 Nicolet, *US Policy,* p. 326; Note for the Record, 23 December 1965: TNA, DO 220/50.
104 Hunt, *Reactions to the UN General-Assembly Resolution,* p. 3, 31 December 1965: DO 220/50, TNA.
105 *Eleftheria,* 30 December 1965.
106 Kuchuk's statement at the UN General-Assembly resolution, 19 December 1965: DO 220/65, TNA.
107 Murray to FO, 1 March 1966: FO 371/185629, TNA.
108 PIO, Press Release, *Joint Communique*, 2 February 1966.
109 Allen to FO, 7 February 1966: DO 220/42, TNA; see exchange of letters between Greek and Turkish representatives to the UN Secretary-General: UN Documents, S/7186, S/7194, S/7296.
110 Extract from Cyprus fortnight summary, 11 February 1966, discussions on the Cyprus problem: DO 220/28, TNA.
111 UN Security-Council, *Report of the UN Secretary-General, 9 December 1965–10 March 1966* (S/7191), paragraph 154.
112 UN Security-*Council, Note by the Secretary-General* (S/7180), 4 March 1966.
113 UN Security-Council, *Report of the UN Secretary-General, March–June 1966* (S/7350), paragraph 157.
114 Paper on Cyprus, Section B, *Aims of the Parties*, April 1966: DO 220/50, TNA.

115 PIO, Press Release, *Interview by President Makarios*, 21 March 1966.
116 UN Security-Council, S/7350, March–June 1966, paragraph 158.
117 Hunt to CRO, 15 February 1966: DO 220/28, TNA.
118 Goulden to Bernard Everett (FO), 19 November 1966: DO 220/42, TNA.
119 Lewis to Peters, 13 April 1966: DO 220/50, TNA.
120 Note from Ministry of Foreign Affairs No. 5, 23 February 1967: FA1/1899, Cyprus State Archive; UN Security-Council, *Report of the Secretary-General on the UN Operations in Cyprus*, 8 December 1966 (S/7611), paragraph 178.
121 Hunt to CRO, 16 April 1966: DO 220/50 TNA.
122 Note for the Record (Nicosia), 25 January 1966: DO 220/28, TNA.
123 Adair to CRO, 29 April 1966: DO 220/51, TNA; Cross, Nicosia to DoS, 24 January 1966, Doc. 219: US DoS, https://history.state.gov/historicaldocuments/frus1964-68v16.
124 Nicolet, *US Policy*, p. 330.
125 Dodson to Roger Jackling (New York), 29 April 1966: DO 220/51, TNA.
126 Ibid.
127 U Thant's Ideas on Cyprus, 6 June 1966: DO 220/51, TNA.
128 Allen to FO, 11 May 1966: DO 220/51, TNA.
129 Nicosia to Ottawa and London, 28 June 1966: FO 371/185629, TNA.
130 Ibid.
131 Diggines to Henry Brind (Ottawa), 13 July 1966: DO 220/51, TNA.
132 More information about the talks conducted from June to December 1966: Giannos N. Kranidiotis, *Το Κυπριακό Πρόβλημα: Η ανάμειξη του ΟΗΕ και οι Ξένες Επεμβάσεις στην Κύπρο 1960–1974 [The Cyprus Problem: UN Involvement and the Foreign Interventions in Cyprus]* (Athens: Themelio, 1984), pp. 326–379.
133 *The Guardian*, 8 December 1966.
134 Costar, *Prospects for a Solution to the Cyprus Problem*, p. 9, 9 March 1967: FCO 9/65, TNA.
135 Goulden to Edes, 1 November 1966: FO 371/185630, TNA.
136 Ibid.
137 *Άπαντα Αρχιεπισκόπου Κύπρου Μακαρίου III, Τόμος Ι', [Collected Works of Archbishop Makarios III, Vol. 10]* (Nicosia: Arch. Makarios III Foundation, 2000), pp. 330, 335.
138 Nicolet, *US Policy*, p. 336; Note for the Record (Nicosia) 16 November 1966: FO 371/185630, TNA.
139 Peters to Tyler, 20 March 1967: FCO 27/53, TNA.
140 Note of conversation with Spinelli, Nicosia,17 January 1967: FCO 27/99, TNA.
141 Costar to CO, 26 January 1967: FCO 27/83, TNA.
142 *Cyprus Mail*, 24 January 1967.
143 Peters to Richard Parsons (Ankara), 8 February 1967: FCO 27/83, TNA; *Cyprus Mail*, 2 March 1967.

144 Pemberton-Pigott to FO, 28 January 1967: FCO 27/83, TNA.
145 Murray to FO, 27 January; Peters to Diggines, 28 January 1967: FCO 27/83, TNA.
146 Fortnight Summary, 7–20 April 1967, UN initiative for improvements in Cyprus: FCO 27/83, TNA.
147 Peters to Tyler, CO, 13 May 1967: FCO 27/83, TNA.
148 Costar to CO, 26 May 1967: PREM 13/1371, TNA.
149 Peters to Tyler, 15 May 1967: FCO 27/83, TNA.
150 Costar to CO, 19 April 1967: FO 27/83, TNA.
151 Intelligence Report No. 36/67, Archbishop's Peace Plan, 6 September 1967: WO 386/5, TNA; Costar to FO, 5 October 1967: FCO 9/73, TNA.
152 Intelligence Report No. 39/67, Normalization measures, 27 September 1967: WO 386/5, TNA.
153 PIO, Press Release, *The Archbishop Replies to Questions,* 18 November 1965.
154 CO to Nicosia, 25 January 1967: FCO 9/65, TNA.
155 Costar to John Moreton (CO), 19 October 1967: FCO 9/73, TNA.
156 Costar: *Prospects of a Solution to the Cyprus Problem,* p. 9, 9 March 1967: FCO 9/65, TNA.
157 Hunt: *First Impressions*, Summary, 8 July 1965: FO 371/179973, TNA.
158 Ibid.
159 Interview with Glafkos Clerides, Nicosia, 23 September 2011.
160 Note for the Record (Nicosia), 18 May 1966: DO 220/51, TNA.
161 Memorandum of Conversation (New York), 4 December 1964, Doc. 168: US DoS, https://history.state.gov/historicaldocuments/frus1964-68v16; Note from Adair, 24 May 1965: DO 220/168, TNA.
162 Peters to Humphrey Arthington-Davy (CRO), 29 January 1966: DO 220/149, TNA.

Chapter 5

1 Allen to FO, 11 April 1967: FCO 9/65, TNA.
2 See TNA files: FCO 9/65-66, FCO 9/82-83, FCO 27/50-52, PREM 13/1372.
3 Claude Nicolet, *United States Policy towards Cyprus, 1954–1974, Removing the Greek-Turkish Bone of Contention* (Möhnesee: Bibliopolis, 2001), pp. 350–351.
4 Costar to FO, 5 October 1967: FCO 9/73, TNA.
5 Michael Harbottle, *The Impartial Solider* (London: Oxford University Press, 1970), p. 98.
6 Parker T. Hart, *Two NATO Allies at the Threshold of War: Cyprus: A Firsthand Account of Crisis Management, 1965–1968* (Durham: Duke University Press, 1990), p. 95.
7 Costar, *The Crisis of November 1967*, p. 4, 28 December 1967: FCO 27/91, TNA.

8   Roger Allen (Ankara), *The Cyprus Crisis*, 9 December 1967: FCO 27/91, TNA.

9   UN Security-Council *Special Report by the Secretary-General on Recent Developments regarding Cyprus*, 3 December 1967 (S/8246/Add.6).

10 Hart, *Two NATO Allies*, pp. 52–55; Hart to DoS, 18 November 1967, Doc. 311: US DoS, https://history.state.gov/historicaldocuments/frus1964-68v16.

11 Ibid.

12 Cyprus Conference: Morning Session, 29 January 1968: FCO 9/74, TNA.

13 Cyprus: Draft Policy Planning Paper, Present Situation, January 1968: FCO 9/74, TNA.

14 Note of Meeting (DoS), 5 December 1967, Doc. 342: US DoS, https://history.state.gov/historicaldocuments/frus1964-68v16; Sir Michael Steward (Athens) to Brown, 28 December 1967: FCO 27/71, TNA.

15 Harbottle, *The Impartial Soldier*, p.164.

16 Draft Paper: November 1967 crisis, '*Seeking the Concurrence of the Cyprus Government*': FCO 27/51, TNA.

17 Costar, *The Crisis of November 1967*, p. 1, 28 December 1967: FCO 27/91, TNA.

18 Draft Policy Planning Paper, Present Situation, p. 2, January 1968: FCO 9/74, TNA.

19 Suha Bolukbasi, *The Superpowers and the Third World: Turkish-American Relations and Cyprus* (Lanham: University Press of America, 1988), pp. 141–144.

20 Ibid.

21 Polyvios G. Polyviou, *Cyprus: Conflict and Negotiations, 1960–1980* (London: Duckworth, 1980), p. 56.

22 Cyprus Conference: Morning Session, 29 January 1968: FCO 9/74, TNA.

23 Draft Policy Planning Paper, Present Situation, January 1968: FCO 9/74, TNA.

24 Allen to FO, 19 January 1968: FCO 27/91, TNA.

25 Cyprus Conference: Morning Session, 29 January 1968: FCO 9/74, TNA.

26 Michael A. Attalides, *Nationalism and International Politics* (Möhnesse: Bibliopolis, 2005), p. 153.

27 Lord Caradon to FO, 29 January 1968: FCO 27/92, TNA; Pemberton-Piggott to FCO, 6 February 1968: FCO27/92, TNA.

28 Statement by Fazil Kuchuk, 10 January 1968, Doc. 2: FA2/284, Cyprus State Archive.

29 Costar to CO, 29 December 1967: FCO 9/62, TNA.

30 'Executive Council Members': Defence (including Internal Affairs and Foreign Relations), Agriculture and Natural Resources, Health, Education, Social–Municipal–Cooperative and Religious Affairs, Judicial Affairs, Economic Affairs, Financial and Budgetary Affairs, Communication and Works.

31 Costar to CO, 29 December 1967: FCO 9/62, TNA.

32 Costar to CO, 29 December 1967: FCO 27/76, TNA.
33 Allen to FO, 31 December 1967: FCO 9/62, TNA.
34 Ibid.
35 Costar to CO, 29 December 1967: FCO 9/62, TNA.
36 Costar to CO, 29 December 1967: FCO 27/76, TNA.
37 Memorandum of Conversation (DoS), 16 January 1968, Doc. 357: US DoS, https://history.state.gov/historicaldocuments/frus1964-68v16.
38 Costar to CO, 30 December 1967: FCO 27/76, TNA.
39 John Dodds (Ankara) to FO, 5 March 1968: FCO 27/49, TNA.
40 Allen to FO, 30 December 1967: FCO 9/62, TNA.
41 FO to Ankara, 29 December 1967: FCO 27/76, TNA; CO to Nicosia, 1 January 1968: FCO 27/76, TNA; Costar to CO, 13 January 1968: FCO 27/76, TNA.
42 John Edmonds (Ankara) to FO, 16 January 1968: FCO 9/63, TNA.
43 Dean to FO and CO, 6 February 1968: FCO 27/77, TNA; Allen to FO, 30 December 1967: FCO 9/62, TNA.
44 Alan Davidson (FO), *Cyprus*, 1 January 1968: FCO 9/62, TNA.
45 Memorandum of Conversation (DoS), 16 January 1968, Doc. 357: US DoS, https://history.state.gov/historicaldocuments/frus1964-68v16. Washington to FO, 30 December 1967: FCO 27/76, TNA; See correspondence between the British and Canadian high commissions and American and Italian embassies in Cyprus from January to March in FCO 9/63 and FCO 9/64 TNA.
46 Costar, *An Exercise in Archiepiscopal Brinkmanship*, p. 3, 28 March 1968: FCO 27/78, TNA.
47 Ibid.
48 Record of Conversation, 30 January 1968: FCO 27/92, TNA.
49 Costar to CO, 15 February 1968: FCO 27/77, TNA.
50 Hart to DoS, 6 March 1968, Doc. 363: US DoS, https://history.state.gov/historicaldocuments/frus1964-68v16; Pemberton-Piggot to FO, 2 March 1968: FCO 9/64, TNA.
51 FO to Washington and Washington to FO, 8 March 1968: FCO 27/77, TNA.
52 Costar to CO, 13 March 1968: FCO 27/77, TNA.
53 Costar to CO, 16 March 1968: FCO 27/77, TNA.
54 Costar, *An Exercise in Archiepiscopal Brinkmanship*, p. 7, 28 March 1968: FCO 27/78, TNA.
55 Ibid., p. 1.
56 Ibid.
57 Ibid., pp. 7–8.
58 Niyazi Kizilyurek, *Glafkos Clerides: Thepath of a Country* (Nicosia: Rimal Publications, 2008), p. 114.
59 Roderick Sarell (Ankara) to FCO, 27 April 1971: FCO 9/1354, TNA.
60 *Cyprus Mail*, 5 January 1968.
61 *Phileleftheros*, 13 January 1968.

62 Costar to CO, 13 January 1968: FCO 27/79, TNA.
63 Memorandum of Conversation (Washington), 16 January 1968, Doc. 357: US DoS, https://history.state.gov/historicaldocuments/frus1964-68v16.
64 Costar to CO, 13 January 1968: FCO 27/79, TNA.
65 Costar to CO, 18 January 1968: FCO 27/29, TNA.
66 Daunt to Tyler, 18 January 1968: FCO 27/79, TNA.
67 Ibid.
68 Costar to CO, 15 January 1968: FCO 27/79, TNA; PIO, Press Release, *About Elections*, 15 February 1968.
69 Takis Evdokas was an enosist politician who argued against the Zurich–London Agreements. He challenged Makarios in 1968 because, as he stated, 'any rival candidate has no chances of winning the elections, but people should go to the polls so that Makarios should not be seen as the only representative'. *Cyprus Mail*, 10 February 1968; James to Tyler, 31 March 1968: FCO 27/80, TNA.
70 Daunt to Tyler, 18 January 1968: FCO 27/79, TNA.
71 Costar to CO, 13 January 1968: FCO 27/79, TNA.
72 *Cyprus Mail*, 18 January 1968.
73 Daunt to Tyler, 26 January 1968: FCO 27/79, TNA.
74 Ibid.; Intelligence Report No. 4/68, 24 January 1968, Cyprus Elections: WO 386/6, TNA.
75 Clement Dodd, *The History and Politics of the Cyprus Conflict* (Basingstoke: Palgrave Macmillan, 2010), p. 92.
76 Intelligence Report No. 5/68, 31 January 1968: WO 386/6, TNA.
77 UN Security-Council, 1386 Meeting. *Resolution 244* (1967).
78 Intelligence Report No. 1/68, 3 January 1968: WO 386/6, TNA.
79 Nicolet, *US Policy*, p. 380.
80 UN Security-Council, *Report by the Secretary-General on the United Nations Operation in Cyprus* (S/8446), 9 March 1968.
81 Record of Conversation, Secretary of State – Cyprus foreign minister, 30 January 1968: FCO 9/73, TNA; *Cyprus Mail*, 18 January 1968.
82 Edmonds to FO, 15 February 1968: FCO 27/49, TNA.
83 Ankara to FO, 9 February 1968: FCO 27/92, TNA.
84 Costar to CO, 5 March 1968: FCO 27/92, TNA.
85 John Beith (FO) to Allen, 3 April 1968: FCO 27/48, TNA.
86 Edward Tomkins (Washington) to Beith, 20 May 1968: FCO 27/93, TNA.
87 *Eleftheria*, 29 March 1968.
88 Ἅπαντα Ἀρχιεπισκόπου Κύπρου Μακαρίου III, Τόμος I [Collected Works of Archbishop Makarios III, Vol. 10] (Nicosia: Makarios III Foundation, 2000), pp. 489–494.
89 Tomkins to Beith, 20 May 1968: FCO 27/93, TNA.
90 Glafkos Clerides, *My Deposition, Vol. II* (Nicosia: Alitheia, 1989), p. 216.
91 Oliver Richmond, *Mediating in Cyprus: The Cypriot Communities and the United Nations* (London: Frank Cass, 1998), p. 110.

92   Clerides, *My Deposition, Vol. II*, p. 217.
93   *Special News Bulletin*, 30 April 1971: FA2/92, Cyprus State Archive.
94   Nicolet, *US Policy*, p. 391.
95   Attalides, *Nationalism and International Politics*, p. 113.
96   Rasmbotham, *Turkish-Cypriot students*, 10 April 1970: FCO 9/1172, TNA.
97   Polyviou, *Conflict and Negotiations*, p. 96.
98   Clerides, *My Deposition, Vol. III*, p. 88.
99   Clerides, *My Deposition, Vol. II*, p. 273.
100 Ibid., p. 21.
101 Ibid., p. 273.
102 Costar, *Vested Interests and the Cyprus Problem*, p. 8, 11 September 1968: FCO 9/786, TNA.
103 Ramsbotham, *Archbishop Makarios III, President of the Republic of Cyprus*, p. 3, 29 March 1971: FCO 9/1364, TNA.
104 Costar, *Vested Interests and the Cyprus Problem*, pp. 1, 11, 11 September 1968: FCO 9/786, TNA.
105 Ibid.
106 Cyprus News Digest, Turkish-Cypriot Press, 14 June 1968: FA2/286, Cyprus State Archive.
107 Intelligence Report No. 25/68, 19 June 1968: WO 386/6, TNA.
108 Polyviou, *Conflict and Negotiations*, p. 88.
109 Denktash to Clerides, 24 June 1969: FCO 9/782, TNA.
110 Costar to CO, 8 April 1968: FCO 27/92, TNA.
111 Call of David Bendall (FCO) by Denktash on 2 November 1970: FCO 9/1150, TNA.
112 Meeting of minister of commerce with Kemal Rustem, 29 August 1968: Glafkos Clerides Archive.
113 Costar to CO, 20 June 1968: FCO 27/97, TNA.
114 Ramsbotham to FCO, 8 October 1969: FCO 9/782, TNA.
115 Costar, *Vested Interests and the Cyprus Problem*, p. 9, 11 September 1968: FCO 9/786, TNA.
116 Hakan Arslan, *The Political Economy of State–Building: The Case of Turkish-Cypriots (1960–1967)* (PhD Thesis, İstanbul Bilgi University, 2014), p. 629.
117 Bolukbasi, *The Superpowers*, p. 147.
118 Kizilyurek, *Glafkos Clerides*, pp. 124–125.
119 Niyazi Kizilyurek, 'Rauf Denktash: Fear and Nationalism in the Turkish-Cypriot Community', in A. Aktar, N. Kizilyurek and U. Özkırımlı (eds), *Nationalism in the Troubled Triangle: Cyprus, Greece and Turkey* (Basingstoke: Palgrave Macmillan, 2010), p. 186.
120 Arif Hasan Tahsin, *Η Άνοδος του Ντενκτάς στην Κορυφή [Denktash's Rise]* (Nicosia: Diafania, 2001), p. 122.
121 Ibid., p. 117.

122 Clerides, *My Deposition, Vol. II*, p. 239.
123 Richard A. Patrick, *Political Geography and the Cyprus Conflict, 1963–1971* (Waterloo: Department of Geography, Faculty of Environmental Studies, University of Waterloo, 1976), p. 157.
124 Ibid.
125 Clerides-Denktash's meeting, 15 July 1968: Glafkos Clerides Archive.
126 Ibid.
127 Report on Turkish-Cypriot activities, Cyprus Intelligence Service, 30 September 1969: Glafkos Clerides Archives.
128 Peter Smart (Washington) to FCO, 10 January 1969: FCO 9/785, TNA; Hart, *Two NATO Allies,* p. 121.
129 Meeting of minister of commerce with Kemal Rustem, 29 August 1968: Glafkos Clerides Archive.
130 Ibid.; Ankara to Ottawa, 17 October 1968: FCO 9/778, TNA.
131 Costar to FCO, 28 March 1969: FCO 9/780, TNA.
132 Costar to CO, 9 April 1969: FCO 27/92, TNA.
133 Clerides, *My Deposition, Vol. III*, p. 29.
134 Costar to FCO, 14 February 1969: FCO 9/785, TNA.
135 Ramsbotham to FCO, 19 November 1969: FCO 9/786, TNA.
136 Ibid.

Chapter 6

1 Glafkos Clerides, *My Deposition*, *Vol.* II (Nicosia: Alitheia, 1989), p. 218.
2 Ibid.
3 Record of Conversation, Commonwealth Secretary–Cyprus Foreign Minister, 28 June 1968: FCO 27/94, TNA.
4 Costar to Robin Edmonds (CO), 20 June 1968: FCO 27/94, TNA.
5 Costar to Edmonds, 20 June 1968: FCO 27/94, TNA.
6 First phase of Inter-communal talks, 23 June–28 August 1968: Glafkos Clerides Archive.
7 Ibid.
8 Clerides-Denktash's meeting, 15 July 1968: Gafkos Clerides Archive.
9 Clerides, *My Deposition, Vol. II*, p. 240.
10 Ibid., p. 247.
11 Clerides-Denktash's meeting, 8 July 1968: Glafkos Clerides Archive.
12 Ibid.
13 Clerides-Denktash's meeting, 4 July 1968: Glafkos Clerides Archive.
14 Clerides-Denktash's meeting in Beirut, 16 June 1968: Glafkos Clerides Archive; Belcher to DoS, 2 August 1968: Doc. 369: US DoS, https://history.state.gov/historicaldocuments/frus1964-68v16.
15 Clerides-Denktash's meeting, 15 July 1968: Glafkos Clerides Archive.
16 Clerides-Denktash's meeting, 24 July 1968: Glafkos Clerides Archive.

17 Record of Conversation, Commonwealth Secretary–Cyprus Foreign Minister, 28 June 1968: FCO 27/94, TNA; Ian Smart (Washington) to John Macrae (FO), 11 October 1968: FCO 9/778, TNA.

18 Costar to Edmonds, 23 August 1968: FCO 27/94, TNA.

19 Costar to Edmonds, 20 June 1968 & 23 August 1968: FCO 27/94, TNA; Record of Conversation, Commonwealth Secretary–Cyprus Foreign Minister, 26 September 1968: FCO 27/94, TNA.

20 Costar to Edmonds, 23 August 1968: FCO 27/94, TNA.

21 Meeting Clerides-Gorge, 9 September 1968: Glafkos Clerides Archive.

22 Costar to CO, 11 October 1968: FCO 9/778, TNA.

23 Clerides-Denktash's meeting, 29 August 1968: Glafkos Clerides Archive.

24 Polyvios G. Polyviou, *Cyprus: Conflict and Negotiations, 1960–1980* (London: Duckworth, 1980), pp. 71–72.

25 Costar to Edmonds, 26 September 1968: FCO 27/94, TNA.

26 Meeting between Clerides and Belcher, 25 September 1968 and meeting between Clerides and Osorio-Tafall and Gorge, 1 October 1968: Glafkos Clerides Archive.

27 Costar, *Cyprus: Inter-Communal Talks, Phase II,* p. 2, 29 January 1969: FCO 9/779, TNA.

28 Proposals of Clerides to Denktash on Local Authorities, 9 December 1968: Glafkos Clerides Archive.

29 Ibid.

30 Costar to FCO, 13 December 1968: FCO 9/779, TNA.

31 Costar to Edmonds, 4 October 1968: FCO27/94, TNA.

32 Clerides, *My Deposition, Vol. II,* p. 263.

33 Costar to CO, 4 October 1968: FCO 9/778, TNA.

34 Clerides-Belcher's meeting, 25 September 1968: Glafkos Clerides Archive.

35 Ibid.; Note of the minister of commerce, 2 October 1968: Glafkos Clerides Archive.

36 Clerides-Denktash's meeting, 16 September 1968: Glafkos Clerides Archive.

37 Ibid.

38 Note of the minister of commerce, 2 October 1968: Glafkos Clerides Archive.

39 Costar to CO, Nicosia, 4 October 1968: FCO 9/778, TNA.

40 Peter Smart (Washington) to FCO, 10 January 1969: FCO 9/785, TNA.

41 Note from Zafiriou, Ankara, 27 December 1968: Glafkos Clerides Archive.

42 Ibid.

43 Costar to CO, 31 October 1968: FCO 9/778, TNA.

44 Clerides and Greek ambassador's meeting, 23 September 1968: Glafkos Clerides Archive.

45 Costar to CO, 19 November 1968: FCO 9/778, TNA.

46 CO to Nicosia, 26 September 1968: FCO 27/94, TNA.

47 Clerides-Pipinelis' meeting in Athens, 25–27 November 1968: Glafkos Clerides Archive.

48 CO to Nicosia, 26 September 1968: FCO 27/94, TNA.
49 Intelligence Report No. 40/68, 2 October 1968: WO 386/6, TNA.
50 Clerides, *My Deposition, Vol. II*, pp. 266–272.
51 Costar to FCO, 5 December 1968: FCO 9/778, TNA.
52 Clerides, *My Deposition, Vol. II*, p. 274.
53 Costar to FCO, 26 October 1968: FCO 9/778, TNA.
54 Allen to FCO, 5 November 1968: FCO 9/778, TNA; Edmonds to FCO, 3 January 1969: FCO 9/779, TNA.
55 Daunt to FCO, 19 December 1968: FCO 9/779, TNA.
56 Clerides-Pipinelis' meetings, 11–12 September 1969: Glafkos Clerides Archive.
57 Interview by Makarios on 14 December 1969, Doc. 156: FA2/90, Cyprus State Archive.
58 *Phileleftheros,* 31 December 1968.
59 Costar to FCO, 31 December 1968: FCO 9/779, TNA.
60 Costar to FCO, 3 January 1969: FCO 9/779, TNA.
61 Ramsbotham to FCO, 23 May 1969: FCO 9/781, TNA.
62 Costar, *Valedictory Dispatch*, p. 1, 26 March 1969: FCO 9/785, TNA.
63 Clerides, *My Deposition, Vol. II*, p. 312.
64 Cyprus News Digest, News and Developments, 4 March 1969, Doc. 34: FA2/287, Cyprus State Archive Note: Parastatal organizations in Cyprus: CYTA (Cyprus Telecommunications Authority), EAC (Electricity Authority Cyprus), etc.
65 Clerides-Denktash's meetings, 3 and 10 February 1969: Glafkos Clerides Archive.
66 Clerides-Denktash's meeting, 17 February 1969: Glafkos Clerides Archive.
67 Costar to FCO, 3 April 1969: FCO 9/780, TNA.
68 Steward to FCO, 20 February 1969: FCO 9/779, TNA.
69 John Freeman (Washington) to FCO, 14 March 1969: FCO 9/780, TNA.
70 Lord Caradon to FCO, 25 March 1969: FCO 9/780, TNA.
71 Allen to FCO, 2 April 1969: FCO 9/780, TNA.
72 Tyler (FCO), 25 March 1969: FCO 9/781, TNA.
73 Claude Nicolet, *United States Policy towards Cyprus, 1954–1974, Removing the Greek-Turkish Bone of Contention* (Möhnesee: Bibliopolis, 2001), p. 394.
74 Steward to FCO, 3 April 1969: FCO 9/780, TNA.
75 Dodson to FCO, 9 April 1969: FCO 9/780, TNA.
76 Ibid.
77 Clerides-Denktash's meeting, 24 April 1969: Glafkos Clerides Archive.
78 Ibid.
79 Ibid.
80 Michael James (Athens) to FCO, 24 April 1969: FCO 9/781, TNA.
81 Secretary of State (Washington) to US Embassy (London), 2 May 1969: FCO 9/781, TNA.
82 Cyprus News Digest, Turkish Press, 28 April 1969, Doc. 126: FA2/89, Cyprus State Archive.

83 Allen to FCO, 30 April 1969: FCO 9/781, TNA.
84 Ramsbotham to FCO, 2 May 1969: FCO 9/781, TNA.
85 Clerides-Denktash's meeting, 11 August 1969: Glafkos Clerides Archive.
86 Counter-Proposals on Autonomous Local Government Authorities, by Rauf Denktash: FCO 9/782, TNA.
87 Ramsbotham to FCO, 14 August 1969: FCO 9/782, TNA.
88 Ibid.
89 Ramsbotham to FCO, 29 August 1969: FCO 9/782, TNA.
90 Clerides, *My Deposition, Vol. II*, p. 330.
91 Daunt to FCO, 12 September 1969: FCO 9/782, TNA.
92 Sarell to FCO, 27 November 1969: FCO 9/783, TNA.
93 Daunt to FCO, 12 September 1969: FCO 9/782, TNA.
94 Clerides to Makarios, 13 October 1969: Glafkos Clerides Archive.
95 See UN secretary-general Reports for 1969–1970: S/9233, S/9521, S/9814, S/10005.
96 Ramsbotham to FCO, 28 January 1970: FCO 9/1147, TNA.
97 Clerides, *My Deposition, Vol. II*, p. 347.
98 Ramsbotham to FCO, 20 February 1970: FCO 9/1147, TNA.
99 For example: Makarios Drousiotis, *Δύο Απόπειρες και μια Δολοφονία: Η Χούντα και η Κύπρος: 1967–1970 [Two Attempts and one Assassination: The Junta and Cyprus 1967–1970]* (Nicosia: Alfadi, 2009); House of Representatives, *Πόρισμα για το Φάκελο της Κύπρου*, 17 Μαρτίου 2011, *[The Findings of the Cyprus File 11 March 2011]*, pp. 58–63.
100 Rambotham to FCO, 19 August 1970: FCO 9/1148, TNA.
101 Joint Document by Clerides-Denktash, August 1970: FCO 9/1149, TNA.
102 Murray to Davidson, 11 April 1968: FCO 27/93, TNA.
103 Clerides, *My Deposition, Vol. III*, p. 22.
104 Ramsbotham to FCO, 27 August 1970: FCO 9/1148, TNA.
105 *Άπαντα Αρχιεπισκόπου Κύπρου Μακαρίου III, Τόμος ΙΒ [Collected Works of Archbishop Makarios III, Vol. 12]* (Nicosia: Makarios III Foundation, 2002), pp. 489–494.
106 Ramsbotham to FCO, 27 August 1970: FCO 9/1148, TNA.
107 Ramsbotham to FCO, 4 September 1970: FCO 9/1148, TNA.
108 Ramsbotham to FCO, 23 September 1970: FCO 9/1149, TNA.
109 Paul Sant Cassia, 'The Archbishop in the Beleaguered City: An Analysis of the Conflicting Roles and Political Oratory of Makarios', *Byzantine and Modern Greek Studies*, 8/1 (1982), p. 198.
110 *Machi*, 6 February 1969.
111 Christophoros Christophorou, 'The Evolution of the Greek-Cypriot Party Politics', in James Ker-Lindsay and Hubert Faustmann (eds), *The Government and Politics of Cyprus* (Oxford: Peter Lang, 2008), p. 88.
112 Peter Loizos, *The Greek Gift: Politics in a Cypriot Village* (Möhnesee: Bibliopolis, 2004), pp. 233–288.

113 Belcher to DoS, 8 November 1968, Doc. 372: US DoS, https://history.state.gov/historicaldocuments/frus1964-68v16.
114 Ibid.
115 Costar to FCO, 14 February 1969: FCO 9/785, TNA.
116 Interview with Lellos Demetriades, Nicosia 27 May 2014.
117 Loizos, *The Greek Gift*, p. 237.
118 Costar to FCO, 22 November 1968: FCO 9/778, TNA.
119 Clerides, *My Deposition, Vol. II*, p. 315.
120 Costar to FCO, 21 February 1969: FCO 9/785, TNA.
121 Kyriacos Markides, *The Rise and Fall of the Cyprus Republic* (London: Yale University Press, 1977), p. 77.
122 Ramsbotham to FCO, 22 August 1968: FCO 9/785, TNA.
123 *Cyprus Mail*, 23 May 1969.
124 *The Guardian*, 13 May 1969.
125 Άπαντα Αρχιεπισκόπου Κύπρου Μακαριου III, Τόμος IA *[Collected Works of Archibshop Makarios III, Vol. 11]* (Nicosia: Makarios III Foundation, 2001), pp. 221–229.
126 Sant Cassia, 'The Archbishop', p. 201.
127 Sia Anagnostopoulou, 'Makarios III, 1950–1977: Creating the Ethnarchic State', in Andrekos Varnava and Michalis N. Michael (eds), *The Archbishops of Cyprus in the Modern Age: The Changing Role of the Archbishop-Ethnarch, Their Identities and Politics* (Newcastle upon Tyne: Cambridge Scholars Publishing, 2013), p. 283.
128 Ramsbotham to FCO, 7 January 1970: FCO 9/1153, TNA.
129 Άπαντα, Τόμος IB, pp. 406–421.
130 Rambotham to FCO, 7 January 1970: FCO 9/1153, TNA.
131 Rambotham to FCO, 19 June 1969: FCO 9/782, TNA.
132 Nicolet, *US Policy*, p. 396.
133 Daunt to FCO, 29 October 1969: FCO 9/786, TNA; See also various reports between July–August 1969 in FCO 9/782.
134 Ramsbotham to FCO, 19 June 1969: FCO 9/782, TNA.
135 Intelligence Reports 5/69, 4 June 1969 & 6/69, 18 June 1969: WO 386/7, TNA.
136 Ramsbotham to FCO, 28 June 1969: FCO 9/782, TNA; Glafkos Clerides Archive: period June–December 1969.
137 Daunt to FCO, 29 August 1969: FCO 9/782, TNA.
138 John Snodgrass (FCO) to Ankara, 1 August 1969: FCO 9/782, TNA.
139 Oliver Miles (Nicosia) to FCO, 11 March 1970: FCO 9/1154, TNA.
140 *Alitheia*, 29 June 1970.
141 David Beattie (Nicosia) to FCO, 10 June 1970: FCO 9/1151, TNA.
142 Ramsbotham to FCO, 20 July 1970: FCO 9/1151, TNA.
143 More Information on elections' results in: Andreas Hatzikyriakos and Christophoros Christophorou, Βουλευτικές: Ιστορία, Αριθμοί, Ανάλυση *[Parliamentary Elections: History, Numbers, Analysis]* (Nicosia: Intercollege Press, 1996), pp. 12–21.

144 Ramsbotham to FCO, 21 July 1970: FCO 9/1155, TNA.
145 Sarell to FCO, 13 March 1970: FCO 9/1148, TNA.
146 Richard A. Patrick, *Political Geography and the Cyprus Conflict, 1963–1971* (Waterloo: Department of Geography, Faculty of Environmental Studies, University of Waterloo, 1976), p. 162; Rasmbotham, *Turkish-Cypriot students,* 10 April 1970: FCO 9/1172, TNA; See press reports in FA2/109 and FA2/309, Cyprus State Archive.
147 Cyprus News Digest, Turkish Press, 15 April 1970: FA2/109, Cyprus State Archive; Also see various documents in FA2/260 Cyprus State Archive.
148 Ramsbotham, *Turkish-Cypriot Economic Development*, p. 5, 10 September 1969: FCO 9/803, TNA.
149 Cyprus Intelligence Service to secretary-general, Ministry of Interior, 21 October 1969: Glafkos Clerides Archive.
150 Clerides to Komodromos, 12 December 1969: Glafkos Clerides Archive.
151 *Special News Bulletin*, 21 July 1970: FA2/109, Cyprus State Archive.
152 Ramsbotham, *Turkish-Cypriot Economic Developmen*t, p. 8, 10 September 1969: FCO 9/803, TNA.
153 Ibid.
154 Memo on Inter-communal Talks, December 1969: FCO 9/783, TNA.
155 Ramsbotham to FCO, 8 October 1969: FCO 9/782, TNA.
156 Cyprus News Digest, Turkish Press, 30 May 1970, Doc. 105: FA2/109, Cyprus State Archive.
157 Cyprus News Digest, National Solidarity Programme, 28 May 1970, Doc. 102: FA2/109, Cyprus State Archive.
158 Ibid.
159 Sarell to FCO, 5 June 1970: FCO 9/1155, TNA.
160 Ramsbotham, *Cyprus: Inter-Communal Talks, End of Phase III*, p. 14, 9 September 1970: FCO 9/1148, TNA.
161 Clerides, *My Deposition, Vol. III*, p. 39.
162 Ibid.
163 Clerides to Denktash, 9 April 1971: FCO 9/1353, TNA.
164 *Eleftheria,* 10 December 1970.
165 Ramsbotham to FCO, 20 January 1971: FCO 9/1353, TNA.
166 Ramsbotham to FCO, 9 December 1970: FCO 9/1150, TNA.
167 Clerides, *My Deposition, Vol. III*, p. 44.
168 Ibid.
169 Ibid.
170 Beattie to FCO, 23 December 1970: FCO 9/1150, TNA.
171 Ramsbotham to FCO, 26 February 1971: FCO 9/1353, TNA.
172 Rambsotham to FCO, 3 March 1971: FCO 9/1353, TNA.
173 Clerides, *My Deposition, Vol. II*, p. 295.
174 Ramsbotham to FCO, 1 October 1969: FCO 9/782, TNA.
175 Daunt to FCO, 7 January 1970: FCO 9/1147, TNA.

176 Clerides-Denktash's meetings, 15 February and 8 March 1971, Doc. 32 & Doc. 42: FA2/92, Cyprus State Archive.
177 Ἅπαντα, Τόμος IB, p. 282.
178 Robin Fearn (FCO) to Nicosia, 2 April 1971: FCO 9/1353, TNA.
179 For example see: Cyprus Turkish Information Office, *The Question of Cyprus: Can Makarios Abandon Enosis?* (Nicosia: s.n., 1971).
180 Michael Scott (Nicosia) to FCO, 7 April 1971: FCO 9/1353, TNA.
181 Clerides, *My Deposition, Vol. III*, p. 55.
182 Ibid., p. 50.
183 Robert Edmonds, *Inter-Communal Talks: The Last Phase?*, p. 15, 27 August 1971: FCO 9/1355, TNA.
184 Note from Fearn, 1 September 1971: FCO 9/1355, TNA.
185 UN Security-Council, *Report by the Secretary-General on the United Nations Operation in Cyprus* (S/10005) 2 December 1970, paragraph 115.
186 John Powell-Jones (Athens) to FCO, 18 September 1970: FCO 9/1149, TNA.
187 Beattie to FCO, 6 October 1970: FCO 9/1149, TNA.
188 *Phileleftheros*, 15 December 1970.
189 Ramsbotham to FCO, 27 January 1971: FCO 9/1353, TNA.
190 Ibid.
191 Ibid.; Ἅπαντα, Τόμος IB, pp. 253–259.
192 Ramsbotham to FCO, 2 February 1971: FCO 9/1353, TNA.
193 Sarell to FCO, 18 May 1971: FCO 9/1367, TNA. Note: Nihat Erim was a law professor who played an important role in the formation of Turkey's policy regarding Cyprus in the 1950s and especially during the Zurich–London Agreements. About Erim's policy papers on Cyprus in 1956: Haralambos Kafkarides, Τουρκία-Κύπρος 1923–1960: Η Τουρκική Πολιτική στο Κυπριακό από τον Ατατούρκ στον Μεντερές [Turkey-Cyprus 1923–1960: The Turkish Policy towards the Cyprus Problem from Ataturk to Menderes] (Nicosia: Amorgos, 2010), pp. 284–293.
194 Clerides-Denktash meeting, 9 August 1971, Doc. 163: FA2/92, Cyprus State Archive.
195 Sarell to FCO, 18 May 1971: FCO 9/1367, TNA.
196 Sarell to FCO, 20 April 1971: FCO 9/1353, TNA.
197 Edmonds, *Turkish-Cypriot Administration*, p. 3, 25 October 1972: FCO 9/1499, TNA.
198 Ibid.
199 Edmonds, *Annual Review 1971*, 1 January 1972: FCO 9/1494, TNA.
200 Cyprus News Digest, Turkish Press, 18 April 1971: FA2/91, Cyprus State Archive.
201 Edmonds, *The Mood of the Turkish-Cypriot Leadership*, p. 2, 22 October 1971: FCO 9/1356, TNA.
202 Beattie to FCO, 24 November 1971: FCO 9/1357, TNA.
203 Sarell to FCO, 29 April 1971: FCO 9/1367, TNA.

204 Ibid.
205 Clerides, *My Deposition, Vol. III*, p. 68.
206 Constantinos Panayiotacos, Στην πρώτη γραμμή αμύνης *[At the First Line of Defence]* (Athens: Photosinthetiki, 1979), p. 97.
207 Clerides, *My Deposition, Vol. III*, pp. 69–75.
208 Ibid., p. 75.
209 Ibid., p. 82.
210 Ibid., p. 80.
211 Van Coufoudakis, 'US Foreign Policy and the Cyprus Problem: An Interpretation', *Millennium, Journal of International Studies*, 5/3 (1976), pp. 245–268 (p. 257); Michael A. Attalides, *Nationalism and International Politics* (Möhnesse: Bibliopolis, 2005), p. 132; House of Representatives, Πόρισμα για το Φάκελο της Κύπρου, σελ.133.
212 Robin Hooper (Athens) to FCO, 11 June 1971: FCO 9/1368, TNA; Sarell to FCO, 16 September 1971: FCO 9/1367, TNA.
213 Nicolet, *US Policy*, p. 401.
214 Panayiotacos, Στην πρώτη γραμμή, p. 97.
215 Ibid., p. 98.
216 Clerides, *My Deposition, Vol. III*, pp. 111–115.
217 See reports in FCO 9/1365, TNA.
218 Record of meeting: minister of state for foreign and Commonwealth affairs with foreign minister of Cyprus, 12 October 1971: FCO 9/1356, TNA.
219 Alec Douglas-Home (FCO) to New York, 12 October 1971: FCO 9/1356, TNA; Edmonds to FCO, 12 October 1971: FCO 9/1356, TNA.
220 Clerides, *My Deposition, Vol. III*, p. 165.
221 Record of meeting: minister of state for foreign and Commonwealth affairs with foreign minister of Cyprus, New York, 12 October 1971: FCO 9/1356, TNA.
222 Brian Crowe (New York) to FCO, 15 October 1971: FCO 9/1356, TNA.
223 Clerides, *My Deposition, Vol. III*, p. 171.
224 Edmonds to FCO, 19 October 1971: FCO 9/1356, TNA; Panayiotacos, Στην πρώτη γραμμή, p. 118.
225 Edmonds to FCO, 23 November 1971: FCO 9/1357, TNA.
226 John Harisson (Ankara) to FCO, 18 January 1972: FCO 9/1492, TNA.
227 William Wilberforce (FCO), 12 January 1972: FCO 9/1494, TNA.
228 Polyviou, *Conflict and Negotiations*, p. 144.
229 Ramsbotham to FCO, 23 May 1969: FCO 9/781, TNA.
230 FCO to Washington, 6 January 1969: FCO 9/779, TNA.
231 Costar to FCO, 17 October 1968: FCO 9/778, TNA.
232 Call of Bendall by Denktash, 2 November 1970: FCO 9/1150, TNA.
233 Washington to FCO, 30 December 1968: FCO 9/779, TNA.
234 Ibid.
235 FCO to Washington, 6 January 1969: FCO 9/779, TNA.
236 Record of Conversation, Commonwealth Secretary–Cyprus Foreign Minister, 28 June 1968: FCO 27/94, TNA.

237 Cyprus Conference: Morning Session, 29 January 1968: FCO 9/74, TNA.
238 Ramsbotham to FCO, 9 September 1970: FCO 9/1148, TNA.
239 Edmonds, *Turkish-Cypriot Administration*, p. 8, 25 October 1972: FCO 9/1499, TNA.
240 Memo by the minister of commerce and industry, 12 March 1969: Glafkos Clerides Archive.
241 Ἅπαντα Ἀρχιεπισκόπου Κύπρου Μακαρίου III, Τόμος IA [Collected Works of Archibshop Makarios III, Vol. 11] (Nicosia: Makarios III Foundation, 2001) p. 132.
242 Edmonds to FCO, 27 August 1971: FCO 9/1355, TNA.
243 Oriana Fallaci, Συνάντηση με την Ιστορία [Interview with History] (Athens: Papiros, 1976), p. 538.

Chapter 7

1   Michael Brown (Ankara) to Reginald Seconde (FCO), 7 December 1971: FCO 9/1357, TNA.
2   John Powell-Jones (Athens) to William Wilberforce (FCO), 12 January 1972: FCO 9/1492, TNA.
3   Michael Dekleris, Κυπριακό: Η Τελευταία Ευκαιρία 1972–1974 [The Cyprus Problem: The Last Chance 1972–1974] (Athens: Sideris, 2003), p. 95; Kenneth Jamieson (New York) to Wilberforce, 26 January 1972: FCO 9/1492, TNA; Edmonds to FCO, 21 January 1972: FCO 9/1492, TNA.
4   Glafkos Clerides, *My Deposition, Vol. III* (Nicosia: Alitheia, 1989), p. 175.
5   Jamieson to Wilberforce, 26 January 1972: FCO 9/1492, TNA.
6   Clerides, *My Deposition, Vol. III*, p. 124.
7   Edmonds to FCO, 14 September 1971: FCO 9/1368, TNA; Edmonds to FCO, 18 September 1971: FCO 9/1367, TNA.
8   Edmonds, *The Arms and the Man*, 22 May 1972: FCO 9/1509, TNA.
9   Stanley Mayes, *Makarios: A Biography* (London: Macmillan, 1981), p. 217.
10   Douglas-Home to Athens & Hooper to FCO, 11 February 1972, FCO 9/1507, TNA.
11   Sarell to FCO, 16 June 1972: FCO 9/1501, TNA.
12   Ibid.
13   Edmonds, *The Arms and the Man*, p. 18, 22 May 1972: FCO 9/1509, TNA.
14   Ibid.
15   Ibid.
16   Douglas-Home to Ankara, 3 May 1972: FCO 9/1492, TNA.
17   Edmonds to FCO, 9 June 1972: FCO 9/1492, TNA.
18   Edmonds to FCO, 25 July 1972: FCO 9/1493, TNA.
19   Clerides, *My Deposition, Vol. III*, p. 210; Hooper to FCO, 24 October 1972: FCO 9/1493, TNA.
20   Michael Dekleris, Κυπριακό: Η Τελευταία Ευκαιρία 1972–1974 [The Cyprus Problem: The Last Chance 1972–1974] (Athens: Sideris, 2003), p. 154.

21 Ibid., p. 158.

22 Ibid.; Sir Stephen Olver (Nicosia) to FCO: *The Enlarged Inter-Communal Talks*, Annex B, 24 October 1973: FCO 9/1666, TNA. Note: In Polyviou, *Conflict and Negotiations*, p. 105, it is reported that there was a 'two-stage negotiation, whereby the mediator would first hold talks with the two sides separately [...] and finally direct and face-to-face meetings between all parties [...], two-stage negotiation with the active participation of the mediator'. According to both the Greek Constitutional expert, Dekleris, and various reports in the FCO 9/1493 and FCO 9/1666, Polyviou's argument is problematic. Moreover, Turkey's disagreement over an active involvement of the UN is already explained. Ankara would have never accepted such a process.

23 Clerides, *My Deposition, Vol. III*, p. 238.

24 Dekleris, Κυπριακό 1972–1974 [*The Cyprus Problem: The Last Chance 1972–1974*], p. 175.

25 Ibid.

26 David Beattie (Nicosia) to Peter Davies (FCO), 4 December 1972: FCO 9/1493, TNA.

27 Davies to Beattie, 28 November 1972: FCO 9/1500, TNA.

28 Ibid.

29 Dekleris, Κυπριακό 1972–1974 [*The Cyprus Problem: The Last Chance 1972–1974*], p. 194.

30 Ibid., p. 184.

31 Clerides, *My Deposition, Vol. III*, p. 256.

32 Goodison, *The Internal Situation in the Pre-election Period*, 31 January 1973: FCO 9/1668, TNA.

33 Dekleris, Κυπριακό 1972–1974 [*The Cyprus Problem: The Last Chance 1972–1974*], p. 194.

34 Claude Nicolet, *United States Police towards Cyprus, 1954–1974, Removing the Greek-Turkish Bone of Contention* (Möhnesee: Bibliopolis, 2001), p. 410.

35 Clerides, *My Deposition, Vol. III*, p. 269.

36 Richard Fyjis-Walker (Ankara) to Brian Hitch (FCO), 27 February 1973 and Fyjis-Walker to Goodison, 19 March 1973: FCO 9/1665, TNA.

37 Sarell to FCO, 16 June 1972: FCO 9/1501, TNA; Record of Conversation (New York), 28 September 1971: FCO 9/1367, TNA.

38 Keith Hamilton and Patrick Salmon (eds), *Documents on British Policy Overseas. Ser. 3, Vol. 5, The Southern Flank in Crisis 1973–1976* (London: Whitehall History Publishing, 2006), p. 20.

39 Dekleris, Κυπριακό 1972–1974 [*The Cyprus Problem: The Last Chance 1972–1974*], p. 240.

40 Olver to FCO, 12 September 1973: FCO 9/1665, TNA; Dekleris, Κυπριακό 1972–1974, pp. 222–226.

41 Hamilton and Salmon, *Documents on British Policy*, p. 16.

42 Ibid., p. 37.

43 Ibid.; Dekleris, Κυπριακό 1972–1974 [*The Cyprus Problem: The Last Chance 1972–1974*], p. 252.

44 Clerides, *My Deposition, Vol. III*, p. 293.
45 Dekerlis, *Κυπριακό 1972–1974 [The Cyprus Problem: The Last Chance 1972–1974]*, pp. 254–263.
46 Clerides, *My Deposition, Vol. III*, p. 309.
47 Hamilton and Salmon, *Documents on British Policy*, p. 23.
48 Ibid., p. 40.
49 Dekleris, *Κυπριακό 1972–1974 [The Cyprus Problem: The Last Chance 1972–1974]*, p. 184.
50 About internal political problems/antagonism within the Turkish-Cypriot community in FCO 9/1499 and FCO 9/1671, TNA.
51 Dekleris, *Κυπριακό 1972–1974 [The Cyprus Problem: The Last Chance 1972–1974]*, p. 54.

Conclusion

1 Paschalis Kitromilides, 'From Coexistence to Confrontation: The Dynamics of Ethnic Conflict in Cyprus', in Michael A. Attalides (ed), *Cyprus Reviewed* (Nicosia: The Jus Cypri Association, 1977), p. 59.
2 Indicative studies: Van Coufoudakis, 'US Foreign Policy and the Cyprus Question: An Interpretation', *Millennium, Journal of International Studies*, 5/3 (1976), pp. 245–268; Marios L. Evrivades, 'The Problem of Cyprus', *Current History*, 70/412 (1976), pp. 18–21, 38–42.
3 Hunt, *Reactions to the Cyprus Resolution of the UN General Assembly*, p. 2, 31 December 1965: DO 220/50, TNA.
4 Michael A. Attalides, *Cyprus: Nationalism and International Politics* (Möhnesse: Bibliopolis, 2005), p. 107.
5 Ibid., p. 114.
6 Ramsbotham, *Turkish-Cypriot Economic Development*, p. 7, 10 September 1969: FCO 9/803, TNA.
7 See Reports by the secretary-general on the UN operations in Cyprus for 1969–1971: S/9233, S/9521, S/9814, S/10005, S/10199, S/10401.
8 Rambsotham, *Archbishop Makarios III, President of the Republic of Cyprus*, p. 11, 29 March 1971: FCO 9/1364, TNA.
9 See, for example, *The Economist*, 29 November 2014, http://www.economist.com/news/europe/21635025-hopes-settling-cyprus-problem-are-starting-look-unrealistic-intractableor-insoluble [Accessed 30 November 2014].

Sources and Bibliography

Unpublished Sources

1. The National Archives of the United Kingdom, Kew

CAB 191: Overseas Joint Intelligence Groups: Fragmentary Records, 1947–1974 (191/7, 191/10)

DO 215: Commonwealth Relations Office and Commonwealth Office: Economic General Department: Registered Files (EGD Series), 1964–1967 (215/150)

DO 220: Commonwealth Relations Office: Mediterranean Department: Registered Files (2-MED Series), 1963–1966 (220/11, 220/28, 220/38, 220/41, 220/49, 220/50, 220/56, 220/57, 220/65, 220/86, 220/87, 220/101, 220/110, 220/117, 220/118, 220/220/120, 220/121, 220/129, 220/132, 220/133, 220/135, 220/150, 220/152, 220/168, 220/178)

FCO 9: Foreign Office, Central Department and Foreign and Commonwealth Office, Southern European Department: Registered Files (C and WS Series), 1967–1982 (9/62, 9/63, 9/64, 9/65, 9/66, 9/67, 9/73, 9/74, 9/82, 9/83, 9/778, 9/779, 9/780, 9/781, 9/785, 9/786, 9/778, 9/779, 9/780, 9/781, 9/782, 9/783, 9/785, 9/786, 9/803, 9/1147, 9/1148, 9/1149, 9/1150, 9/1151, 9/1153, 9/1154, 9/1155, 9/1172, 9/1353, 9/1354, 9/1355, 9/1356, 9/1357, 9/1364, 9/1365, 9/1367, 9/1368, 9/1492, 9/1493, 9/1494, 9/1499, 9/1500, 9/1501, 9/1507, 9/1509, 9/1665, 9/1666, 9/1668, 9/1671)

FCO 27: Commonwealth Office: Middle East, Western and United Nations Department and Mediterranean Department: Registered Files (M Series), 1967–1968 (27/48, 27/49, 27/50, 27/51, 27/52, 27/53, 27/70, 27/71, 27/76, 27/77, 27/78, 27/79, 27/80, 27/83, 27/91, 27/92, 27/93, 27/94, 27/97, 27/99, 27/156)

FO 371: Foreign Office: Political Departments: General Correspondence 1906–1966 (371/174770, 371/179973, 371/179996, 371/185620, 371/185629, 371/185630)

LAB 13: Ministry of Labour and successors: International Labour Division and Overseas Department: Registered Files, 1923–1980 (13/2205)

PREM 13: Prime Minister's Office: Correspondence and Papers, 1964–1970 (13/792, 13/1371, 13/1372)

WO 386: War Office and Ministry of Defence: Headquarters Middle East and successors: Records – Intelligence Reports: Joint Intelligence Group (Cyprus) 1964–1974 (386/2, 386/3, 386/4, 386/5, 386/6, 386/7)

2. National State Archives of the Republic of Cyprus, Nicosia

FA1, FA2: Ministry of Foreign Affairs – General Files: 1960–1980

3. Private Papers

Major-General Sir Alec Bishop (Imperial War Museum)
Glafkos Clerides Archive (http://www.glafkosclerides.com.cy/Archives.aspx)
　　[Accessed from 2011–2014]

4. Doctoral Theses

Arslan, Hakan. *The Political Economy Of State-Building: The Case of Turkish-
　　Cypriots (1960–1967)*. İstanbul Bilgi University, 2014.
Assos, Demetris. *Makarios: A Study of Anti-Colonial Nationalist Leadership,
　　1950–1959*. University of London, 2009.
Ker-Lindsay, James. *The Origins of the United Nations Force in Cyprus
　　(UNFICYP): International Politics on the Road to United Nations Security
　　Council Resolution 186 (1964)*. University of Kent at Canterbury, 1997.
Strong, Paul Nicholas. *The Economic Consequences of Ethnonational Conflict
　　in Cyprus: The Development of Two Siege Economies after 1963 and 1974*.
　　London School of Economics, 1999.

Newspapers

(The below newspapers have been consulted only for the dates used in the
Endnotes.)

Αγών (Agon)
Αλήθεια (Alitheia)
Ελευθερία (Eleftheria)
Κύπρος (Kipros)
Μάχη (Machi)
Πατρίς (Patris)
Τελευταία Ώρα (Teleutaia Ora)
Φιλελεύθερος (Phileleftheros)
Χαραυγή (Haravghi)
Cyprus Mail
Special News Bulletin (Turkish-Cypriot publication in English)
The Economist
The Guardian
The Morning Record
The New York Times
The Observer

Interviews

Glafkos Clerides, 23 September 2011, Nicosia, Cyprus
Vassos Lyssarides, 29 November 2011, Nicosia, Cyprus
Lellos Demetriades, 27 May 2014, Nicosia, Cyprus

Books

Άπαντα Αρχιεπισκόπου Κύπρου Μακαρίου Γ, Τόμοι Η-ΙΒ] [Collected Works of Archibshop Makarios III, Vol. 8–13]. Nicosia: Makarios III Foundation, 1997–2004.

Anagnostopoulou, Sia. Ή Κυπριακή Δημοκρατία, Καθρέφτης Πολλαπλών Ανακλάσεων: Τουρκία και Τουρκοκυπριακή Κοινότητα, 1960–1983' [The Cyprus Republic, Mirror of Many Reflections: Turkey and the Turkish-Cypriot Community]. In Pericleous, Chrysostomos (ed), *Κυπριακή Δημοκρατία 50 Χρόνια: Η επώδυνη Πορεία [Republic of Cyprus 50 Years: A Painful Course]*. Athens: Papazisi Publications, 2010, pp. 293–327.

Anagnostopoulou, Sia. 'Makarios III, 1950–1977: Creating the Ethnarchic State'. In Varnava, Andrekos and Michael, Michalis N. (eds), *The Archbishops of Cyprus in the Modern Age: The Changing Role of the Archbishop-Ethnarch, Their Identities and Politics*. Newcastle upon Tyne: Cambridge Scholars Publishing, 2013, pp. 240–290.

Attalides, Michael A. 'The Turkish-Cypriots: Their Relations to the Greek-Cypriots in Perspective'. In Attalides, Michael (ed), *Cyprus Reviewed*. Nicosia: The Jus Cypri Association, 1977, pp. 71–97.

Attalides, Michael A. *Cyprus: Nationalism and International Politics*. Möhnesse: Bibliopolis, 2005.

Averoff-Tossizza, Evangelos. *Lost Opportunities: The Cyprus Question, 1950–1963*. New Rochelle, NY: A.D. Caratzas, 1986.

Ayla, Gürel. *Turkish-Cypriot Legal Framework, Displacement in Cyprus – Consequences of Civil and Military Strife, 4*. Nicosia: PRIO Cyprus Centre, 2012.

Bahceli, Tozun. 'Cyprus in the Politics of Turkey since 1955'. In Salem, Norma (ed), *Cyprus: A Regional Conflict and Its Resolution*. London: Macmillan Press, 1992, pp. 62–70.

Berridge, G. R. *Diplomacy: Theory and Practice*. Basingstoke: Palgrave, 3rd edition, 2005.

Bolukbasi, Suha. *The Superpowers and the Third World: Turkish-American Relations and Cyprus*. Lanham: University Press of America, 1988.

Christodoulou, Demetrios. *Inside the Cyprus Miracle: The Labours of an Embattled Mini-Economy*. Minnesota Mediterranean and East European Monographs. Minneapolis: University of Minnesota, 1992.

Christophorou, Christophoros. 'The Evolution of the Greek-Cypriot Party Politics'. In Ker-Lindsay, James and Faustmann, Hubert (eds), *The Government and Politics of Cyprus*. Oxford: Peter Lang, 2008, pp. 83–106.

Clerides, Glafkos. *Cyprus: My Deposition (Volumes I–IV)*. Nicosia: Alithia, 1989.

Crawshaw, Nancy. *The Cyprus Revolt: An Account of the Struggle for Union with Greece*. London: Allen and Unwin, 1978.

The Cyprus Development Corporation Ltd. *Annual Reports* 1963–1974. Nicosia: 'Proodos' Print & Publ. Co Ltd, 1964–1976.

Cyprus Planning Bureau. *The Second Five-Year Plan: 1967–1971*. Nicosia: Government Printing Office of the Republic of Cyprus, 1967.

Cyprus Planning Bureau. *The Third Five-Year Plan (1972–1976)*. Nicosia: Government Printing Office of the Republic of Cyprus, 1972.

Cyprus Turkish Information Office. *The Question of Cyprus: Can Makarios Abandon Enosis?* Nicosia: s.n., 1971.

Dekleris, Michael. *Κυπριακό: Η Τελευταία Ευκαιρία 1972–1974 [The Cyprus Problem: The Last Chance 1972–1974]*. Athens: I. Sideris, 2003.

Dodd, Clement. *The History and Politics of the Cyprus Conflict*. Basingstoke: Palgrave Macmillan, 2010.

Drousiotis, Makarios. *The First Partition: Cyprus 1963–1964*. Nicosia: Alphadi, 2008.

Drousiotis, Makarios. *Δύο Απόπειρες και μια Δολοφονία: Η Χούντα και η Κύπρος: 1967–1970 [Two Attempts and One Assassination: The Junta and Cyprus 1967–1970]*. Nicosia: Alfadi, 2009.

Ertekün, M. Necati Münir. *The Cyprus Dispute and the Birth of the Turkish Republic of Northern Cyprus*. Nicosia: K. Rustem, 1984.

Fallaci, Oriana. *Συνάντηση Με Την Ιστορία [Interview with History]*. Athens: Papiros, 1976.

Faustmann, Hubert. 'The Colonial Legacy of Division'. In Ker-Lindsay, James and Faustmann, Hubert (eds), *The Government and Politics of Cyprus*. Oxford: Peter Lang, 2008, pp. 45–62.

Garoufalias, Petros E. *Ελλάς Και Κύπρος: Τραγικά Σφάλματα, Ευκαιρίες Που Χάθηκαν (19 Φεβρουαρίου 1964–15 Ιουλίου 1965) [Greece and Cyprus: Tragic Mistaces and Missed Opportunities]*. Athens: Bergadi Publications, 1982.

Gazioglu, Ahmet C. and Moran, Michael (eds), *Past-Masters of Illegality*. Lefkosa: CYREP, 2000.

Hadjikyriakos, Andreas and Christophorou, Christophoros. *Βουλευτικές: Ιστορία, Αριθμοί, Ανάλυση, [Parliamentary Elections: History, Numbers and Analysis]*. Nicosia: Intercollege Press, 1996.

Hamilton, Keith and Salmon, Patrick (eds), *Documents on British Policy Overseas. Ser. 3, [1960–]. Vol. 5, The Southern Flank in Crisis 1973–1976*. London: Whitehall History Publishing in association with Frank Cass, 2001.

Harbottle, Michael. *The Impartial Soldier*. London: Oxford University Press, 1970.

Hart, Parker T. *Two NATO Allies at the Threshold of War: Cyprus: A First-Hand Account of Crisis Management, 1965–1968*. Durham: Duke University Press, 1990.

Holland, Robert. *Britain and the Revolt in Cyprus 1954–1959*. Oxford: Oxford University Press, 1998.

House of Representatives. *Πόρισμα για το Φάκελο της Κύπρου, 17 Μαρτίου 2011 [The Findings for the Cyprus Problem, 17 March 2011]*. Nicosia: House of Representatives, 2011.

Hudson, John and Dymiotou-Jensen, Marina. *Modelling a Developing Country: A Case Study of Cyprus*. Aldershot: Avebury, 1989.

Hunt, David. *On the Spot: An Ambassador Remembers*. London: P. Davies, 1975.

Kafkarides, Haralambos. *Τουρκία-Κύπρος 1923–1960: Η Τουρκική Πολιτική Στο Κυπριακό Από Τον Ατατούρκ Στον Μεντερές [Turkey-Cyprus 1923–1960: The Turkish Policy on the Cyprus Problem from Ataturk to Mederes]*. Nicosia: Amorgos, 2010.

Kakoullis, Loukas. *Η Αριστερά και οι Τουρκοκύπριοι: το κυπριακό από μια άλλη σκοπία [The Left and the Turkish-Cypriots: The Cyprus Problem from Another Angle]*. Nicosia: Kasoulides Printings, 1990.

Kasoulides, Andreas. *Πολιτική, Εκπαιδευτική Πολιτική και Διδασκαλικός Συνδικαλισμός στην Κύπρο (1960–1974) [Politics, Educational Politics and Teachers Unions]*. Nicosia: Epifaniou Publishings, 2016.

Kitromilides, Paschalis. 'From Coexistence to Confrontation: The Dynamics of Ethnic Conflict in Cyprus'. In Attalides, Michael A. (ed), *Cyprus Reviewed*. Nicosia: The Jus Cypri Association, 1977, pp. 35–70.

Kizilyurek, Niazi. *Η Κύπρος: Το αδιέξοδο των εθνικισμών [Cyprus: The Dead-End of Nationalisms]*. Athens: Black List, 1999.

Kizilyurek, Niazi. *Οι Τουρκοκύπριοι, Η Τουρκία Και Το Κυπριακό [Turkish-Cypriots, Turkey and the Cyprus Problem]*. Athens: Papazisi Publications, 2004.

Kizilyurek, Niazi. *Glafkos Clerides: The Path of a Country*. Nicosia: Rimal Publications, 2008.

Kizilyurek, Niazi. 'Rauf Denktash: Fear and Nationalism in the Turkish-Cypriot community'. In Aktar, Ayhan, Kizilyürek, Niyazi and Özkirml, Umut (eds), *Nationalism in the Troubled Triangle: Cyprus, Greece and Turkey, New Perspectives on South-East Europe*. Basingstoke: Palgrave Macmillan, 2010, pp. 175–193.

Kranidiotis, Giannos N. *Το Κυπριακό Πρόβλημα: Η Ανάμειξη Του ΟΗΕ Και Οι Ξένες Επεμβάσεις Στην Κύπρο 1960–1974 [The Cyprus Problem: The UN Involvement and the Foreign Interventions in Cyprus 1960–1974]*. Athens: Themelio, 1984.

Kranidiotis, Nikos G. *Ανοχύρωτη Πολιτεία, Κύπρος 1960–1974 [The Unfortified State, Cyprus 1960–1974]*. Vols 1–3. Athens: Estia, 1985.

Kyriakides, Stanley. *Cyprus: Constitutionalism and Crisis Government*. Philadelphia: University of Pennsylvania Press, 1968.

Loizos, Peter. *The Greek Gift: Politics in a Cypriot Village*. Möhnesee: Bibliopolis, 2004.

Lyras, Eleni and Psaltis, Charis. *Formerly Mixed Villages in Cyprus: Representation of the Past, Present and Future*. Cyprus: PRIO, 2011.

Markides, Kyriacos. *The Rise and Fall of the Cyprus Republic*. New Haven: Yale University Press, 1977.

Markides, Diana Weston. *Cyprus 1957–1963: From Colonial Conflict to Constitutional Crisis; the Key Role of the Municipal Issue*. Minnesota Mediterranean and East European Monographs. Minnesota: University of Minnesota, 2001.

Mayes, Stanley. *Makarios: A Biography*. London: Macmillan, 1981.

Mehmet, Ozay. *Sustainability of Microstates: The Case of North Cyprus*. Salt Lake City: University of Utah Press, 2010.

Miller, Linda B. *World Order and Local Disorder: The United Nations and Internal Conflicts*. Princeton: Princeton University Press, 1967.

Navaro-Yashin, Yael. 'Confinement and Imagination: Sovereignty and Subjectivity in a Quasi State'. In Hansen, Thomas Blom and Stepputat, Finn (eds), *Sovereign Bodies: Citizens, Migrants, and States in the Postcolonial World*. Princeton: Princeton University Press, 2005, pp. 103–119.

Necatigil, Zaim M. *The Cyprus Question and the Turkish Position in International Law*. Oxford: Oxford University Press, 1989.

Nicolet, Claude. *United States Policy towards Cyprus, 1954–1974: Removing the Greek-Turkish Bone of Contention*. Möhnesee Bibliopolis, 2001.

Nicolet, Claude. 'The Turkish Cypriot Failure to Return to Cypriot Government in 1964: A View from the US Archives'. In Charalambous, John and Chrysostomou, Alicia et al. (eds), *Cyprus, 40 Years from Independence: Proceedings from a Conference Held at the University of North London 16–17 November 2000*. Möhnesee: Bibliopolis, 2002, pp. 61–69.

Panayiotacos, Constantinos. *Στην Πρώτη Γραμμή Αμύνης [At the First Defence Line]*. Athens: Fotosinthetiki, 1979.

Papadopoulos, Tassos. 'Labour and Social Insurance'. In Greek Communal Chamber (ed), *Cyprus: A Handbook on the Island's Past and Present*. Nicosia, 1964, pp. 209–222.

Papageorgiou, Spyros. *Από Την Ζυρίχη Εις Στον Αττίλα [From Zurich to Attila]*. 3 Vols. Athens: G. Ladia, 1980.

Patrick, Richard A. *Political Geography and the Cyprus Conflict, 1963–1971*. Waterloo: Department of Geography, Faculty of Environmental Studies, University of Waterloo, 1976.

Polyviou, Polyvios G. *Cyprus: Conflict and Negotiations, 1960–1980*. London: Duckworth, 1980.

Republic of Cyprus. *The First Five-Year Plan (1962–1966)*. Nicosia: Printing Office of the Republic of Cyprus, 1961.

Republic of Cyprus. *Πρακτικά Της Βουλής Των Αντιπροσώπων, Σύνοδος Ε. (1 Ιανουαρίου -15 Αυγούστου 1965) [Minutes from the House of Representatives, Session E]*. Nicosia: Government Printing Office of the Republic of Cyprus, 1966.

Republic of Cyprus. *The Second Five-Year Plan (1967–1971)*. Nicosia: Planning Bureau, 1967.

Republic of Cyprus. *The Third Five-Year Plan (1972–1976)*. Nicosia: Planning Bureau, 1972.

Richmond, Oliver P. *Mediating in Cyprus: The Cypriot Communities and the United Nations. Cass Series on Peacekeeping, No. 3*. London: Frank Cass, 1998.

Richmond, Oliver P. 'UN Mediation in Cyprus, 1964–65: Setting a Precedent for Peace-Making'. In Richmond, Oliver P. and Ker-Lindsay, James (eds), *The

Work of the UN in Cyprus: Promoting Peace and Development. Basingstoke: Palgrave, 2001, pp. 101–126.

Solomou, Emilios and Faustmann, Hubert (eds), *Colonial Cyprus, 1878–1960: Selected Readings from the Cyprus Review.* Nicosia, Cyprus: University of Nicosia Press, 2010.

Soulioti, Stella. *Fettered Independence: Cyprus, 1878–1964.* Vols 1–2. Minnesota Mediterranean and East European Monographs. Minnesota: Modern Greek Studies, University of Minnesota, 2006.

Statistics and Research Department, Ministry of Finance: *Economic Review 1961.* Nicosia: Printing Office of the Republic of Cyprus, 1963.

Stavrinides, Zenon. *The Cyprus Conflict: National Identity and Statehood.* Nicosia: Loris Stavrinides Press, 1976.

Stegenga, James A. *The United Nations Force in Cyprus.* Columbus: Ohio State University Press, 1968.

Stephens, Robert. *Cyprus: A Place of Arms. Power Politics and Ethnic Conflict in the Eastern Mediterranean.* London: Pall Mall Press, 1966.

Tansu, İsmail. *In Reality No One Was Asleep: A Secret Underground Organization, with State Support … TMT.* Nicosia: Bolan Printing Limited, 2007.

Tahsin, Arif Hasan. *Η Άνοδος Του Ντεκτάς Στην Κορυφή [Denktash's Rise].* Nicosia: Dafania, 2001.

The Cyprus Development Corporation Ltd. *Annual Reports* 1963–1974. Nicosia: "Proodos" Print & Publ. Co Ltd, 1964–1976.

Theocharis, Renos. 'A General Review of the Cyprus Economy'. In Greek Communal Chamber (ed), *Cyprus: A Handbook on the Island's Past and Present.* Nicosia: Publications Department, Greek Communal Chamber, 1964, pp. 183–208.

Thorp, Willard. *Cyprus: Suggestions for a Development Programme.* New York: United Nations, 1961.

Tornaritis, Criton George. *Cyprus and Federalism.* Nicosia: s. n., 1974.

Tornaritis, Criton George. *Cyprus and Its Constitutional and Other Legal Problems.* 2nd edition. Nicosia: s.n., 1980.

Articles

Bryant, Rebecca and Hatay, Mete. 'Guns and Guitars: Stimulating Sovereignty in a State of Siege'. *American Ethnologist,* 38/4 (2011): 631–649.

Coufoudakis, Van. 'US Foreign Policy and the Cyprus Problem: An Interpretation'. *Millennium, Journal of International Studies,* 5/3 (1976): 245–268.

Evriviades, Marios L. 'The Problem of Cyprus'. *Current History,* 70/412 (1976): 18–21 & 38–42.

Haass, Richard. 'Ripeness and the Settlement of International Disputes'. *Survival: Global Politics and Strategy,* 30/3 (1988): 232–251.

Lanitis, Nicholas C. 'Our Destiny'. *Cyprus Mail*, 3–7 March 1963.

Mikes, George. 'Letter from Cyprus'. *Encounter* (March 1965): 87–92.

Navaro-Yashin, Yael. 'Affect in the Civil Service: A Study of a Modern State-System'. *Postcolonial Studies*, 9/3 (2006): 281–294.

Nevzat, Altay and Hatay, Mete. 'Politics, Society and the Decline of Islam in Cyprus: From the Ottoman Era to the Twenty-First Century'. *Middle Eastern Studies*, 45/6 (2009): 911–933.

Özersay, Kudret. 'The Excuse of State Necessity and Its Implications on the Cyprus Conflict'. *Perceptions*, IX (2004–2005): 31–70.

Panagides, Stathis. 'Communal Conflicts and Economic Considerations: The Case of Cyprus'. *Journal of Peace Research*, 5/2 (1968): 133–145.

Papadakis, Yiannis. 'Reflections on the 1st October Commemoration of the Independence of Cyprus'. *The Cyprus Review*, 22/2 (2010): 61–66.

Sant Cassia, Paul. 'The Archbishop in the Beleaguered City: An Analysis of the Conflicting Roles and Political Oratory of Makarios'. *Byzantine and Modern Greek Studies*, 8/1 (1982): 191–212.

Sant Cassia, Paul. 'Patterns of Covert Politics in Post-Independence Cyprus'. *European Journal of Sociology*, XXIV (1983): 115–135.

Electronic Sources

Cyprus Legislation: http://www.cylaw.org/index.html [Accessed 1 December 2014]

Glafkos Clerides Archive: http://www.glafkosclerides.com.cy/Archives.aspx [Link no longer available – Accessed from 2011–2014]

US Department of State Archives:

Miller, James E. (ed), *Foreign Relations of the United States, 1964–1968, Volume XVI, Cyprus; Greece; Turkey* (Washington: United States Government Printing Office, 2000). http://history.state.gov/historicaldocuments/frus1964-68v16 [Accessed 2 December 2014]

Press and Information Office: Press releases from 1 January 1962–28 February 1994 and 1 October 2003–31 December 2013: http://www.piopressreleases.com.cy/easyconsole.cfm/id/1 [Accessed 1 December 2014]

The Yearbook of the United Nations: http://unyearbook.un.org/ [Accessed 25 November 2014]

United Nations Documents: http://www.un.org/en/documents/ [Accessed 25 November 2014]

United Nations Oral History: Dag Hammarskjöld Library: Interview with Galo Plaza Lasso, 28 March 1984. http://dag.un.org/handle/11176/89710 [Accessed 2 March 2017]

Index

Acheson, Dean 19, 24, 25–7, 54–5, 102–3
agriculture 75, 77, 78, 81, 86, 89, 90, 171, 182
AKEL (Progressive Party of Working People) 9, 13–14, 55–7, 146, 147, 174, 175, 180, 181
Aldikacti, Orhan 196, 206, 207, 209, 211
Ali, Ihsan 157, 181
Ali, Vasif 107
Alitheia 105
Allen, Roger 132
Anagnostopoulou, Sia 10
Anastasiou, Antonakis 165
anti-communism 10, 175
Arab–Israeli conflict
    Six-Day War of 1967 3, 129
    Yom Kippur War of 1973 3, 209
archival material 5–6
Ataturk, Kemal 10
Attorney-General of the Republic v. Mustafa Ibrahim and others 44, 63, 65

Beha, Ozar 64
Belcher, Toby 138, 165, 168, 175
Benjiamin, Christodoulos 164
Berberoglu, Ahmet 57, 183
Bernardes, Carlos 55, 57, 58, 110, 116, 117, 120, 124
Bey, Fuad 107
Britain
    archival material 5
    decolonization strategies 3, 11–12
    involvement in the Cyprus problem 2–4, 9, 10, 17–18, 25, 29, 35, 36, 39, 97, 99–100, 105, 111, 117, 118, 137, 145, 158, 168, 177, 197, 213

reaction to *Enosis* 10–11, 15
British Intelligence Reports 37

Caglayangil, Ihsan Sabri 114, 158, 168, 169, 174
Cassia, Paul Sant 2, 10, 177
Charter of Minority Rights 102, 108, 137
Clerides, Glafkos 6, 13, 15, 16, 38, 57, 80, 92, 108–9, 109, 111, 124, 139, 140, 141, 144, 146, 151, 152–4, 155–66, 169–71, 173–80
Clerides, Ioannis 13
construction sector 85, 86, 89
Costar, Sir Norman 91, 92, 123, 133, 138–9, 140, 147, 148, 150, 159, 161, 166, 198
Costopoulos, Stavros 101–2
Council of Europe 96
coup d'état, 1974 1, 8, 120, 134, 155, 203, 205, 209, 212
Cyprus
    arms crisis 16, 28, 70, 71, 120, 121, 149, 204–7
    under British rule 9–11
    Cabinet 12, 46, 111, 141, 152, 164, 181, 185, 201
    Constitution, 1960 1, 11–12, 15–17, 19, 28, 29, 36, 37, 42, 43, 44–50, 52, 54–5, 57, 58, 59, 62, 65, 73, 75, 79–80, 95, 97, 99, 103, 107, 111, 113, 116, 124, 135, 136, 142, 143, 145, 148, 149, 155, 157–61, 192, 203, 207, 211, 214, 216
    elections, 1970 173, 180–1
    GDP 76, 89
    historical background 8–19
    House of Representatives 13–14